PALGRAVE GREAT DEBATES IN LAW

GREAT DEBATES IN
LAND LAW

(Previously GREAT DEBATES IN PROPERTY LAW)

DAVID COWAN
Professor of Law and Policy, University of Bristol Law School

LORNA FOX O'MAHONY
Professor of Law, University of Essex

NEIL COBB
Senior Lecturer in Law, University of Manchester

Second Edition

 macmillan education   palgrave

First edition 2012
This edition published 2016 by
PALGRAVE

Palgrave in the UK is an imprint of Macmillan Publishers Limited, registered in England, company number 785998, of 4 Crinan Street, London, N1 9XW.

Palgrave Macmillan in the US is a division of St Martin's Press LLC, 175 Fifth Avenue, New York, NY 10010.

Palgrave is a global imprint of the above companies and is represented throughout the world.

Palgrave® and Macmillan® are registered trademarks in the United States, the United Kingdom, Europe and other countries.

ISBN 978–1–137–48165–8

This book is printed on paper suitable for recycling and made from fully managed and sustained forest sources. Logging, pulping and manufacturing processes are expected to conform to the environmental regulations of the country of origin.

A catalogue record for this book is available from the British Library.

A catalog record for this book is available from the Library of Congress.

Printed and bound by CPI Group (UK) Ltd, Croydon, CR0 4YY

CONTENTS

PREFACE

The subject of land law has the potential to be an endlessly fascinating area of study. We all usually need to live somewhere, to be somewhere, and so to exist in some relationship with land. Yet, while its importance is in one way reflected in its status as a foundational subject for any LLB degree, for too long land law has been regarded by undergraduate students as a difficult, inaccessible and insufficiently relevant area of law to their everyday lives. This book seeks to change that, by introducing readers to land law as a fluid and ever-changing entity, developed over centuries of debate and cultural change; and by enabling readers to appreciate that to understand the current rules requires a sense of where those rules have come from, how they might change in the future and why they matter in the real world. The book takes a contextual approach throughout, encouraging students to think critically about the nature of land law, its political, social, cultural and economic contexts, and the values which are inherent to the system as it has developed in England and Wales.

This book broadly follows the structure of most conventional undergraduate land law or property law courses as they are delivered in UK law schools. However, we are seeking to provide something quite different from other books, which typically introduce the subject by providing an exposition of the principles from within the closed system of land law's logical and rationally ordered boundaries. Such approaches start from the law, work through the law and often end with the law. While we have all taught land law courses that follow a largely conventional format in respect of the topics covered, we strongly believe that there is much more to discover in these foundational topics than doctrinal approaches alone can hope to reveal. Indeed, by placing the law as it is formally constituted at the centre of the picture, we would argue that such approaches conceal at least as much as they expose.

What we hope to have produced, therefore, is not just another land law book, but a searching volume designed to support the study of our subject by uncovering the (often messy, frequently politicized and heavily value-laden) real-world environment in which real actual people negotiate their way around (and sometimes outside) legal principles; and how those principles interact with wider socio-economic contexts, policies and values. While the book is modelled around the key topics delivered on typical undergraduate courses, it seeks to engage readers in the 'why' of land law, as well as the 'what' and 'how' set out in traditional texts. Our rationale for writing this book, then, is to re-invigorate the subject for a new generation of readers, emphasizing the relevance of these debates for contemporary society. This is the approach that we ourselves adopt, as scholars and teachers of property, to engage with and understand our subject. We believe that, by capturing some of these ideas and perspectives, mapped onto the topic areas of the conventional land law course, our approach offers a new pathway through which to enhance and develop the ways that land law is understood by students and by researchers. Our bold aim in writing this book has been to enable and encourage others to see land law as we do: as an attractive, exciting and valuable subject.

CASES

LEGISLATION

1

THEMES OF PROPERTY

INTRODUCTION

Books on land law sometimes begin with a discussion around the question: what is land? There are various ways these discussions can be structured, incorporating some or all of the following (and, no doubt, others): students are usually served up the 'bundle of rights' theory, best exemplified by Honoré's classic argument that, rather than focus on the thing itself (that is, land), land law is focused on various rights in the thing and responsibilities which derive from one's ownership of the thing.[1] Students may also be served up the 'thin air' argument which broadly, and slightly more contextually, asks us to think about the relationships between people and space. Again, commonly but perhaps with less sophistication, we are enjoined to think about the difference between property and personal rights by reference to the ineffable characteristic of property rights (that they bind third parties). Land law then becomes a definitional struggle between property and the personal.

Our approach in this chapter and in this book is rather different. Rather than take issue with those starting points, we sidestep them because our search is to identify key themes which govern land – the term 'govern' is used here to suggest that these key themes offer a certain mentality of property, or at least the way property is used in law. They produce what seem to be truths about land and these truths run deep so that, when they are brought out into the open and questioned, their logic seems, paradoxically, both unassailable but also assailable. We deal with this paradox below.

One such truth is about the value of ownership. Ownership is, in our sense, a governing function of property. It is imbricated in the fabric of liberal govern-ance. It appears in various aphorisms and metaphors about property – owners live in 'homes', they are 'homeowners', investors, their home is theirs; renters are 'othered' – that is, portrayed as 'not one of us' – by that narrative, except to the extent that homeownership is assumed to be their ambition.[2] These aphorisms

---

[1] A. Honoré, 'Ownership', in A. Guest (ed.), *Oxford Essays in Jurisprudence* (Oxford University Press, 1961); see also M. Warnock, *Critical Reflections on Ownership* (Edward Elgar, 2015).
[2] C. Gurney, 'Lowering the Drawbridge: A Case Study of Analogy and Metaphor in the Social Construction of Home-Ownership' (1999) 36(10) *Urban Studies* 1705.

and metaphors have a striking importance in modern society in England and Wales, and, importantly, are replicated in government policy documents, which emphasize the 'naturalness' of homeownership.[3] As was suggested in 1976 (and is equally the case today):

> Even the use of English language is affected in government statements. ... Owner occupiers have homes, tenants have dwellings. Council tenants have homes when they are being urged to buy them. The use of the emotive word in the one context rather than the other reflects the attitudes of those making the statements.[4]

In this introduction, however, we set out the governing themes of property law, as we see them. These themes are alienation, citizenship, exclusion, rationality, responsibility and space.[5] They are not insulated from each other or, indeed, the changing social, economic, political and cultural debates that shape property law's role in governing the use, allocation, acquisition and management of resources in the social world. There is a complex interaction between our themes and that interaction shifts over time. They keep each other in check, and problems are likely to result when one becomes overly dominant, as the 'property crisis' that has followed the global financial crisis and austerity politics has demonstrated.[6] The themes are intimately related with the ways in which property is viewed in society. We explain each in turn below, but, before doing so, there is another important point we need to make about the nature of our subject – indeed, one which goes to its root.

This is where we do take issue with the presentation of our subject. Perhaps because land law is a foundational subject for the professional bodies in the UK, it is somehow regarded by many as 'bounded' by the needs of the profession; and property law teaching is often geared to imply that the subject exists to under-pin conveyancing practice. For us, by contrast, land law is not the mere starting point for practical conveyancing but a destination subject, playing a crucial and fascinating role in shaping, as well as responding to, contemporary social issues and problems. Land law lives and breathes in society (and vice versa), and it offers us a powerful 'socio-legal object' through which to understand law in society.[7] Indeed, of all areas of law, it is property – particularly as it relates to housing and home – that affects people most consistently and directly; yet, the traditional methodologies of land law scholarship – centred on the *status quo* of established rights, obligations and duties – tend to marginalize the human 'subjects' of the property system.[8] Rather than focus on the abstract interplay of individual rights

---

[3] C. Gurney, 'Pride and Prejudice: Discourses of Normalisation in Public and Private Accounts of Home Ownership' (1999) 14(2) *Housing Studies* 163.

[4] A. Murie, P. Niner and C. Watson, *Housing Policy and the Housing System* (Allen & Unwin, 1976) p. 171.

[5] Cf. the identification of 'traditional' key themes by Birks in 'Five Keys to Land Law', in S. Bright & J. Dewar (eds.), *Land Law: Themes and Perspectives* (Oxford University Press, 1998).

[6] J. Clarke & J. Newman, 'The alchemy of austerity' (2012) 32(2) *Critical Social Policy* 299.

[7] E. Cloatre, 'TRIPS and Pharmaceutical Patents in Djibouti: An ANT Analysis of Socio-Legal Objects' (2008) 17(2) *Social and Legal Studies* 263.

[8] L Fox O'Mahony, 'Property Outsiders and the Hidden Politics of Doctrinalism' (2014) 62 *Current Legal Problems* 409.

and responsibilities in the thing, in this book we approach land law by giving equal attention to people, land and the contexts in which land law governs human access to resources.

The politics of land law and the ways that we think and talk and argue about legal principles, doctrines and decisions vary from one jurisdiction to another. For example, while much of the leading US property scholarship explicitly engages

---

AUTOBIOGRAPHICAL NOTES

In this book, we intersperse our analysis with ideas about property from within our own and our friends' lives to illustrate some of the central themes inherent in property (and scholarship about it), which are discussed above and below. This is the first such note.

Nailing it! A fragment of a housing history

When we bought our first place together in 1997, my then partner (who is a lawyer, but not a property lawyer) remarked that at last she was able to hammer nails into a wall. Up until that point, her housing pathway had been through renting either privately or from friends. Rather than entering into the spirit of that remark, it became chalked up as a possible framework for a paper.

This short biographical note seems important for a number of reasons. First, and most importantly, it speaks of property but in a rather complex and dynamic way. It does not just speak of property, it drips it, or, to put it yet another way, it *performs* property. This metaphor performs an appropriation of space, making something hers and, indeed, ours; it was designed to perform an ongoing ideal of belonging, making us belong to the space and the space belong to us. It constitutes an affective characteristic of property. The point, if you will forgive the pun, was about creating and performing 'home', a private space for us and a site of control.

The simple act to be performed illustrates a further element of property, one which has been said to be of the highest order of property, that is, exclusion. In making it hers and ours, she was also saying that it belonged to us and nobody else. It created a boundary between us and the rest of the world (although, strictly, our mortgage lender could have taken possession of the property at any time, subject to the terms of the agreement between us all, which we didn't read (!)). Stretching it a bit, her metaphor was also about the value(s) of private property against the social, whether that be the 'intentional community', group-based property principles or publicly provided housing (sometimes now described as 'social housing').

Next, her comment performed not just property but a deeper sense of tenure. Ownership was counterposed in this comment to (formal and informal) renting relationships. Whether she was correct or not in asserting that she had been unable to hammer a nail in a wall when renting, a matter to be resolved in relational contract, the metaphor was designed to raise ownership to a different level over and above renting.

---

with the individual rights and distributional consequences of particular configurations of rules and decisions through appeals to competing values, the dominance of doctrinal methods in English property scholarship – reflecting to some extent the traditions of English judicial decision making in private law – has shaped a purportedly apolitical style of judicial reasoning and scholarly analysis. The separation between 'law/doctrine' (viewed as a legitimate space for legal analysis and debate) and 'politics/policy' (argued by some to be outside the realm of private law) has significant implications for the way that English scholars think about, debate and reason through 'property problems'. An important consequence of this is the designation of some aspects of land regulation (for example, the distributional consequences of decisions relating to land, especially for people who have less or no property) as 'politics' not 'law'. This distinction, in turn, strategically locates land inequalities and injustices beyond legal scrutiny. Resisting those inequalities and injustices in law proves both problematic and beyond what seems possible.[9]

The dominant values of much land law reasoning (for example, certainty, efficiency, autonomous individualism) are presented as apolitical, neutral, abstracted from the real impacts of legal reasoning on the people for whom the outcome of the case may have major implications,[10] sometimes to the point of life and death. For example, Andre van der Walt has written about cases in South Africa, and elsewhere, in which property rights bump up against other, 'non-property' rights, including the right to life, dignity and equality;[11] and in Chapter 6 we reflect on the human costs of the erosion of adverse possession under the Land Registration Act 2002, and the criminalization of squatting in England and Wales in 2012. Yet, despite the heady influence of the politics of the day, land law systems are shaped by plural values, which jostle for position and are accorded more or less prominence depending on the question under consideration, the competing interests at stake and the relative power of the actors and institutions involved. To further this discussion, let us now introduce the core themes of this book.

ALIENATION

The first core theme of land law concerns alienation – the flow of property in land within England and Wales through sale and transfer, connecting with the global in a variety of ways, and facilitating and furthering the dominance of the capitalist ideal. Property talks in this way through its monetary (or 'exchange') value. Much popular and political conversation about land is about house price deflation

---

[9] See, for example, the framing of the claim to the use value of unused council housing as necessity in *Southwark LBC* v. *Williams* [1971] Ch 734; and Keenan's discussion of two legal challenges to the Northern Territory National Emergency Response Act 2007: 'Property as Governance: Time, Space and Belonging in Australia's Northern Territory Intervention', (2013) 76(3) *Modern Law Review* 464.

[10] *Ibid.*.

[11] AJ van der Walt, *The Modest Systemic Status of Property Rights*, 1 J. L. Prop. & Soc'y 15 (2014), http://alps.syr.edu/wp-content/uploads/2015/02/JLPS-2014-11-vanderWalt.pdf.

or inflation – and, more broadly, about the price we put on property; sometimes, it seems, property is only worthy when it is worth something; measured by its financial – rather than intrinsic – value.

The core of the system of land law in England and Wales was designed to facilitate the flow of money. Consider the following description of the 'epoch-making' legislation in the law of property:

> The main objects of the 1925 amendments are to assimilate the law of real and personal property whenever practicable, and to simplify and improve the practice of conveyancing, without interfering, more than is essential, with beneficial interests. For many years past the ideal of law reformers has been to enable land to be dealt with as readily as stocks and shares, subject to the necessary modifications inherent to the subject-matter.[12]

That 1925 legislative settlement was primarily designed to achieve this purpose through an agenda which was founded on simplification of the land law and conveyancing systems; simplification was viewed as supporting certainty of title which, in turn, would encourage the greater circulation and flow of property. The 1925 legislation set out to address an emergent problem of *un*certainty in land law and conveyancing, resulting from the development of the doctrine of notice. The systems of registration (of either interest [land charges] or land [land registration] or both) were intended to avoid what Lord Wilberforce subsequently referred to as 'the hazards' of the doctrine of notice:

> The system of land registration, as it exists in England, which long antedates the Land Registration Act 1925, is designed to simplify and to cheapen conveyancing. It is intended to replace the often complicated and voluminous title deeds of property by a single land certificate, on the strength of which land can be dealt with. In place of the lengthy and often technical investigation of title to which a purchaser was committed, all he has to do is to consult the register; from any burden not entered on the register, with one exception, he takes free. Above all, the system is designed to free the purchaser from the hazards of notice – real or constructive – which, in the case of unregistered land, involved him in enquiries, often quite elaborate, failing which he might be bound by equities. The Law of Property Act 1925 contains provisions limiting the effect of the doctrine of notice, but it still remains a potential source of danger to purchasers. By contrast, the only provisions in the Land Registration Act 1925 with regard to notice are provisions which enable a purchaser to take the estate free from equitable interests or equities whether he has notice or not. (See, for example, section 3(xv) s. v. 'minor interests'). The only kind of notice recognised is by entry on the register. (*Williams & Glyns Bank* v. *Boland* [1981] AC 487, 503–4)

This is a foundational statement of land registration, and it is one through which the triptych of simplicity–certainty–alienation (the core drivers of property law) seamlessly moves.

---

[12] Sir B. Cherry, D. Parry, and J. Maxwell, *Wolstenholme & Cherry's Conveyancing Statutes* (Stevens & Sons, 12th edn., 1932) p. 12.

Importantly also, the 1925 legislation created the conditions which make the flow of money around land – through mortgages – possible. Again, the agenda was one of radical simplicity, creating a simple new form of mortgage (the charge by deed by way of legal mortgage) and facilitating multiple mortgages over the same property. The only thing stopping the lender was what might have been termed, albeit inadequately, 'prudence', and which has more recently been labelled 'responsible lending' and 'treating customers fairly'.[13] Yet, at the same time, the flow of capital also put the outright purchase of property practically out of reach for ordinary mortals.[14] Following the latest global financial crisis – a crisis that was triggered by the meltdown of the sub-prime mortgage market in the US – the rise of 'generation-rent' and the inaccessibility of homeownership to two-thirds of people aged 30 today has led a geography scholar, Danny Dorling, to describe widespread homeownership as a 'one-generation' phenomenon.[15] Whether or not that is the case, and we do not have a crystal ball, it is the case that the mortgage market is in a state of flux.

The centrality of alienation – and the emergence of a 'strong ownership' ideology – was furthered by a rather mundane turn of events in the inter-war period which had quite dramatic consequences. English property law's core doctrinal commitments to certainty, autonomous individualism and efficiency were reinforced by legislative policies in 1925 – and again in the Land Registration Act 2002 – that vigorously pursued a political agenda to facilitate the flow of money through property transactions. The 1925 legislation was highly successful in according 'trump value' to 'strong rights',[16] with an emphasis on legal over equitable, registered over unregistered. This doctrinal hierarchy was designed to promote the pro-buyer agenda and make land a more marketable commodity. Indeed, in treating property in land – including the owned home – as an exchangeable asset, the 1925 legislation set the scene for the emergence, much later in the century, of the idea that owned housing is an investment, and, subsequently, for the re-construction of the owned home as a 'pot' of money to draw against for a whole range of financial needs – from supplementing living expenses to paying for adult social care.

The deep assumptions of the 1925 property values (hierarchy of proprietary claims; security of individual property rights; stability of the property regime) – although often ignored by housing scholars – have had a seemingly intractable

---

13 The emphasis on 'responsibility' in respect of mortgage lending – both for lenders and borrowers – is discussed in Chapter 10.

14 As one housing scholar put it, "There is a 'magnificent contradiction': on the one hand, the construction of dwellings is fundamentally necessary for labour, but those who labour do not receive salaries or wages sufficient to purchase that property": S. Merrett, *Owner-Occupation in Britain* (Routledge, 1992) p. 72.

15 D Dorling, *All That is Solid: How the Great Housing Disaster Defines Our Times and What We Can Do About It* (Penguin, 2015).

16 In the 'rights paradigm', 'property rights [are] stronger than personal rights...rights always trump no-rights;...and stronger rights always trump weaker rights or no-rights'; AJ van der Walt, *Property in the Margins*, (Hart, 2009), p. 27.

effect on English property culture. The 1925 legislation did not merely coincide with a rise in the proportion of owners; it also facilitated that rise. But it was not the only cause; indeed, its existence was entirely coincidental.

The trigger for the rise of homeownership was neither ideologically driven nor built on a rising popular aspiration to own; nor was it *directly* the result of legal or market intervention – although perhaps indirectly so. Instead, the growth of the owner-occupied sector was driven by housing need, which could not be met by the (previously dominant) private rental sector. The evolution of statutory control over the rents which private landlords could charge (and the mortgage interest they paid) constrained the delivery of housing through private landlords which, in turn, created pent-up demand for alternative housing. Only part of that pent-up demand – evidenced by multiple households living together – could be dealt with through the development of the public housing sector. At the same time, building societies had a ready supply of money to lend and on terms favourable to owner-ship (rather than the then predominant tenure of the time, renting). Building costs began to reduce. Major marketing campaigns were developed, which – at this point, strategically or fortuitously – piggy-backed on new social policy debates. Ownership became associated with building 'a bulwark against bolshevism and all that bolshe-vism stands for'.[17] The building society movement, which, at its heart, emphasized thrift and mutual self-help, offered a readily available supply of money for property purchase; it also offered an alternative to public subsidy and ownership. Such was the need for building societies to lend that they engaged in what we might now refer to as 'dodgy practices' – relationships with builders which produced jerry-built housing.[18] While it was these social and economic drivers that propelled housing market growth, the 1925 legislation ensured that land law kept pace with the fash-ion for alienation, as land was commoditized in England and Wales as never before.

In Chapter 3 we explore the lasting legacy of the 1925 legislation in embed-ding the theme of 'alienation' in English land law. Indeed, such is the stark power of the theme of alienation in English land law that, even when subsequent legislation has specifically set out to correct the assumptions of alienation, the juggernaut remains unmoved. The Trusts of Land and Appointment of Trustees Act 1996, discussed in that chapter, was designed to correct the position under the Law of Property Act 1925, which implied that, where property was held by two or more people in equity, there was an explicit duty to sell the property and a (lesser) power to postpone. The primacy of the duty to sell was reinforced by the practices of the law.[19] Yet, the almost pathological core theme of alienation

---

[17] H. Bellman, *The Building Society Movement* (Methuen, 1927) p. 54.

[18] These histories can be found in a range of texts, but by far the most significant is P. Craig, 'The House That Jerry Built? Building Societies, the State and the Politics of Owner-Occupation' (1986) 1(2) *Housing Studies* 87; see also M. Ball, *Housing Policy and Economic Power: The Political Economy of Owner Occupation* (Methuen, 1983); D. Cowan & M. McDermont, *Regulating Social Housing: Governing Decline* (Routledge, 2006), ch. 8.

[19] See, in particular, *Re Mayo* [1943] Ch 302. Perhaps the most significant thing about this case is its brevity, which emphasizes just how obvious the outcome seemed to be.

remains in the jurisprudence which has emerged under the 1996 Act. Perhaps those remnants might have been anticipated – in the real world, the past has a lengthy shadow on the present – but they are, nevertheless, significant.

CITIZENSHIP

A key feature of our approach is to consider land law in its broader social, economic and political contexts. Our second theme, 'citizenship', relates to the relationship between 'land law' – narrowly defined as a system of rights, interests and entitlements – and the broader legal and social systems that frame our discipline.

In his 1970s essay, 'Citizenship and Social Class',[20] T.D. Marshall conceived of liberal democratic citizenship in the West as an almost inevitable progression towards the acquisition of civil, political and social or welfare rights. Accepting for a moment Marshall's contentious 'rights-based' construction of citizenship, it is clear that property – and, particularly, landownership – has been a prominent feature in wider debates about democracy, human rights and state welfare. The eventual extension of the right to vote in the UK beyond the property-owning classes through the gradual dismantlement of property qualifications in electoral laws, and then universally, was pivotal to the democratization of Western citizenship from the late nineteenth century.[21] State provision of housing was part and parcel of the development of an approach to citizenship (although one which initially emphasized the differentiated nature of such citizenship).[22] And the right to peaceful enjoyment of property, with a particular nod towards the protected sphere of the home, has been central to past and present conceptions of liberal freedom.[23]

The role of property in citizenship discourse in the West remains fiercely contested, however, across each of these areas of rights acquisition. For instance, the idea that liberal citizenship is defined through property rights and the privacy of the home has been critiqued for its prioritization of property-owning insiders, reinforcing economic inequality and social exclusion. First, the rights of property acquisition and ownership form the bedrock of capitalist economic structures, and their enforcement – including through land law – embeds political resistance to the redistributive measures that some argue are required to address the vast economic inequalities in society. Second, the conception of a protected private sphere of 'home', a space in which one has the right 'to be left alone', has often circumscribed the power of the state to protect the citizenship entitlements of the most vulnerable. The liberal private sphere has been especially problematic

---

[20] T.D. Marshall, 'Citizenship and Social Class', in J. Manza & M. Sauder (eds.), *Inequality and Society* (W W Norton and Co, 2009).

[21] M. Ignatieff, 'Myth of Citizenship' (1987) 12(3) *Queen's LJ* 399.

[22] See D. Cowan & A. Marsh, 'From Need to Choice, Welfarism to Advanced Liberalism: Some Problematics of Social Housing Allocation' (2005) 25(1) *Legal Studies* 22.

[23] J. Waldron, *The Right to Private Property* (Clarendon, 1988).

for those who understand the home as a site of exclusion. Most notably, freedom from state interference in the home has often meant control and unpunished violence by men over women within the private sphere.[24] Third, these kinds of embedded understandings overwrite other, contrasting understandings which are then pushed to the margins and made other. You only need to think about the ways in which Gypsy and Traveller populations are treated within land and associated planning systems, or the ways in which Indigenous populations' understandings have been overwritten to appreciate the violence that dominant understandings produce (citizen/anti-citizen).[25]

The social right to housing provides a useful example of the politics of citizenship in land law. Since the 1980s and 1990s, social citizenship in Britain – both in the specific context of social housing and across all areas of welfare provision – has been recast in terms of neoliberal individuality and self-responsibility, rather than collective needs-based state protection. Self-reliance on the part of a new 'active citizen' offers a claimed solution to the perceived bureaucracy and dependency culture created by the welfare state. In land law, this was epitomized in the 'right to buy' legislation, which gave effect to Thatcher's aim of rolling back the welfare state, while also normalizing homeownership as an expectation of good citizenship. This was a highly political move, which used the opportunity to link citizenship and landownership in an attempt to tap into the ancient Greek civic republicanism of an, inevitably conservative, property-owning democracy. It simultaneously located citizenship at odds with the social provision of the welfare state, including social housing, so creating a new division between citizens (owners) and 'anti-citizens' (tenants).[26]

The recent politics of citizenship suggests four things about the relationship between citizenship and property. First, while Western citizenship is often understood to be synonymous with the acquisition of rights, it can also be conceptualized in terms of the duties citizens owe to each other (and often the state). This is an important aspect of what it means to be an owner: to understand the responsibilities, as well as the rights, that flow from ownership of land. Yet, if these responsibilities are not encapsulated in law – but left as a matter of personal morality for the individual owner – there is a risk that land law's concept of ownership may become overly skewed towards the exclusion of others from access to the benefits of property, so exacerbating the powerlessness experienced by many within the constructed private sphere. This has been an important theme in recent debates about the regulation of access to public and quasi-public spaces.[27]

[24] S. Walby, 'Is Citizenship Gendered?' (1994) 28(2) *Sociology* 379; R. Lister, *Citizenship: Feminist Perspectives* (Palgrave Macmillan, 1997).

[25] See, for example, P. Niner, 'Accommodating nomadism? An examination of accommodation options for Gypsies and Travellers in England', (2004) 19(2) *Housing Studies* 141; Keenan, op cit n 9 above.

[26] J. Flint, *Housing, Urban Governance and Anti-Social Behaviour: Perspectives, Policy and Practice* (Policy Press, 2006).

[27] See A. Layard, 'Shopping in the Public Realm: The Law of Place' (2010) 37 *Journal of Law and Society* 412.

Secondly, it might be said that the current model of citizenship employed in the law of property is one of *differentiated* citizenship – embedding a political agenda that privileges certain groups of people (property insiders) over others (property outsiders).[28] This is a binary which has become sharper in the last 30 or so years as an increasing, more despotic, form of control has been exercised in areas such as anti-social behaviour and deviance, such that the insider/outsider binary has been combined with citizen/anti-citizen, with more intrusive mechanisms of transformation of the subject.[29]

Legal decision making is always 'framed': by facts, by law, by policies or purposes and by values; and the frame determines the (in)visibility of differentiated impact on insiders and outsiders.[30] It must follow that the relative impact of the legal frameworks applied to property problems on insiders and outsiders is an important criterion against which to explore, understand and evaluate legal decisions.

Thirdly, we need to treat with caution claims that the progressive acquisition of rights of citizenship in and around property is irreversible. Our relationship to property, as citizens, exists temporally, and rights relating to land can morph in the face of new policies and modes of thinking, resulting in greater inclusion or exclusion. While the push and pull of exclusion and inclusion – and the importance of having, acquiring or retaining property rights to shore up one's citizenship – run through many of the discussions in this book, perhaps the most explicit struggles over citizenship in the context of property rights are to be found when we look across from the criminalization of squatting (Chapter 6), the articulation of human rights claims in land disputes (Chapter 8) and the interface of equalities law with housing law regimes (Chapter 9).

EXCLUSION

It has been said that exclusion – the right to exclude all comers – is of the highest order of property.[31] It is this right which claims to deliver property's promises of autonomy, liberty and security. The exclusion by owners of non-owners (or of those who have 'weaker' property rights by those who have stronger rights) produces discrimination both inherently and as an outcome. For one thing, it requires boundaries and, in mapping out those boundaries, it produces a

---

[28] L. Fox O'Mahony, 'Property Outsiders and the Hidden Politics of Doctrinalism' (2014) 62 *Current Legal Problems* 409.

[29] For discussion, see N. Rose, 'Government and control', (2000) 40(3) *British Journal of Criminology* 321; D. Garland, *The Culture of Control* (OUP, 2001); L. Hancock and G. Mooney, '"Welfare ghettos" and the "broken society": Territorial stigmatization in the contemporary UK', (2013) 30(1) *Housing Theory and Society* 46; R. Levitas, 'The just's umbrella: Austerity and the Big Society in Coalition policy and beyond', (2012) 32(3) *Critical Social Policy* 320.

[30] See, for example, Z. Bankowski & G. Mungham, *Images of Law*, (Routledge & Kegan Paul, 1976); D. Cowan and D. Wincott, 'Exploring the legal', in D. Cowan and D. Wincott (eds.), *Exploring the Legal in Socio-Legal Studies*, (Palgrave, 2016).

[31] J. Penner, *The Idea of Property in Law* (Oxford University Press, 1997).

governable territory (which, in turn, facilitates alienation).[32] This latter point is also foundational to our idea of government. Rose puts it like this:

> A telling picture hangs in the Australian National Art Gallery in Canberra. It shows traces of hills, rivers, trails, borders, overlaid by a vast eye. It is entitled 'The Governor loves to go mapping'. Cartography – the activity of mapping – exemplifies the ways in which spaces are made presentable and representable in the hope that they might become docile and amenable to government. To govern, it is necessary to render visible the space over which government is to be exercised. This is not simply a matter of looking; it is a practice by which the space is re-presented in maps, charts, pictures and other inscription devices. It is made visible, gridded, marked out, placed into two dimensions, scaled, populated with icons and so forth. In this process, and from the perspective of its government, salient features are identified and non-salient features rendered invisible.[33]

We look at the significance of mapping and space further below, and in Chapter 5 when we consider the project of title by registration in the Land Registration Act 2002.

The theme of exclusion is both definitional, in establishing the territorial boundaries, and also controlling – shouting 'hands off, it's mine!', or 'stay out! Private property!' For some property theorists, particularly in the North American tradition, exclusion – and specifically the right to exclude – is regarded as the defining feature, or 'essence', of ownership.[34] This view has been challenged by competing, 'pluralist' and 'progressive' accounts of property, which identify elements of both rights of exclusion (for insiders) and rights of access (for outsiders) within the myriad contexts and circumstances in which land law rules are applied.[35]

One consequence of the dominance of the doctrinal tradition in the English land law mould is that the political content of land law is less likely to be the explicit object of analysis, to be openly debated and scrutinized, or to be evaluated with reference to its differentiating impacts on people according to their property/citizenship position (as more or less propertied parties). But this does not make the theme of exclusion, underpinning the meanings we ascribe to property values, and their distributive effects, any less present in English land law, as our discussion of the criminalization of squatting in Chapter 6 will show. A focus on the right to exclude also gives rise to 'defensive homeownership', as a reaction to

---

[32] J. Nedelsky, 'Law, Boundaries and the Bounded Self' (1990) 30(1) *Representations* 162; cf. N. Blomley, 'The Borrowed View: Privacy, Propriety and the Entanglements of Property' (2005) 30(3) *Law and Social Inquiry* 661.

[33] N. Rose, *Powers of Freedom: Reframing Political Thought* (Cambridge University Press, 1999) p. 36.

[34] T.W. Merrill, 'Property and the Right to Exclude' (1998) 77 *Neb L Rev* 730; J. Penner, *The Idea of Property in Law* (OUP, 1997); T.W. Merrill & H.E. Smith, 'The Morality of Property' (2007) 48 *Wm & Mary L Rev* 1849; L. Katz, 'Exclusion and Exclusivity in Property Law' (2008) 58 *U Toronto L J* 275.

[35] For a summary of these debates, see A.J. van der Walt, 'The Modest Systemic Status of Property Rights', (2014) 1 *J. L. Prop. & Soc'y* 15, http://alps.syr.edu/wp-content/uploads/2015/02/JLPS-2014-11-vanderWalt.pdf; see also D. Cooper, 'Opening up ownership: Community belonging, belongings, and the productive life of property', (2007) 32(3) *Law and Social Inquiry* 625.

the insecurity of everyday life. That insecurity '... has generated an imperative for the control and handling of domestic territory that seeks autonomy and refuge from dangers, as well as connecting to prevailing ideologies that celebrate personal autonomy and control'.[36] The notion of defensive homeownership territorializes risk and has, as its foundations, the link between property and crime control strategies. Defensive homeownership is a response to '... the two major social facts of the last third of the twentieth century: *the normality of high crime rates* and *the acknowledged limitations of the criminal justice state*'.[37] One visible consequence has been the demand for architectural and urban planning to enhance security.[38] Manifestations of this security are all around us (such as CCTV, lighting, etc.).

The 'gated community', discussed in Chapter 7, is a particularly valuable example of the link between the understandings of exclusion at the root of property law and our everyday lives. The gate – both literal and metaphoric – operates as a defensive mechanism against the savage and barbarous exterior, a kind of safe haven and exclusion of the other.[39] McKenzie links their rise to developers, local government and middle- and upper-class consumers, in all of whose interests the gate exists. Although the term 'gated community' is a contested concept in itself,[40] one common thread is of interlocking legal rights and obligations, often through the use of covenants, to enforce community norms: '... a legal framework which allows the extraction of monies to help pay for maintenance of common-buildings, common services, such as rubbish collection, and other revenue costs such as paying staff to clean or secure the neighbourhood'.[41] As such, they represent the apotheosis of the logic of property law – a community divided off from the outside by its own relational local law and norms in which everything from allocation to security to refuse collection is private.

The limits of the exclusion thesis can be exemplified by, and in, the debate over the conviction of Tony Martin, a farmer who took it upon himself to shoot two burglars, one of whom died as a result. Martin was convicted of murder (which was subsequently reduced to manslaughter on the grounds of diminished responsibility).[42] The case became something of a *cause célèbre* for those who (unsuccessfully) sought to argue that the logic of landownership, with the right to exclude at its core, conferred a right to act defensively in this way to defend one's home. And when Radio 4's *Today Programme* held a poll asking what subject

---

[36] R. Atkinson & S. Blandy, 'Panic Rooms: the Rise of Defensive Homeownership' (2007) 22(3) *Housing Studies* 443, 444.

[37] D. Garland, *The Culture of Control: Crime and Social Order in Contemporary Society* (Oxford University Press, 2001) p. 106 (emphasis in original).

[38] See, for example, O. Newman, *Defensible Space: People and Design in the Violent City* (Architectural Press, 1972).

[39] See M. Davis, *City of Quartz: Excavating the Future of Los Angeles* (Verso, 1990); E. McKenzie, *Privatopia: Homeowner Associations and the Rise of Residential Private Government* (Yale University Press, 1994).

[40] See A. Bottomley, 'A Trip to the Mall: Revisiting the Public/Private Divide', in H. Lim and A. Bottomley (eds.), *Feminist Perspectives on Land Law* (Glasshouse-Routledge, 2007).

[41] R. Atkinson & S. Blandy, 'Introduction: International Perspectives on the New Enclavism and the Rise of Gated Communities' (2005) 20(2) *Housing Studies* 177.

[42] *R* v. *Martin (Anthony Edward)* [2003] QB 1.

should form a Private Members' Bill in Parliament in 2003–2004 the winning proposal (which attracted 37 per cent of the 26,000 votes) was to allow homeowners to use 'any means' to defend their homes.[43]

As students, scholars and practitioners of land law – indeed, in any field of law – it is important that we remain alert to the 'under the radar' influence of 'taken-for-granted' ideas in determining how we understand land problems; how we think and talk and argue for solutions to these problems; and how we see the place of land law in the legal system and in society. This challenge of reaching past the 'taken-for-grantedness' of the discipline's norms is particularly acute when it comes to our next theme, rationality.

RATIONALITY

The fourth theme which cuts across the law and governance of land is rationality. An emphasis on rationality pervades much of legal scholarship and education. For many legal scholars, the idea that law has an emotional dimension – that is, that legal doctrine and decision making is, or should be, influenced by emotional considerations – may seem surprising at least, and even antithetical or heretical. As students of the law, we are taught that law is objective and impartial, that legal training teaches one to 'put emotions to one side' and to adopt purely rational analyses.[44] From this perspective, the idea that emotional responses and analyses might have a role to play in law conjures up the spectre of a subjective, irrational and partial system, which is anathema to our idea of 'what law is'. Formally, land law is objective; it has a status above the parties to a dispute and above what those parties think they have created (as discussed particularly in Chapter 4 on leases).

Yet, to see land law this way blinkers us from seeing and understanding the relationship of belonging between a person and their property. For when we focus exclusively on the drivers of land law as alienation, exclusion and rationality, we miss out on a singularly important facet of land: its affective capacity; or what Cooper describes as the sense of 'belonging' that is a core element of the experience of landownership.[45] In similar vein, Keenan uses empirical examples of property in action to argue that '... there is a merging of property as a subject's rights over an object (subject-object belonging) and property as a part of the subject's identity (whole-part belonging), with both types of belonging, or what could be seen as the merging of the two, having a material effect on the surrounding space'.[46] Keenan goes on to argue that seeing property like this can produce subversive property, a way of challenging hegemonic relations. A

---

[43] See http://news.bbc.co.uk/1/hi/uk/3360765.stm.
[44] See, generally, D. Sugarman, 'Legal Theory, the Common Law Mind, and the Making of the Textbook Tradition', in W. Twining (ed.), *Legal Theory and the Common Law* (Blackwell, 1986).
[45] Cooper, n.35, 629.
[46] S. Keenan, 'Subversive property: Reshaping malleable spaces of belonging', (2011) 19(4) *Social and Legal Studies* 423, 436.

further example is provided in Ewick and Silbey's research: when it snows in New Jersey, car owners clear a space and put a chair there to denote their owner-ship; the chair is a sign of ownership and what others refer to as 'networks of belonging'.[47]

Rationality is frequently presented as the unquestioned and unquestionable foundation of land law thinking: land law, so the argument goes, must behave in ways that are rational if it is to achieve its other purposes. Rationality is seen as necessary if the law is to achieve certainty, and to enable people to know where they stand in relation to property, so supporting the policy goals of trade in land and facilitating market transactions discussed above (alienation). Land law does not deal well with irrationality or with emotion. Yet, at the same time – and although much legal analysis is posited on the presumption that law is and should be rooted in logic and rational choice (we speak of judicial reasoning), based on fact rather than feeling – there are many contexts in which (even) property law must respond to emotional phenomena. Examples might include recognizing, and responding to, the emotional attachment that occupiers have to their homes as a special type of property based on its materiality as well as its emotional and psychological significance (see Chapter 5), or where the setting for the property problem is the emotional relationship between property subjects (see Chapter 11). And we should also remember that the craft of judging is an act of emotional labour in its own right.[48]

Rationality underscores land law in two important respects. The first is through the ideal-type deep rationality that underpins the classical exposition of property law – and particularly English land law – as rational, logical, abstract and juridical in character. Land law is treated as a juridical category which must be internally coherent, and the rules of which are worked out only by reference to its internal logic. There is no role, in a system of pure logic, for external, policy-informed goals: rather, land law is viewed as non-instrumentalist, and its doctrine is judged according to consistency and coherence with its internal schema (for example, the meanings of the core juridical concepts of ownership, title, possession and so on). This view of land law supports a dispassionate, logical mode of reasoning; it is not concerned with the effects of rules or decisions on parties, or with the fairness of outcomes.

Non-instrumentalist approaches to private law emphasize its inner character rather than its external effects, seeking to find coherence in the internal charac-teristics of private law without external referents in the form of policy or social interests. In these accounts of private law, the theorists seek to detach the reason of the law from political and policy issues based on their conviction that private

---

[47] See P. Ewick & S. Silbey, *The Common Place of Law: Stories from Everyday Life*, (University of Chicago Press, 1998); S. Silbey, 'J. Locke, op. cit.: Invocations of Law on Snowy Streets', (2008) 5(2) *Journal of Comparative Law* 66.
[48] See, for example, S. Roach Anleu and K. Mack, 'Magistrates' Everyday Work and Emotional Labour'. (2005) 32(4) *Journal of Law and Society* 590.

law is not a legitimate vehicle by which to achieve social policy goals.[49] The emphasis on deep rationality in such approaches to property excludes (re-)distributive considerations (for example, underlying inequalities). Those approaches are concerned with abstract rights rather than the welfare of parties. While they do not deny that other values (efficiency, welfare, etc.) are persuasive within their own moral and political orders, those values are simply not relevant (so the reasoning goes) to the juridical order governing private transactions between individuals.

Abstract, deep rationality approaches to land law do not recognize the (complex, differentiated) characteristics of the parties to particular property problems. They reason that (formal, procedural) equality requires that all subjects of land are treated equally in law.

Critics of abstracted approaches to land law argue that this ignores the reality of substantive inequality, in terms of unequal social, economic, knowledge or power resources. For example, feminist theorists have argued that the presentation of legal doctrine as 'abstract', 'objective' and 'impartial' privileges what are perceived to be masculine values.

A second, related meaning of rationality, also prevalent in land law debates, is economic rationality. This perspective on land law accepts the role of policy goals, but bases those goals on the values of economic efficiency (rather than, for example, social welfare). This is sometimes described as the classical market-individualist model. According to this model, the legal 'subject' of land law is an imagined person who is economically rational, expected to understand legal rules and procedures, and to behave in a self-interested, welfare-maximizing way.

From this perspective, property transactions are viewed as opportunities for individuals to maximize their own welfare (i.e., profit), in an adversarial game from which each party – so long as they follow the rules of the game (which under the political ideology of liberal individualism includes respecting the autonomy and equal opportunities of others to do likewise) – aims to wrest as much as they can to their own self-interest. This perspective positions land law within an adversarial transactional environment in which the parties' responsibilities are to their own self-interests and not to each other.

The economic rationality model of land law, and its construction of the legal subject as a rational agent aggressively pursuing his or her own self-interest, is said to be justified on several grounds. These include the need to ensure the security of long-term expectations, the reliability of investment strategies, the rationality of decision making about future land use, stable forward planning, the need to protect titles taken by purchasers and creditors, and the importance of ensuring that the substantial wealth tied up in land should not be rendered economically sterile. Economic rationalists emphasize the need to facilitate land transactions as smoothly and effectively as possible.

---

[49] See, for example, E. Weinrib, *The Idea of Private Law* (Harvard University Press, 1995).

Critics of this model of property challenge its emphasis on interpersonal justice – between the parties to the transaction – rather than social justice, taking account of the wider implications of legal decisions and doctrines.

The unreality of the rational economic subject – which doesn't take account of differences between parties' actual (social, economic, knowledge, power) situation – was highlighted by the critical school of legal realism,[50] on the basis that they operate as a shield for the implicit smuggling of assumptions that are calibrated to the privileged – for example, people with more land or more financial capability – with (hidden) political consequences.[51] Legal doctrine and institutions are not 'neutral' but have distributive consequences, perpetuating and reflecting political choices, social disadvantage and relations of inequality and oppression. Law – including land law – affects distributions of risk, wealth and power. Legal methods which claim to strip away the context in which transactions occur and the individual characteristics of the parties may have regressive or progressive outcomes. The point is that when the impact of doctrines and decisions is concealed, we lose sight of when, and how, land law affects real people in different contexts and social settings.

RESPONSIBILITY

As the discussions above have shown, the values that frame land law have direct, and sometimes explicit, implications for the ways in which responsibility for losses or harms is allocated. From a deep rationality perspective, questions about whether one person is *responsible* for another's loss employ highly theorized and abstract concepts rooted in the rights and correlative duties (or responsibilities) of the parties. According to this view, parties choose by their own free will to participate as subjects of private law, and so must bear responsibility for their own losses unless it can be positively shown that another party has *caused* that loss (and so is responsible for harming the losing party) in a legally significant way.[52]

For liberal theories of law – which acknowledge the role of property in achieving the goals of liberal/market individualism – the question is 'what are our responsibilities to one another as efficiency-maximizing liberal subjects?' The

---

[50] See, for example, E. Bonthuys, 'Accommodating Gender, Race, Culture and Religion: Outside Legal Subjectivity' (2002) 18 *SAJHR* 41 at 55; see also C. Smart, 'Law's Power, the Sexed Body, and Feminist Discourse' (1990) 17 *Journal of Law and Society* 194 at 210; M Mossman, 'Feminism and Legal Method: the Difference It Makes' (1986) 3 *AJLS* 30.

[51] Bonthuys, n.50.

[52] See, for example, Ripstein's 'individual responsibility' thesis, which posits that '[a] society of equals – a just society, if you like – is also a society that supposes people are responsible for their choices': A. Ripstein, *Equality, Responsibility and the Law* (Cambridge University Press, 1999) p. 1; or Honoré's theory of 'outcome responsibility', which argues that being held responsible for the outcomes of our choices is 'central to the identity and character of the agent ... our responsibility for what we do and for its outcome is inseparable from our status as persons': T. Honoré, *Responsibility and Fault* (Hart Publishing, 1999) p. 10.

value of autonomy and choice are central to the view that land law's function is to hold individuals responsible, as rational agents, for the choices they have made based on their own preferences. This is because (hypothetically, given fair circumstances and a level playing field) people are assumed to choose rationally according to what they value most,[53] and holding parties responsible for the autonomous choices they make, no matter how badly they turn out, is a hallmark of our liberal commitment to respect free and equal moral agency.

According to this model, the parties to property transactions have no positive duties or responsibilities towards each other or to the wider community. This proposition is challenged by competing theories which argue that the functions of property law include matters of distributive justice such as welfare policy and social context considerations.[54] Such theories adopt a more explicitly distributive perspective on how we conceive of our responsibilities in respect of property, not only between parties to the transaction as individuals but also as members of a community within which property is a valued resource and private owner-ship of property is a privilege. As Akhil Reed Amar argued[55] (and the new wave of 'progressive property' scholarship has echoed): if we seek to uphold private property values for the benefit of privileged 'insiders', mustn't we also – in a free and democratic society based on equality, dignity and respect[56] – recognize the importance of a minimum entitlement to property for socio-economically disad-vantaged outsiders? As Amar put it: 'Private property is such a good thing that every citizen should have some.'

The idea that property has a social context broadens the meaning of respon-sibility for property law, and raises important questions about the types of goals that are supported or privileged by our land law system.

Should the work that the legal system does to protect property rights be driven (only) by the goals of economic efficiency, or should it be responsive to broader social and welfare considerations?

Coming back to the argument that what we are studying is law, not politics (and if we imagine that the two can be separated), we might also ask: if land law does *not* consider social as well as economic values, what level of confidence can we have that the state/politics can, or will, adequately discharge this responsibility? If social and welfare considerations fall outside the scope of property law, and are pushed outside the realm of the minimalist state, does this force us to the conclusion that

---

[53] See, generally, R. Dworkin, *Sovereign Virtue: The Theory and Practice of Equality* (Harvard University Press, 2000).

[54] See, for example, J. Purdy, *The Meaning of Property: Freedom, Community, and the Legal Imagination* (Yale University Press, 2010); J Purdy, 'A Freedom-Promoting Approach to Property: A Revived Tradition for New Debates' (2005) 72 *U Chi L Rev* 1237.

[55] A.R. Amar, 'Forty acres and a mule: a republican theory of minimal entitlements' (1990) 13 *Harvard J Law & Public Policy* 37, 37.

[56] Joseph Singer has argued that 'property law is a constitutional problem because the norms and values of a free and democratic society limit the kinds of property rights that can be created'. J.W. Singer 'Property as the law of democracy' (2014) 63 *Duke LJ* 1287, 1304.

the social welfare of the parties is part of their own self-responsibility, to sink or swim as 'autonomous consumer-citizens'? And what does this, in turn, mean for the 'outsiders', for the socio-economically not-privileged? We know that resources and resilience – to 'sink or swim' in the market – are not evenly distributed in society; that property 'insiders' enjoy advantages when it comes to succeeding in the market; and that, by extension, these outcomes matter not only for property but also for citizenship.[57] Through this lens, are we still content that land law abdicate responsibility for outcomes?

The relationships between land law, on the one hand, and social-welfare considerations on the other, are explored in a recent body of scholarship (referred to as 'progressive property'). That scholarship seeks to temper the economic individualism of classical property theory with the idea of society as an interconnected web, in which an ethic of mutual responsibility around property plays a central role in achieving the common good.[58] Progressive property emphasizes the *social* values of property, including community, autonomy, personhood, environmental protection and personal security. In addition to our liberal commitments to freedom and autonomy, progressive property highlights our democratic commitments to respect for life, dignity and equality. The community of rights invoked in this model of property emphasizes our shared commitment to the values of '… life and human flourishing, the protection of physical security, the ability to acquire knowledge and make choices, and the freedom to live one's own life on one's own terms';[59] and (echoing Amar's argument, discussed above) reasons that, to the extent that we as members of communities that value private property as necessary for our human flourishing, we have a moral obligation to support social matrices and legal strategies that promote human flourishing for others.

Law plays an important role in shaping the expectations of responsibility placed on land law's subjects, whether we frame the parties to land law's interactions as self-responsible subjects, or as members of a community that values the property needs of others within the community. One manifestation of the notion of community responsibility for property subjects is the idea that being a private property owner carries some responsibility or duty in respect of the use of the property itself. This can be illustrated, by way of example, by the idea of an ethic of stewardship in respect of land, discussed in relation to the doctrine of adverse possession in Chapter 6. The stewardship justification[60] – that is, the ethical argument that landownership imposes a moral duty or responsibility of

---

[57] Fox O'Mahony, n.8.

[58] G. Alexander, 'The Social-Obligation Norm in American Property Law' (2009) 94 *Cornell LR* 745, 818–19.

[59] G. Alexander, E. Peñalver, J. Singer & L. Underkuffler, 'A Statement on Progressive Property', (2009) 94 *Cornell L R* 743.

[60] See, for example, J. Karp, 'A Private Property Duty of Stewardship: Changing Our Land Ethic' (1993) 23 *Environmental Law* 735; L. Caldwell and K. Shrader-Frechette, *Policy for Land: Law and Ethics*, (Rowman & Littlefield, 1993) ch. 7.

effective stewardship on the owner to look beyond their own self-interest and to ensure that this limited and vital commodity is managed fairly on behalf of the community as a whole – was one of the traditional justifications for the doctrine of adverse possession.

As the discussion in Chapter 6 demonstrates, the reform of adverse possession in the Land Registration Act 2002 marked a significant turning point (from a doctrine that required effective stewardship on the part of the landowner as a condition of retaining private ownership, on pain of potentially losing the right to recovery to a squatter) to a model of responsibility in which the state, through its bureaucratic system of title by registration, effectively relieved private landowners from those responsibilities in respect of land that may be occupied by squatters. This departure also has implications, discussed in Chapters 5 and 6, for how we conceive of land – as the material, organic and tangible physical entity that is used and occupied to satisfy material needs (for example, possessed by the squatter, or occupied as a home by the owner-occupier subject to a mortgage), or as an abstract commodity (as an entry on the land register, or as securitization rights, to be traded on the secondary mortgage market). These distinctions – which can also be characterized as 'place' (the social, material manifestation of land) and 'space' (the abstract representation of real property) – are considered further in the next section.

SPACE

Gray and Gray ask us to think about property using the notion of 'propriety' – which emphasizes the 'proper' in property, 'a claim to the legitimacy of one's personal space in this land'. This idea, which they describe as 'pre-legal',[61] makes an important claim, and one which links property law with parallel cross-disciplinary developments between law and geography.[62] Space is an active participant in land law, one which changes over time, according to disputes and the ways in which it is envisioned. We saw above how the crucial function of mapping out space enables government processes. One can take this further. The production of the map – particularly in colonial settings – enabled land to be carved up and sold as free space, or *terra nullius*, through the doctrine of discovery. As Mawani puts it, describing the indigenous inhabitants – regarded by colonial map-makers as 'non-subjects', and so excluded from their official maps – 'They were here (once upon a time), but now they are gone'.[63] Rob Home makes a similar point about the mapping of Palestine: 'The mosaic of land

---

[61] Gray and Gray, *Elements of Land Law* (Oxford University Press, 2009), para 1.5.43 and footnote 2.
[62] See the two important collections: N. Blomley, D. Delaney and R. Ford, *The Legal Geographies Reader* (Blackwell, 2001); J. Holder & C. Harrison, *Law and Geography* (Oxford University Press, 2003).
[63] R. Mawani, 'Genealogies of the Land: Aboriginality, Law, and Territory in Vancouver's Stanley Park' (2005) 14(2) *Social and Legal Studies* 315, 324.

parcels was plotted, a cadastral survey plan superseded verbal descriptions and the authoritative definition of land parcels, and new survey points were physically fixed on the ground.'[64]

Scholars working at the interface of law and geography go much further than this in thinking about boundaries and using alternative methodologies to understand land law's human subjects.[65] It is, perhaps, trite to note that land law seems to construct its own spatial boundaries through a series of apparent binaries – public/private, privacy/propriety, property/personal, community/outsider, inclusion/exclusion – which offer powerful descriptions through which space (abstract and objective) becomes place (social, cultural, material).

Law/geography scholars often seek to disrupt such binaries. Blomley, for example, in a study of gardening in Strathcona, Canada, disrupts the apparent binary between privacy and propriety. The garden was described as 'the public face of the family' – but he pushes on to argue that '... the evidence here suggests that people live in a much more emulsive world when it comes to property' so that the boundaries of property are broken down. He argues that we do not live according to these binaries; rather,

> ... we think of property as a way of being in the world. By this, I mean that it entails, at the very least, a set of beliefs, dispositions, and taken-for-granted norms, as well as embodied practices that relate to the world of things. Storytelling, lawmaking, mapmaking, adjudication, and fence building are all examples. Gardening, in part, is a symbolic and practical enactment of property. Property is put to work in multiple settings, of which the courtroom is only one.

By contrast, Layard, drawing on a case study of the regeneration of the city centre shopping area in Bristol, illustrates how these binaries were set up, how public was reduced to private through coalitions of expertise, resulting in the prohibition of certain 'spatial practices'.[66] Her rich theoretical analysis enables her to make some striking points about the effects of space becoming place. So, for example, she argues that '"good" or "anti-social" behaviour is determined by the vision of place, most famously by the banning of wearing "hoodies" from some shopping centres. ... Currently, the signs that adorn the side of the buildings at the entrance to the retail-led developments make these prohibitions [dog-walking, guitar-playing, skateboarding, photography] graphically clear.'[67]

Never before has space played such a significant role in the everyday lives of land. Space has been globalized and the social setting of place is often transformed into the signals, the neurons, the bytes transmitted electronically (through social

[64] R. Home, 'An "Irreversible Conquest"? Colonial and Postcolonial Land Law in Israel/Palestine' (2003) 12(2) *Social and Legal Studies* 291, 298.

[65] See, for example, N. Blomley, *Law, Space, and the Geographies of Power* (Guilford Press, 1994); D. Cooper, *Governing out of Order: Space, Law and the Politics of Belonging* (Rivers Oram, 1998).

[66] A. Layard, 'Shopping in the Public Realm: A Law of Place' (2010) 37(3) *Journal of Law and Society* 412.

[67] Ibid. 436–37.

media, or just as our chapters of this book have been electronically transmitted between us).[68] This global market – and its national, and local, effects – had a particularly significant impact on property at the time of the crisis from 2007. The origins of the crisis lay within the US mortgage market and its use of devices to make mortgages transportable, bundled up as sellable commodities on the open market (devices collectively referred to as 'securitization').[69] The extra-territorial links created by the internationalization of capital led to 'spillover effects' across nation states,[70] when capitalized profit gave way to socialized loss. The ways in which these effects impact on the UK mortgage market, and for individual subjects of English land law, is discussed in Chapter 10.

Land law in England and Wales may seem rather mundane when set against these international imaginations of space, but it nevertheless retains a salience by its apparent silence. Land law does not bat an eyelid at self-certified mortgages or 125 per cent mortgages or loan-to-income ratios that do not stack up or a city that nobody occupies because it is owned by non-residents as part of their capital accumulation strategies. This reflects, again, the significance of our alienation theme, replicated in the commodification of the loan document itself, and a version of the responsibility thesis. Land law is indifferent to bad bargains (even though some might say that the people who were caught in this trap were badly advised or that their imprudent lenders should bear the responsibility for their losses).

CONCLUSIONS

In this chapter, our purpose has been to identify what, for us, are the key themes in property law. These key themes run through this book in diverse ways, sometimes obvious and seen, and sometimes lurking beneath the surface. Each of them is, or has, disrupting influences. Like a temperamental teenager, there is contrariness within each of these themes and some, frankly, are just rebellious. But that doesn't mean we should ignore them or not take them seriously. It can hardly be a surprise that there are tensions at the root of the principles of law governing such a finite, powerful resource. There are no easy answers – anybody who suggests there are is trying to get one over on you – but, if there is one key message to take from this chapter, it is that land law has an everyday material reality which is obscured by a focus on doctrine; the way in which we use it and the law views it,

---

[68] See the brilliant analysis in A. Riles, *Collateral Knowledge: Legal Reasoning in the Global Financial Markets* (University of Chicago Press, 2011).

[69] See, generally, T. Wainwright, 'Laying the Foundations for a Crisis: Mapping the Historic-Geographical Construction of Residential Mortgage Backed Securitization in the UK' (2009) 33(2) *International Journal of Urban and Regional Research* 372; P. Langley, 'Sub-Prime Mortgage Lending: A Cultural Economy' (2008) 37(4) *Economy & Society* 469.

[70] S. Sassen, 'When Local Housing Becomes An Electronic Instrument: The Global Circulation of Mortgages – A Research Note' (2009) 33(2) *International Journal of Urban and Regional Research* 411, 420.

and the problems which it causes all have their roots in the complex, messy social world in which we all live.[71]

Further Reading

G. Alexander, E. Peñalver, J. Singer and L. Underkuffler, 'A Statement on Progressive Property' (2009) 94 *Cornell LR* 743.

N. Blomley, 'The Borrowed View: Privacy, Propriety and the Entanglements of Property' (2005) 30(3) *Law and Social Inquiry* 661.

M. Davies, *Property: Meanings, Histories, Theories* (Routledge-Cavendish, 2007).

S. Keenan, 'Subversive property: Reshaping malleable spaces of belonging', (2011) 19(4) *Social and Legal Studies* 423

A. Layard, 'Shopping in the Public Realm: A Law of Place' (2010) 37(3) *Journal of Law and Society* 412.

J. Nedelsky, 'Law, Boundaries and the Bounded Self' (1990) 30(1) *Representations* 162.

---

[71] Our sense is that each of us (the authors and you, the reader) has a different identity of the 'social' (and note the definite object, which one might also question). So, for example, Latour argues '... the social is not a type of thing either visible or to be postulated. It is visible only by the *traces* it leaves (under trials) when a *new* association is being produced between elements which themselves are in no way "social"': B. Latour, *Reassembling the Social: An Introduction to Actor-Network-Theory* (Oxford University Press, 2005) p. 8 (emphasis in original).

2

TENURE AND ESTATES

INTRODUCTION

If all property is theft, then the doctrines of tenure and estates are a double theft. Not only do they legitimate (and define) the ownership of land as well as rights over it, but they also de-naturalize the law from experience. That is the great debate with which this chapter engages.

What we mean by de-naturalizing law from experience is that these doctrines, which are taught to most students in the opening classes of land law, take our subject out of our ordinary everyday appreciation of our symbiotic relationship with land. Imposed aside from that relationship are a series of technical legal concepts which perform the double feat of apparent political neutering as well as introducing a technical character to legal, as opposed to ordinary, knowledge. This is what makes law 'law', so to speak: neutral, objective and technical. As Riles suggests, 'This view of technical law as neutral and removed from the rough and tumble of fights over how to allocate scarce resources in society itself has political consequences.'[1] Students are taught that we cannot 'own' the land (that is the right of the Sovereign, the doctrine of tenure), and that what landowners own is merely what Gray and Gray refer to as an 'interposed abstraction'[2] between the owner and the land (the abstraction being time, the doctrine of estates).

What would land law look like, if, rather than labelling it like that, we labelled it the 'law of the home' or 'the law of place'?[3] We would be forced to think about the empirical question, what is a 'home' or a 'place', a more natural question

---

[1] A. Riles, *Collateral Knowledge: Legal Reasoning in the Global Financial Markets* (University of Chicago Press, 2011) p. 67.

[2] K. Gray and S. Gray, *Elements of Land Law* (Oxford University Press, 2009), para 1.3.3.

[3] Both such terms are in regular usage in academic scholarship, giving rise to major conceptual advances – see, for example, L. Fox, *Conceptualising Home: Theories, Laws and Policies* (Hart, 2007); A. Layard, 'Shopping in the Public Realm: A Law of Place' (2010) 37(3) *Journal of Law and Society* 412. The understanding of property as 'proper' or as 'propriety' has similarly been a significant mine for understandings – see M. Davies, *Property: Meanings, Histories, Theories* (Routledge-Cavendish, 2007); N. Blomley, 'The Borrowed View: Privacy, Propriety and the Entanglements of Property' (2005) 30(3) *Law and Social Inquiry* 661.

rooted in the social realities of everyday life; and, although there might be temptation to essentialize, we would be forced to recognize that the doctrines of tenure and estates do radical injustice to our relationship with where we live; and indeed, to recognize that 'where we live' may well include nowhere, may be mobile and/ or a site of repression/oppression.[4]

All of this does not suggest that technical law should be overlooked – quite the reverse, for we need to appreciate its contours in order to understand the strategies it uses to govern everyday life without, in fact, being seen to govern, until one needs to engage with it. Let us unpack that comment a little. Law is not so much the tip of the iceberg but rather an abstraction through which we are governed, but we don't see it, and land law actually bears little relation to our everyday lives.[5] We talk about either owning or renting, living in a hostel or B&B and, in so doing, elide unsatisfactorily land law with our everyday lives. Rather like the Borg,[6] we have assimilated land law into our talk but without some essential components. Nevertheless, land law is also all around us. It comes to the fore at certain crisis moments, tipping points which assimilate us as they force us to 'go to law' and result in some rather awkward conclusions.

After a brief description of the doctrines of tenure and estates, this chapter is split into three parts, which are designed around these issues. In the first part, we outline research around tenure from the housing policy literature. In this research, various authors have considered the attributes of 'home' ownership as opposed to renting. This material enables us to frame our appreciation of the social reality of the doctrine of tenure and estates – or the way in which law is inadequately interwoven with, and translated in, society. We then develop these ideas through three case studies: long leaseholds, sale and rentback, and shared ownership. The great debate as regards long leaseholds can be summarized by the title of an important article, 'Owners yet tenants?'; with sale and rentback, it concerns land law's particular appreciation of temporal realities and the prioritisation of mortgage lenders over the other participants in the transaction. Lastly, the great debate as regards shared ownership, a modern creation (well, about 40 years old), is the way it passively uses the leasehold regime without amendment, causing considerable uncertainty for the 'owners'; what we find in relation to shared ownership is that the elements of the label 'shared' and 'ownership' are a nonsense in law; yet, this label is what is being peddled.

---

[4] See, for example, the highly suggestive discussion of the 'homeless vehicle' by Neil Smith: 'Contours of a Spatialized Politics: Homeless Vehicles and the Production of Geographical Scale' (1992) 33 *Social Text* 54.

[5] N. Rose and M. Valverde, 'Governed by Law?' (1998) 7(4) *Social and Legal Studies* 541.

[6] According to Wikipedia, 'The Borg are a fictional pseudo-race of cybernetic organisms depicted in the *Star Trek* universe associated with Star Trek' (http://en.wikipedia.org/wiki/Borg_%28Star_Trek%29, accessed 13.04.2012).

TENURE AND ESTATES

The doctrine of tenure is an entirely incidental, historical anachronism in English law, although it can become the subject of intense debate even today.[7] In essence, it derives from the conquest by William I and his method of keeping hold of power. Sitting atop the feudal pyramid, he granted lands in return for services, the land being held of the monarch. Tenure in this sense merely means 'holding of' the crown. Put another way, it is said that the crown has radical title, that is, absolute ownership over land. But all of this simply explains the limits of what can be owned by us ordinary mortals, and what we can own is this abstraction called the estate. The doctrine of tenure provides that explanation; its lack of utility as a concept lies in the ways in which, and the reasons why, tenure itself became redundant following in particular the Statute Quia Emptores 1290 and the Abolition of Tenures Act 1660.

The estate being what is owned is of much greater importance and interest. The great success of the Law of Property Acts of 1922 and 1925 was to reach a position where the number of estates capable of existing at law was reduced to two: the fee simple absolute in possession and the term of years absolute.[8] So important was this shift, and so dramatic, that it is contained in the opening words of the opening section of that great Act of consolidation in 1925, the Law of Property Act. These estates are translated into the colloquialisms of freehold and leasehold. The freehold (in this sense) is the best type of right which can exist in relation to land, for it is temporally finite only by being indefinite. In other words, its temporal limitation is that it lasts indefinitely. The leasehold interest is, as discussed in greater detail in Chapter 4, definite in duration, but it also implies a relationship between the grantor (the lessor, or landlord) and the grantee (the lessee, or tenant). Practically all flats are held leasehold for the simple reason that this was the only way of ensuring mutually interlocking obligations between those living horizontally (so to speak). Many houses are also owned in this way, although this is often for historical reasons due to the way in which various large landowners have carved up their property.

The more interesting estate is the leasehold, and here a little history is essential. Rather than being a property right, the historical derivation of the leasehold estate was as a chattel. It was convenient for it to be regarded as such at the time, but damages for trespass to a leasehold were not sufficient; so, in the ways in which lawyers have historically done, fictional mechanisms were devised to enable the leaseholder to recover possession. Over time, the fiction was able to be dropped so that the leasehold has a curious status in the law of property, being defined properly now as a 'chattel real'. The notion of a chattel real is antithetical but conveys

---

[7] See the discussion in *Mabo* v. *Queensland* (1989) 166 CLR 186 concerning the prior rights of indigenous peoples over the Crown's radical title.

[8] Law of Property Act 1925, s. 1.

something hugely important about the lease: its basis lies both in contract and property. For some of the time, this antithesis is hidden, for it may be neither relevant to a dispute nor relevant to our everyday lives. At times, though, it is productive of huge controversy, particularly when contract and property offer different solutions to a dispute or when the feudal status of the tenant becomes manifest.

As regards the former, consider Lord Browne-Wilkinson's analysis in the case of *Hammersmith and Fulham LBC* v. *Monk*.[9] In this case, the question was whether a tenancy granted to two persons jointly could be ended by the unilateral service of a notice to quit by one of them. The House of Lords held that the one could do so by analogy with contractual rights. Lord Browne-Wilkinson said:

> In certain cases a contract between two persons can, by itself, give rise to a property interest in one of them. The contract between a landlord and a tenant is a classic example. The contract of tenancy confers on the tenant a legal estate in the land such legal estate gives rise to rights and duties incapable of being founded in contract alone. The revulsion against Mrs. Powell being able unilaterally to terminate Mr. Monk's rights in his home is property based: Mr. Monk's property rights in the home cannot be destroyed without his consent. The other reaction is contract based: Mrs. Powell cannot be held to a tenancy contract which is dependant for its continuance on the will of the tenant.[10]

As regards the problems which arise when the feudal status of the tenant becomes manifest, consider the everyday situation of the tenant of a 99-year lease having to pay a ground rent to their landlord; a landlord seeking to levy a sizable service charge against their tenant; or where the tenant of what was originally a 99-year lease finds that the remaining term in the property is unmortgageable (because lenders will not lend against the remaining period of the term). There has been much law reform on the two latter issues but, in truth, the law has been poorly drafted and it is complex so that disputes often arise.[11]

Debate 1

How is 'tenure' translated in society?

Compared to these legal meanings, tenure appears to be used in a completely different sense – and one which is driven to a large extent by housing policy – in society. Housing policy tenures are owner-occupation, private renting, local authority renting or housing association renting.[12] The map of tenure presented

---

[9] [1992] 1 AC 478.
[10] At 491.
[11] As one commentator put it, the law was 'too restrictive, too complex, and too expensive': D. Clarke, 'Occupying "Cheek by Jowl": Property Issues Arising from Communal Living' in S. Bright and J. Dewar (eds.), *Land Law: Themes and Perspectives* (Oxford University Press, 1998) p. 400.
[12] See D. Cowan, *Housing Law and Policy* (Cambridge University Press, 2011), ch. 1.

bears little relation to that inherent in land law. Of course, one can say that a freehold estate is ownership in practical terms, but what of long leaseholders? Are they renters? The answer seems to be that they are not, at least for housing policy, but that does not really help us either because we then must ask: at what point does a long lease tip from being renting to owning? What is important here is to understand the ways in which housing policy has promoted ownership above all else, and the effects of that promotion on the ways in which tenure (in the housing policy sense) is viewed in society. There is now a bank of empirical work on the subject.

PROMOTING OWNERSHIP

The starting point is to note the massive evolution in tenure during the twentieth century. From a position in which practically all households rented (around 90 per cent), the latest statistics show that around 63 per cent of households are owners.[13] Undoubtedly, one cause of that evolution was the failure of private renting and, although there are different ways of looking at the causes of that failure, the key period in this transition occurred during the inter-war years. It was during this period that diverse factors came together to push households into ownership. One factor was the economic climate which meant that building societies had considerable capital to lend for ownership and they manipulated mortgage law to make the cost of mortgages cheaper (such as increasing mortgage terms so as to reduce monthly repayments); another that construction for ownership became more profitable than building for rent; another that there was pent-up demand for accommodation; another that the introduction of security of tenure and rent control had limited the availability of property for rent.[14] As Ball puts it:

> [Owner-occupation] became relatively cheaper, provided new comparatively spacious suburban housing attuned to the consumer goods that were beginning to come onto the market, and as all of the households that could afford to buy flocked into owner occupation it rapidly developed a social kudos. Conversely non-ownership began to become synonymous with the negative social status of being unable to afford house purchase.[15]

Studies of housing policy documents have also demonstrated the way in which owner-occupation became regarded rhetorically as both 'homeownership' and

---

[13] Department for Communities and Local Government, *Dwelling Stock Estimates: 2014, England* (London: DCLG, 2015) – this represents a decrease by 7 per cent since 2002.

[14] The best discussions of this period can be found in A. Holmans, *Housing Policy in Britain* (Croom Helm, 1987), ch. 3; and M. Ball, *Housing Policy and Economic Power: The Political Economy of Owner Occupation* (Methuen, 1983). For discussion of the ways in which the mortgage lending industry changed during this period, see P. Craig, 'The House That Jerry Built? Building Societies, the State and the Politics of Owner-Occupation' (1986) 1(1) *Housing Studies* 87.

[15] Ball, n.14, at 25.

'natural'. This promotion chimes with the neoliberal settlement of private, marketized relations creating bonds of obligation in private law.

As we saw in Chapter 1, the suggestion was that tenures other than ownership did not provide 'homes' and were somehow unnatural.[16] The zenith of this discursive formation was probably during the 1970s when ownership was paraded as 'a basic and natural desire' or as a 'deep and natural desire' for independent control over one's home.[17] Gurney's analysis of the 1995 housing White Paper makes a similar point:

> 'Home' as a normalising discourse is expressed in *Our Future Homes* through ideas of love, warmth, comfort, pride, independence, and self-respect. The chapter concerning homeownership is dripping with these ideas. This is normalisation through repetition and association. Significantly 'home ownership' is preferred to the more formal-legal terminology of 'owner-occupation' except in relation to specific proposals for legislation.[18]

Similarly, the Conservative party manifesto in 2015 told us that 'Conservatives believe passionately in home ownership' and that they are 'the party of home ownership'.[19] These sentiments about ownership, and the moral and ethical values underpinning it, find their purest expression in the self-help literature of the nineteenth century and that deriving from the building society movement in the early twentieth century.[20]

The development of the welfare state did not really touch housing in the same way as it did other areas of social insurance – indeed, Cole and Furbey have suggested that 'Adolf Hitler proved a more decisive influence than William Beveridge in shaping the housing requirements of post-war Britain'.[21] The involvement of the state in the provision of housing, through local authorities, had always been regarded as contingent on the failure of the private sector; but it was anticipated that, as soon as the private sector was able to re-take the reins, the state's role would simply fall away.[22] As a retrospective, one can see that analysis

---

[16] A. Murie, P. Niner and C. Watson, *Housing Policy and the Housing System* (London: Allen & Unwin, 1976) p. 171; see also J. Kemeny, *The Myth of Home Ownership: Private versus Public Choices in Housing Tenure* (London: Routledge & Kegan Paul, 1981).

[17] Respectively, Department of the Environment, *Housing Policy: A Consultative Document* (London: DoE, 1977) p. 50, and *A Fair Deal for Housing* (London: HMSO, 1971) p. 4. It was at or about this time that the ghost was being given up on private renting: see F. Berry, *Housing: The Great British Failure* (London: Croom Helm, 1974) p. 123, and D. Cowan and A. Marsh, 'There's Regulatory Crime and Then There's Landlord Crime: from "Rachmanites" to "Partners"', (2001) 64(6) *MLR*, 831, 840–42.

[18] C. Gurney, '*Pride and Prejudice*: Discourses of Normalisation in Public and Private Accounts of Home Ownership' (1999) 14(2) *Housing Studies* 163, 173.

[19] *The Conservative Party Manifesto*, (London: Conservative Party, 2015) p 51.

[20] See, further, D. Cowan and M. McDermont, *Regulating Social Housing: Governing Decline* (Routledge Glasshouse, 2006) pp. 163–68.

[21] I. Cole and R. Furbey, *The Eclipse of Council Housing* (Routledge, 1994) p. 60.

[22] See the discussion in P. Malpass, 'The Wobbly Pillar? Housing and the British Postwar Welfare State' (2003) 32(4) *Journal of Social Policy* 589; and P. Malpass, *Housing and the Welfare State: The Development of Housing Policy in Britain* (Palgrave Macmillan, 2005).

holding good in the settlement of social housing after 1979, with various partial privatization mechanisms being employed (both individual and collective).[23]

UNDERSTANDINGS ABOUT OWNERSHIP

Although the evidence predates the current economic crisis and the major problems in the banking industry, as well as the attempt to revive the reputation of social housing, there is considerable evidence about the hierarchy of tenures in society. These largely mirror understandings in housing policy. Ownership is what is prized and aimed for, and anything else is somehow lesser. These findings have been controversial, though. The starting point is probably Peter Saunders' book, *A Nation of Home Owners*, in which he argues from his own survey data in three towns that homeownership provides ontological security. Rather than having petty and other rules imposed on the household by a landlord, the homeowner has the power to create their own world through the lens of their home:

> Two principal motives are mentioned time and time again when people are asked why they prefer to own rather than rent their homes. One is financial – buying is seen as cheaper in the long run, or rent is seen as a waste of money, or rising prices are seen as a means of saving for the future or accumulating capital. The other has to do with the sense of independence and autonomy which ownership confers – the freedom from control and surveillance by a landlord and the ability to personalize the property according to one's tastes.[24]

Saunders argued that owners tended to associate 'home' with relaxation and personal possession, whilst renters defined it in terms of family or neighbourhood. The differences were most marked for council house purchasers. Tenants were 'much less inclined to develop attachments to their houses than owners'. Because of local authority control through the tenancy agreement, tenants were less likely to have personalized their homes (particularly because they had little or no choice over the property allocated to them).[25] However, the bigger point made by Saunders was that a 'consumption sector cleavage' had opened up between those who could afford to buy, and reaped the benefits of apparently inexorable capital gain, and those who could not, who then languished in the rented sector.

Saunders' work was hugely controversial, in part because it ascribed certain values to an apparently homogeneous class. It was the subject of an instant critique, which emphasized the diversity of experiences and the fragility of the sector.[26] Further, Forrest and Murie referred to a 'paradox that, as owner occupation

---

[23] Principal amongst these are the right to buy and the large-scale voluntary transfer of stock from local authorities to housing associations; see, in particular, H. Pawson and D. Mullins, *After Council Housing: Britain's New Social Landlords* (Palgrave Macmillan, 2010).

[24] P. Saunders, *A Nation of Home Owners* (Methuen, 1990) p. 84.

[25] See D. Cowan and A. Marsh, 'From Need to Choice, Welfarism to Advanced Liberalism: Problematics of Social Housing Allocation' (2005) 25(2) *Legal Studies* 22.

[26] R. Forrest, A. Murie and P. Williams, *Home Ownership: Differentiation and Fragmentation* (Unwin Hyman, 1990).

has expanded, it has become progressively what it is not supposed to be. It has become dependent in its present form on large-scale public support.'[27] Other studies noted that homeownership should be construed as a 'continuum' with a low-income end which is indistinct from renting – evidence from a study conducted in the late 1970s of areas of low-income homeownership in Birmingham and Liverpool suggested that homeownership was 'a squalid trap':

> Unlike many owners who might expect capital gains on their property and the possibility of movement to a different strata of the market, these owners may suffer real capital losses and far from being able to move they will be forced to stay in a deteriorating asset which will be in a deteriorating condition.[28]

There were studies of intersectional disadvantage in the housing system, which effectively forced certain households into ownership, and studies which suggested that, for some, ownership is a form of coerced exchange.[29]

Nevertheless, what comes out of Gurney's data is a rich picture of a social hierarchy of tenure, with ownership at the top and local authority renting at the bottom.[30] Gurney drew attention to the construction of tenure which came from his qualitative interviews through the use of well-known aphorisms and metaphors about homeownership, for example: 'an Englishman's home is his castle', 'it's yours at the end of the day' and 'renting's just money down the drain'. These aphorisms and metaphors formed part of the everyday understandings of his sample and were value-laden expressions of 'common-sense'; they constructed '... a housing tenure knowledge [which] is both stereotypical and prejudiced'.[31] His interviewees also constructed a morality about housing tenure through providing prejudicial accounts of renting and moral fables. Council housing was '... a metaphor for a stereotypical feckless class'.[32]

THINKING TENURE

Although housing policy researchers were once counselled to get rid of the fetishism of tenure,[33] there is little doubt that it retains a hold over researchers and society. Barlow and Duncan wondered aloud '... how the term [tenure] jumped the gap between this specialised, legal use and the much broader, quasi-scientific use

---

[27] R. Forrest and A. Murie, *Selling the Welfare State: The Privatisation of Public Housing* (Routledge, 1990) p. 174.

[28] V. Karn, J. Kemeny and P. Williams, *Home Ownership in the Inner City: Salvation or Despair?* (Gower, 1985) p. 106.

[29] Summarized in Cowan, n.12, ch. 2.

[30] C. Gurney, 'Lowering the Drawbridge: A Case Study of Analogy and Metaphor in the Social Construction of Home-Ownership' (1999) 36(10) *Urban Studies* 1705.

[31] Ibid. 1706.

[32] Ibid. 1716.

[33] F. Gray, 'Owner Occupation and Social Relations', in S. Merrett, *Owner Occupation in Britain* (Routledge and Kegan Paul, 1982) ch. 5.

by housing researchers. ... The process of transition between legal and quasi-scientific usage would be a useful subject for research in the sociology of knowledge, precisely because it seems unjustified'.[34] Now it is that very translation which is both interesting and uneasy. It is interesting because, as Cowan has suggested, it reflects a certain 'legal consciousness', a translation of the apparently neutral values of law into the political valves and values of society.[35] Perhaps that imperfect translation has occurred over time for policy reasons – it became important to know the numbers and proportions of households who are owners – or simply mirrored the way in which ownership was marketed as a homogeneous device. It is uneasy because, in its inaccurate rendering of the position in law, it is productive of major fault lines in the experiences of ownership. Housing policy finds this particularly hard to deal with; and when faced with the cold reality of the apparently objective neutral position of property law that imperfect translation of legal doctrines in policy and society becomes manifest.

Debate 2

Between ownership and renting (1): Are long leaseholders owners?

This problem was set up in the introduction to the previous section. It concerns the fit of 'long leaseholds' with understandings of ownership and tenure both in law and in society. We do not need to set out what we mean by 'long' in this context – as was noted above, it is unclear when a leasehold interest becomes categorized as an ownership interest – but we should note the imprecision and inelegance in the use of such a term.[36] It is (of course) outside the realm of land law, which ascribes no such time period to the existence of a leasehold estate in land. But what the term leasehold does imply are the following characteristics: (a) a relationship between landlord and tenant; (b) the payment of a ground rent, often at a peppercorn or low value, and often a service charge; and (c) mutually enforceable obligations between landlord, tenant and other occupiers of the building, with the consequences of non-performance potentially dire (including, in the case of tenant non-performance, the loss of their entire interest).

The growth of long leaseholds of property occurred at a number of key moments in time, each of which gives rise to quite separate sets of concerns.[37] First, during the nineteenth century, there were so-called 'building leases', usually

---

[34] J. Barlow and S. Duncan, 'The Use and Abuse of Housing Tenure' (1988) 3(4) *Housing Studies* 219, 220.

[35] See D. Cowan, 'Housing and Property' in P. Cane and H. Kritzer (eds.), *Oxford Handbook of Empirical Legal Studies* (Oxford University Press, 2010), drawing on P. Ewick and S. Silbey, *The Common Place of Law: Stories from Everyday Life* (University of Chicago Press, 1998).

[36] The idea of a long lease is probably one for more than 21 years, as that is the threshold beyond which certain statutory protections 'kick in'.

[37] See A. Stewart, *Rethinking Housing Law* (Sweet & Maxwell, 1996) p. 110 ff.

of 99 years, granted to build a property on a plot of land which would then be rented out. Second, in the period between the world wars, there was significant construction of mansion blocks. Third, during the 1950s and 1960s, a significant number of long leasehold properties were sold to 'sitting tenants'. Fourth, a significant number of flats have been sold since 1980 to former local authority tenants under the right to buy.

The research evidence suggests that long leaseholders' idea of themselves as 'owners', an idea which implies certain self-determining power over their physical accommodation, is not necessarily borne out by the reality of the relationships. And it can come as a real surprise to the 'owners'. As Cole and Robinson, drawing on their qualitative research with leaseholders, suggest:

> Leaseholders commonly balked at referring to themselves as tenants, prefer-ring instead to consider themselves owner occupiers. Their legal status had been made clear to them, however, by the limited control and freedom they were able to exercise over significant aspects of their occupation. To many, unaware of or misunderstanding their legal position as leaseholders, this came as a surprise.[38]

The problems identified in that study '... were rooted in the freedom freeholders have to exercise authority without concern for the wishes of lessees'.[39] Inadequate repairs and maintenance, which were only reactive and not proactive (meaning costs eventually were higher and could not be offset); maintenance and service charges were high and increasing; and there were delays on the 'wasting asset' of the remainder of the term.[40]

Stewart considers the reasons for the growth of the market in the reversionary interest of the freehold. She makes the following significant point:

> The relationships between owners and occupiers have been transformed by the development of a market for the sale of flats. Once this market had emerged, there developed a dual market in flats ... The value of flats for owner occupation became greater than their value to landlords for renting. In these market conditions, traditional residential investment companies are replaced by an aggressive breed of speculative break up companies who are not 'landlords' but asset strippers.[41]

The new breed of corporate freeholder sought profit from their investment. Profit could come in one of two ways: from waiting until the end of the lease (which was not long, of course, in relation to the nineteenth-century leases); or increasing service charges and administration costs. As Robertson puts it, the source of greatest resent-ment is that while the leaseholders live in the property and pay for the management and maintenance they are beholden to the freeholder who does neither.[42]

---

[38] I. Cole and D. Robinson, 'Owners Yet Tenants: The Position of Leaseholders in Flats in England and Wales' (2000) 15(4) *Housing Studies* 595, 608, citing one of their respondents as saying 'It was a shock really, to find out that your life wasn't really your own.'

[39] Ibid. 602.

[40] Ibid. 603.

[41] Stewart, n.37, 114.

[42] D. Robertson, 'Cultural Expectations of Homeownership. Explaining Changing Legal Definitions of Flat "Ownership" in Britain' (2006) 21(1) *Housing Studies* 35, 43.

At the level of policy, the arguments range from 'pure' freedom of contract principles and 'pure' property rights to 'abuse' and 'exploitation' by 'neglectful' landlords.[43] One might suppose that party political lines would be clearly drawn on this issue – the Conservatives on the one side and Labour on the other – but that would be an inaccurate representation. Leasehold reform became a cross-party political issue. The Conservatives, during the 1980s and 1990s, saw leasehold reform '... as a natural and (vote-winning) extension of its ideological commitment to homeownership ... [F]reeholders' control was seen as restricting the liberty of people to own their homes'; Labour supported leasehold reform as a social justice issue.[44] The London *Evening Standard* has also campaigned on the issue for some time.

Leasehold reform has come 'thick and fast' since the Leasehold Reform Act 1967.[45] There are now controls over service charges, insurance, management, consultation, enfranchisement (buying the freehold individually or collectively), right of first refusal, buying a further term of years, restrictions on the landlord's right to forfeit the lease for non-payment of service charge, a right to manage for leaseholders and indeed an entirely new form of tenure, commonhold.[46] Amidst this welter of law, though, one thing is clear: in seeking to balance the principles of freedom with the rights of the users, the law is extremely complicated and it is more than easy to get lost in that complexity. The balance struck leaves the lease itself in place and there are many disputes which arise as a result of the poor drafting of those leases. Many disputes are the province of the Tribunal system and a brief reading of the reports of their judgments and appeals merely exemplifies that complexity.

A considerable number of everyday problems remain despite this welter of law,[47] and these can particularly impact on right-to-buy leaseholders (who often are the least likely to be able to afford to pay). Right-to-buy leaseholders will usually have properties which remain managed by the local authority (or possibly a housing association).[48] Other properties in the block are likely to remain as social housing lettings. By virtue of government housing policy in the 2000s, social landlords were required to bring their properties up to the 'decent homes standard' by 2010.[49] Decades of underinvestment in the stock had left much of it in poor repair, and the programme did a great deal of good, but it also cost a lot (around £22 billion for housing and communities alone).

---

[43] Cole and Robinson, n.38, p. 600.

[44] S. Blandy and D. Robinson, 'Reforming Leasehold: Discursive Events and Outcomes, 1984–2000' (2001) 28(3) *Journal of Law and Society* 384, 399.

[45] Robertson, n.43, p. 42.

[46] See, generally, S. Bright, *Landlord and Tenant Law in Context* (Oxford: Hart, 2007) ch. 13. As regards commonhold, this has not proved particularly attractive and is not discussed further here – for discussion, see D. Clarke, 'Long Residential Leases: Future Directions' in S. Bright (ed.), *Landlord and Tenant Law: Past, Present and Future* (Hart Publishing, 2006).

[47] See the Nearly Legal blog for a sample of these: www.nearlylegal.co.uk/blog.

[48] See H. Carr, 'The Right to Buy, the Leaseholder, and the Impoverishment of Ownership' (2011) 38(4) *Journal of Law and Society* 519.

[49] DETR/DSS, *Quality and Choice: A Decent Home for All* (DETR/DSS, 2000) para. 7.7.

The costs of these works resulted in local authorities levying bills for thousands of pounds on largely unsuspecting long leaseholders. As the London Assembly put it:

> Preliminary discussions with stakeholders and leaseholders suggest that there are a number of factors surrounding the levying and payment of service charges that are proving problematic. These include:
>
> ⟩ The level of services charges that are variable and depend on the level of work undertaken;
> ⟩ Poor awareness of the need to pay service charges;
> ⟩ Those on low incomes or struggling with mortgage/rent payments may not be able to cover large bills; and
> ⟩ The transparency of the programming of repairs and the services charged for may not be great.[50]

The document notes that of the 4000 cases before the Tribunal about 1500 are service charge related. The freeholder is only entitled to what is 'due' and 'reasonably incurred',[51] and it is usually the latter which causes the problem. What might seem 'reasonably incurred' to a landlord, however, might be regarded as unreasonable by a long leaseholder on the basis of cost.[52] However, it is perfectly open to the manager to take account of the means of the leaseholders to pay the service charge: 'the financial impact of major works on lessees through service charges and whether as a consequence works should be phased is capable of being a material consideration when considering whether the costs are reasonably incurred ...'.[53]

In summary, it can be said that the problematic of long leaseholders is that they 'buy into' ownership but are, as a matter of law, left in a subservient position. Ameliorating legislation has sought to redress the balance but only by tinkering at the edges and not at the fundamental issue, the lack of relation between ownership and leasehold. It is, then, an unfortunate clash between popular understandings of law in society and real, hard law in fact.

Debate 3

Between ownership and renting (2): What problems exist in sale and rentback transactions?

Sale and rentback transactions in relation to homes have tended to be relatively common at times of economic hardship and as part of mortgage rescue programmes. They involved tenure shifting – the owner sells the property and

---

[50] London Assembly, *Proposed Review of Service Charges in London*, (GLA, 2011).
[51] Landlord and Tenant Act 1985, s. 19(1)(a); *Forcelux* v. *Sweetman* [2001] 2 EGLR 173, [39]–[40].
[52] Appendix 1 to the London Assembly document notes one local authority's '£13,275,183 service charge bill was then allocated respectively to 6,500 individual leaseholders on the basis of actual cost of work incurred'.
[53] *Garside* v. *RFYC Ltd* [2011] UKUT 367 (LC), [14].

the buyer, usually a property company, grants that former owner a tenancy of the property instead. These transactions should not be entered into lightly and, at least in relation to those transactions executed before the Financial Services Authority (FSA) began to regulate them in 2009, cause some major problems for property law. The FSA now require the seller to be given clear warnings about the consequences of the transaction and its inadvisability.[54] One would have hoped that would have cured the significant problems which have arisen and lead to professionalism in the sector. That professionalism was, as the cases recount, lacking at least in some firms. As a result, the cases raise questions about unconscionability, construction of tenancy agreements, breach of contract, proportionate evictions and overriding interests.[55] In short, they have become property law's growth area and are likely to be the next 'big' thing. As a further result, these transactions were effectively shut down and heavily regulated.[56] As the 2012 FSA review of the market put it, 'The review identified widespread poor practice among SRB firms. The main conclusion is that the majority of SRB sales were either unaffordable or inappropriate. This means consumers have entered into agreements that have either already led to a detrimental outcome, or are highly likely to in the future. This is unacceptable, and we are taking immediate action to address this.' In summary, 'the FSA reported that most sale and rentback transactions were unaffordable or unsuitable and should never have been sold, but that in practice the entire market had shut down. They are now very rare'.[57]

The usual type of sale and rentback transaction goes like this: the seller sells, the buyer buys with the aid of a mortgage, and subsequently the seller obtains a tenancy agreement (and often that tenancy agreement is poorly constructed and of limited utility). Often, the buyer makes representations concerning the enforceability of the tenancy agreement as part of the negotiations leading to the sale (e.g. that the seller will be able to stay in the property for a set period or their life, rent will be reduced for a period or such like matter), sufficient in certain circumstances potentially to give rise to a proprietary estoppel (see Chapter 11).

The question raised in the sale and rentback cases is to the type of interest that the seller has between exchange of contracts and completion of the sale. And, if they have an interest, whether the buyer's mortgage lender takes priority over the seller's tenancy. The 2012 FSA review of the transactions found that when they examined the files, most did not show that the lender had agreed to the letting to the seller.[58]

---

[54] See, generally, FSA, *Sale and Rent Back (Full Regime)* CP10/04 (FSA, 2010).
[55] *Scrowther* v. *Watermill Properties* [2009] EW Misc 6 (EWCC); *Redstone* v. *Welch* [2009] EG 98; *Purdie and Bellwood* v. *Miller*, High Court, 20.10.2011; *In re North East Property Buyers Litigation* [2010] EWHC 2991 (Ch).
[56] For current regulation, see http://www.fca.org.uk/firms/financial-services-products/mortgages/sale-and-rent-back.
[57] *Scott* v. *Southern Pacific* [2014] UKSC 52, [2], Lord Collins.
[58] Para 2.4.

This was the problem which confronted the Supreme Court in *Scott* v. *Southern Pacific Mortgages Limited*.[59] The facts of these cases for present purposes, because they were largely assumed, were that a number of owner occupiers entered into an agreement with nominees for an organization called the North East Property Buyers. The terms of the agreement were that the nominee would buy the property and, on sale, would then rent the property back to the sellers. The nominees were not particularly well-versed in either land or landlord and tenant law. They promised different terms to each of the sellers and different rent levels, but many were told they could stay in the property for as long as they liked provided they kept to the terms of the tenancy. NEPB financed each transaction with a buy-to-let mortgage. Crucially, they did not disclose to the lender that the seller/s would remain in the property or the terms of the tenancy agreement (something which the FSA guidance now explicitly requires). Exchange of contracts and completion, including the execution of the charge, took place on the same day. NEPB became insolvent later and vanished. The lenders wanted possession.

The overarching question was whether the representations and agreements made between NEPB and the sellers created rights which bound the lenders. The Supreme Court held that this argument was not open to the sellers. The reason was that the buyers could not create binding property rights between exchange and completion. They could only create personal rights enforceable between seller and buyer (which were, of course, useless to Ms Scott as the NEPB had vanished) at that time. On completion of the contract, that personal right is fed with proprietary consequences because only at that time is the buyer able to make such a grant. This is a hugely significant decision not just in relation to these transactions but all transactions where the buyer seeks to grant property rights between contract and completion.

But if the buyer was capable of granting proprietary rights at completion, would those rights not take effect before the grant of the mortgage? This raises the question addressed in *Abbey National BS* v. *Cann*.[60] In that case, the House of Lords held that in an 'ordinary' property transaction involving a mortgage, where the buyer could not proceed without the aid of the mortgage, there is not a moment in time (*scintilla temporis*) between the buyer's purchase and the grant of the mortgage. If there was, then it would have been perfectly possible for rights adverse to the buyer to arise in that moment. The significance of this rule is that, in principle, those rights would bind the mortgage lender in certain circumstances because the rights were created prior in time (a moment) before the grant of the mortgage. That rule made sense in those transactions which involved an acquisition mortgage. But it clearly causes unfairness to the innocent party (in that case, Daisy Cann; in these cases, Ms Scott and the other sellers).

Even so, the majority in *Scott*[61] would have extended this rule if necessary (this was *obiter dicta*, but the point was argued extensively before the Court), so that,

---

[59] [2014] UKSC 52.
[60] [1991] 1 AC 56.
[61] Baroness Hale dissented.

even if Ms Scott did have a proprietary right between contract and completion, there is no gap between those events for these purposes. In other words, the mortgage lender would have taken free of those interests anyway. This seems to compound the unfairness of the *Cann* rule. The majority were at pains to suggest that, although this extended rule was in line with conveyancing practice, they were not influenced by that practice.[62]

Baroness Hale expressed disquiet about the conclusion on the following two grounds:

> First, *Cann* was not a case in which the vendor had been deceived in any way or been made promises which the purchaser could not keep. Should there not come a point when a vendor who has been tricked out of her property can assert her rights even against a subsequent purchaser or mortgagee? Second, *Cann* was not a case in which the lenders could be accused of acting irresponsibly in any way. Should there not come a point when the claims of lenders who have failed to heed the obvious warning signs that would have told them that this borrower was not a good risk are postponed to those of vendors who have been made promises that the borrowers cannot keep? Innocence is a comparative concept. There ought to be some middle way between the "all or nothing" approach of the present law.[63]

If we step back a moment and think about how this significant decision impacts on the themes of land law, it is clear that what the Court did in *Scott* was to facilitate alienability. Despite Lord Collins' comment that it was not relevant to the reasoning that the incidental effect of the outcome was that it facilitated conveyancing practice, one cannot gainsay that the decision did, in fact, do so. Mortgage lenders can now operate without concern as to the possibility that a seller creates rights binding on them between contract and completion. This means that lenders don't need to worry about unfair conduct by buyers or even acting irresponsibly, as Baroness Hale suggests; put another way, they are protected and that protection will facilitate the flow of mortgage capital.[64]

Debate

Between Ownership and Renting (3): How does shared ownership fit?

BACKGROUND

In the 1980s, ownership was heavily promoted by the Thatcher governments; as we have seen, this continued a pattern of preference established by preceding governments, but the Thatcher governments also did rather more to promote it than others. They introduced a range of what were known as 'low cost home

---

[62] [88].
[63] [122].
[64] The same analysis can apply to two of the other 'big' cases in land law: *City of London BS* v. *Flegg*; and *Cann*.

ownership' initiatives, ranging from the right to buy to providing cash payments for purchase. Shared ownership was initially developed as one of these initiatives, but it became heavily promoted in the period after the 1980s. The policy reason was relatively simple; it became a tenet of government housing policy that owner-ship had reached its sustainable limit (as was shown by the crash in the early 1990s) and alternatives were required beyond the mere bolstering of private rent-ing. At the same time, it was also clear that many people were being priced out of ownership and affordability became a major issue.

Shared ownership provided a convenient mechanism through which sustainable low-cost ownership could be achieved. The policy model was relatively simple: the buyer bought (and buys) a percentage share in the prop-erty; over time, they can buy a greater percentage share, if and when they can afford it; eventually, they would end up owning the whole thing. It was a model which could also be delivered by the then government's preferred provider of social housing, housing associations, and it is fair to say that they were relatively keen to do so because, in an era of fiscal constraint, they would receive a decent proportion of public funding for this purpose; all of which still holds true.

Successive governments have promoted shared ownership as not just the solution to a problem but also as a policy priority. It is regarded as fulfilling the homeownership aspirations of households. This was the original aim of the shared ownership programme, enabling households to progress to full ownership;[65] and it has remained the case.[66] The 2010 Coalition government's agreement specifically contained a promise in the following terms: 'We will promote shared ownership schemes and help social tenants and others to own or part-own their home'; the 2015 Conservative government is clearly seeking to develop shared ownership as a low cost homeownership solution, particularly in high value areas.

This rationale for the programme has developed over time so that its purpose is now to facilitate access to *sustainable* homeownership by increasing the supply of *affordable* homeownership.[67] In fulfilling the promotion of this policy, a huge amount of public funding has been ploughed into its development, accounting for a proportion of total capital spend on social housing by housing associations

---

[65] Department of the Environment, *Shared Ownership: A Stepping Stone to Full Ownership* (HMSO, 1982) p. 21.

[66] DETR/DSS, *Quality and Choice: A Decent Home for All*, The Housing Green Paper (DETR, 2000) para. 4.2; Office of the Deputy Prime Minister, *HomeBuy – Expanding the Opportunity to Own*, Consultation Paper (ODPM, 2005) para. 1; Department for Communities and Local Government, *Homes for the Future: More Affordable, More Sustainable*, Cm 7191 (DCLG, 2007) p. 70.

[67] Home Ownership Task Force, *A Home of My Own*, The Report of the Government's Low Cost Home Ownership Task Force (Housing Corporation, 2003) para. 6.1 (a suite of recommendations largely accepted, or accepted in principle, in the Government's response: Office of the Deputy Prime Minister, *Government Response to the Recommendations of the Home Ownership Task Force* (ODPM, 2003) pp. 6–7).

of between 11 and 25 per cent.[68] The National Audit Office noted the following in relation to shared ownership and equity loans:

> In 2004–05 the Government spent almost £470 million on these two products. The products are absorbing a growing proportion of the support made available to the affordable housing sector, from 13 per cent in 1999–2000 to almost 30 per cent in 2004–05.[69]

The benefit to housing associations has been that they are able to recycle the receipts paid by the borrowers into certain of their other housing activities.

Although not one of the original key aims of the schemes, a significant objective now is that shared ownership is designed to meet housing need in one or both of two ways – buyers are most usually either on local authority or housing association waiting lists for housing (many of which are now held jointly or in common) or occupying social rented housing.[70] In purchasing a property (which they are not currently occupying), the buyer will be removed from the waiting list or move out of their social rented accommodation into their property. In this way, the length of the waiting list is reduced and/or a unit of social rented accommodation is freed for another household.[71] It is also regarded as a method of preventing homelessness[72] and contributes to the development of mixed-tenure estates, regeneration and sustainability, as well as enabling more people to share in asset wealth.[73] That identity of shared ownership as meeting housing need, and provided by social housing organizations, also creates a tension in the nature of the product itself – for the product is both social housing and, in policy terms, ownership.[74] The protection of the public investment in the property is also a telling factor against the power of the buyer as owner.[75] For example, the model leases generally required the buyer to give the provider a right of pre-emption so that the property can be recycled for other households in need.

---

[68] G. Bramley and S. Dunmore, 'Shared Ownership: Short-Term Expedient or Long-Term Major Tenure?' (1996) 11(1) *Housing Studies* 105, 109–10; S. Hills and A. Lomax, *Whose House is it Anyway? Housing Associations and Home Ownership* (Housing Corporation, 2007) p. 15.

[69] National Audit Office, *A Foot on the Ladder: Low Cost Home Ownership Assistance*, HC 1048 Session 2005–06, (NAO, 2006).

[70] See, for example, the eligibility criteria for such schemes: Office of the Deputy Prime Minister, *HomeBuy*, n.66, para. 1.4; Housing Corporation, *Capital Funding Guide* (Housing Corporation, 2006) para. 2.1.

[71] See A. Clarke, 'Shared Ownership: Does It Satisfy Government and Household Objectives?' in S. Monk and C. Whitehead (eds.), *Making Housing More Affordable: The Role of Intermediate Tenures* (Wiley Blackwell, 2010), who describes this is as the 'double whammy' effect. The empirical basis for the success of this objective is less clear, partly because of the need for buyers to have financial security (in order to obtain a mortgage on the part they are buying) and partly because some social housing occupiers may well have left the sector at some point in the future in any event: National Audit Office, n.69, paras 44–47.

[72] DCLG, *Homelessness Code of Guidance for Local Authorities* (DCLG, 2006) para. 1.28.

[73] See, generally, Office of the Deputy Prime Minister, *HomeBuy*, n.66, para. 2.1.

[74] A. Wallace, *Achieving Mobility in the Intermediate Housing Market: Moving up and Moving on?* (Joseph Rowntree Foundation/Chartered Institute of Housing, 2008) p. 1. Shared ownership falls within the definition of 'social housing': Housing and Regeneration Act 2008, ss. 68 and 70.

[75] The buyer, under the model leases, is not entitled to make physical alterations to the property without the landlord's written consent and cannot make structural alterations.

That having been said, there are a large number of private schemes, usually run by building companies and particularly marketed during economic downturns (when the market for 'normal ownership' is less secure). There is limited knowledge of these schemes, but what is known is that in some areas there are issues over competition between housing associations and these private companies.[76]

TRANSLATING THE MODEL

If shared ownership at the level of policy ticks all the right boxes, it creates a considerable headache for the lawyers implementing it. The problem is that shared ownership does not appear in our land law lexicon. It does not exist except in the minds of housing policy experts who dreamt it up and those who have turned that dream into a reality. Like Frankenstein's monster, the lawyers have fashioned the different bits of tenure available to them at the time into the shape of something equivalent to shared ownership, and, with a jolt of electricity, it came to life. And, continuing the Frankenstein theme, they are having considerable difficulty controlling it, for it has taken on a life of its own.

The mechanism used to deliver it is our friend, the long leasehold, or through a mortgage relationship (see Chapter 10). As Bright and Hopkins have suggested, the trust of land would have been a much better device to use (see Chapter 3),[77] but that device was not available until 1997 by which time the leasehold relationship was cast in regulatory stone. The conventional form is the long leasehold, which accounts for the majority of such properties. The buyer, then, takes a lease usually of 99 or 125 years over their share in the property. The lease contains standard provisions and some unusual ones. One of the latter is a clause which gives comfort to the buyer's mortgage lender if they have to claim possession of the property, for the housing association agrees to pay their costs. Such a provision was designed because shared ownership, as a new 'product', needed to be sold to lenders as well to make them willing, first to lend money, and second at affordable rates. Strangely, it might seem, the shared owner also takes responsibility for all the repairs, maintenance and service charges; so, even if they buy (say) a 25 per cent share, they are responsible for 100 per cent of those costs. The buyer pays a sub-market rent on the share they haven't bought, which *must* be set at no more than three per cent of the open market valuation of the provider's share with strict limits on the level of rent increases.[78]

Although the lease is long, it will usually attract the protection of the Housing Act 1988 and is usually an assured tenancy.[79] This can create a major problem

---

[76] G. Burgess, F. Grant and C. Whitehead, *Low Cost Home Ownership and the Credit Crunch: A Report on Regional Markets and Competition with Private Developers* (TSA, 2009).

[77] S. Bright and N. Hopkins, 'Home, Meaning and Identity: Learning from the English Model of Shared Ownership', (2011) 28(4) *Housing Theory and Society*, 377, 380.

[78] HCA/CML/NHF, *Shared Ownership: Joint Guidance for England* (HCA/CML/NHF, 2010), para. 15, p. 11.

[79] The exclusions to security of tenure in Housing Act 1988, sch. 1 are unlikely to apply because of the high rental element.

because the buyer can be evicted if they fail for whatever reason to make two months' payment at the date of the relevant notice and they are still two or more months in arrears at the date of the hearing of the claim for possession.[80] The court has no discretion to refuse possession; it must make an order on this particular ground for possession.[81] The effect of such an order is the equivalent of forfeiture: the buyer loses not just the property but also their financial stake as well as any increase in value. It is an outrage, but, once the provider has chosen this route, the die is cast; there does not seem to be anything which can be done about it other than through the use of human rights law (as to which, see Chapter 8 for discussion in this context). Bright and Hopkins observe:

> Shared owners are, therefore, less secure than traditional owner-occupiers. They have to pay rent in respect of the 'non-owned' share, and (usually) will also have mortgage payments to make. Default in either can lead to loss of possession. Where default relates to rent, loss of possession may be mandatory, thus denying the purchaser the final procedural protection (available on mortgage default) of recourse to the court's discretion. Given the relatively low comprehension of how shared ownership 'works' it may be that purchasers are not conscious of this higher level of risk.[82]

What we have with shared ownership, then, is the marketing of a relatively innovative product as something which palpably it is not: ownership. As an empirical study of shared owners demonstrates, buyers are just as confused as the lawyers.[83] They *want* to think about themselves as owners but, at certain moments, it becomes clear to them that they are something else. Consider the following quotation from one of the research participants:

> *I don't know what I am. I don't know what they think I am. I think I'm the owner, but I'm also partly a tenant, but I'm a tenant that they don't really care about. But they'll look after their real – their tenants, who don't own their properties. They'll go and do everything for them. I don't get anything.*[84]

Quite apart from the existential angst, this person is identifying the fundamental problem with this new form of tenure – that it is something and nothing.

Land lawyers are conventional and law is traditional (a fact emphasized by the use of the doctrine of precedent), and the doctrines of tenure and estates too powerful to escape. Again, Bright and Hopkins provide a powerful critique, arguing that their study of shared ownership demonstrates '... the inadequacies of tenure classification: it is ill-suited to acknowledge the heterogeneity that exists within housing; or to provide a meaningful account of the rights and responsibilities that exist between people and their housing'.[85]

---

[80] Housing Act 1988, ground 8, sch. 2.
[81] *North British HA* v. *Matthews* [2005] 1 WLR 3133.
[82] Bright and Hopkins, n.77, p. 389.
[83] D. Cowan, A. Wallace and H. Carr, *Exploring Experiences of Shared Ownership Housing: Reconciling Owning and Renting* (Bristol: University of Bristol Law School, 2015).
[84] P. 85.
[85] Ibid. p. 393.

CONCLUSION

The doctrines of tenure and estates retain a powerful hold over property lawyers. Their translation in law and society, in policy and lay terms, inadequately reflects their nature and effects. The belief of, and in, ownership as having a set of under-pinning values is easily exposed by the problematic of the long leasehold and shared ownership relations. The problems of long leaseholds are well-known in practice but they continue to cause real heartache precisely because the legislative 'solutions' have not particularly impacted on the root cause of the problem, the continuing landlord and tenant relationship. As regards shared ownership, there is a mismatch between the rhetoric of policy and the legal mechanisms designed to bring it into effect. There is, of course, a crossover between the two – both use long leasehold relationships – but the significant difference is that in respect of shared ownership, policy-makers are directly implicated in the problematic.

There is a further theoretical point to be made by way of reflection on the material in this chapter. A simple analysis, which focuses on the rationalities and techniques of government, needs to be supplemented here with an understanding of jurisdiction.[86] The ability of the provider in the leasehold relationship to obtain possession on a mandatory ground, thus cutting the long leasehold interest and capital payment away from the buyer, as a result of a simple jurisdictional choice (viz. the security of tenure implied by the Housing Act 1988), creates the conditions within which this policy and set of practices is extremely likely to cause major problems.

Further Reading

S. Bright, 'Of Estates and Interests: A Tale of Ownership and Property Rights', in S. Bright and J. Dewar, *Land Law: Themes and Perspectives* (Oxford University Press, 1998).

H. Carr, 'The Right to Buy, the Leaseholder, and the Impoverishment of Ownership' (2011) 38(4) *Journal of Law and Society* 519.

I. Cole and D. Robinson, 'Owners Yet Tenants: The Position of Leaseholders in Flats in England and Wales' (2000) 15(4) *Housing Studies* 595.

D. Cowan, A. Wallace and H. Carr, *Exploring Experiences of Shared Ownership Housing: Reconciling Owning and Renting* (Bristol: University of Bristol Law School, 2015).

C. Gurney, *'Pride and Prejudice*: Discourses of Normalisation in Public and Private Accounts of Home Ownership' (1999) 14(2) *Housing Studies* 163.

---

[86] See M. Valverde, 'Jurisdiction and Scale: "Legal Technicalities" as Resources for Theory' (2009) 18(2) *Social and Legal Studies* 139.

3

THE 1925 LEGISLATION

INTRODUCTION

There is no clearer illustration of the themes discussed in Chapter 1, or of the tensions that have shaped the development of English land law in the twentieth and twenty-first centuries, than the great debates that informed the 1925 legislation.[1] In 1925, a set of legislation was introduced in England and Wales that reshaped the system of land law and created the structural framework that governed landownership and transfer until the introduction of the Land Registration Act 2002. Although most of the central concepts of property law are common law-based, the 'Englishness' of English land law is often identified by reference to this 1925 legislation, a collection of statutes which sought to modernize and simplify conveyancing, with the explicit objective of making land a more marketable commodity. Although this system has been moulded and shaped since it came into effect on 1 January 1926, to meet the changing political, economic and social demands made of the English land law system, a striking and enduring feature of English land law is the lasting impact of the 'property values' embedded in the 1925 legislation (certainty, simplicity, alienability) on contemporary doctrine and decision making.

While the common law of land took its tone from the English common law's underlying 'liberal' philosophy – characterized by 'ideas about the priority of the individual, the need for a distinction to be made between the regulation of the public as compared to the private spheres, limited government, liberty, freedom from individual interference as well as personal autonomy, equality before the law and the importance of the rule of law'[2] – the core doctrinal commitments this embedded were reinforced by legislative policies in 1925 and again in the Land Registration Act 2002, geared towards a political agenda to facilitate the flow of money through property transactions. The 1925 legislation was highly successful in according 'trump value' to 'strong rights' (with an emphasis on legal over equitable, registered over unregistered), within a doctrinal hierarchy designed to promote the pro-purchaser agenda and make land a more marketable commodity.

---

[1] The Law of Property Act 1925, Land Charges Act 1925, Land Registration Act 1925, Settled Land Act 1925, Administration of Estates Act 1925.
[2] T Hutchinson, 'Doctrinal Research: Researching the Jury' in D Watkins and M Burton (eds.), *Research Methods in Law* (Abingdon: Routledge, 2013), p. 16.

The framers of the legislation were explicit in seeking to encourage people with capital – 'property insiders' – to invest in land as freely as they would in stocks and shares. This political and economic aim shaped the deep assumptions of the 1925 property values (hierarchy of proprietary claims; security of individual property rights; stability of the property regime), which have had a lasting – indeed, intractable – effect on English property culture.

The first debate considered in this chapter reflects on the degree to which land law is – and should be – geared towards supporting the market in land. This touches on a prominent issue in contemporary property theory debates around the world, between 'monist' land law systems – legal frameworks with one clear dominant goal – and 'pluralist' systems – which recognize a range of competing political, economic, social and cultural values which interact to determine legal solutions depending on the context. The second debate moves on to reflect on the values that were embedded by the 1925 legislation. The third debate – which picks up on the regulation of co-owned land – explores how land law's unshakeable commitment to the (monist) themes and values of 1925 has withstood the explicit will of Parliament, by surviving legislation that was specifically enacted to bolster the 'weak right' claim of domestic co-owners against the 'strong right' of a secured creditor (Trusts of Land and Appointment of Trustees Act 1996). Finally, we suggest that the remarkable resilience of the themes of 1925 – distinct from discussions about the evolution of the machinery of conveyancing, discussed in Chapter 5 – is perhaps best understood as a function not only of the structural power of the legislation itself, but of its confluence with the dominant narratives of English property politics, particularly since the 1980s.

Debate 1

How can, or should, the property framework be structured to support the market in land?

The 1925 legislation represented a decisive break from the past for English land law. In seeking to place the law on a modern footing, it swept away many of the features of land law that were associated with the old system of aristocratic rule stemming from feudal times. The political driver for the reforms was the free-market philosophy identified by the early economist Adam Smith:[3] the 1925 legislation was designed to create a free market in land. The policy by which it sought to achieve this was,

> ... to assimilate the law of real and personal estate and to free the purchaser from the obligation to enquire into the title of him from whom he purchases, any more than he would have to do if he were buying a parcel of stock.[4]

---

[3] See, for example, A. Smith, *An Inquiry into the Nature and Causes of the Wealth of Nations*, ed. E. Cannan (Methuen and Co Ltd, 5th edn., 1904, first published 1776).

[4] Lord Birkenhead in a letter to *The Times*, 15 December 1920.

The main strategies of the legislation were:

(i)   to reduce the number of legal estates and interests, as discussed in Chapter 2, with other estates and interests taking effect only in equity;
(ii) to introduce a system of registration of land charges (for *unregistered land*) which was intended to cope with the increased number of equitable interests flowing from strategy (i), the reduction of legal estates and interests;[5]
(iii) to introduce a system of title registration (Chapter 5);
(iv) to extend the concept of overreaching (this chapter, Debate 1, 2);
(v)   to reform the law relating to co-ownership (this chapter, Debate 3); and
(vi) to reform the law relating to mortgages (Chapter 10).

While many of these aims will be explored later in this book, this chapter begins by focusing on the 'shape' of the system, before going on to consider the impact of the 1925 strategies for overreaching and co-ownership.

Before 1925, the range of legal estates that could exist in land was wide-ranging (examples of now defunct estates included the fee tail and the life estate, which can no longer exist *at law*); there were also various subsidiary interests which could exist in the land, as legal interests; in addition to this various equitable estates and equitable interests were capable of subsisting in the land. When land was transferred from one person to another, purchasers had to investigate the title to the land to be sure of what they were buying. However, with a wide range of different legal and equitable estates and interests potentially capable of binding purchasers, the process was complex, slow, expensive and potentially still uncertain.

The priority of these legal and equitable estates and interests was determined according to the rules of notice, and it was these rules which were at the root of much conveyancer and purchaser anxiety. The core principles of the notice rules were that legal rights bind all the world, and equitable rights bind all the world *except* a bona fide purchaser for value of the legal estate without notice (*equity's darling*). Notice could be actual (the purchaser knew about the equitable interest), constructive (the purchaser could have discovered the existence of the equitable interest had they made reasonable inspections and enquiries) or imputed (an agent of the purchaser – e.g. solicitor – had actual or constructive notice of the equitable right).

Legal rights presented a major obstacle for purchasers, as they were always binding and, although they had to be created by deed, there was no comprehensive, nationwide system for recording and discovering deeds. Equitable rights were even harder to discover, and potentially binding on purchasers even when they didn't have actual notice of the right. The real problem was seen to be with

---

[5]   One consequence of *reducing* the number of *legal* estates in land was that the volume of *equitable* interests *increased*. The land charges system sought to deal with these equitable interests by enabling the interest holder to register their interests as a land charge. The land charges register introduced a system whereby certain equitable interests had to be registered as a land charge if they were to bind purchasers. These interests were classified in six categories, labelled A to F. The list can now be found in section 2 of the Land Charges Act 1972.

constructive notice, as purchasers were *treated* as if they knew about the burden on their land, even though they did not *actually* know about it. The courts were wary of constructive notice, since it treats a third party purchaser or creditor as having knowledge which he did not in fact have.[6] However, since a purchaser is not affected by notice of any interest if that interest could not have been discovered by carrying out reasonable inspections and inquiries, the doctrine of notice placed an onus on the purchaser to protect his or her title by making the necessary inspections and inquiries prior to accepting the title as security. Since this created more work for the purchaser, took more time and generated more expense, it ran counter to the 'alienability' theme of the 1925 regime.

The standard of reasonable inspections and inquiries depended on the individual case, and while it was generally sufficient if the third party satisfied the standard conveyancing practices appropriate for such a case, it was hard for purchasers to know for sure if they had done enough to protect themselves. The limited guidance which purchasers had to go on emerged from the courts, which judged what was 'reasonable' on a case-by-case basis. One key area of concern related to possible claims from people in occupation of the land: it was established that '... if a person purchases an estate which he knows to be in occupation of another than the vendor, he is bound by all the equities which the party in such occupation may have had in the land.'[7] The fact of occupation constituted notice to third parties that the occupier might claim an interest in the land.[8]

In order to establish a clear title, the 'purchaser' (this includes someone who buys the land, a bank who takes security over the land or a tenant under a lease) had to ensure that the seller had good title to the land. The purchaser also had to find any hidden rights and interests that might exist in the land and affect the title. The purchaser would investigate a range of different types of factors, including:

Possession – the fact that someone was in possession of land was usually (but not always) an indication that they had some estate in the land. Common law presumed that the person in possession had a fee simple estate *unless and until the contrary was shown* (i.e. unless someone showed a relatively better title through documentation).

Documentary evidence – purchasers also needed to inspect the deeds to the property (this is a collection of all the documents that provide evidence about the seller's title). Purchasers needed to trace title back through the documents to follow the history of the title. This was described as showing a 'good root of title'.[9] The root of title was usually indicative of legal title

---

[6] '[T]he doctrine is a dangerous one. It's contrary to the truth. It is wholly founded on the doctrine that a man does not know the facts, and yet it is said that constructively he does know them'; *Allen* v. *Seckham* (1879) 11 ChD 790 at 795, per Lord Esher.

[7] *Jones* v *Smith* (1841) 1 Hare 43 at 60.

[8] *Barnhard* v. *Greenshields* (1853) 9 Moo PC 18.

[9] Statute has limited the requirement for a good root of title from 60 years to 40 (1874) and now to 15 years (Law of Property Act 1969, s. 23).

only, although documents would sometimes show the equitable estates or interests existing in relation to the land. A purchaser was also deemed to have constructive notice of anything they could have discovered from the title documents.

Physical inspection of the property – this was also necessary in order to discover some interests, especially equitable interests which might not have been created in writing and might not have been apparent from the title deeds.

Enquiries – the purchaser also had to make enquiries from the vendor to discover interests that might not have been apparent from the title deeds or on physical inspection (for example, an easement). The purchaser also had to make enquiries from other persons in occupation of the property. If a purchaser failed to make reasonable enquiries, they would be deemed to have constructive notice of any interests that could have been discovered from making enquiries.

These steps cost a purchaser time and money, each time the land was transferred; even if there had been a recent sale, the purchaser could not rely on the previous inspections and enquiries but had to re-do the whole process. At the heart of the reform agenda was anxiety that the entire system hinged on the doctrine of notice. Purchasers could find themselves bound by hidden interests even though they did not have actual knowledge of the interests before buying the land. On the other hand, if you were the person with an equitable interest, you could not always rely on the doctrine of constructive notice to ensure that your interest survived the transfer of the land to the purchaser, since there was no clear rule about what had to be done to avoid constructive notice.

As we saw in Chapter 2, section 1, Law of Property Act 1925 limited the types of legal rights (those which bind purchasers automatically) that can exist in land to two legal estates (fee simple absolute in possession, and the term of years). Section 1(2) listed the other interests (not estates) which are available at law: easements, rentcharges,[10] charges by way of legal mortgage, similar charges not created by an instrument (this covers statutory charges) and certain rights of entry.[11] Any other interests in land that fall outside the statutory list can be *equitable* only. One consequence of this is that a wide range of equitable interests in land are vital to the working of the modern law of property. For example, as we will see below, the 1925 legislation made extensive use of trusts to regulate co-ownership of land. Another important aspect of the new system was the emphasis on registration of rights and interests, to ensure that so far as possible, purchasers would know what they were buying.

---

[10] A right to a money payment from land. Like rent, but paid by a freeholder. Increasingly unusual, and its creation was severely limited by the Rentcharges Act 1977. They can only be created now where there is a trust of land, or for an estate rentcharge, imposed to ensure the performance of covenants by the owner of land.

[11] The right to enter on breach of covenants in a legal lease, and a right of entry attached to a legal rentcharge.

Yet, while the reduced categories of legal estates and interests and the introduction of systems of registration to protect certain interests went some way to protect the purchaser from undiscovered claims against the land, this was not considered sufficient to support the market in land, so further measures were thought necessary. A key gap in the protection afforded to purchasers was caused by 'unregistrable interests', which did not fall within any of the categories of registrable interest and so were not *capable* of being registered. The most significant and substantial unregistrable interest was the interest of a beneficiary under a trust relating to land. The framers of the 1925 legislation recognized that this presented a flaw in the overall scheme, making the market in land riskier for purchasers. The technique they used to manage that risk was to 'overreach' the unregistrable interest. Sections 2 and 27 of the Law of Property Act 1925 (LPA 1925) provided that, where a trust affecting land has two or more trustees, and on condition that the money from any sale was paid to all trustees, the equitable estates of any beneficiaries under the trust would be 'overreached'. This meant that the purchaser would acquire a clear title to the land; the beneficiary's equitable interest would detach from the land, and attach instead to the proceeds of sale in the hands of the trustees.[12]

The overreaching rule applied regardless to whether the purchaser had notice of the beneficiaries' interests. As such, it illustrates one of the central pillars of the 1925 property legislation: that land, including a person's home, was treated as a 'fungible' resource, as merely another form of capital, a commercial asset, as readily exchangeable as any other. This designation of land as 'any other asset' created a way of thinking land law that has fuelled several major debates in recent years. For one thing, it is inclined to de-contextualize land law: if land is just an item of capital, is it relevant to legal doctrine or decision making whether a particular piece of land is used as a home, or a farm, or a factory, or an office block, or a hospital and so on? Does – and should – the social function that land plays in society, as well as in the economy, have any bearing on how we think and talk about land law, or when balancing competing claims to a particular piece of land? The 1925 legislation played an important role in reducing the meanings and values of land to a money value, limiting the space in land law discourse for other types of concern – from social justice to sustainability. This was played out most recently in England and Wales in the debates surrounding the criminalization of squatting (Chapter 6), which were heavily influenced by the idea of land as a mere capital asset.

As well as providing a useful illustration of the values that underpinned the 1925 legislation (discussed in the next section), the doctrine of overreaching also offers a useful case study illustrating the difficulties which subsequent reformers have faced in displacing the ethos of the 1925 legislation. The use of overreaching in the LPA 1925 – particularly, it has operated to treat a family home as mere

---

[12] The classic illustration is contained in *City of London BS* v. *Flegg* [1988] AC 54.

capital – has been heavily criticized by both the Law Commission[13] and the Court of Appeal,[14] with the decision in *National Westminster Bank plc* v. *Malhan*[15] suggesting that it amounted to a discriminatory interference with the occupier's right to respect for home under Article 8 of the European Convention on Human Rights and/or the right to peaceful enjoyment of possessions under Article 1 of the First Protocol. Yet, the strength of land law's commitment to the theme of alienation has enabled the doctrine of overreaching to withstand – so far – these challenges.

Debate 2

What types of value does the private property system recognize with respect to land?

As the discussion above has shown, in addition to its significance in formulating the structures and systems of today's land law, the 1925 legislation embedded a particular perspective and way of valuing land which, despite subsequent developments, continues to have a major impact on contemporary land law. It offers the first clear example of the strength of *policy* in land law, as expressed in the rise of protections specifically oriented towards purchasers and designed to facilitate and build confidence in land transactions. Even where aspects of the 1925 legislation have been replaced (for example, much of the framework for land registration, originally set out in the Land Registration Act 1925, has been updated by the Land Registration Act 2002), the values that inform the current law remain heavily influenced by the explicit policies of the 1925 legislation.

This section explores a debate concerning the functions and *value* of land, focusing particularly on tensions between land as an asset for occupation and use (*use value*), and land as an investment asset (*exchange value*). While land, as an item of property, holds many different values, political, economic and legal discourses often focus on its use value and exchange value. Adam Smith (whose moral philosophy is often identified as the foundation for neoclassical economics) described 'value' as having '... two different meanings ... [It] sometimes expresses the utility of some particular object, and sometimes the power of purchasing other goods which the possession of that object conveys. The one may be called "value in use"; the other, "value in exchange".'[16] The tensions between use value and exchange value are also highlighted in Marxist critiques of political economy, which distinguish between an idea of 'use value', which is based on the intrinsic,

---

[13] Law Commission, *Trusts of Land: Overreaching*, Working Paper No 106 (London: HMSO, 1988); and Law Commission, *Transfer of Land – Overreaching Beneficiaries in Occupation*, Law Com No 188 (HMSO, 1989).

[14] *State Bank of India* v. *Sood* [1997] Ch 276.

[15] [2004] EWHC 847.

[16] A. Smith, *An Inquiry into the Nature And Causes of the Wealth of Nations*, ed. E. Cannan (Methuen and Co Ltd, 5th edn., 1904, first published 1776), Book One, Of the Causes of Improvement in the Productive Powers of Labour, And of the Order according to which its Produce is Naturally Distributed among the Different Ranks of the People; see chapter IV, 'Of the Origin and Use of Money'.

material characteristics of the product and its usefulness in terms of satisfying a human want or need; and 'exchange value', which is the price that can be realized in the market on sale. Land provides a paradigmatic example of both of these ways of thinking about value. It has inherent use value, in light of the complex array of: '... organic human uses ... within a complex, interactive web of life ...';[17] while at the same time representing a significant financial resource with strong exchange value in the market, and whose value is not consumed by use.

The way in which these competing functions are recognized and given effect in property theory and law is not fixed but has evolved over time as the demands that policy goals have made on property law have changed.

In *The Historical Foundations of the Common Law*, Milsom wrote that:

> From the earliest settlements until the Industrial Revolution the economic basis of society was agrarian. Land was wealth, livelihood, family provision, and the principal subject matter of the law ... [land] was also government and the structure of society.[18]

In this agrarian society, peasant farmers 'owned' the plots of land on which they lived and worked, under the system of feudal tenure.[19] These original owner occupiers valued the land primarily in terms of its use value rather than its exchange value. There was a strong material connection between the peasant landowners and the soil which supported them.[20] These landowners were unlikely to use their land as a financial asset, either by selling or mortgaging the land.[21] This reluctance to trade with land was rooted in the symbolic importance of the land for peasants, as well as the belief that transacting in land would transform it to an item of exchange, and so dissipate its symbolic value.[22] Peasant landowners regarded their land as having a unique, social, use value, which they did not wish to lose by treating the land as an exchangeable item.

The idea that each piece of land has a unique value was explicitly swept away by the 1925 legislation, which set out to remove most of the remnants of the feudal system of landowning and to place the law on a modern footing. The economic agenda of the reforms was clear. The functions of property in land were

---

[17] L. Caldwell and K. Schrader-Frechette, *Policy for Land: Law and Ethics* (Rowman & Littlefield Publishers Inc, 1993) p. 5.

[18] S. Milsom, *Historical Foundations of the Common Law* (Butterworths, 1981) p. 99.

[19] MacFarlane claimed that, using its commonsense meaning, England was a 'peasant society' between the thirteenth and eighteenth centuries: A. MacFarlane, *The Origins of English Individualism* (Blackwell, 1978) p. 9.

[20] W. Ashley, *An Introduction to English Economic History and Theory* (Vol. 1) (Longmans, 3rd edn., 1901), see pp. 33–38.

[21] MacFarlane, n.19, p. 23. Although MacFarlane recognized some evidence that English peasants were involved in the market and transacted on the land as a commodity, he argued that the land retained a special status until long after private property as a basic concept had been accepted: 'Although small pieces of land may be bought and sold to even out demographic differences between households or in crises, it is very clear that an extensive and open market in land, which treats land as just another commodity, is absent in traditional peasantries.' (p. 23).

[22] Ibid..

fundamentally transformed by the rise of commercialism following the Industrial Revolution. Atiyah described the move to this new commercialist, transaction-focused society as a,

> ... transition from a law of property [the land itself] to a law of contract relating to property [the transfer of land]... the significance of property rights changed from their use value to their exchange value.[23]

The growth of credit as a means of doing business in a commercial society also impacted on the ways that we think and talk about land law. Where landowner-ship had previously been rooted in the tangible fact of *possession*, the role of land in the credit society was centred on the contractual *obligation*. Where landowner-ship in the pre-industrial society revolved around physical, tangible things, the rise of the commercial society revolved around the exchange value of property as wealth. Kahn-Freund argued that the object of the abstract right – the land itself – had become so insignificant that it no longer mattered: '... it may be a block of flats, an agricultural estate, a factory, or so many South African gold shares. The property object has become capital.'[24] As we have seen in other contexts, land law – in this case, in shifting from a traditional conception of land as symbolic property to the modern representation of land as capital – had an important part to play in both following and furthering these social, political and economic changes.

The development of the theme of alienation in land law was also associated with the emergence of the theme of (economic) rationality and a liberal market-individualist political orientation – what Atiyah described as an ethos of: '... newer individualism, stressing risk-taking, free choice, rewards to the enterprising and sharp and devil take the hindmost'.[25] As the discussion in Chapter 1 has noted, English land law, particularly following the 1925 property reforms, has been dominated by an ethos of logic and rationality. Gray and Gray have claimed that in relation to dealings between strangers, for example, private landlords and tenants or creditors and occupiers,

> ... relationships are strictly commercial, bargaining is hard-nosed, social bondings are minimal and the value attached to land is primarily, perhaps even exclusively, an 'exchange value'. Altruism is in very short supply; we are talking money.[26]

It is important to recognize that this characterization of land law is not the only way that we can think about these questions. Far from being inherent to our discipline, it is the result of a very clear policy agenda – primarily, the legislative commitment to alienation. The idea that land, including a person's home, should be valued as a piece of exchangeable capital (rather than for its subjective value

---

[23] P. Atiyah, *The Rise and Fall of Freedom of Contract* (Clarendon Press, 1979) p. 103.

[24] O. Kahn-Freund, 'Introduction' in K. Renner, *The Institutions of Private Law and Their Social Functions* (Routledge & Paul, 1949), p. 28.

[25] Atiyah, n.23, p. 176.

[26] Gray and Gray, *Elements of Land Law* (Oxford University Press, 2009), p. 241.

to the occupier who used the land, for example) was one of the central pillars of the 1925 legislation. The 1925 legislation sought to make land as easily and securely transferable as possible, as readily exchangeable as any other asset, and to deny the idea that land had any special meaning just because it was occupied as a home. As such, it clearly emphasized the *exchange value* of land over its *use value*. Indeed, the strength of the underlying core principles put in place by 1925 was such that – even after the parliamentary debate was resolved in favour of a more occupation-oriented conception of co-owned land – it has been extremely difficult to displace the values of the 1925 regime (see Debate 3).

AUTOBIOGRAPHICAL NOTE

A legal journey: Lorna's perspective on property

There can be no doubt that the 1925 legislation pursued a particular policy agenda, and according to many of the conventional land law texts, the merits of this agenda are taken as read. Unlike those who are reading this book as students, my first encounter with land law was not through the medium of the English system. Studying, and later teaching, in Northern Ireland, a number of important differences characterized both the detail and (it seems) the underlying philosophy of land law. One of these differences is that the 1925 legislation never crossed the Irish Sea. While modern Northern Irish land law has developed as a hybrid of English and Irish influences, as well as including some particular approaches that are all its own, the absence of this behemoth of commercialist, pro-purchaser policy may (alongside other cultural differences) go some way to explaining the different stance which the Northern Ireland Law Commission has taken on some key contemporary property law debates, compared to its English counterpart. For example, in its recent report and recommendations for the reform of land law, the Northern Ireland Law Commission not only declined to follow the English approach of effectively abolishing adverse possession, but proposed strengthening the position of the squatter in some significant respects (see Chapter 6).

The effect of a different starting point in the way I think about land law was brought home to me a few years ago when I wrote a journal article about the Northern Ireland proposals. The peer-reviewers of the article (who I guess were anchored in English land law) asked me to be clearer in unpacking the reasons why the Northern Irish approach neither presumptively followed the English approach, nor found it necessary to explain this 'departure'.

A key point of departure was that, in its analysis and proposals, and on matters ranging from registration to mortgages to adverse possession, the NI Law Commission did not apply a strong pro-purchaser/legal title holder agenda, but appeared to approach key issues from an arguably more open initial position. There are practical, technical and political reasons why the NI Law Commission did not take the English approach as its starting point – for example, land registration has not advanced at the same pace in Northern Ireland as it has in England and Wales – but there are also philosophical and ideological differences. Most notably, perhaps, the Northern Ireland proposals appear to swim against what in England has been a fairly relentless tide towards a tighter system of registration, strongly focused on protecting legal title holders against informal claims such as those brought by squatters or the off-title interests of persons in occupation of land.

The fact that others found it necessary for these reasons to be explained, where I had thought them obvious, served as a useful reminder of one of the first lessons of legal research: we all carry baggage in the way that we perceive, define, approach and analyse the questions that we set ourselves as researchers. Sometimes (perhaps often) we are not aware of that baggage (or 'researcher bias'), yet the values that we bring to the project of legal analysis implicitly influence what we choose to write about and how we make our arguments. The same point can also be made about judges and the way that they understand the law and adjudicate disputes: the law itself is shaped by how judges were taught, the textbooks and commentaries they read, the values they were inducted to uphold and apply. Stepping back from the 1925 legislation to reflect on its remarkable success in setting an agenda and defining the values with which we think about property law in England brings this process of value acquisition, and its consequences for legal analysis and argument, into sharp relief.

Debate 3

What does English law regard as the purpose of co-owning land?

The law regulating co-ownership provides a useful case study through which to illustrate the themes of this book, the debates set out in this chapter and, particularly, the strength of the underlying core principles put in place by 1925, such that – even in the face of Parliamentary intervention – it has been extremely difficult to displace the values of the 1925 regime.

One key respect in which the machinery of the 1925 legislation sought to achieve the goal of transforming land into a capital asset was through the statutory 'trust for sale', imposed on all jointly owned property under the Law of Property Act 1925.[27] For most of the twentieth century, applications for the sale of co-owned land were governed by the statutory framework set out in the Law of Property Act 1925. The provisions concerning co-owned land in the 1925 legislation were very much in keeping with the overall policy goals of the reforms. Prior to 1925, problems had existed in relation to co-owned land, particularly with respect to informal equitable co-ownership – for example, under an implied trust – since these interests did not appear on the face of the title to the property, and so were sometimes

---

[27] LPA section 35 stated that: '... land held upon the "statutory trusts" shall be held upon the trusts and subject to the provisions following, namely, upon trust to sell the same and to stand possessed of the net proceeds of sale'.

difficult for purchasers to discover. The drafters of the 1925 legislation sought to facilitate the transfer of co-owned land by two principal means. First, all interests in co-owned land would be held behind a trust, with the trustees – identifiable from the legal title – empowered to execute transactions affecting the land; in addition, the doctrine of overreaching meant that purchasers dealing with two or more trustees could be confident that they would obtain good title. Second – as explored in this section – to ensure the effective management of co-owned land, the statutory trust imposed upon it was imbued with a presumption in favour of sale.

THE TRUST FOR SALE

The statutory trust for sale imposed on all co-owned land by the LPA 1925 applied a legislative presumption that the primary object of property ownership – for example, between spouses or partners – was investment and sale rather than use and occupation. This has had major implications for the meanings and values associated with co-owned land. As the Law Commission has noted:

> The defining feature of the trust for sale ... is that the trustees are under a duty to sell the trust land. Implicit in this is the notion that this land should be held primarily as an investment asset rather than as a 'use' asset.[28]

Co-owned land was valued as a capital asset only, and meanings associated with the personal use and occupation of the land – for example, as a home – were excluded. One of the features of this trust was the duty that was imposed on all legal owners of the co-owned land (the 'trustees for sale') to sell the property immediately. Although the obligation to sell was tempered by a power to postpone sale,[29] in cases where the trustees chose to exercise this power to postpone sale, 'any person interested' could apply to the court under section 30 of the Law of Property Act 1925 for a judicial order forcing the sale of the property, such order to be granted at the discretion of the court.

The impact of the trust for sale was not merely ideological, but highly significant in practice. Section 30 was often used by creditors seeking to force the repossession and sale of jointly owned land. Typically, the court exercised its discretionary power to order sale by giving way to the creditor's interest in realizing the debtor's assets against the interests of any parties who opposed sale. When sale was opposed, this was usually on the grounds that the occupiers wanted to retain the property for their own use, for example, for occupation as a home. However, the object of the 1925 provisions was to facilitate the alienability of real property. That legislative policy characterized the judicial approach towards granting orders for sale under section 30 of the 1925 Act: when balancing the competing interests, the court did not start from a neutral position but by asking whether it was

---

[28] Law Commission, *Transfer of Land: Trusts of Land,* Law Comm No 181 (HMSO, 1989), para 3.1.
[29] Law of Property Act 1925, s. 25.

inequitable *not* to allow the applicant to realize his capital share of the property.[30] Thus, and although the decision lay within the court's discretion, the legislative policy in support of alienability, and the designation of land – including the home – as merely another form of capital, created a presumption of sale to give effect to the purpose of the trust. In practice, this meant that the creditor's interest, which lies in the sale of the debtor's property, typically prevailed over the co-owning occupier who wished to retain the land for occupation and use.[31]

As we have remarked in Chapter 1, in 1925, owner-occupation accounted for a small but growing proportion of the housing sector in the United Kingdom, although the government had already embarked upon a homeownership campaign which aimed to encourage citizens to buy their own homes.[32] The broad outcome of these policies was that by 2009, around 69 per cent of households in the UK either owned, or were in the process of buying, their own homes,[33] although the impact of the global financial crisis that began in 2007 meant that by 2011 this had dropped to 64 per cent – as high house prices, low wage growth and tighter lending requirements coincided with the first fall in homeownership since 1918.[34] One of the paradoxes of land law as it butts up against housing policy in England and Wales is that the government strategy in promoting homeownership in the United Kingdom was geared towards a belief that homeownership supports a culture of citizenship, encouraging owners to feel that they had a 'stake in the nation'.[35] Yet, while these housing policies sought to *encourage* occupiers to invest – economically, socially and emotionally – in their homes through owner-occupation, the 1925 legislation – which set the scene for the legal framework of property law that governs owner-occupation – ran counter to this ideology with its designation of land as nothing special, just another form of capital.

It is perhaps not surprising that these policies ran at cross-purposes: for one thing, the framers of the 1925 legislation could not have anticipated the dramatic growth of owner-occupation in the twentieth century – from 23 per cent in 1918;[36] nor, later, the radical social changes that saw women moving out of the shadows of land law to share (sometimes equitable) ownership with their husbands and partners. The 1925 legislation was,

> ... neither premised upon the existence of mass owner-occupation, nor aimed at providing a legal framework to govern such a pattern of ownership ... [the drafters of the 1925 legislation were] not concerned to provide a conveyancing regime tailored to the needs of the modern owner-occupied sector.[37]

[30] *Jones* v. *Challenger* [1960] 2 WLR 695.
[31] *Re Citro (a Bankrupt)* [1991] Ch 142.
[32] The role of the government in promoting the 'owner-occupier mortgaged to a building society' society is discussed in Chapter 10.
[33] C. Randall, *Housing*, Social Trends 41, (London, Office for National Statistics, 2011).
[34] ONS, *A Century of Home Ownership and Renting in England and Wales* (2011 Census analysis).
[35] See further, D. Cowan and M. McDermont, *Regulating Social Housing: Governing Decline* (Routledge-Glasshouse, 2006) ch. 8.
[36] ONS, above, n. 34.
[37] W. Murphy and H. Clark, *The Family Home* (Sweet & Maxwell, 1983) pp. 18–19.

In fact, the policy of treating land as capital was geared to meet the needs of the commercial, industrialized society of the late nineteenth and early twentieth centuries.[38]

There is nothing unusual about social change outpacing legal development. However, what is important about English land law's debate about the purpose of co-owning land is the resistance of the 1925 philosophy to evolution in line with changing social circumstances. The LPA's focus on co-ownership was driven by the particular hazards that undiscovered interests in co-owned land could present for purchasers, and the solution was the strongly pro-purchaser trust for sale.

This had obvious, potentially adverse, consequences for non-transacting co-owners: a co-owner of land, who might reasonably have believed that – niceties of land law aside – they had an interest in the land itself, could find the property sold, and their interest transferred to the proceeds of the sale. In fact, this 'conversion' of the co-owner's property interest took place long before the point of sale: from the point of acquisition of co-owned land, any equitable interest was designated as an interest in the capital value, rather than an interest in land. The doctrine of 'conversion' gave practical effect to the policy of treating property in land as mere capital, rather than a specific interest in a particular item of real property. Yet, by the time the LPA was enacted, it was arguably already out of sync (or nearly so) with the ways in which householders were beginning to use land, particularly in the domestic context.

THE DOCTRINE OF CONVERSION

The parliamentary debates preceding the Law of Property Act attested to the government's policy of assimilating land with other forms of property, so that land would carry no special meaning. Some members of the House of Commons opposed the policy, arguing that '[y]ou cannot compare the transfer of stocks and shares with the transfer of property':[39]

> You may want one special piece of land ... no one wants one special stock certificate ... There is no magic in one stock certificate ... [on the other hand] land is a special property. A man may want one particular piece of land, and it may be that no money can compensate him for the loss of it.[40]

These arguments were unsuccessful. The provisions of the 1925 legislation – specifically, the trust for sale and the doctrine of conversion – ensured that land would be valued according to its exchange value rather than its material and organic use value. This was achieved through the trust for sale, the defining feature of which was that the trustees were under a duty to sell the land, with the implicit assertion that the objective of this form of ownership was investment rather than

---

[38] See 155 HL Deb (5th Series) col 709–710 (16 June 1922), Sir Donald McLean.
[39] 154 HC Deb (5th Series) col 145 (15 May 1922).
[40] Ibid., col 124.

use. The doctrine of conversion operated to ensure that, from the outset of the co-ownership – not merely on the point of sale – the beneficiaries' interests were interests in the proceeds of sale only: they were not interests in the land.

The effect of the doctrine of conversion was to treat the land itself as 'perfectly replaceable' by money. For example, in *Irani Finance Ltd* v. *Singh*,[41] the court recognized that while '... In a non-technical use of language, the beneficiary may be said to have a real interest in the land ...',[42] in legal terms,

> ... the beneficial interest of a person whose interest arises under a trust for sale ... is not one which is appropriately described as being 'an interest in the land' ... [so that] he has no estate or interest in the land itself.[43]

The lasting implications of conversion – particularly as both homeownership, and the prominence of (female) partner claims to shared ownership of domestic property, grew throughout the twentieth century – have attracted considerable criticism. In a series of cases following *Irani Finance Ltd* v. *Singh*, the courts wavered between treating proprietary interests in co-owned land as interests in the land itself, on the one hand, and viewing the claim as one against capital value, on the other.[44] In *Williams & Glyn's Bank Ltd* v. *Boland*,[45] Lord Wilberforce described the proposition that an interest in co-owned land under a statutory trust for sale was an interest in the proceeds of sale only – through the operation of conversion – as 'just a little unreal' in the case of a *home* that had been purchased for the purposes of occupation. Indeed, the automatic application of conversion to co-owned land was ultimately altered by TLATA, although, as the discussion below will show, the theme of alienation had by then been so firmly entrenched in English land law that the new philosophy of TLATA had little practical effect.

BANKRUPTCY

The 1925 property reforms provided the courts with the ideology, the language, the tools and the justification to adopt a presumption in favour of sale, to value land as a capital asset only and to disregard the non-financial interests of occupiers in their homes. This ethos was so strongly embedded in legal discourse that even when section 336, Insolvency Act 1986 was enacted, with a view to attaching greater weight in bankruptcy proceedings to the use and occupation of property

---

[41] [1970] 2 WLR 117 (ChD); [1971] Ch 59 (CA).
[42] [1971] Ch 59 at 69; per Buckley J.
[43] Ibid..
[44] In *National Westminster Bank Ltd* v. *Stockman* [1981] 1 WLR 67 the interest was construed as an interest in land for the purposes of the Charging Orders Act 1979, to enable an interest in a trust for sale to form the subject matter of a charge). *Perry* v. *Phoenix Assurance* [1988] 1 WLR 940 held that it did not amount to an 'order affecting land' under the Land Charges legislation; however, in *Clark* v. *Chief Land Registrar* [1993] 2 WLR 141, the order was allowed as one where 'the interest was to charge the land not the proceeds of sale'. In *Elias* v. *Mitchell* [1972] Ch 652, an interest in the proceeds of sale under a statutory trust for sale was described as a 'minor interest in land' for the purposes of the Land Registration Act 1925.
[45] [1981] AC 487, at 507.

as a *family home*, at least for a limited period, the commercial interests of creditors continued to prevail. Section 336 of the Insolvency Act 1986 required the court, when exercising its discretion to order the sale of a family home, to have regard to a range of factors, including,

> ... the interests of the bankrupt's creditors, the conduct of the spouse or former spouse ... the needs and financial resources of the spouse or former spouse, the needs of any children, and all the circumstances of the case other than the needs of the bankrupt.[46]

Yet, while this provision purported to provide the court with grounds on which to recognize the interests of the debtor's family in retaining their home, it was tempered by section 336(5), which required the court, once a year had passed from the instigation of bankruptcy proceedings, to: '... assume, unless the circumstances of the case are exceptional, that the interests of the bankrupt's creditors outweigh all other considerations'. The court's policy with regard to section 30 applications by trustees in bankruptcy was epitomized by the decision in *Re Citro (a Bankrupt)*,[47] in which Nourse LJ considered the scope of exceptional circumstances. As he put it:

> What then are exceptional circumstances? As the cases show, it is not uncommon for a wife with young children to be faced with eviction in circumstances where the realisation of her beneficial interest will not produce enough to buy a comparable home in the same neighbourhood, or indeed elsewhere; and, if she has to move elsewhere, there may be problems over schooling and so forth. Such circumstances, while engendering a natural sympathy in all who hear of them, cannot be described as exceptional. They are the melancholy consequences of debt and improvidence with which every civilised society has been familiar.[48]

Notwithstanding the discussion in the next section, the provisions of the Insolvency Act 1986 remain in force and the courts continue to follow the approach set out in *Re Citro (a Bankrupt)*.[49]

THE 'TRUST OF LAND': FROM SALE TO HOME?

With the enactment of the Trusts of Land and Appointment of Trustees Act 1996 (TLATA), the overwhelming dominance of the alienation theme appeared set to be tempered with the idea that co-owned land has a particular 'use value', in addition to its value on exchange. The explicit purpose of TLATA was to recognize that landowners (and particularly, in the case of co-ownership, homeowners) do not,

---

[46] Insolvency Act 1986, s. 336(4).
[47] [1991] Ch 142.
[48] Ibid., at 157.
[49] [1991] Ch 142. Although there may have been a slight softening following on from the Human Rights Act – see *Barca* v. *Mears* [2004] EWHC 2170 (Ch) at [40]–[42]; cf. *Nicholls* v. *Lan* [2006] EWHC 1255 (Ch), at [43].

in reality, value their property merely as an investment asset, but also for its use value as a home. By replacing the 'trust for sale' on co-owned land with a 'trust of land', TLATA set out to re-establish the *use value* of the land itself, so displacing what had become an overwhelming emphasis on exchange value, while retaining the protections for the purchaser in the 1925 Act (overreaching, and indeed strengthening, the powers of the trustees).

It was the unreality of the trust for sale in the new context of widespread ownership which propelled the reform.[50] As the Law Commission put it, '[A] system devised for one set of social circumstances is being used for very different circumstances'.[51] The Law Commission recognized that co-ownership was widely used by owner-occupiers, and that, for them, an important element of their ownership was the use and occupation of the property *as a home*, alongside any investment interest in the property as a saleable asset.[52] The main purpose of the new legislation was to recognize that land – especially the owned home – was likely to bear particular meaning and value for occupiers as '... the place where the beneficiaries live, or want to live in the future'.[53] TLATA was, therefore, intended to reassert the material, organic value of property in land as a specific, unique, not-always-substitutable–with-capital asset; an approach described by Lord Browne-Wilkinson as '... at last ... a little bit of common sense ...'.[54]

TLATA sought to address both the preference for sale at the heart of the trust for sale, and the implications of the doctrine of conversion. By abolishing the doctrine of conversion, the proposition that a co-owner's interest in land was limited to the proceeds of sale was re-shaped to establish the right as an interest in land.[55] TLATA also removed the duty to sell, thus seemingly diminishing the *prima facie* advantage previously enjoyed by parties applying for an order for sale of co-owned land. The Law Commission claimed that the section 30 discretion had been unduly governed by the 'duty to sell' and that this had 'confined the development of judicial doctrine to the formulation of reasons why sale should not take place'.[56] Section 15 set out new criteria to guide the court's discretion to make orders affecting the land, including the order for sale, which included regard for the intentions of the person who created the trust, the purpose for which the trust was formed (for example, occupation as a home), and the welfare of any minor occupant, as well as the interests of any secured creditor. Section 15(3) also directed the court to consider the interests of persons of full age entitled to interests in possession – that is, adult co-owners – with a consideration of the value of their interests. This can be understood as a shift from a 'monist' approach (pursuing one dominant value, alienation/sale) to a 'pluralist' approach – balancing

---

[50] Law Com No 181 (1989), para. 1.3; Law Com WP No 94, paras 3.2, 6.4.
[51] Law Commission, Trusts of Land, Working Paper No 94, (HMSO, 1987), para. 3.17.
[52] Law Com WP No 106, para. 3.2.
[53] Ibid., para. 3.10.
[54] 569 HL Deb (5th Series) col 1725 (1 March 1996).
[55] TLATA, s. 3.
[56] Law Comm No 181 (1989), para 3.6.

a range of competing values, set out in section 15. Yet, the extent to which new terminology, changing the stated purpose of the trust and including these new criteria to guide the court, has changed the way in which the courts have exercised their discretion to make orders affecting co-owned land has varied according to the circumstances and depending on who the parties to the dispute are. In disputes between co-owners, there are a range of cases which demonstrate the courts taking account of section 15 (see, for example, *Chun* v. *Ho*,[57] *Rodway* v. *Landy*,[58] *Holman* v. *Howes*,[59] *Ellison* v. *Cleghorn*.[60]) However, in cases where the party seeking sale is a creditor, the section 15 guidelines have only very occasionally displaced the presumption of sale, with the courts remaining largely faithful to the ethos of the 1925 legislation, continuing to order sale in most cases.[61] So, for example, in *Bank of Ireland Home Mortgages* v. *Bell*, a case in which the bank had received no interest payments from the occupier beneficiaries for some time, the court was particularly concerned that, if an order for sale were refused, it would have '... condemned the bank to go on waiting with no prospect of recovery [of their money] and with the debt increasing all the time, the debt already exceeding what could be realised on a sale'.[62] The factors to be balanced the other way were viewed as slight by comparison: the house had originally been bought as a matrimonial home and there were children. Yet, the male partner had left and thus the purpose was no longer relevant, and the son was not far short of 18 years old.

The point about the bank waiting for its money was applied in (quite remarkable) circumstances in *First National Bank plc* v. *Achampong*, in which the bank had been slow to bring a claim for possession. As the judge in the county court had put it, 'The fact remains that the bank started these proceedings in 1993 with a debt of some £63,000 which because of their own inaction has...rise[n] to some £180,000.'[63] Blackburne J, however, argued that delay was neither here nor there because, in the meantime, Ms Achampong had received the use of the property,[64] and so had not been prejudiced. The further argument for Ms Achampong was that, although her husband had left her – and so the immediate purpose of the trust to use the property as a home for them had failed – she was living in the property with her grandchildren, one of whom was severely disabled. That argument was brushed aside, partly on an evidential ground, and partly because:

---

[57] [2002] EWCA Civ 1075.
[58] [2001] Ch 703.
[59] [2007] EWCA Civ 877.
[60] [2013] EWHC 3 (Ch).
[61] See for example, *TSB Bank plc* v. *Marshall* [1998] 39 EG 308; *Bank of Ireland Home Mortgages Ltd* v. *Bell* [2001] 2 FLR 809; *First National Bank plc* v. *Achampong* [2003] EWCA Civ 487; *Mortgage Corporation Ltd* v. *Lewis Silkin* (25 February 2000, unreported).
[62] [2001] 2 FLR 809 at [31], Peter Gibson LJ.
[63] [2003] EWCA Civ 487 at [55].
[64] Ibid. at [62].

Insofar as the purpose of the trust – and the intention of the Achampongs in creating it – was to provide a family home and insofar as that is a purpose which goes wider than simply the provision of a matrimonial home, I am unpersuaded that it is a consideration to which much if any weight should be attached. The children of the marriage have long since reached adulthood. One of them is no longer in occupation. It is true that the elder daughter, Rosemary, is a person under mental disability and remains in occupation but to what extent that fact is material to her continued occupation of the property and therefore to the exercise of any discretion under section 14 is not apparent.[65]

One exception to this line of authority seems to be *Edwards* v. *Lloyds TSB*,[66] in which Park J refused to make an order for sale. He regarded two particular facts of that case as salient: first, there was sufficient equity in the property to pay the debt; and second, the actual property itself was relatively modest and Ms Edwards would not be able to afford adequate alternative accommodation. Even so, he postponed sale for five years, until the youngest child was 18 years old.[67]

The difference in approach to cases of conflict between co-owners, on the one hand, and conflicts between co-owners/occupiers and a creditor, on the other, offers an interesting illustration of the themes we have been considering. For one thing, it is notable that, in this area of land law, the context appears to make a difference to the way in which the courts resolve the case. Perhaps this is not too surprising, since TLATA as a whole – and sections 14 and 15 specifically – were driven by the view that the earlier law (LPA 1925, section 30) was not fit for purpose to meet the new context of homeownership. Yet, on the other hand, creditors almost invariably prevail under section 14, even though the reason they need to use the provision is that they have failed to secure priority over a co-owner's interest, so that the interests of the co-owner in occupation have priority as a matter of property law. This demonstrates the strength of the pro-creditor norm in English land law: between co-owners, the court can be flexible, but when the interests of capital are at stake, the pro-purchaser, alienation ethos of the 1925 legislation appears to remain resistant to reform.

CONCLUSIONS

The impact of the 1925 theme of alienation has been identified in many other contemporary land law contexts. For example, Hunter and Nixon's analysis of judicial attitudes in mortgage possession actions emphasized the significance of the market ethos in respect of owner-occupation. They found that, in cases involving default, both legal principles and judicial decision-making processes have been

---

[65] Ibid. at [65].
[66] [2005] 1 FCR 139.
[67] He also ordered that no interest was to be paid in the meantime and that the parties had liberty to apply to vary the length of the postponement – an order which might be regarded as at the margins of discretion.

influenced by the underlying assumptions that: [f]or lenders their primary interest is in the commercial/exchange value of their property rights [while] social land-lords have primarily been seeking, within certain constraints, to provide use value rights ... [68]

Hunter and Nixon tracked this assumption through to the outcomes of cases involving the exercise of the court's discretion, concluding that:

> The way in which judges exercise their discretion [in mortgage cases] provides evidence of the dominance of market forces and the primary importance of the exchange value of the dwelling ... judges take a very different view of the rights which have to be protected in cases against tenants from those involving borrowers.[69]

While the mortgage possession cases they reviewed displayed a monist, exchange value approach to ordering possession, in cases involving social landlords, the courts were more likely to adopt a plural values orientation, recognizing the use value of the property to the tenants as well as its exchange value on the market. This echoes Gray and Gray's observation – discussed above at note 26 – that when it comes to relationships between 'strangers':

> Relationships are strictly commercial, bargaining is hard-nosed, social bondings are minimal and the value attached to land is primarily, perhaps even exclusively, an 'exchange value'. Altruism is in very short supply; we are talking money.[70]

In light of the debates considered in this chapter, we elaborate on this to note that while the values put in place by the 1925 legislation have been tempered by the TLATA – in the 'newer' context of (typically family) disputes between co-owners – where a third party purchaser/creditor is involved, the dominant theme of aliena-tion continues to shape property law's ideological orientation.

The 1925 legislation had a significant and lasting effect on English land law and culture. Through its emphasis on alienation, it 'commodified' land, which came to be valued according to its 'exchange value' or 'market value' in a free market economy. Margaret Radin has observed that a key feature of commodified assets is that:

> All commodities are fungible and commensurable – capable of being reduced to money without changing in value, and completely interchangeable with every other commodity in terms of exchange value.[71]

This has significant implications for people who use land, and for whom it bears more specific, personal or practical values. The TLATA recognized that the 1925

---

[68] C. Hunter and J. Nixon, 'Better a Public Tenant Than a Private Borrower Be: The Possession Process and the Threat of Eviction' in D. Cowan (ed.), *Housing: Participation and Exclusion* (Ashgate, 1998) pp. 94, 95, 98.

[69] Ibid..

[70] Gray and Gray, n.26, p. 241.

[71] M. Radin, *Contested Commodities: The Trouble with Trade in Sex, Children, Body Parts and Other Things* (Harvard University Press, 1996) p. 3.

frame for thinking about land did not sit well against the growth of mass home-ownership, and that the dominance of the alienation theme was not well-aligned to ways that we think about our owned homes. The particular devices considered in this chapter – the trust for sale and the doctrine of conversion – both explicitly rejected the idea of land as a special or unique type of property, and valued it only in terms of its exchange value. In addition to closing out considerations of use, this also excluded consideration of the emotional dimension of property in land, and of property as a socially meaningful 'place' rather than an abstract, commoditized space. As a mere commodity, a capital asset to be traded in the marketplace, the owned home was reduced to a house and its owner regarded as a property investor. The limited traction of the TLATA in countering this framework demonstrates how deep our 'property values' – values that are not inherent, but were politically constructed in 1925 – run in English land law.

Further Reading

S. Anderson, 'Land Law Texts and the Explanation of 1925' (1984) *Current Legal Problems* 63.
S. Anderson, 'The 1925 Property Legislation: Setting Contexts', in S. Bright and J. Dewar, *Land Law: Themes and Perspectives* (Oxford University Press, 1998).
L. Fox, 'Creditors and the Concept of Family Home: A Functional Analysis' (2005) 25(2) *Legal Studies* 201.

4

LEASES

INTRODUCTION

In the previous chapter, we discussed some of the issues arising from co-ownership of property. In this chapter, we deal with a set of issues deriving from a different type of property right – the lease, also known as a tenancy. Part of the consideration here is about the dividing line between property and personal rights, to be sure, but the relationships created out of, or because of, a tenancy agreement are just as significant to our discussion. The themes outlined in Chapter 1 are equally relevant here, but the key theme here is legal rationality. The law puts to one side what the parties think they are doing and, instead, by law's own logic, provides an 'objective' solution that is rather different from what the parties thought they were doing. A whole set of sub-disciplines have been formed around this logic (landlord and tenant law; housing law).

There is also a perhaps contradictory tendency – a real temptation – to get sucked in by the law, to over-privilege it, and miss your own perspective. The law is a backstop which is irrelevant in most agreements. With that in mind, the opening section asks you to think about your own experience as occupier and draws on landlord perspectives to illustrate the significance of respect and responsibility, which underlie the relationship between occupier and the person/s or bodies to whom these responsibilities might be owed. This is Debate 1, which concerns the everyday life of tenancy law. The following section looks at the dividing practices of the technical law, which divides off property from personal rights, paying particularly close attention to the notions of intention and exclusion. This is Debate 2, which concerns property rights versus personal rights. The next section discusses the law's construction of tenant's rights, noting the narrow constructions given to those rights. This is Debate 3, about rights and their amelioration. The final section considers problems arising when the landlord seeks to determine a tenancy agreement. That is Debate 4, about how a tenancy is determined. One significant omission from that final section is the intervention of human rights law, which is considered in Chapter 8 and is closely related to this chapter.

Debate 1

What is the 'everyday life' of tenancy law?

We used to begin tutorials on leases by asking our students whether they had read their tenancy agreement. Most had not done so. Some, particularly those living with non-law students, had been asked by their fellow occupiers to read the agreement. None appreciated the extent of their rights and responsibilities in the property. The observation follows that if they do not read the document or understand their rights and responsibilities, they cannot necessarily expect others to do so.

In a study of harassment and unlawful eviction in the late 1990s, one of the comments from a landlord that stood out was that they regarded the tenancy agreement as an entirely secondary, consequential aspect of the relationship between themselves and the occupiers.[1] They believed that leaving a bottle of wine (for male tenants) or a bunch of flowers (for female tenants) in the property at the start was a far greater control on the behaviour of the occupiers than the formality of the tenancy agreement. On the other hand, some social landlords now engage in tenancy signing ceremonies with their future occupiers, the aim of which is to make occupiers appreciate the extent of their obligations under the agreement so that enforcement of the tenancy agreement might become less necessary.[2]

These observations of landlords and tenants are, in fact, two sides of the same coin of legality and lead on to a broader point. Both the private landlord and the social landlords were seeking, in different ways, to get the occupier to take responsibility for the property; the social landlords have an extended meaning of the property here, to encompass the neighbourhood and community to whom the obligations of the tenancy agreement can also be said to be owed, a matter of less significance to the private landlord who is likely to be more concerned with the internal state of the property.[3] The students were enacting their everyday under-standings of the extent of their agreement with the landlord, whether or not they read their agreements, through the payment of a sum of money and (we have no doubt, from personal experience) varying approaches to respecting the internal condition of the property. In sum, the versions of legality in these relationships are often extra-contractual but enact and perform assumptions about respect and responsibility.

---

[1] A. Marsh, P. Niner, D. Cowan, R. Forrest and P. Kennett, *Harassment and Unlawful Eviction in the Private Rented and Park Homes Sector* (DETR, 2000).

[2] See, in particular, J. Flint, 'Reconfiguring Agency and Responsibility in the Governance of Social Housing in Scotland', (2004) 41(1) *Urban Studies* 151; J. Flint and J. Nixon, 'Governing Neighbours: Anti-Social Behaviour Orders and New Forms of Regulating Conduct in the UK', (2006) 43(5/6) *Urban Studies* 939; J. Flint and H. Pawson, 'Social Landlords and the Regulation of Conduct in Urban Spaces in the United Kingdom', (2009) 9(4) *Criminology and Criminal Justice* 415.

[3] See D. Cowan and H. Carr, 'Actor-Network Theory, Implementation and the Private Landlord' (2008) 35 (Special Research Issue) *Journal of Law and Society* 149.

The tenancy continues not because of the contract but because of the relational assumptions of respect and responsibility which underlie it.[4] These can, however, break down. Research into harassment and unlawful eviction usually finds, in relation to private landlords, that the landlord does not necessarily think about using due process of law to evict the occupier, but, rather, bases their decision-making processes on the understanding that the property is 'theirs'.[5] That understanding is often also shared by police officers, who, it is found, sometimes unwittingly assist landlords in their unlawful activity.[6] In such circumstances, and others where resort to law is necessary, it is only at that point when the actual agreement takes on a presence and is translated into and through the process of 'going to law'.

This leads on to a further problem about the limits of law. A tenant who complains to the landlord about the state of the property (because there is damp or no central heating, for example), or about the landlord's broader management role, does so at their own risk. They may have every right to do so, but they may also recognize that a complaint often leads to eviction. This is the unquantifiable problem of 'retaliatory eviction', which arises when the landlord feels, for example, that there is a breakdown in trust with the occupier.[7]

This practice is not likely to change even though there is now provision which is designed to stop retaliatory eviction in certain circumstances.[8] That is because the circumstances in which the notice will be invalid rely on a number of conditions being satisfied:

(a) Before the section 21 notice was given, the tenant made a complaint in writing to the landlord regarding the condition of the dwelling-house at the time of the complaint.
(b) The landlord –
    (i) did not provide a response to the complaint within 14 days beginning with the day on which the complaint was given,
    (ii) provided a response to the complaint that was not an adequate response, or
    (iii) gave a section 21 notice in relation to the dwelling-house following the complaint.
(c) The tenant then made a complaint to the relevant local housing authority about the same, or substantially the same, subject matter as the complaint to the landlord.
(d) The relevant local housing authority served a relevant notice in relation to the dwelling-house in response to the complaint, and

---

4 See, generally, I. Macneil, 'Economic Analysis of Contractual Relations: Its Shortfalls and the Need for a "Rich Classificatory Apparatus"' (1981) 75(3) *Nw LR* 1018; P. Vincent-Jones, *The New Public Contracting* (Oxford University Press, 2006); H. Collins, *Regulating Contracts* (Oxford University Press, 1999).
5 See D. Nelken, *The Limits of the Legal Process: A Study of Landlords, Law and Crime* (Academic Press, 1983); D. Cowan, 'Harassment and Unlawful Eviction in the Private Rented Sector: A Study of Law (in-) Action' [2001] *Conveyancer and Property Lawyer* 249.
6 See, for example, http://nearlylegal.co.uk/blog/2010/07/illegal-eviction-and-the-police/.
7 See D. Cowan, *Housing Law and Policy* (Cambridge University Press, 2011) ch. 11.
8 S. 33, Deregulation Act 2015.

(e) If the section 21 notice was not given before the tenant's complaint to the local housing authority, it was given before the service of the relevant notice.

It all depends on how long the occupier thinks they have left in the property – which may not necessarily correspond with their rights to remain in the property after the expiry of a fixed term – but it tends to reflect what has become known as the 'status of moveability' of occupiers.[9] Most private rented tenancies take effect under an assured shorthold tenancy, which only lasts for at least six months (or such period as the parties agree). In brief, such a tenancy can be terminated by means of a notice giving the tenant two months; such notices also require the court to make an order for possession (although this is not usually something of which many tenants are aware and, in any event, they may find themselves liable for court costs of the possession claim). It is easier for the tenant to move on to alternative accommodation. The relational nature of the tenancy agreement is rarely acknowledged in property law, nor in landlord and tenant law – it appears that merely putting the word 'law' after 'property' and 'landlord and tenant' neutralizes the relational understandings which are translated into legal rights and remedies – but it is clearly significant to everyday life.

The above points are further illustrated through the work of Diane Lister on the governance of tenancy relationships in the private sector. Lister's data consisted of qualitative interviews with younger tenants and their landlords. She demonstrates how the formal contract between landlord and tenant gave way to informal sets of understandings developed at the outset through the interactions between landlord and tenant. Neither party expected to negotiate about terms and rents. If the tenant sought to negotiate, '... it was perceived [by the landlord] as denoting financial insecurity and a potential risk'.[10] Lister's point was that by focusing on legal requirements, '... social factors of relationships are overlooked which are significant and have a greater impact on behaviour than at first credited ...'.[11] Thus, social expectations of the relationship, combined with the emotional or sentimental attachments (including to the property) should be regarded as significant. Lister emphasizes the role of trust, which might be regarded as a central aspect of all ongoing relations. When trust breaks down between the parties, attachments can become more evident through unlawful action. Alternatively, and using language more associated with criminology, she refers to the overt and covert surveillance techniques used by landlords both inside the property and outside.[12] That being said, though, national landlord associations often draw distinctions

---

[9] See, for example, J. Morgan, 'Housing Security in England and Wales: Casualisation Revisited' (2009) 1(1) *International Journal of Law in the Built Environment* 42.

[10] D. Lister, 'The Nature of Tenancy Relationships – Landlords and Young People in the Private Rented Sector' in S. Lowe and D. Hughes (eds.), *The Privately Rented Sector in a New Century* (Policy Press, 2001) p. 99.

[11] 'Controlling Letting Arrangements in the Private Rented Sector?' in D. Hughes and S. Lowe (eds.), *The Private Rented Housing Market: Regulation or Deregulation?* (Ashgate, 2007) p. 72.

[12] 'Controlling Letting Arrangements? Landlords and Surveillance in the Private Rented Sector' (2005) 2(4) *Surveillance and Society* 513.

between what they see as the landlord's proper role – controlling behaviour inside the property's boundaries – and that outside the property, which is the proper province of the public police.[13]

Lister's findings chime also with the critique of the anti-regulationists – the economists who assume that regulation of the market, and particularly rent, is a moral and practical hazard, causing declines in property quality and availability.[14] Margaret Radin argues against the idea that housing should be treated as an ordinary market commodity.[15] From the individual tenant's perspective, 'The intuitive general rule is that preservation of one's home is a stronger claim than preservation of one's business, or that noncommercial personal use of an apartment as a home is morally entitled to more weight than purely commercial landlording'.[16] As opposed to the landlord's commercial interest in the property, the tenant's personal interest in the property becomes bound up with their selfhood. Now, this dichotomy may well not hold good in this jurisdiction, where most landlords own or manage a portfolio usually of only one or two properties, which they regard as their 'own'; but what it does emphasize are the reciprocal obligations and, perhaps most importantly, the polyvocality of 'home'.

Debate 2

Is a tenancy a property or a personal right?

Conventionally, in property law, one distinguishes a lease – a proprietary right – from a licence or other personal right. That proprietary right, however, obscures the complex nature of the relationship between landlord and tenant, which exists both contractually and as a matter of property – in other words, the answer to this question is that it is both a property and a personal right. The reason for that crossover is largely historical but its enduring power remains. The dual nature of the relationship becomes particularly significant at different moments, when one or the other becomes pre-eminent. It also causes problems, such as in the enforcement of covenants between the parties when the original landlord or tenant has transferred their interest so that there is no 'privity of contract'.[17]

There has been considerable case law on the distinction between leases and licences, although it has diminished (both in scale and importance) since the implementation of the Housing Act 1988 because of the decline in security of tenure and rent regulation/control which had been in place previously; and, as

---

[13] See H. Carr, D. Cowan and C. Hunter, 'Policing the Housing Crisis', (2007) 27(1) *Critical Social Policy* 100.
[14] See, for example, Institute for Economic Affairs, *Verdict on Rent Control* (IEA, 1972); and the sophisticated analysis by B. Turner and S. Malpezzi, 'A Review of Empirical Evidence on the Costs and Benefits of Rent Control', (2003) 10 *Swedish Economic Policy Review* 11.
[15] M. Radin, 'Residential Rent Control', (1986) 15 *Philosophy & Public Affairs* 350; see also the sophisticated account provided by D. Cooper, 'Opening Up Ownership: Community Belonging, Belongings, and the Productive Life of Property', (2007) 32(3) *Law and Social Inquiry* 625.
[16] Radin, n.15, p. 360.
[17] Issues largely resolved by the Landlord and Tenant (Covenants) Act 1995.

regards council tenants, the Housing Act 1985 provisions concerning security of tenure apply equally to leases and certain licences.[18] The lease was a powerful right; now less so (as discussed above). These shifts have effectively neutralized the power of the law so that this law might be regarded almost as a passive bystander in most disputes.[19] That does not mean it is unimportant – a body of law which is largely symbolic remains important for what it represents (and it is not symbolic all the time). In this case, it represents a struggle both outside the law and inside the law as to the significance of different types of intention; or, to put it another way, different versions of truth.

A BRIEF DIVERSION

It is impossible to get a handle on the complicated law in this area unless account is taken of the parallel rise and fall of security of tenure and rent control/regulation.[20] As originally conceived in 1915, security of tenure (by which is meant that a landlord required a court order before the tenant could be evicted, such order only to be made on certain grounds of possession) and rent control (rent rises being set centrally) were linked to control over the levels of mortgage interest payable.[21] In the short term, this made sense,[22] but the conjunction was subsequently disturbed so that central control over mortgage interest was stopped.

It was assumed also that when wartime controls were no longer necessary, the rent control provisions at least would be discontinued. There was a succession of official reports, each of which was tasked to consider not only the technical law but also whether the provisions should be continued. As Cowan and McDermont suggest, 'what is apparent in these reports is that the private sector should be made as free as possible and, when it is, it was thought that it should be able to cater for the population. The evident belief was that the free market would provide decent quality housing at an affordable rent, if it was given the chance. It was a belief in the value of enterprise, conceived as a "social service".'[23] The wavering commitment to rent control can be shown by the process of allowing 'creeping decontrol' – new lets being exempted from the rent control provisions – and, from the mid-1960s, a shift to rent regulation. Security of tenure remained largely in place until the Housing Act 1980 allowed landlords, under certain restrictive

---

[18] *Westminster CC* v. *Clarke* [1992] 2 AC 288; Housing Act 1985, s. 79(3).
[19] Vincent-Jones describes the leading case in the field, *Street* v. *Mountford* [1985] AC 809 as a 'shallow victory' as a result: P. Vincent-Jones, 'Exclusive Possession and Exclusive Control of Private Rented Housing: A Socio-Legal Critique of the Lease-Licence Distinction' (1987) 14(4) *Journal of Law and Society* 445, 455.
[20] Security of tenure and rent control/regulation have usually gone hand-in-hand, one being regarded as impossible without the other.
[21] The history of these provisions is set out in Cowan, n.7, ch. 1.
[22] Indeed, it was not wholly disadvantageous to landlords: A. Holmans, *Housing Policy in Britain* (Croom Helm, 1987) p. 388.
[23] D. Cowan and M. McDermont, *Regulating Social Housing: Governing Decline* (Routledge, 2006) p. 147.

conditions, to grant less secure tenancies; by the Housing Act 1988, however, that limited form was given freer rein through the creation of the assured shorthold tenancy. The latter allows occupiers a minimum of six months' security. It is now the default tenancy arrangement in the private rented sector. Rent control/regulation is limited, in essence, to a market-based regime.

What the previous paragraph does not convey, however, is the *politics* of private renting. Until the 1990s, there appeared to be sharp divides between the Conservative and Labour parties, and debates about security and rent were conducted with considerable fervour.[24] Those debates seem like an age ago and have been rarely stimulated until recently.[25] The Labour Party manifesto at the 2015 general election contained a promise to ensure that rent increases had an upper limit.[26]

There is also what seems (if anything) a distant memory of judicial antipathy to rent control/regulation legislation regarded as ill-fitting,[27] and problematic relations between landlords and tenants. These latter points are best encapsulated in the bitter start of an article written by Roger Street, the principal protagonist in the law considered below:

> The Rent Acts are grossly unfair to landlords. A stranger obtains a weekly tenancy of a house: half a century may pass before the owner can have his property again. In the meantime he can only charge a so-called 'fair' rent which in many cases does little more than cover the cost of keeping the property in repair. As a result of all this, the capital value of the property drops to between one-third and one-half of the vacant possession value. Little wonder that over the years landlords and their legal advisers have sought various ways of avoiding the potentially horrendous consequences of being caught by the legislation.[28]

Street's concerns were tempered by the well-known knowledge that there were other well-worn routes through which landlords could avoid the security of tenure and rent regulation legislation – for example, the grant of 'holiday lets' and 'winter lets'.[29]

However, the essential point of this section is that the debates about the distinction between proprietary and personal rights are shot through with considerations which are both extraneous and politicized. At their heart, as Roger Street discursively demonstrated, the distinction offers a far greater appreciation of our core themes of ownership, alienation and exclusion than is suggested by the apparently neutral case law discussed below.

---

[24] There is a full discussion in P. Kemp, *Private Renting in Transition* (CIH, 2004).

[25] See, for example, the occasional calls for rent control, particularly in London (see, for example, B. Dillon, 'Only rent controls will help to solve London's housing crisis', *International Business Times*, 15 July 2015); and the various campaigns led by Generation Rent.

[26] See www.labour.org.uk/issues/detail/renting (last visited 15 October 2015).

[27] See C. Hand, 'The Statutory Tenancy: An Unrecognised Proprietary Interest?' [1980] *Conveyancer and Property Lawyer* 351.

[28] R. Street, 'Coach and Horses Trip Cancelled? Rent Act Avoidance after Street v Mountford' [1985] *Conveyancer and Property Lawyer* 328, 328.

[29] At 335; see also House of Commons Environment Committee, *The Private Rented Sector*, HC 40-I (HMSO, 1982).

AUTOBIOGRAPHICAL NOTE

Renting in the halcyon days

When I was a law student in the distant past, I had no idea about such matters as security of tenure or the like. We students were expected to move out of halls and into the private rented sector. That was what everybody did. That was in the halcyon days of student grants and free tertiary education. So, I moved out with my then partner and a couple of other students into a rented property. The landlord was a sweetie (more about him in a moment). Our rent was set by the rent officer at £14 per week each and we each received housing benefit to pay for it. I didn't know that this was a regulated tenancy under the Rent Act 1977, which granted us considerable rights to security. The following year, however, housing benefit vanished and my rent seemed to increase exponentially to £40 per week or thereabouts. And our landlord insisted on us signing something called an 'assured shorthold tenancy' contract.

I couldn't work it out at all – why should my rent jump by such an amount and why should my housing benefit disappear? I was less concerned by this new tenancy agreement. To be honest, in those days there were other more pressing concerns such as where my next drink was going to be had, and the questions soon disappeared in an alcoholic and cigarette haze.

But it is now clear to me after all these years that my legal education took place on the cusp of major shifts in security of tenure and towards market rents for properties. In that year, the impact on me of the deregulation of the private rented sector was felt most strongly at the local pub and tobacconist. My landlord clearly expected us to stay for the whole academic year and then move out (under both types of tenancy), and we did so.

Under the Rent Act tenancy, however, we could have stayed until a ground for possession emerged. Under the Housing Act assured shorthold tenancy, if it was properly granted, the landlord could have got us out with a simple two-month notice under section 21, Housing Act 1988, and a court order.

And back to my lovely landlord. We regularly used to come home after a day at the library (or wherever) to find him in 'our' place, making a cup of tea. He used to make me one too, which I thought was very nice of him. I didn't appreciate that this was wrong (Protection from Eviction Act 1977), nor that it was a breach of the implied covenant of quiet enjoyment. Such things didn't bother me then.

Knowing what I know now, as a lawyer, I suspect that I might have approached matters rather differently then; but, as a socio-legal academic, I recognize the relational quality of the relationship between landlord and tenant, so that formal law may well be less relevant than the ongoing day-to-day experience of our interactions. However, I am also acutely aware that my experience is not necessarily shared by students and other renters, for whom harassment and unlawful eviction together with terrible conditions in rented property can be an everyday affair. The day-to-day experience of barristers specializing in housing law is often precisely these types of cases. I hope it doesn't happen to you, but, if it does, talk to your local authority tenancy relations officer about it and get their help. They are a fantastic resource.

GENERAL PRINCIPLES

It is of the essence of a lease that it conveys the right to exclusive possession on the tenant; that is, the right in the tenant to exclude allcomers from the property, including the landlord.[30] That is now regarded as so trite that it almost needs no authority in support. There must also be a term, one which is certain at the outset.[31] It is said that there must also be a rent, but this assertion is, in most cases, incorrect.[32] As it confers a property right on the occupier, it must also be properly granted at law or in equity.[33]

Certain agreements which confer on an occupier exclusive possession for a term may, however, not be leases: where there is no intention to enter into legal relations; where the landlord has no power to grant a tenancy;[34] or where the occupation is referable to some other relationship (e.g. employment, seller/buyer, tolerated trespasser).[35] These were regarded as 'exceptional categories' in *Street* v. *Mountford*[36] but their exceptionalism is an empirical question, the answer to which is likely to depend in part on the reception of the prevailing statutory regulation.

Where there is more than one person who takes under the agreement (or agreements), the question also arises whether they are joint tenants, in the co-ownership sense.[37] If there is no express joint tenancy created, then the question is whether one can be inferred from the surrounding circumstances. Here, one needs to find the 'four unities' – possession, interest, time, title – but there appears to be a fundamental disagreement on the authorities. The problem usually arises where the occupiers take under separate agreements containing separate obligations in relation to the rent. How can one nevertheless get unity of interest and title from those facts? In *Antoniades* v. *Villiers*,[38] the House of Lords

---

[30] *Street* v. *Mountford* [1985] AC 809; note that the reservation by the landlord of limited rights of entry confirms the exclusivity of the tenant's possession for, otherwise, there would have been no need to make such a reservation: at 818C.

[31] There is a line of authority going back to *Say* v. *Smith* (1530)1 Plowd 269, affirmed by the House of Lords in *Prudential Assurance* v. *London Residuary Body* [1992] 2 AC 386; for the effects, see *Berrisford* v. *Mexfield Housing Co-operative* [2011] UKSC 52.

[32] *Street*, cf. *Ashburn Anstalt* v. *Arnold* [1989] Ch 1, pointing out that the definition of a term of years absolute in the Law of Property Act 1925 does not require a rent; note, however, s. 54(2), which requires a proper rent for informally created legal leases.

[33] Law of Property Act 1925, ss. 52 & 54(2); Law of Property (Miscellaneous Provisions) Act 1989, s. 2.

[34] Compare *Camden London BC* v. *Shortlife Community Housing* (1992) 90 LGR 358 and *Bruton* v. *London & Quadrant Housing Trust* [2000] 1 AC 406. In the latter, although L&Q had no relevant estate, a tenancy by estoppel was created from the fact of a grant of exclusive possession for a term to an occupier who accepted it.

[35] *Errington* v. *Errington* [1952] 1 KB 290, 297.

[36] [1985] AC 809 at 821.

[37] It is unclear, at best, why it was assumed that the parties were either joint tenants or licensees, and no consideration was given to whether they might be tenants in common – see the classic article by Peter Sparkes, 'Co-Tenants, Joint Tenants and Tenants in Common' (1989) 18(2) *AALR* 151; for further discussion, see S. Bright, *Landlord and Tenant Law in Context* (Hart, 2007), p. 99.

[38] [1990] 1 AC 417.

felt able to engage in a process of legal alchemy by reading two separate agreements together, Lord Templeman regarding them as interdependent (as opposed to independent of each other). By contrast, in apparently similar circumstances, the Court of Appeal in *Mikeover* v. *Brady* were unable to read the two separate agreements together '... because the monetary obligations of the two parties were not joint obligations and there was accordingly no complete unity of interest'.[39] The judgments appear irreconcilable (and it is no answer to that irreconcilability to say that one of the occupiers moved out subsequently in *Mikeover*, because the relevant date for determining the nature of the agreements is the date on which they were entered into).

The body of law described above proceeds by reference to the rationality theme in relation to the law's construction of the actual agreement itself. The agreement rules, although the labels the parties give to the agreement are irrelevant – it is the effect in law of the agreement which is crucial.[40] By contrast to that line of authority is another line which requires a rather different evaluation which goes beyond the tenancy agreement. Here, the question is whether the agreement itself (or clauses in it) is, in fact, a 'pretence'.[41] Originally, Lord Templeman had referred to the need for the courts to be '... astute to detect and frustrate sham devices and artificial transactions whose only object is to disguise the grant of a tenancy and to evade the Rent Acts'.[42] The problem with the latter formulation was the excessively narrow formulation of the doctrine of 'sham' developed in a different context.[43] The shift to 'pretence' was, one might infer, a recognition that this doctrine was designed to be more wide-ranging.

THE QUESTION OF 'TERM'

It is of the essence of an estate in land that it exists for a certain period. If there is an uncertain term, it will be void in law. The rule is that one needs to be able to tell, at the outset of the term, the maximum possible duration. Thus, in *Prudential Assurance* v. *London Residuary Body*,[44] a term which allowed the occupier to take the property until the landlord required it for road widening was held to be void. A periodic tenancy, which rolls on from one period to the next, is valid only because the period itself (be it weekly, monthly or yearly) is certain, even though the tenancy may run on for an uncertain period until it is determined. However, 'A power for nobody to determine or for one party only to be able to determine is inconsistent with the concept of a term from year to year.'[45]

---

[39] (1989) 21 HLR 513, 523.
[40] *Street* at 819E-F.
[41] *Antoniades*, 462H.
[42] *Street*, 825H.
[43] *Snook* v. *London & West Riding Investments Ltd* [1967] 2 QB 786, 802, Diplock LJ.
[44] [1992] AC 386.
[45] At 394F.

In *Berrisford* v. *Mexfield Housing Co-Operative Ltd*,[46] the Supreme Court was able, on ancient authority, to circumvent this strict rule. The problem arose because Ms Berrisford (like many other tenants of a co-operative) had entered into a tenancy which provided that the term of the tenancy was to be from month to month. If it had stopped there, then that term would have been valid. However, it did not do so. Clause 6 of the agreement provided that the co-operative could 'ONLY' determine the tenancy by exercise of a right of re-entry on four limited grounds. Mexfield served notice to quit on Ms Berrisford after she fell into rent arrears (although those arrears were paid off). Mexfield did not purport to exercise their right of re-entry under clause 6, but to argue that as the contractual term was void due to uncertainty as a result of the fetter on their right to determine the monthly tenancy, it became a periodic tenancy.

In the Court of Appeal, Ms Berrisford's defence was that the agreement retained its validity in *equity* when the original contracting parties remain in place.[47] The arguments here were finely balanced – should equity follow the law and hold that the restriction on the landlord's right to determine has no effect, or does equity have some life beyond the law, so that the contract can be given effect by way of specific performance?[48] The Court of Appeal, by majority, accepted the former proposition, on the basis that, in the absence of a trust or estoppel or unconscionability, equity should normally follow the law (a reading which may well be too narrow).

Before the Supreme Court, however, the focus for Ms Berrisford's argument shifted, and decisively so, in her favour. Her argument was that the contractual term was void; that it was incapable of being a tenancy as a matter of law; but that prior to the LPA 1925 it would have taken effect as a tenancy for life (determinable earlier on the events in clause 6 of the agreement); and, after 1925, it became a tenancy for 90 years determinable earlier on the basis of the contractually agreed methods of termination (as a result of section 149(6), LPA 1925). The Supreme Court accepted this analysis. The majority also held that, in any event, as the parties were the original contracting parties, either way the contract into which they had entered was enforceable between them. This point serves as a warning to us land lawyers never to forget that property rights bite when issues of durability arise, but that the contractual obligations between the original contracting parties are enforceable in the ordinary way.

Nevertheless, it is the process of reasoning by which the Supreme Court, Lord Neuberger giving the leading judgment, reached that conclusion which is important. Mexfield first argued that, on a proper construction of the agreement, it created a monthly tenancy, determinable by one month's notice in accordance with established common law principles. This argument was rejected on the basis

---

[46] [2011] UKSC 52. For an excellent commentary, see K. Low, 'Certainty of Terms and Leases: Curiouser and Curiouser' [2012] 75(3) *MLR* 401.

[47] *Berrisford* v. *Mexfield Housing Co-Operative Ltd* [2011] 2 WLR 423; the point being that in *Prudential*, the House of Lords were concerned with successors in title and not the original contractors.

[48] Of interest is that proprietary estoppel had not, hitherto, been relied upon by Ms Berrisford.

of principles of ordinary contractual interpretation: what would the reasonable person think that this agreement created as a term?[49] It was clear on the face of the agreement that Mexfield could *only* determine the agreement in accordance with clause 6. Furthermore, '... given the circumstances in which the Agreement was entered into, it seems unlikely that Ms Berrisford's security was intended to be so tenuous as to be determinable by Mexfield on one month's notice at any time from the day the Agreement was made'.[50] Now, it must be said that this explanation about the law corresponding with the parties' intentions was only a passing thought, as a response to the deep rationality of the position taken at land law. And, as Baroness Hale put it, '... it is not difficult to imagine circumstances in which the same analysis would apply but be very far from the intentions of the parties. And that analysis is not available where the tenant is a company or corporation. So there the court is unable to give effect to the undoubted intentions of the parties.'[51]

On the second question, whether the agreement could constitute a tenancy as a matter of law, Ms Berrisford conceded that it could not, following a line of authority culminating in *Prudential*. This gave rise to many comments about the unsatisfactory state of the certainty rule in leases, although the Supreme Court felt that, on the facts of this case, they could not overrule such a long-standing principle. That was for Parliament. They expressed their opinions in characteristically forthright terms, as had Lord Browne-Wilkinson in *Prudential*.[52]

On the third proposition, there was plenty of authority to demonstrate that, before 1925, a tenancy with an uncertain term would have been regarded as a tenancy for life. Furthermore, that seemed to have been the intention of the agreement in this case, subject to earlier determination on the basis of clause 6 (as well as Ms Berrisford's right to determine the tenancy earlier, in clause 5). However, importantly, as noted above, the same rule would seem to apply even if the parties did not intend for such an outcome.

On the fourth ground, section 149(6) LPA 1925 clearly rewrites tenancies for life into terms of 90 years which are determinable on the same bases as the previous common law allowed. The fact that such arguments were not pursued in the leading cases of *Lace* v. *Chantler* and *Prudential* was neither here nor there because the point was not argued in those cases.[53] It now appears, as Lord Neuberger (who was the unsuccessful counsel in *Prudential*) put it, 'Some of the statements about the law by Lord Greene and Lord Templeman can now be seen to be extravagant

---

[49] See, for example, *Mannai Investment Co Ltd* v. *Eagle Star Life Assurance Co Ltd* [1997] AC 749.
[50] [19]; Baroness Hale, [94]. The agreement was entered into as part of a mortgage rescue scheme – Mexfield re-paid the mortgage which Ms Berrisford could not afford and granted the tenancy to her.
[51] [94].
[52] [34], Lord Neuberger; [80], Lord Hope; [93]–[96], Baroness Hale; [105] and [111], Lord Clarke; [115] and [119] Lord Dyson.
[53] [1944] KB 268, [53]. It is to be noted that this point would not have saved the tenancy agreement in *Prudential* in any event, as the original lessee was probably dead and a company cannot take a tenancy for 'life' as it has no 'life'.

or inaccurately wide, but it is only fair to them to repeat that this was, at least in part, because the tenancy for life argument was not raised before them.'[54]

This does raise an oddity, though: the rule only applies where the tenant is an individual and not a corporate entity. As Lord Dyson put it, 'To treat an individual and a corporate entity differently in this respect can only be explained on historical grounds. The explanation may lie in the realms of history, but that hardly provides a compelling justification for maintaining the distinction today.'[55] There are other oddities of the decision. So, for example, its constitution as a 90 year lease subject to earlier determination meant that it required registration for it to have effect at law; and, although Ms Berrisford was able to stay in her home, she lost extremely valuable rights that are otherwise available to tenants where the tenancy is for less than seven years.[56]

In *Southward Housing Co-operative Ltd* v. *Walker*, Hildyard J had to consider a not dissimilar tenancy agreement to that in *Berrisford*, on which Southward restricted its ability to seek possession to certain grounds, including rent arrears. The occupiers racked up rent arrears, in part because the DWP applied sanctions in respect of their entitlement to benefits. Southward sought possession. Hildyard J found that, although the tenancy was uncertain, it was not the intention of the parties that the occupiers were to have a tenancy for life.[57] Further,

> with diffidence and anxiety, I have eventually concluded that there is a solution which does give effect to the intention of the parties. The solution revolves around the difference between, on the one hand, accepting (as plainly one must) that the 'rule' can be applied in circumstances where the parties had no inkling or intention that it would, and, on the other hand, accepting that its application is mandatory even where the parties' intentions were to the contrary and their agreement contains fundamental terms that simply cannot be carried over into a 90 year lease.[58]

He concluded that, although the rule operated independently of the parties' intentions, the rule could be disapplied where those intentions and fundamental aspects of the agreement were confounded by it.[59] Now, it has to be said that this is an entirely novel approach, which appears to be out of step with the way in which the deep land law logic was treated by the Supreme Court. One might say that Hildyard J's subjective reaction to the inexorable objective logic of land law was natural but, almost certainly, problematic. He went on to consider, if he was wrong, how the tenancy could be determined. In *Berrisford*, the Supreme Court appeared to suggest that the tenancy could be determined in accordance with

---

[54] [53].
[55] [119].
[56] S. 11, Landlord and Tenant Act 1985.
[57] [2015] EWHC 1615 (Ch), [71]: '... it is plain that even if the parties envisaged that the Defendants in this case would stay at the property for a long time, it was not the intention of the parties that they should be legally entitled to enjoy the premises for life'.
[58] [87].
[59] [91].

the terms of the agreement, either by virtue of section 149(6) or by virtue of the contractual agreement (although this was *obiter*). Hildyard J, however, proceeded on an alternative path, which was that the relevant clause was an 'innominate process for termination'.[60] He was concerned that, otherwise, 'the long lease into which the Agreement, on the hypothesis underlying this part of this judgment, is transmogrified is not subject to any termination provision at all. In my view, that is so unpalatable, and so alien to the parties' intentions, that some solution must be found.'[61] It is likely that, once again, this emotional response to land law logic led him into error.

THE USES OF INTENTION

The previous section was neutral on the uses of intention in the creation of proprietary interests (other than *Southward*, which is controversial at best). However, intention is *the* central consideration. In the opening question of whether, on the face of the agreement, exclusive possession for a term has been granted, the intention is not the subjective intention of the parties. That is why the labels the parties give to the agreement are irrelevant. The question is whether, as a matter of law, the occupier has been granted exclusive possession on the face of the agreement. Here, it is also said, the regulatory protections of the Rent and Housing Acts are also irrelevant ('... they must not be allowed to alter or influence the construction of an agreement'),[62] although perhaps the whole basis for the judgment in *Street* was to halt the practice of landlords contracting out of those very protections (certainly, that was the reason why the case was so significant at the time).

As regards the exceptional categories, intention is being used rather differently. Here, the courts are encouraged to look at the identity of, and relationship between, the parties in considering whether there was an intention to enter into legal relationships. If the parties are friends or relations, one might begin to wonder whether they really did intend to enter into legal relations, with the consequences which might subsequently occur. If a lease is created, then the Rent/Housing Acts become relevant – did they really mean to convey those protections (a less relevant question after the Housing Act 1988 assured shorthold tenancy regime). Rent becomes an important, albeit not decisive, indicator. If no rent is paid, again one might wonder whether they intended to enter into legal relations. The key point, though, is that we are moving into the realms of subjective intention.

A tenancy by way of estoppel, however, offers an odd conjunction of both objective and subjective intentions. In *Bruton* v. *London and Quadrant Housing Trust*,[63] the

---

[60] [112].
[61] [111].
[62] *Street*, 825H.
[63] [2000] 1 AC 406.

House of Lords were faced with this problem of intention. Lambeth council had a property in Brixton which they wanted to re-develop into flats. In the meantime, they entered into a licence agreement with L&Q for use as short-term accommodation for homeless persons. It was clear that Lambeth had no power to do more than that.[64] The licence agreement explicitly stated that L&Q could only grant licences to those homeless households to occupy the property. L&Q could not grant tenancies. The licence agreement between L&Q and Mr Bruton accordingly said:

> As has been explained to you, the above property is being offered to you by [L&Q] on a weekly Licence from 6 February 1989. The Trust has the property on licence from [Lambeth] who acquired the property for development ...'and pending this development, it is being used to provide temporary housing accommodation. It is offered to you on the condition that you will vacate upon receiving reasonable notice from the Trust, which will not normally be less than four weeks. You understand and agree that while you are living in the property, you will allow access at all times during normal working hours to the staff of the Trust, the owners and agents for all purposes connected with the work of the Trust.

Mr Bruton also agreed 'To permit the Trust or its agents, surveyors or consultants to enter the property for the purpose of inspecting the state of repair and cleanliness of the property or any purpose connected at all reasonable hours of the day.' Mr Bruton was to pay £18 per week for his occupation of the property.

The question arose for the House as to whether, despite these clear circumstances and facts, Mr Bruton in fact was entitled to the benefit of certain statutory repairing covenants.[65] He would only have been so entitled if he had, in fact, a tenancy. How could a tenancy be manufactured from such unpromising facts? The starting point is the objective intention of the parties: did Mr Bruton have exclusive possession for a term at a rent? It was held that he did. Lord Hoffmann said '... [T]he classification of the agreement as a lease does not depend upon any intention additional to that expressed in the choice of terms. It is simply a question of characterising the terms which the parties have agreed. This is a question of law.'[66] The reservation of the right of entry to inspect the property for the state of repair and cleanliness merely emphasized that Mr Bruton had exclusive possession.[67] The argument that L&Q had no power to grant a tenancy and did not represent that they had such a power was irrelevant (which surely meant that one of the essential elements of the estoppel [the representation] was absent) was met by Lord Hoffmann with the observation that,

> ... it is not the estoppel which creates the tenancy, but the tenancy which creates the estoppel. The estoppel arises when one or other of the parties wants to deny one of the ordinary incidents or obligations of the tenancy on the ground that

---

[64] Housing Act 1985, s. 32(3).
[65] Landlord and Tenant Act 1985, s. 11.
[66] See also Lord Hobhouse's pithy observation: 'The relevant question is simply one of ascertaining the effect in law of the agreement which the parties made.'
[67] Following Lord Templeman's remark to the same effect in *Street*, at 818.

the landlord had no legal estate. The basis of the estoppel is that having entered into an agreement which constitutes a lease or tenancy, he cannot repudiate that incident or obligation.

The House was forced to emphasize the contractual element of the landlord–tenant relation.[68] Leases usually convey property rights, and L&Q had no property rights to convey to Mr Bruton – that is, as an ordinary application of the rule, *nemo dat quod non habet* (you can't give what you don't have). But here, Lord Hoffmann circumvented that rule with the observation that '... it is the fact that the agreement is a lease which creates the proprietary interest. It is putting the cart before the horse to say that whether the agreement is a lease depends upon whether it creates a proprietary interest.'[69]

Counsel for L&Q argued, however, that, even if the agreement had all the attributes of a tenancy, it was an example of an 'exceptional' case so as to take it outside the domain of landlord and tenant. Attention was drawn to the socially valuable functions of L&Q, and the circumstances of the case – all parties including Lambeth had never said or agreed that Mr Bruton could have a tenancy. Furthermore, at least Lords Slynn and Jauncey recognized that their judgment would cause problems in terms of future provision for homeless households as these types of arrangements would be curtailed by the effect of their judgment.[70] However, this was not one of the exceptional cases because the character of the landlord and the agreement with Mr Bruton was irrelevant. As regards the latter, the key point was that 'one cannot contract out of' the security of tenure legislation by claiming the agreement was something that it was not.[71] So, Mr Bruton was left with a very odd type of right – he could enforce the landlord and tenant covenants, especially of repair, against L&Q, but it was a tenancy by estoppel, a type of non-proprietary lease which would have limited effect, if any, on third parties. Indeed, it could be defeated by L&Q doing what they, in fact, did: surrendering their interest to Lambeth. That led to another story, about human rights, which is discussed in Chapter 8.

The same point about the relevance of subjective intention is equally relevant in co-ownership cases. It is significant that, in *Antoniades* v. *Villiers*,[72] Lord Templeman quotes from the evidence given by Mr Villiers and Ms Bridger, the occupiers:

He [Antoniades] kept going on about it being a licence and not in the Rent Act. I didn't know either but was pleased to have a place after three or four months of chasing. I didn't understand what was meant by exclusive possession or licence. Signed because so glad to move in. Had been looking for three months.[73]

---

[68] For discussion, see M. Wonnacott, *Possession of Land* (Cambridge University Press, 2006) pp. 15–17; cf. J.-P. Hinjosa, 'On Property, Leases, Licences, Horses and Carts: Revisiting *Bruton v London & Quadrant Housing Trust*' [2005] *Conveyancer and Property Lawyer* 114.

[69] At 415C.

[70] At 410D, 412B.

[71] At 414D–E.

[72] [1990] 1 AC 417.

[73] At 462.

Antoniades clearly intended both subjectively and on the face of the agreement to grant a licence. That was what the occupiers took and knew that they had taken. There was a clause in the agreement which allowed Antoniades to introduce further occupiers into the property, should he so wish. However, the property was only suitable for those living in 'quasi-connubial bliss'.[74] The reservation of that right was inconsistent with the Rent Acts and could not be enforced; separately, though, it was clearly not a genuine reservation of the right and it was, therefore, a pretence. In order to ascertain its genuineness the evidence extended beyond the agreement to the surrounding circumstances as well as the parties' subsequent conduct.[75]

The significance of the evidence of the occupiers is that the basis for the doctrine of pretence is the same as that for the Rent/Housing Acts – a broad-based jurisdiction concerned with inequality of bargaining power, premised on an assumption of disequilibrium between landlord and tenant in a situation of over-demand for a limited supply of accommodation.[76] The empirical basis for that justification is questionable. It is clear that the private rented sector is made up of a number of heterogeneous sub-sectors, such as the student market, the housing benefit market, the 'top end', etc.[77] Different considerations apply in each sub-sector. There are also geographical differences between areas as to the supply of private rented housing.

The key issue on the nature of intention in 'pretence' cases regards the subjective intentions of the parties. In *Antoniades*, the clause clearly was not genuine. However, in *Bankway Properties Ltd* v. *Pensfold-Dunsford*,[78] there was a genuine clause which the parties clearly intended would be enforced. At the outset, the rent was £4680 per annum payable by equal monthly instalments of £390 per month. Mr Pensfold-Dunsford was in receipt of housing benefit, a fact known to Bankway (a company owned by the mega-wealthy Pears family). After 12 months, however, clause 8(2)(iii) of the tenancy agreement said that the rent would rise to £25,000 p.a., a figure which all parties knew would not be paid by the housing benefit authority. This was a genuine clause in the sense that Bankway expected it to be enforced. However, its enforcement would also (at that time) take the agreement outside the protection of the Housing Act 1988 because it was outside the rent limits. The agreement had been intended to create an assured tenancy by Bankway.[79] The Court of Appeal held that this rent increase 'device' was not genuine. In part this was based on the surrounding circumstances – the clause had not been individually negotiated and Bankway only demanded the increased rent

---

[74] *Street*, 825G.

[75] At 475.

[76] J. Hill, 'Intention and the Creation of Proprietary Rights: Are Leases Different?' (2000) 16(2) *Legal Studies* 200, 214.

[77] See, for example, J. Rugg and D. Rhodes, *The Private Rented Sector: Its Contribution and Potential* (Centre for Housing Policy, 2008).

[78] [2001] 1 WLR 1369.

[79] That may have enabled them to take advantage of tax concessions at that time.

at a time subsequent to when they could have demanded it, essentially to obtain possession without the need to prove a relevant ground under the 1988 Act.[80] However, Arden LJ went further:

> In my judgment, when the facts of this case are examined as a whole, it is clear, that, as the Judge found, clause 8(b)(iii) was merely a device. It was in reality a provision which would enable the landlord to obtain possession of the premises. As such, clause 8(b)(iii) masqueraded as a provision for an increase of rent: it was not in substance a provision for the payment of rent. It was introduced to enable the landlord to bring the assured tenancy to an end when it chose. In some cases the tenant might be expected to leave voluntarily. In other cases such as this, the landlord would have to make an application to the court but (subject to the outcome of this appeal) that would only be a formality since the rent was much higher than a tenant could be expected to pay. The landlord, therefore, did not have to give the tenants the last opportunity which they obtain in the usual way to pay the rent arrears at the door of the court to avoid an order for possession. The landlord may, as Miss Padley submits, have intended to demand rent but it had no genuine expectation that it would ever receive any rent under clause 8(b)(iii).[81]

She preferred to base her judgment on the basis that Bankway had effectively sought to contract out of the statutory protection, something which could not be done in the scheme of the 1988 Act. Pill LJ preferred to base his concurring judgment on the principle that the clause was inconsistent with the 1988 Act.[82] Bright concludes her comment on this case with the observation that: 'No longer will it be sufficient to ask if something is genuine, or allowed; instead the test will be whether "in substance" it is allowed. This will be a much more difficult question to answer.'[83]

Debate 3

Should the law interfere in tenancy bargains?

Most tenancy agreements will contain a list of obligations on one or both of the parties. This list usually relates to the core terms of the bargain – the rent to be payable and the term of the agreement – as well as peripheral terms. The great debates here are, first, over the extent to which it is proper for the law to interfere in bargains, and the second over the proper judicial approach. It has always been accepted that these obligations generally only apply to leases, and not licences, although the justification for that division seems rather unclear today.[84]

---

[80] See Susan Bright's critical commentary on these reasons, 'Avoiding Tenancy Legislation: Sham and Contracting Out Revisited' (2002) 61(1) *CLJ* 146, 165: 'Devious the clause may be, but it is hard to see how it is an unlawful contracting out of the legislation given that the legislation permits the landlord and tenant to agree the initial rent and any provisions for reviewing it.'
[81] At [55].
[82] At [68], which Bright also critiques at 166–67.
[83] At 168.
[84] See Law Commission, *Renting Homes*, Law Com No 284 (Law Commission, 2003), paras 6.19–20.

As regards the former, the debate was settled in the nineteenth century, perhaps paradoxically at the zenith of the free market movement, in favour of certain limited interventions justified on the ground of public health.[85] Many such interventions remain in place, largely unamended,[86] their justification now being to do with length of existence together with a more generalized recognition of an inequality in the bargaining power between landlord and tenant; one might say that such justifications lack empirical validity but the law is a blunt instrument.

As regards the proper judicial approach, it can certainly be argued that the interpretation given by judges to these obligations has been to narrow them at almost every turn, thus ameliorating the potential burden on landlords.[87] That is not to say that fairly trenchant criticisms of the law have not been made, but that judges have felt constrained often to take a narrow view.[88]

Certain terms are implied into certain agreements either by the common law or by statute. A principal such statutory implied term, in leases of less than seven years, is the duty on the landlord to keep the property and its services in repair.[89] It has been said that one local authority spent more in defending disrepair claims at one stage than it did in actually conducting repairs to its housing stock. Those days are likely to be over now.[90] In any event, the nature of the obligation is limited and only begins when the landlord has notice of the defect.[91] However, there are two other issues which should be considered: unfair terms in tenancy agreements, and tenancy deposits.

What seem to be potentially powerful rights for the tenant turn out to be rather limited. So, for example, the right to 'quiet enjoyment' means something rather less than this. In *Southwark LBC* v. *Mills*,[92] the tenants in a block of flats were continually disturbed by their neighbours because of a lack of sound insulation – essentially, the tenants could hear everything going on in their neighbours' flats. As Lord Hoffmann put it, the flat is not quiet and the tenants are not enjoying it; yet the covenant simply meant that the tenant has a right to enjoy the flat free of substantial interference from their landlord or those claiming under the landlord.

---

[85] Cowan, n.7, pp. 9–11.

[86] See, for example, the now mostly useless statutory implied condition of habitability: Landlord and Tenant Act 1985, s. 8, and the discussion in *Quick* v. *Taff-Ely BC* [1986] QB 809; cf. the Renting Homes (Wales) Bill 2015.

[87] This is the position taken in J. Reynolds, 'Statutory Covenants of Fitness and Repair: Social Legislation and the Judges' (1974) 37(3) *MLR* 377; cf. M. Robinson, '"Social Legislation" and the Judges: A Note by Way of Rejoinder' (1976) 39(1) *MLR* 43.

[88] Most prominently, see *Quick* v. *Taff-Ely BC* [1986] QB 809.

[89] Landlord and Tenant Act 1985, s. 11.

[90] The Pre-Action Protocol for Housing Disrepair Cases has effectively made most claims for breach of this covenant settle at a much earlier stage.

[91] *O'Brien* v. *Robinson* [1973] AC 912; for discussion and critique, see Reynolds, n.87. As regards the development of the regulatory oversight of local authorities to the current 'health and safety rating system', see R. Burridge and D. Ormandy, 'Health and Safety at Home: Private and Public Responsibility for Unsatisfactory Housing Conditions' (2007) 34(4) *Journal of Law and Society* 544.

[92] [2001] 1 AC 1.

UNFAIR TERMS

The Office for Fair Trading has regulatory oversight for the jurisdiction opening up through the Unfair Terms in Consumer Contracts Regulations 1999,[93] over contracts entered into between a 'seller or supplier' and a 'consumer'. These provisions have been held to apply to both private and public landlords as well as between a letting agent and non-business landlord.[94]

Where a term is not 'core' to the agreement, and has not been individually negotiated, it '... shall be regarded as unfair if, contrary to the requirement of good faith, it causes a significant imbalance in the parties' rights and obligations arising under the contract, to the detriment of the consumer'.[95] Core terms are those which are the essence of the contract: the price and the main subject matter of the contract, as these were regarded as more likely to have been negotiated between the parties.[96] The requirement of good faith is 'one of fair and open dealing', which might be expressed as transparency and not taking advantage of the consumer.[97] All terms, core or not, must be drafted in plain, intelligible language and, where there is doubt about their meaning, 'the interpretation most favourable to the consumer shall prevail'.[98]

The Office of Fair Trading (OFT) produces written guidance setting out certain terms which it regards as potentially unfair as well as how the regulations are interpreted by them.[99] This notes, for example, that fairness depends not only on how a contractual term is intended to be used, but also how it could be used (which depends on its breadth).[100] In relation to rights of the landlord to re-enter the property on the tenant's default (forfeiture clauses), the OFT states that it does not object to the inclusion of such clauses provided that the landlord makes clear the circumstances under which the landlord is entitled to re-enter. In other words, a right of re-entry on its own is unlikely to be viewed as unfair; although such terms must be in plain language and cannot give the landlord greater powers to end the tenancy than they would have under the law.[101]

TENANCY DEPOSITS

The story of tenancy deposits is a story of the interaction between, on the one hand, the concern about over-regulation of the private rented sector being overridden by other concerns about landlord behaviour, perhaps due more to political

---

[93] SI 1999/2083, implementing Council Directive 93/13/EEC.

[94] *R (Khatun)* v. *Newham LBC* [2002] HLR 29; *Office of Fair Trading* v. *Foxtons Ltd* [2009] EWHC 1681.

[95] Reg. 5.

[96] *Abbey National plc* v. *Office of Fair Trading* [2009] EWCA Civ 116, at [52].

[97] *Director General of Fair Trading* v. *First National Bank plc* [2002] 1 AC 481, at [17], Lord Bingham.

[98] Reg. 7; on the limitations of plain English, see R. Assy, 'Can the Law Speak Directly to Its Subjects? The Limitations of Plain Language' (2011) 38(3) *Journal of Law and Society* 376.

[99] Office of Fair Trading, *Guidance on Unfair Terms in Tenancy Agreements* (OFT, 2005).

[100] Para. 2.6.

[101] Paras 4.16–4.18.

considerations than knowledge, and, on the other hand, judicial concerns about over-regulation resulting in an extremely narrow view being taken, so as to render the law practically useless. It provides an excellent case study, then, of the different motivations in play between landlords and tenants, as well as law and policy.

The starting point is the campaign that was run for some time by the Citizens Advice Bureau about the inadequate protection given to tenancy deposits, which reflected a view among certain politicians about the need to rein in private landlords, and concerns over their management practices. Private landlord associations and organizations were on the defensive but seemed to accept the need for at least some regulation because it would improve the image of the landlord. Self-regulation was deemed unsuccessful, but the evaluation of that regime wondered whether there was a need for any further regulation at all. However, at a late stage in the debates leading to the Housing Act 2004, the then government introduced the new regime.

The current law is, to say the least, confused and confusing, being the product of layered statutory interventions responding to judicial interventions which pulled the original provisions in different directions. All tenancy deposits paid by tenants to landlords under an assured shorthold tenancy must be dealt with in accordance with an authorized scheme from the time that they are received.[102] A deposit is defined as any money intended to be held by the landlord or otherwise as security for the performance of the tenant's obligations or the discharge of any of the tenant's liability arising under or in connection with the tenancy.[103] The 'initial requirements of an authorised scheme' must have been complied with by the landlord within 30 days of receipt of the deposit.[104] The landlord must provide certain information to the tenant about the scheme, initial requirements and the operation of these statutory provisions in a prescribed form or to the same effect as such a form within 30 days of receipt of the deposit.[105] The parties cannot contract out of these provisions.

Failure to comply with the initial requirements of an authorized scheme, failure to provide the information in the correct format or, in effect, being misinformed by the landlord that a scheme applies to the deposit, entitles the tenant or any person who pays the deposit on behalf of the tenant to apply to the county court for certain relief.[106] One element of that relief includes the severe penalty of the landlord paying the tenant up to three times the amount of the deposit;[107] there are also restrictions on the landlord's ability to obtain possession through a section 21 notice. [108]

---

[102] s. 213(1). The definition of a landlord includes 'a person or persons acting on [the landlord's] behalf in relation to the tenancy or tenancies'.
[103] s. 212(8).
[104] s. 213(3)–(4).
[105] s. 213(5)–(6).
[106] s. 214(1)–(2).
[107] s. 214(4).
[108] s. 215.

The history of the judicial construction of these provisions is confused. No clear parameters or purposes have really emerged. This has led to a complex legislative structure, applying different rules to different tenancy agreements depending on when those agreements were created. This is not the place for a complete summary of those rules, in part because the mind-numbing complexity is a feature of housing law and not land law.[109] The potential of the original incarnation of the law was said to have been 'eviscerated' by the majority decision of the Court of Appeal in *Tiensia* v. *Universal Estates, Honeysuckle Properties Ltd* v. *Fletcher*.[110] In *Tiensia*, the Court of Appeal (Sedley LJ strongly dissenting) held that a landlord in default of protecting the deposit within the prescribed period was not liable to pay the penalty if they protected the deposit at any time prior to the county court hearing.[111] The policy reason for the decision was as follows:

> Such interpretation appears to me to be not only firmly supported by what I would regard as the carefully chosen statutory language, it is also a properly precise, or strict, one to apply to legislation such as section 214 that is manifestly penal in intent. Moreover, it is an interpretation that is consistent with the purpose of the legislation. That purpose is to achieve the due protection of deposits paid by tenants, ideally within the [relevant] period but, if not, then later. It cannot be its purpose to punish landlords who may for example, for innocent reasons, be just a day late in securing such protection.[112]

In *Gladehurst Properties Ltd* v. *Hashemi*,[113] the Court of Appeal continued that process of evisceration by holding that the penalty could not apply after the tenancy had come to an end. Part of the Court's reasoning turned on the observation that the tenant has it in their hands to secure the enforcement of the rules by bringing a claim, just as with other covenants[114] (an argument with an air of unreality to it when one considers the strong possibility that, as a result, the tenant may well be faced with an eviction or, at a more base level, losing trust with the landlord). The Court also noted the anomalies which would be caused by the tenant's argument, but of course, the Court's construction itself creates anomalies, for it protects both the scrupulous landlord who returns the deposit (subject to any necessary deductions) and the unscrupulous landlord who does not (or makes unnecessary deductions).[115] If the scheme had any purpose, it was to resolve costly and unnecessary legal disputes between the parties, but the effect of *Gladehurst* is that they will return.[116]

---

[109] Readers with sufficient interest should see http://nearlylegal.co.uk/2015/08/making-sense-of-deposits-nearly/.

[110] [2011] HLR 10, at [51], Sedley LJ.

[111] [2011] HLR 10; for rich discussion, see http://nearlylegal.co.uk/blog/2010/11/tenancy-deposit-protection-eviscerated/.

[112] At [40].

[113] [2011] EWCA Civ 604; for excellent discussion, see http://nearlylegal.co.uk/blog/2011/05/eviscerated-now-also-drawn-and-quartered/.

[114] At [38]–[39].

[115] At [40]–[42].

[116] Indeed, in *Gladehurst* itself, one issue was over the landlord's retention of an amount from the returned deposit, the amount of the retention being in dispute.

The problems caused by these hastily drafted provisions were recognized by legislators. In the Localism Act 2011, an attempt was made to ameliorate them through various technical amendments, and, in particular, a more reflexive penalty.[117]

But there was more. In *Superstrike Ltd* v. *Rodrigues*, the question was whether a landlord could rely on a section 21 notice where the tenancy, which had been for a fixed term but had rolled on, had not been protected. The added complication was that the original deposit had been received before the deposit protection regime had come in to force. The question was whether the landlord had to protect the deposit when the statutory periodic tenancy, which came into being once the fixed term had ended, commenced. The Court of Appeal held that the landlord had to do so. The statutory periodic tenancy was a new tenancy. While the facts of the case were of rather marginal significance, as not many assured shorthold tenancies continue on for that long or move into a statutory periodic phase, the Court of Appeal's judgment was significant because a periodic tenancy is a tenancy in its own right, and each new succeeding tenancy is a new tenancy. Even if the landlord protected the deposit correctly with an initial fixed or periodic term, the logic of land (and housing) law seemed to suggest that the deposit was required to be protected again and again.

That outcome was clearly not going to be either practical or desirable. The Deregulation Act 2015 contains provisions designed to ameliorate the *Superstrike* decision. But, it can be said with confidence that the current position is as clear as mud.

Debate 4

How can a tenancy be determined?

GENERAL PRINCIPLES

Residential occupancies generally have to be determined by court order.[118] There are exceptions, but the usual situation today is that either the tenant has the protection of the Housing Act 1988 or the Housing Act 1985, or the more limited protection conferred by the Protection from Eviction Act 1977. Although tenancies for a fixed term are, as a matter of land law, determined at the end of the fixed term by effluxion of time, if they fall within the protection of the Housing Acts, there is provision for them to roll on for further periods determined by the period for which rent is payable.[119]

Under the 1977 Act, the landlord must give the tenant or licensee a notice to quit a tenancy or a periodic licence which must be in writing, containing certain information, and give at least four weeks (or the contractual period, if longer)

---

[117] Localism Act 2011, s. 184.
[118] As regards commercial occupancies, see S. Bright, *Landlord and Tenant Law in Context* (Hart, 2007) Part 7.
[119] Housing Act 1985, s. 86; Housing Act 1988, s. 5.

before it is to take effect.[120] After such a notice has been served, if the occupier continues lawfully residing in the premises, then they may only be evicted by due process of law, that is to say, a court order, a provision which amends the landlord's common law self-help remedy of ejectment.[121] These provisions do not, however, apply to 'excluded' tenancies and licences – where the occupier shares accommodation in certain circumstances with the landlord/licensor or a member of their family.[122]

In *Hammersmith and Fulham LBC* v. *Monk*, the House of Lords held that one of two joint tenants could lawfully end the tenancy by giving the landlord a notice to quit under the common law.[123] This rule has been particularly valuable to social landlords in making provision to deal with alleged perpetrators of domestic violence. The leaving partner is able to determine the tenancy in its entirety, thus leaving the remaining occupier/s effectively as trespassers and, in theory at least,[124] the court must grant the landlord possession of the property. The reasoning of the House of Lords in *Monk* was based on the contractual nature of the tenancy agreement and by analogy with the principles of the law of contract.[125] We discuss the human rights challenge to *Monk* below (see Chapter 8), but it remains a powerful tool at the hands of the landlord and a legitimate device, as well as demonstrating the power of the contractual nature of the lease as a reasoning device.

The general rule beyond this, however, is that the landlord must obtain a court order in accordance with the relevant provisions of the Housing Acts 1985 or 1988.[126] There are some exceptions to the landlords caught by these rules – including mutual co-operatives – who are governed by the common law principles as amended by the 1977 Act. The 1985 and 1988 Acts provide procedural and substantive protections to the occupiers. As regards the former, they require relevant notices to be served; as regards the latter, they limit the grounds on which the landlord is entitled to possession. Under the 1985 Act, all the grounds are discretionary – the landlord has to prove the ground *and* that it is reasonable to grant possession. Under the 1988 Act, some of the grounds are discretionary but there are also mandatory grounds. As we have noted, for an assured shorthold tenancy, the landlord can determine the tenancy by means of a notice, subject to a court order which, in theory at least, must be granted.[127]

---

[120] s. 5(1) and (1A).

[121] s. 3(1) and (2).

[122] ss. 5(1B) and 3(1) and (2).

[123] [1992] 1 AC 478.

[124] This rider refers to the discussion in Chapter 8 concerning the proportionality defence under Human Rights Act 1998, sch. 1, art. 8.

[125] [1992] 1 AC 478, 483–89, Lord Bridge.

[126] The former applies to those landlords which fulfil the landlord condition (s. 79), which are generally 'public'; the latter applies to private landlords, but including certain quasi-private landlords, like housing associations.

[127] 1988 Act, s. 21.

UNLAWFUL EVICTION AND HARASSMENT

Due process is a particularly powerful motif of this area of law. It offers a different and in some ways more humane vision of the balance between the rights of the parties than existed in the nineteenth century. Due process can involve a fairly simple rubber-stamping – as in the accelerated procedure which can be used to determine an assured shorthold tenancy – but the stamp is what is important. Anything less than the stamp will not do unless the occupier has abandoned the property or terminated their occupation. An eviction without due process runs the risk at least of being unlawful; actions short of an eviction, but with the intention of getting the occupier out, run the risk of being unlawful.[128] Potentially, such actions give rise to both criminal and civil liability.[129] That few are prosecuted, and fewer successfully so, is neither here nor there. The likelihood is that this type of conduct occurs more frequently than is seen in the courts but what was referred to above as the 'status of moveability' means that it is easier for occupiers to move on.[130]

Prosecution and regulation of the private rented sector is generally in the hands of the local authority. The police rarely get involved (and, when they do, have been known to assist the landlord in their unlawful acts out of ignorance of the law[131]) despite the evident denial of property rights inherent in the act/s. The local authority is caught facing both ways – on the one hand, it is responsible for the regulation of the private rented sector, but on the other it is also responsible for its promotion, particularly to assist low- and no-income households. Prosecution can act to counter that second motivation.[132] Another counter-motivation lies in the very obscurity inherent in the law and the possibility that, if pursuing a civil claim, the level of damages may not provide adequate recompense for the considerable time and emotional energy engaged in pursuing the claim.[133]

CONCLUSIONS

Superficially, the great debate in this chapter concerns the (thin) dividing line between property and personal rights, as exemplified by the contortions in the distinction between leases and licences, together with the pragmatic reliance on the contract or property element of the relationship when it suits. However, the purpose of this chapter has been to go beyond that formal law and highlight its

---

[128] Protection from Eviction Act 1977, s. 1.

[129] For discussion, see Cowan, n.7, ch. 12.

[130] See further D. Cowan, 'Harassment and Unlawful Eviction in the Private Rented Sector – A Study of Law (in-)Action' [2001] *Conveyancer and Property Lawyer* 249.

[131] See, for example, *Cowan v. Chief Constable for Avon and Somerset Constabulary* [2002] HLR 44.

[132] D. Cowan and A. Marsh, 'There's Regulatory Crime and Then There's Landlord Crime: from "Rachmanites" to "Partners" in Meeting Housing Need' (2001) 64(6) *MLR* 831.

[133] See, for example, *King v. Jackson* (1998) 30 HLR 539.

contexts, for those contexts highlight other great debates about the role (or rule) of law in society. The concerns and interests of property law give way to everyday understandings about the relationship and taken-for-granted assumptions on which the landlord and tenant relationship is based. Attention has been drawn to the tensions which exist in regulating renting; these tensions appear at the meta-level, in terms of ideological assumptions about landlordism. What has become clear, at the level of pragmatic politics, is that landlordism is very much here to stay and that landlords should be protected from over-regulation; the assumption is that over-regulation will stifle the development of private renting.[134]

Further Reading

S. Bright, 'Avoiding Tenancy Legislation: Sham and Contracting Out Revisited' (2002) *CLJ* 146.
D. Cowan, *Housing Law and Policy* (Cambridge University Press, 2011).
Law Commission, *Renting Homes: Status and Security*, Law Commission Consultation Paper No 162 (London: Law Commission, 2002).
J. Reynolds, 'Statutory Covenants of Fitness and Repair' (1974) 37(3) *MLR* 377.
P. Sparkes, 'Co-Tenants, Joint Tenants and Tenants in Common' (1989) 18(2) *AALR* 151.

---

[134] These arguments are further developed and contextualized in Cowan, n.7, ch. 3.

5

LAND REGISTRATION

INTRODUCTION

A central feature of modern English land law is the emphasis placed on registration of title (or, more accurately following the Land Registration Act 2002, title *by* registration) as the definitive authority on the validity and priority of competing interests in registered land. The development of a practice of land registration was one of the key aims of the 1925 legislation (see Chapter 3), although earlier iterations of the system of registered land dated back to the late 1800s. In 1857 the Royal Commission on Registration of Title proposed a system of registration based around a central registry in London with district offices, and the Land Registration Act 1862 provided for the registration of freehold estates in land. The system of registration adopted in England had its origins in a system that had been piloted in South Australia by then Prime Minister of South Australia, Sir Robert Torrens. This model became known as 'Torrens-style' registration and was subsequently adopted in many countries around the world. In this chapter, we address five great debates about land registration which broadly relate to (1) the relationship between mapping land and title; (2) the definitiveness of the register; (3) whether the bureaucratization of land is necessary and justified in the interests of efficiency (and, latterly in England and Wales, the prospect of a shift to e-conveyancing); (4) the dominance of rational, abstract ways of valuing land over material possession of land; and (5) the practical changes resulting from the philosophical shift from registration of title to title by registration.

Debate 1

How does the process of mapping territory affect conceptions of landownership?

Let us begin by distinguishing between two related, but distinct, official systems of mapping land: cadastral mapping, and land registration. A cadastral map is a comprehensive register of the land in a country, based on a detailed survey of territory, often originally compiled for taxation purposes, but also used to support other government administrative purposes such as planning. Land registration systems are designed to provide a public record of ownership of, and transactions in, land. Although this aim can be distinguished from the process of cadastral mapping, the two sometimes overlap, for example, when the land registration system also functions as a cadastre.[1]

The idea of using cadastral mapping as an administrative tool dates back to the Romans, who drew up large-scale plans of the Empire to administer the allocation of land and facilitate the collection of taxes. Many subsequent cadastral mapping projects have linked property and topography with fiscal or juridical bureaucratic schemes.[2] The extent to which a map – even one based on a detailed survey of the territory – can adequately represent the social space to which it refers, and property rights in that space, is controversial; it is argued that 'property and cartography are quite different ways of knowing land: neither is a mirror of nature'.[3] Pottage explained that 'There is an essential distinction between the understandings which arise from the possession or use of land, and which support the attribution or recognition of property rights, and those which are presupposed by cartography.'[4] The map is only ever a representation of the land: representations are always loaded with the meanings and values of the representor, and '[a] pervasive theme in much contemporary commentary on cartography is that topography is never innocent. It serves a range of disguised interests.'[5]

Post-modern and post-colonial geographers have identified the process of surveying and mapping land as a key pillar in colonial policies, and as one of the colonizer's tools for wielding power to dispossess indigenous populations.[6] There is no doubt that drawing cadastral maps was important to enable colonial powers to exercise control and exert administrative authority over territory. In imperialist terms, the cadastral map is viewed as a Western tool imposed on indigenous populations; lands were deemed *terra nullius*, treated as empty of inhabitants with existing legal rights to the territory. The process of cadastral mapping applied the colonizing state's property laws and conceptions of ownership to the mapped territory, so functioning as a tool to subject indigenous peoples to the laws of the colonizer. Thus, colonizers often displaced (or uneasily co-existed with) existing customary conceptions of place, property and landownership, under the moral justification of 'modernization', or the claim of bringing order and civilization to

---

[1] E. Cooke, 'Land Cadastres/Registries in the Developed World' in S. Smith, M. Elsinga, L. Fox O'Mahony, S. Ong and S. Wachter (eds.), *The International Encyclopaedia of Housing and Home* (Elsevier, 2011).

[2] A. Pottage, 'The Measure of Land' (1994) 57(3) *MLR* 361 at 374, fn 64.

[3] Ibid., 362.

[4] Ibid., 362–63.

[5] J. Harley, 'Deconstructing the Map' (1989) 26(1) *Cartographica* 1.

[6] K. Beamer and T. Ka'eo Duarte, 'Mapping the Hawaiian Kingdom: A Colonial Venture' (2006) 2 *Haw JL & Pol* 34; B. Braun, *The Intemperate Rainforest: Nature, Culture and Power on Canada's West Coast* (University of Minnesota Press, 2002); T. Mitchell, *Colonising Egypt* (Cambridge University Press, 1991); E. Stokes, 'Contesting Resources: Maori, Pakeha, and a Tenurial Revolution' in E. Pawson and T. Brooking (eds.), *Environmental Histories of New Zealand* (Oxford University Press, 2002); C. Harris, 'How Did Colonialism Dispossess? Comments from An Edge of Empire' (2004) 94(1) *Annals of the Association of American Geographers* 165.

bear over 'savagery'.[7] When Western imperialists mapped colonial territories, their cadastres tended to reflect a particular, Western understanding of the world and of the meaning of place, which was often imposed notwithstanding its disjunctions with indigenous values, although it should be recognized that surveys and maps produced in 'colonies' varied in the extent to which they reflected, or were based upon, the original inhabitants' conceptions of the land and its boundaries.[8]

When colonial powers mapped indigenous land, this was typically preparatory to making allocations of territory to incomers. A crucial feature of colonial mapping was that the existing use and enjoyment of indigenous occupiers was sometimes overlooked or ignored, with 'lands treated as empty slates that need to be rationally ordered for future land use purposes'.[9] This practice of mapping out existing land use differed significantly from the ways that colonial powers mapped their own 'domestic' land, when pre-existing use formed the basis of the map.[10] In either case, cadastral mapping had clear political and economic implications: it provided a technique for governing territory, usually for the purposes of exploiting its natural resources. While the colonial mapping enterprise differed significantly from mapping within England and Wales, both were driven by a combination of political (control) and economic (maximizing capital gain from the land) goals.

Attempts to embed registered land in England and Wales echoed many of the themes of colonial cadastres as well as resonating with the major themes set out in Chapter 1. Mapping and registration are typically geared towards facilitating alienation of land, marking out exclusive territory for use or transfer, using the abstract, rational tool of the map. As we mentioned in Chapter 1, the production of the map enabled land to be carved up and sold as free space. The registered landowner achieved a level of citizenship which was distinct from that of the indigenous land holder – who was often written out of the 'official' story of the land. And, as we will see as we reflect on the modern land registration project in this chapter, and perhaps most acutely in relation to unlawful occupation of land in Chapter 6, registered title has been progressively elevated over the material, organic use of the land in ways that raise new challenges for property and citizenship.

The English land registration project dates back to 1862 and, over a century and a half, has swung between 'meticulous accuracy in defining the land, cost what it might in money and hostility between landowners'[11] and a combination of broadly defined boundaries combined with physical inspection of the land and discussions

---

[7] Harris, n.6.

[8] Beamer and Ka'eo Duarte, n.6, 35, arguing that colonial maps of the continental US were notable in their lack of regard for the indigenous peoples' conceptions of the land and its boundaries; see also E. Price, *Dividing the Land: Early American Beginnings of Our Private Property Mosaic* (University of Chicago Press, 1995) p. 11.

[9] Beamer and Ka'eo Duarte, n.6, p. 41.

[10] Ibid.; citing J. Scott, *Seeing Like a State* (Yale University Press, 1998) p. 49.

[11] J. Stewart-Wallace, 'Land Registration in England in Relation to Mapping and Surveying' (1931) 17 *Conv* 45, at p. 48.

with persons in actual occupation to ascertain the extent of the property. The latter was the position adopted by the Land Registration Act 1925, which directed that the land be verbally described, with a plan appended to *assist* identification of the property.[12] Under the scheme set up by the Land Registration Rules 1925, the Registry itself was authorized, using the Ordnance Survey maps as the basis for its plans, to produce accurate and co-ordinated maps where land was registered. Technological developments in recent decades have greatly enhanced the quality and accuracy of Ordnance Survey maps even in areas of unregistered land.

As the science of mapping developed, the ways that we think and talk about land have changed, from a narrative topography – the 'topographical story' – which included descriptions of land, reference to local landmarks or activities carried out on the land, and which encapsulated the 'local sense of place and property',[13] to a 'geometric topography'. As mapping methodologies shifted from memory and lived experience to abstract geometrical measurements,[14] so the 'cartographic ideal [became] a sort of "placeless" description, a tracing transferable between localities',[15] to create a 'rational' or 'linear space'.[16] Our methods of understanding, describing and governing the land became generic across the country, rather than specific to a locale. This can be understood as part of the process of assimilating real property to other forms of property – to be 'as easily transferable as stocks and shares' – discussed in Chapter 3. It also echoes the themes of 'space' and 'place' we introduced in Chapter 1. Through mapping and registration systems, the territory was 'rationalized', inasmuch as the map followed principles of standardization, simplification and economy.[17] Although the Land Register for England and Wales is not a cadastral system – it is the title that is recorded, rather than the land itself – it is underpinned by standardized maps and descriptions of the land. Through its promotion of, and reliance on, the science of mapping, both cadastral and land registration systems 'made "land" a calculable and finite surface rather than a lived and remembered medium',[18] bringing into the public domain what was previously a private matter. Pottage has traced the origins of bureaucratization in English land law to the mapping function of land registration:

> Registration extricated land from the network of relations and understandings which formed the 'local knowledge' of different communities, relocated it on an abstract geometric map, and deciphered it according to a highly conventionalised topographic code. This process marked a transformation in the idea of land in law: property ceased to be a contractual construct and became a bureaucratic artefact.[19]

---

[12] Ibid., 49–50.
[13] Pottage (1994), n.2, 365.
[14] Ibid., 366.
[15] Ibid., 368.
[16] Ibid., 370.
[17] Ibid., 381.
[18] Ibid., 381.
[19] Ibid., 363.

This shift has had major implications for our evolving conception of landowner-ship in England and Wales. Some of the effects of re-conceiving property in land in this way – including the stark separation of occupation from ownership – are explored further in Chapter 6.

At first, registration of land in England and Wales was voluntary, but this was not terribly successful: not only was it not compulsory to register the ownership of the land, but once property was registered there was no compulsion to register any subsequent transactions, so that the person registered as owner of the prop-erty might not be the current owner. After 1862, reformers began to consider the prospect of compulsory registration, although they faced considerable opposition from the legal profession. The introduction of compulsory registration in England and Wales under the Land Registration Act 1925 was, therefore, a significant moment.[20] The key aims of the land registration system created in 1925 resonated with the general goals of the 1925 legislation, including easing, facilitating and speeding conveyancing, protecting the interests of purchasers and assuring the security of land transactions. The Land Registration Act 1925 formed the basis for the system of landownership and transfer for over 75 years and still provides much of the structural underpinnings for the current system – although the 2002 Act has made some significant changes to that system.

In 1998, a joint report of the Law Commission and the Land Registry proposed an overhaul of the entire system of title registration. A further joint report, *Land Registration for the Twenty-First Century: A Conveyancing Revolution* was published in 2001, and the substantial changes proposed in this report were implemented in the Land Registration Act 2002 (LRA 2002), which came into force on 13 October 2003.

Debate 2

Can (and should) the register be definitive of interests in land?

At its core, land law is composed of the rules that regulate competing interests, such as those of purchasers on the one hand, and owners or subsidiary interest-holders on the other. The role of any system of registration is underpinned by two key questions: when is it reasonable for the purchaser to be bound by prior subsidiary interests?; and when is it reasonable to require that an interest in land be registered at the risk of defeasibility for non-registration?

There are three types of registration system: (1) registration of deeds, where a copy of any deed affecting the property is kept in a central register (this system has not played a significant role in English land law); (2) registration of specific interests, for example, requiring that some or all equitable interests must be

---

[20] A. Offer, 'Lawyers and Land Law Revisited' (1994) 14(3) *OJLS* 269, arguing that the opposition of practi-tioners to the 1925 reforms was self-interested; and S. Anderson, *Lawyers and the Making of English Land Law, 1832–1940* (Clarendon Press, 1992) p. 227, arguing that these same practitioners were also keen to make a valuable contribution to the reform process.

registered, as in the Land Charges Register for unregistered land in England and Wales; and (3) title registration, the most modern of the three types of system, and radically different from the other systems.

Under the English system of title registration, each title is registered with its own file, which indicates the ownership of the property (a single plot of land may have more than one registered interest, for example a freehold and lease-hold interest); most legal interests must be registered in order to have legal effect, and equitable rights must be protected by entry on the register. Registration is effectively a state guarantee of title to land; although when lesser interests are protected by entry in the register this does not guarantee the existence of the right but merely ensures that, if the right exists, it will bind successors to the title.

The system is underpinned by three core principles. The 'mirror principle' requires that the register reflect the position regarding the ownership of the land and the third party interests affecting it: the register should be a complete and accurate reflection of the state of the title to the land at any given time, so that it is possible to investigate title to land with the absolute minimum of additional enquiries and inspections. The 'curtain principle' requires that the register should be the sole and definitive source of information for purchasers, so that a purchaser does not need to go behind the 'curtain' to ascertain interests that will bind. Finally, the insurance principle refers to the state-backed guarantee that supports the information contained in the register, such that, even if the register is inac-curate, it is authoritative. If any loss is suffered as a result of reliance on an error in the register, compensation can be claimed from a state fund. The principal flaw in the application of these principles to registered land in England and Wales is the category of 'overriding interests' – interests that do not appear on the register, but are still binding on a purchaser.

The extent to which the land registry can be relied on as definitive statement of the rights and burdens affecting land constitutes one of the great debates of contemporary land law in England and Wales. It goes to the heart of the nature of landownership under English law, and the extent to which the government (through the Land Registry) is responsible for protecting a landowners' title once it is recognized through the register (see Chapter 6 on adverse possession). The implications of these foundational debates range from practical questions concerning the extent to which 'overriding interests' are permitted to constitute a 'crack' in the mirror principle, to more fundamental, philosophical questions about the nature of landownership under the Land Registration Act 2002. The debate is positioned between the protection of the existing proprietary interests held by a range of claimants, and the facilitation of transactions by ensuring that purchasers are not bound by these interests unless they were on the register; between the protection of 'on the ground' interests and the transfer of clean title. Echoing the discussion of functions of land (for use and occupation, on the one hand, and its role in exchange, on the other) in Chapter 3, the Land Registration Act 2002 represented a crucial turning point in a related debate between the mate-riality of possession and the bureaucratization of title. Following the decisive steps taken towards the protection of purchasers, registered owners and those interests which are *on* the register (as opposed to often less formal *off* register claims) in the Land Registration Act 2002, this chapter reflects on the implications of our commitment to perfecting the register for the philosophy of land law in England and Wales; and on the shift from landownership rooted in possession and an organic relationship between user and land to a bureaucratic system of title by registration which is increasingly removed from the land itself.

Debate 3

Is the bureaucratization of land necessary – and justified – in the interests of efficiency and e-conveyancing?

The business of title registration is performed by Her Majesty's Land Registry, a non-ministerial government department, with the Chief Land Registrar appointed by the Lord Chancellor. The administration of the system is organized around 24 District Land Registries which keep the register for land in their regions. With the largest property database in Europe, today's Land Registry underpins the British economy by guaranteeing ownership of many billions of pounds worth of property. The economic function of the registry is reflected in the fact that (in normal economic conditions) approximately £1 million worth of property is processed every minute in England and Wales. In 1988, the information held by the Registry became open to the public, and the LRA 2002 allows any person to inspect and make copies of entries,[21] subject to some exclusions for sensitive information and payment of a fee in certain cases. The register currently holds more than 24 million titles,[22] representing about 90 per cent of all titles in England and Wales (although considerably less of the land by volume – approximately 70 per cent – with much of the unregistered land held by institutions, including the Crown).[23]

The Land Registry's principal aims include 'maintaining and developing a stable, effective land registration system, guaranteeing title to registered estates and interests in land, enabling confident dealings in property and security of title by providing ready access to up-to-date and guaranteed land information, and matching the ever more ambitious performance targets set by the Lord Chancellor'.[24] The drive to ensure that the Land Registry is delivering value and efficiency influenced, in part, work seeking to move towards e-conveyancing for land transactions, which the LRA 2002 – described as a 'conveyancing revolution' – was intended to facilitate.

While earlier land registration provisions sought to ensure consistent approaches between unregistered and registered land, the LRA 2002 has moved away from that strategy, and is focused wholly on developing principles

---

[21] LRA 2002, s. 66(1).
[22] www.gov.uk/government/organisations/land-registry/about.
[23] M. Dixon, *Modern Land Law* (Routledge, 7th edn., 2010) p. 95, fn 1.
[24] See Land Registry website www.landregistry.gov.uk/.

appropriate to registered land. A crucial distinction between these two systems (discussed below) is that while unregistered land recognizes the basis of title in *possession,* the basis of title in registered land is *registration.* This philosophy is applied under the LRA 2002 by tightening up the system to ensure that the register is as complete and accurate as possible, by simplifying the system and by reducing the number of ways in which third-party interests can be recorded on the register. The 2002 Act promised to pave the way for electronic conveyancing:

> The fundamental objective of the Bill is that, under the system of electronic dealing with land that it seeks to create, the register should be a complete and accurate reflection of the state of the title to the land at any given time, so that it is possible to investigate title to land online, with the absolute minimum of additional enquiries and inspections.[25]

When the 2002 Act was passed, it was intended that it would enable a shift to electronic conveyancing within three to five years. The development of the e-conveyancing project was identified as an important aspect of the Land Registry's work to improve the quality of the service that it offers in facilitating land transactions – for example, by encouraging open access to chain information, and by providing a mechanism for all payments relating to transactions in a chain to be paid simultaneously and electronically, with automatic registration on completion.[26] It was hoped that this process would 'reduce the delay and anxiety which can be experienced in the house buying process'.[27]

Since electronic conveyancing requires that processes for investigating title can be carried out online, it demands that the register is complete and accurate, with minimal need for additional enquiries and inspections. So, for example, one of the key changes introduced in the LRA 2002 in preparation for e-conveyancing was to remove the requirement that a purchaser present a paper land certificate when applying for registration, in recognition of the philosophy that the register, not the land certificate, is now conclusive of title. It was intended that full electronic conveyancing would be introduced on a staged basis, allowing for a transitional period in which the electronic system would operate alongside the paper-based system until the paper-based system is gradually phased out. The process for achieving this was set out in Part 8 of the LRA 2002 and Schedule 5 (which addressed the practicalities of e-conveyancing). The first stage was to establish an electronic process for e-lodgments (fairly basic transactions such as changes of property address or property description), e-discharges (electronic discharges of registered charges) and e-charges (electronic registration of charges in respect of registered land), with e-conveyancing becoming the only method of transfer once the system became fully operational.[28] The Land Registry has been

---

[25] Land Registry and Law Commission, *Land Registration for the Twenty-First Century: A Conveyancing Revolution,* Law Com 271 (Law Commission, 2001) para. 1.5.
[26] Land Registry, *E-Conveyancing: A Land Registration Consultation* (Land Registry, 2011).
[27] Ibid..
[28] LRA 2002, s. 91.

developing its e-conveyancing proposals since 2007 and during this time some of the secondary legislation required to give effect to the provisions contained in the Land Registration Act 2002 has been drafted.[29] Some aspects of the Land Registry's work to move to electronic conveyancing have been very successful: for example, almost all searches can now be completed online. However, after six years of work, and an investment of £41m to deliver a suite of e-services including an e-conveyancing portal, e-security and a business gateway service, the Chief Land Registrar announced in 2011 that the Land Registry had halted its work on the development of e-transfers to focus on improving its other services. Conveyancing solicitors can now access titles at the Land Registry online, and lenders can discharge mortgages via direct access to the Land Registry. But in light of stakeholder anxieties about electronic land transfers and the risks of fraud and hacking affecting the security of e-signatures, and with a slow housing market curtailing revenue streams for services into the Land Registry and tipping the scales against further investment, the Land Registry decided to put the development of e-transfers on hold until the delivery systems for the receipt of electronic documents prepared in the traditional way have been fully automated.[30]

In 2013 the Law Society announced its plans to launch an e-conveyancing portal, to enable transactions to be handled online. This new 'Veyo' facility, developed as a commercial joint venture with IT services firm Mastek UK, was launched in May 2015 across England and Wales. It brings together all processes, checks and documentation prepared and undertaken by solicitors and conveyancers in the sale and purchase of residential properties, with buyers and sellers able to track their transaction through a mobile phone app. At the time of writing, it remains to be seen how extensively this system will be adopted by solicitors and conveyancers, but, even if successful, remains some way short of e-transfer. The drive for greater simplicity, speed and efficiency in land transactions remains stronger than ever. The next section will reflect on the impact these drivers have had on our concept of land, and on what it means to be a real property owner in English land law.

AUTOBIOGRAPHICAL NOTE: A RESIDENTIAL PROPERTY PURCHASER'S PERSPECTIVE

As well as being academic property lawyers, we are also 'consumers' of land law inasmuch as we – like everyone – need somewhere to live. Our experiences on the 'real world side' of academic inquiries often shed interesting new light on our research, as well as exposing tensions between what election polls might badge as 'public policy' (what we think and argue as land law scholars) and 'family fortunes' (what we think and want as consumers of land).

---

[29] The Land Registration (Electronic Conveyancing) Rules 2008 introduced the facility for e-charges.
[30] Land Registry, *Report on Responses to E-conveyancing Secondary Legislation Part 3* (2011).

In my housing career, I have now bought three properties (and sold two – when it comes to multiple property ownership, my professional and personal views are neatly aligned). Each time we have used a different solicitor, and the conveyancing process has been slow, stressful and bumpy. I have had sales fall through months after they were agreed, and completion dates pushed back because of delays in the process. When we bought our current house, the completion date was lined up with starting new jobs at the other end of the country, moving the children out of nursery, the removals van we had booked, I had even booked a night's accommodation half-way down the country to break the journey.

A week before we were due to complete, and following a comedy of errors which included the building society leaving our mortgage application on a shelf and forgetting to approve it, and a three week delay while the local council (didn't) respond to a local land charges search request, the solicitors had still not managed to confirm exchange of contracts. The vendor announced that they weren't ready to move and wanted to push back the completion date by six days. While in some cases this might not have been a big deal, the logistics of changing the date for a cross-country family move, when you're due to report for duty for your new job six days before the rest of the family can now move, are considerable. By the time I worked my way down the re-arranging list to ask the nursery if they could let the children continue attending for another week, I was an emotional wreck. I will always remember the lovely nursery manager saving the day when she said 'Of course, we would *love* to have the boys for another week.'

My solicitor (who had already counselled me that 'the problem, my dear, is English conveyancing law, it's very complicated, you see...') was sanguine, saying this happens all the time, it's par for the course and just part of the rough and tumble of residential conveyancing. I sometimes wonder if I have form for choosing the wrong solicitor, or if being a land law scholar makes me a bad land law client. I must confess that, if stamp duty wasn't enough to put you off residential land transactions, my transactional experiences of buying (and selling) residential property would disincline me from attempting it too often. Just as well I'm the type who gets attached to home.

So, when I am reflecting on the impact of land registration on the overall meaning and concept of landownership in England, I do also have in mind the 'user experience' of conveyancing. As a user of the Land Registry's services, I will be as delighted as every other land law consumer when we achieve streamlined, secure systems for stress-free (or at least, stress-less) conveyancing. But, as a scholar, I still believe that it is important, as we make progress towards this goal, not to close our eyes, or look away from the political and philosophical implications of our changing approach to land registration, but also to have in view the other values that underpin a pluralist land law system. It is important that we are mindful of the consequences that flow from the choices we are making and the values we are promoting for the ways that we think, and talk, and debate key contemporary issues about land use and exchange.

Debate 4

Has the Land Registration Act 2002 succeeded in establishing abstract rationality over material possession in English land law?

The drivers towards e-conveyancing have had a major influence on both the philosophy of landownership and the technical changes set out in the LRA 2002. The key philosophical change set out in the Act concerned a shift away from a concept of landownership rooted in possession and an organic relationship between user and land, with title obtained through this process registered, to a bureaucratic system of title *by* registration. This bureaucratic system reflects our theme of *rationality* in land law, as discussed in Chapter 1. The philosophy of the LRA 2002 clearly favours the rational, objective and tangible values attributed to interests in land, while the proposition that a property may be socially, psychologically or emotionally meaningful is sidelined within this system. The LRA 2002 marked a decisive shift in the frame of reference underpinning the ownership of land, with the concept of dwelling based on a material, possessive relationship with the land[31] displaced by a new emphasis on the record – the register itself – as the basis of title. While the common law began from the factual situation, the LRA 2002 has largely eliminated considerations relating to the material use of land, in favour of the formal record entered on the register. This is a shift '... from possession to title, from empirically defined fact to state-defined entitlement, from property as a reflection of social actuality to property as a product of state-ordered or political fact. In short, instead of the citizen telling the state who owns land, the state will henceforth tell the citizen.'[32]

The impact of the LRA 2002 in (further) embedding the value of rationality in English land law was recognized by Gray and Gray, when they stated that:

> There has always been an instinctive bias in favour of transactional certainty in the land market and this perceived imperative has now acquired a heightened emphasis with the enactment of the Land Registration Act 2002. By various means this legislation infuses a new quality of rationality into dealings with land ... The 2002 Act accordingly oversees an intensified system of almost universal recordation of property rights in the Land Register, thereby sharpening up the effects of dealings between strangers and reducing potential threats to any title taken by a transferee or mortgagee.[33]

The difference in approach can also be characterized, according to another of our themes, as a movement away from an idea of the land which is the subject of the rights as *place* (that is, as a social setting in which the land – the space – provides the material, organic basis for life's core activities and so is invested with social meaning) to an abstract, rational representation of the land as

---

[31] The importance of 'possession' in the common law relating to landownership reflected 'the organic element in the relationship between man and land': K. Gray and P. Symes, *Real Property and Real People* (Butterworths, 1981) pp. 48–49.

[32] K. Gray and S. Gray, 'The Rhetoric of Realty', in J. Getzler (ed.), *Rationalizing Property, Equity and Trusts: Essays in Honour of Edward Burn* (LexisNexis UK, 2003) p. 245.

[33] K. Gray and S. Gray, *Elements of Land Law* (Oxford University Press, 4th edn., 2005) [2.48].

space.[34] This philosophical conception of landownership also further embeds the theme of *alienability* (see Chapter 1) by prioritizing the exchange value of the land (and the ease of the transaction itself) over interests in use, which are by their nature often created informally. The LRA 2002 changed the system of land registration in England and Wales from one that still recognized vestiges of the 'natural' human interest in possession, the use value of the land, or the material attachment that results from long use, towards a rationally based, abstract, technical system.

The contrast between the traditional, common law-based notion of landownership derived from possession in English law, and the abstract, bureaucratic system perfected in the LRA 2002 can be usefully demonstrated by reflecting on the values underpinning the common law approach. The traditional role of possession in concepts of landownership appeared rooted in an instinctive awareness that the value an item of property represents to the possessor is greater than the value that the property holds for a non-possessor, *because of the material fact of possession*. The philosopher Hume reasoned that the degree of harm caused to a possessor by losing that property would be greater than the harm suffered by depriving the non-possessor of the property, because:

> Men generally fix their affections more on what they are possess'd of than on what they never enjoyed ... it would be greater cruelty to dispossess a man of anything than not to give it to him.[35]

This 'bias in favour of the factual situation'[36] was also reflected in Oliver Wendell Holmes' jurisprudential acknowledgment of the attachments that people form towards property through use:

> It is in the nature of a man's mind. A thing which you enjoyed or used as your own for a long time, whether property or opinion, takes root in your being and cannot be torn away without your resenting the act and trying to defend yourself, however you came by it. The law can ask no better justification than the deepest instincts of man.[37]

Notable English jurists Pollock and Maitland also reasoned that: 'Possession as such deserves protection ... He who possesses has by the mere fact of his possession more right in the thing than the non-possessor has.'[38] Indeed, this principle is exemplified in the pre-LRA 2002 doctrine of adverse possession.

---

[34] See A. Buttimer and D. Seamon (eds.), *The Human Experience of Space and Place* (St. Martin's Press, 1980).

[35] D. Hume, *A Treatise of Human Nature* (Cambridge University Press, 1938, first published 1740), Book III, Part II, Sect. 1.

[36] A. Ehr-Soon Tay, 'Law, the Citizen and the State' in E. Kamenka, R. Brown and A. E.-S. Tay, (eds.) *Law and Society: The Crisis in Legal Ideas* (E Arnold, 1978), p. 11.

[37] O.W. Holmes, 'The Path of the Law' (1897) 10 *Harvard LR* 457, 477.

[38] F. Pollock and F. Maitland, *The History of the English Law before the Time of Edward I* (Cambridge University Press, 2nd edn., 1898) pp. 42–43. This phenomenon is recognized in the modern economic theory of the 'endowment effect': that is, that people place a higher sale price on what they already have than they would pay for the same thing if they did not own it – see C. Camerer, 'Individual Decision Making' in J. Kagel and A. Roth (eds.), *The Handbook of Experimental Economics* (Princeton University Press, 1995) pp. 665–70, for an account of empirical studies of the endowment effect, and some possible psychological explanations for such effects; on the endowment effect as a status quo bias, see W. Samuelson and R. Zeckhauser, 'Status Quo Bias in Decision Making' (1988) 1 *Journal of Risk and Uncertainty* 7.

The traditional English common law approach, in which rights in land were derived from possession, can be contrasted with the registration-based approach of Roman law systems,[39] which provided that: '... a man's right to use and enjoy, to the exclusion of others, flowed from title, from a state-recognised acquisition or transfer of ownership ...'.[40] Alain Pottage has claimed that the move to registered land in 1925 had fundamental conceptual and political implications, which were 'glossed over' as merely easing conveyancing, when in fact it introduced a fundamental 'new grammar of property':[41]

> [R]egistration was not simply a different or better way of doing the job of conveyancing, but rather ... brought with it a change in the understanding of what that job was; it transformed the basic conceptual and institutional resources which supported the process of conveyancing ... it did not simplify existing processes of proof, rather it developed an entirely new understanding of what was being proved and transferred.[42]

The 2002 Act took a further step in transforming the fundamental basis of entitlement to land, from *possession* of land as a good root of title, to *registration* as the source of title.[43] For registered land, the 'basis of title ... is not possession, but the register itself'.[44] As Fiona Burns explained:

> In a title-by-registration system, possession is no longer the bedrock of land law. It is not necessary for a person to demonstrate some kind of physical nexus with the land in order to acquire seisin or other interests in the land. As possession declines as the normative principle, so the legitimacy of registration is amplified because the only way of dealing with the land is through alteration of the register.[45]

Pottage demonstrated that, rather than changing the existing system of land transfer, the introduction of registration in the 1925 Act had 'constructed an entirely new foundation for property in land',[46] based not on deeds, contracts and conveyance but on the register, backed by insurance or indemnity. By removing most of the remaining vestiges of the possession-based system, the LRA 2002 has elevated the rational, measurable, objective, financial exchange interest in landownership as recorded on the register, over the more subjective, emotional and potentially unquantifiable interests associated with material possession and use. This trope had already gained ascendency in the 1925 legislation, and the LRA 2002 simply

---

[39] Which continue to influence property ownership systems in continental Europe.

[40] Tay, n.36, p. 10.

[41] A. Pottage, 'The Originality of Registration' (1995) 15(3) *OJLS* 371, 377.

[42] Ibid., 372.

[43] The Law Commission has acknowledged that: '[a]t its most fundamental level, the basis of title to unregistered land is possession, whereas the basis of registered title is the fact of registration': Law Commission & HM Land Registry, *Land Registration for the Twenty-First Century: A Consultative Document*, Law Com No 254 (HMSO, 1998) [1.6].

[44] Ibid., [2.6].

[45] F. Burns, 'The Future of Prescriptive Easements in Australia and England' [2007] *Melbourne Univ LR* 3, 22.

[46] Pottage, n.41, 386.

further embedded the capital landowner's interest in the exchange value of land. Pottage underlined the substitution of the social basis for landownership with a bureaucratic system: 'Property was no longer grounded in a practice of social mnemonics – the rich medium of practical social memory – but in administrative practice.'[47] The result is that the law and practices governing ownership of land are distanced from the thing – the land – itself, and from the human experiences of the people who use the land.

Debate 5

What practical changes were triggered by this philosophical shift?

The 2002 Act sought to pave the way for electronic conveyancing by making the register more complete in a range of specific ways. It reduced the categories of overriding interests (interests that can bind a purchaser without entry on the register); it encouraged the entry of overriding interests onto the register; it extended the function of registration to more interests (for example, expanding the category of registrable leases); and it limited the cautions that could be made against first registration. The Act also sought to modernize the process of registration through more logical approaches to drafting and the use of modern language, by rationalizing the protection of third-party interests, reforming the law relating to adverse possession, eliminating land certificates and charge certificates, and providing for the independent adjudication of disputes. Specific strategies to reduce the risk posed by third-party interests in land included the prohibition of new cautions against dealings with land; and the category of interests previously known as inhibitions was subsumed into restrictions, so reducing the categories of third-party interests – to which a purchaser needs to be alert – to two: notices and restrictions. A clearer demarcation was made between these two categories and, to allow for its broader range of functions, notices can now be either agreed or unilateral. Finally, the troublesome 'beneficial interest behind a trust of land' – the interest that a co-owner may acquire in (usually family) property – can only be protected by way of restriction.

REGISTRABLE INTERESTS AND DISPOSITIONS

In unregistered land, an interest is created or a transfer takes place when the sale is completed and the deed of conveyance signed; when land is registered, the interest is not created or transfer is not completed until the transfer form has been registered and the name of the purchaser entered into the register.[48] One distinctive feature of transactions in registered land (compared to unregistered land

---

[47] Ibid.; see also Pottage, n.2.
[48] LRA 2002, s. 27.

transactions) is that the legal interest does not pass to the purchaser on exchange of contracts or completion, but vests only on registration.[49] Only certain categories of legal estates and interests can be registered, and these registrable interests have their own files in the Land Registry. The list of registrable interests has been expanded by the LRA 2002,[50] so that the list now includes the fee simple absolute in possession, leasehold estates in possession for longer than seven years (whether the landlord's title is registered or not), future leases (leases which commence later than three months from the date of creation) and discontinuous leases (e.g. a lease of a property for three months every year), rentcharges, legal franchises forever or for a fixed term longer than seven years and legal *profits à prendre* in gross (not attached to the land) forever or for a fixed term of greater than seven years (for example, a right to hunt).

Registrable dispositions – transactions in relation to land that must be completed by registration – tend to relate to legal (rather than equitable) interests and are recorded against an existing registered title. A registrable disposition does not operate at law until it is registered,[51] and such dispositions include transfers of registered land; a grant from registered land of a lease of more than seven years; a lease that takes effect in possession after three months; a lease where the term is discontinuous; or a grant of a legal charge over registered land and certain easements and profits. Only relatively short leases (for less than seven years) do not need to be registered to take effect.[52] This can be contrasted with the pre-2002 position, when the bar for a short lease that did not require registration (but could be an overriding interest) was set at 21 years.[53] Obviously, the more expansive the category of registrable interests and dispositions, the more information is provided to the prospective purchaser on the face of the register, and the less additional inquiry is required to ensure that the purchaser is fully aware of what they are going to get with the title.

In addition to these major aspects of title, registered land can also be affected by burdens and incumbrances (previously known as minor interests), which are not registrable in their own right but (usually)[54] must be entered on the register against the main title to bind a purchaser; and by overriding interests, a category of interest that can bind a purchaser even though they are not registered. The 2002 Act has increased the categories of burden or incumbrance that can be registered by restriction or by notice, again with a view to moving towards a more perfect register in which all interests affecting the land are evident on the face of the file. These categories are residual, in the sense that if the interest in

---

[49] LRA 2002, s. 58.
[50] ss. 2–8.
[51] At best, it can only take effect in equity: LRA 2002, s. 27(1).
[52] LRA 2002, s. 29(4).
[53] LRA 1925, s. 70(1)(k).
[54] Following the 2002 Act, some overriding interests are also registrable (although they may still be overriding without registration), to encourage as much information concerning the title onto the register as possible.

question is not substantively registrable, and is not an overriding interest, it must be protected by registration against the substantive title. Against this objective, overriding interests – which operate outside the register – have been described as constituting a crack in the mirror principle, and regarded as a continuing source of tension within the system of title registration.

OVERRIDING INTERESTS

While the conceptual shift from unregistered to registered land has been compre-hensive, some commentators might argue that so long as the category of over-riding interests continues to exist, the transformation of land law will not be complete. Yet, beyond the bureaucratic aims of title registration, the continued existence of the category of overriding interests also invokes another important debate concerning the protection of certain categories of vulnerable interests (for example, interests created informally) in their proprietary form; that is, against the land itself (in effect, against the purchaser), rather than as a claim for damages against the vendor of the land. This echoes the themes of debates about conversion and overreaching, which were discussed in Chapter 3. Does the goal of alienability and encouraging trade in land justify some parties losing their proprietary interests in the land itself, in order to clear the way for a purchaser's clear title?

In recent years, this debate has, in certain sub-categories of interest, become oriented around the (purchaser-facing) question of the discoverability of the interest: has the purchaser done all she could reasonably be expected to do to identify and overcome any claims that might subsequently be made against the land? The great debate surrounding overriding interests, before and after the LRA 2002, has been about where to draw the line on 'reasonableness' in relation to the inquiries or inspections that a purchaser of registered land should be expected to carry out. What makes an interest discoverable? And is it fair for purchasers to be bound by interests that are not discoverable? It is worth noting that, even as we ask these questions, the power of the dominant theme of alienation has shaped the way that they are formulated, from the purchaser's perspective rather than the interest holder's: we ask when is it fair for a purchaser to be bound; not when is it reasonable for a subsidiary interest holder to lose their proprietary interest in the land.

From a purist perspective, the need to carry out inspections to identify inter-ests affecting the land are reminiscent of the old system of constructive notice in unregistered land, and have no place in a modern bureaucratic system of title registration. Indeed, while the LRA 1925 set out an extensive list of overriding interests,[55] one of the main aims of the LRA 2002 was to make the register as comprehensive as possible and to minimize the number of interests that are

---

[55] LRA 1925, s. 70.

capable of binding without appearing on the register. This has been achieved by retaining the concept of overriding interests but limiting the category to those interests which are proprietary in nature and where it is considered unreasonable, unrealistic or uneconomical to expect the right to be registered. Thus, many interests that were overriding under the LRA 1925 are no longer overriding and now have specific registration requirements (as burdens or incumbrances, see below). Many of the interests that retain their overriding status have been more clearly drafted, so as to limit their application and to avoid uncertainties in their operation, while a general principle has been applied that rights that are expressly created should in principle be subject to registration. For example, informally created legal easements and profits[56] are potentially overriding, but only bind the purchaser in fact if (a) the purchaser had actual knowledge or constructive knowledge (i.e. obvious on a reasonably careful inspection) of the existence of the easement, or (b) the easement has been exercised within the last year. This approach demonstrates the incorporation of the discoverability requirement with respect to even those interests that are informally created, where the argument that the interest-holder could reasonably be expected to take positive steps to protect their interests is significantly weaker. This again reflects the dominance of the purchaser perspective over the interest-holder perspective, and the commitment to formality over recognizing the informalities inherent to certain types of land transaction, at least in relation to easements that have not been recently exercised.

Leases granted for a term not exceeding seven years from the date of grant of lease are overriding,[57] unless the tenant does not take possession until three months after the grant of the lease (these reversionary leases or future leases are more difficult for a purchaser to discover); or if the lease is discontinuous (for example, a lease of a property for a month a year, over three years – again, difficult to discover); and also excluding the grant of certain rights under the Housing Act 1985. The distinction between legal interests (which attract a higher level of protection within the registration system) and equitable interests (which are more readily defeated unless they have been registered) is also maintained, as equitable leases are not overriding unless the tenant is in actual occupation (so making the interest more discoverable).

Most equitable interests or minor interests will bind purchasers if they are protected by entry on the register. If not so protected, they may still bind purchasers if the beneficiary is in actual occupation of the property. The interests of persons in actual occupation attract special protection under Schedule 3, paragraph 2 of the 2002 Act. Interests in actual occupation were originally deemed overriding under section 70(1)(g) of the LRA 1925, which covered 'the rights of every person in actual occupation of the land or in receipt of rents and

[56] Easements created under LPA 1925, s. 62, and easements that are implied under the rule in *Wheeldon* v. *Burrows* (1879) 12 Ch D 31, the doctrine of necessity or common intention: LRA 2002, sch. 3, para. 3; see Chapter 7. Legal easements that are created expressly must be registered as a disposition. Equitable easements must be protected as a minor interest.

[57] LRA 2002, sch. 3, para. 1.

profits thereof, save where inquiry is made of such a person and the rights are not disclosed'. The purpose of this section was to protect the rights of those persons actually living in the property, who might risk losing their interests 'in the welter of registration'.[58] This concept was carried forward into the LRA 2002 through Schedule 3, paragraph 2, which incorporated two components from section 70(1) (g) into the modified version in the LRA 2002 – the existence of a right, and the holder of the right being in actual occupation of the land – but which excluded from the category 'an interest – (i) which belonged to a person whose occupation would not have been obvious on a reasonably careful inspection of the land at the time of the disposition, and (ii) of which the person to whom the disposition is made does not have actual knowledge at that time'.[59]

There must be an interest that is capable being overriding (carried across the transaction). If the claimant has no interest in the land, there is nothing to override the transaction.[60] The person claiming that the interest is overriding must be in actual occupation of the land at the date of disposition. That occupation must have been obvious to the purchaser on a reasonably careful inspection of the land at the time of the disposition, and the purchaser did not have actual knowledge of the interest. This is a new requirement to address concerns that, under the LRA 1925, purchasers were being held to interests that they could not have been expected to discover. Yet, the uncertainties that proved controversial under LRA 1925 section 70(1)(g) have not been fully resolved by Schedule 3, paragraph 2 of the LRA 2002. Indeed, in order to establish that an interest holder was in actual occupation, guidance provided in cases decided under section 70(1)(g) will remain relevant. For example, in determining – as a question of fact – whether someone is in actual occupation, the court will consider the normal usage of the property.[61] Absence from the property for a short period of time does not preclude a person from being considered to be in actual occupation;[62] and actual occupation does not have to be exclusive or continuous, although – illustrating the shift towards purchaser protections – under the LRA 2002, occupation must now be discoverable notwithstanding the occupier's absence from the property. Pre-2002 case law also established that the nature of the property may be relevant to the application of the actual occupation test;[63] that preparatory acts prior to fully moving in will generally not

[58] *Strand Securities Ltd* v. *Caswell* [1965] Ch 958, at 979, Lord Denning.

[59] LRA 2002, sch 3. para. 2(c).

[60] *National Provincial Bank Ltd* v. *Ainsworth* [1965] AC 1175; cf. *Williams and Glyn's Bank* v. *Boland* [1981] AC 487, in which Mrs Boland's equitable interest under a trust, combined with actual occupation, was an overriding interest (and therefore binding on the bank).

[61] See, for example, *Kling* v. *Keston Properties Ltd* (1985) 49 P & CR 212 (using a garage to park cars did not require that there be a car there constantly); and *Malory Enterprises* v. *Cheshire Homes* [2002] 3 WLR 1 (use of property for storage requires keeping it locked and fenced).

[62] *Chhokar* v. *Chhokar* [1984] FLR 313 (absence in hospital while having a baby).

[63] *Lloyd's Bank plc* v. *Rosset* [1989] 3 All ER 915 (where the property was semi-derelict and unfit for occupation, the presence of builders was sufficient).

be considered sufficient to give rise to actual occupation;[64] and that a claimant cannot generally claim actual occupation through the occupation of another.[65]

The continuity between the pre-2002 case law and the 2002 Act demonstrates the convergence of judicial and legislative policy in tilting the debate concerning when the interests of persons in actual occupation are binding in favour of purchasers. Even the new discoverability requirement was pre-empted by the interpretation of actual occupation in cases such as *Abbey National Building Society* v. *Cann*[66] and *Malory Enterprises Ltd* v. *Cheshire Homes Ltd.*[67] While the LRA 2002 has clearly embedded the purchaser-protecting discoverability requirement into its formulation to carry the interests of persons in actual occupation across the transaction, the issues underlying the earlier debate remain extant.[68] This provision strikes a balance between the informally created interests of claimants who cannot reasonably be expected to protect themselves (and so are still included in the retrenched category of overriding interests), and the protection of purchasers who have taken reasonable steps to discover such interests. And the courts continue to mediate the impact of the provision, as the decisions in *Thompson* v. *Foy*[69] and *Link Lending Ltd* v. *Bustard*[70] (dealing with the 'factual question' of actual occupation during temporary, albeit lengthy, absences from the property) have demonstrated. Nevertheless, as Jackson has observed, the existence of overriding interests continues to challenge the policy - deeply engrained in English property law - that land should be freely transferable,[71] so much so that alienability sometimes becomes what Harpum described as an 'unspoken premise',[72] fading into the background of the unspoken assumptions and biases with which we perceive land law.

While the discoverability criterion would appear adequate to protect any purchaser who has taken reasonable steps, any remaining vulnerability of purchasers to the interests of a beneficiary under a trust can be eliminated through the principle of overreaching, where the purchaser pays the purchase money to two or more trustees. According to the interpretation applied by the courts in *Williams & Glyn's Bank Ltd* v. *Boland*,[73] the doctrine of overreaching applies in registered

---

[64] *Abbey National Building Society* v. *Cann* [1991] 1 AC 56 (furniture and laying of carpets not actual occupation).

[65] *Strand Securities Ltd* v. *Caswell* [1965] Ch 958 (step-father trying to claim actual occupation through step-daughter as his agent; *Hypo-Mortgage Services Ltd* v. *Robinson* [1997] 2 FLR 71 (parents cannot claim through their children).

[66] [1991] 1 AC 56.

[67] [2002] Ch 216. See also *Hodgson* v. *Marks* [1971] Ch 892; *Lloyd's Bank plc* v. *Rosset* [1989] Ch 350; *Ferrishurst* v. *Wallcite Ltd* [1999] Ch 355; and J. Stevens, 'Is Justice a Priority in Priorities? Law Reform and the Re-Introduction of Morality to Registered Conveyancing' in F. Meisel and P. Cook (eds.), *Property and Protection: Essays in Honour of Brian Harvey* (Hart Publishing, 2000).

[68] N. Jackson, 'Title by Registration and Concealed Overriding Interests: The Cause and Effect of Antipathy to Documentary Proof' (2003) 119 *LQR* 660.

[69] [2009] EWHC 1076.

[70] [2010] EWCA Civ 424.

[71] Ibid., 662.

[72] C. Harpum, 'Property in An Electronic Age' in E. Cooke (ed.), *Modern Studies in Property Law* (Hart Publishing, 2001) p. 4.

[73] [1981] AC 487.

land, so that it is only if the claimant's interest is not overreached that it may be overriding and so bind the purchaser through the actual occupation provision. Conversely, where the claimant's interest has been overreached, there can be no question of it overriding the transaction, even if the beneficiary is in actual occupation.[74] The availability of overreaching has significant implications for the protection of the occupier's interest in property *as a home*. Where occupiers' interests are subject to overreaching, the interest is converted from ownership of the home to a claim against the capital realized on sale, thus undermining the idea that home holds any value beyond its capital value.[75]

CONCLUSIONS

In Chapter 1 we considered a series of central themes which we have identified as significant in contemporary property law debates. Several of these themes are represented in the shift from a possession basis for landownership (pre-registration) to the bureaucratic characteristics of registered land, as perfected in the LRA 2002. The goals of land registration are clearly aligned with the drive towards alienability in the 1925 legislation, which was reinforced in the 2002 Act; the orientation of land registration is rationalist, particularly as this has been understood within the economic model of rationality, valuing the security of long-term expectations; the reliability of investment strategies; the rationality of decision making about future land use; stable forward planning; the need to protect titles taken by purchasers and creditors; the importance of ensuring that the substantial wealth tied up in land should not be rendered economically sterile; and the objective of facilitating property transactions as smoothly and effectively as possible. Finally, the development of land registration reflects a conception of land law based on abstract *space* rather than socially meaningful *place*: it closes out the idea of property as a way of 'being in the world', of land as the physical, organic basis for human activity, in favour of a vision of property as a commodified asset to be traded as efficiently as possible in pursuit of capital gain. Pottage claimed that 'Registration sought entirely to remove property from its natural habitat, from the realm of practical presuppositions and expectations which underpin the attribution of formal property rights.'[76] Both property in land, and the topography through which the physical manifestation of the land was represented, were reduced to entries on the register.[77] Studies of bureaucratic organizations reveal the aptness of the perfected model of land registration in pursuing these goals. Bureaucratic organizations

---

[74] *City of London Building Society* v. *Flegg* [1988] AC 54 (the beneficial interest of the trustees' parents was overreached by payment to two trustees. As the interest was overreached, there was no 'interest in land' that could become overriding by virtue of actual occupation).

[75] For a discussion of the range of values which home represents to occupiers, see L. Fox, *Conceptualising Home: Theories, Laws and Policies* (Hart Publishing, 2006).

[76] Pottage, n.2, 361–62.

[77] Ibid., 362.

are defined by rule-bound procedures; they respond to written rather than verbal discourse; their procedures are enacted by experts using specialized and technical language; and their aims are to achieve speed, precision, clarity and objectivity in carrying out their functions.[78] The rise in bureaucratic values in land law is instrumental in closing out concerns for human behaviour or emotions. As Weber argued, bureaucracy:

> ... develops the more perfectly the more the bureaucracy is 'dehumanized', the more completely it succeeds in eliminating from official business love, hatred, and all purely personal, irrational, and emotional elements which escape calculation.[79]

As the system of title registration as a means of regulating dealings affecting land becomes increasingly procedural, it embeds the reduction of *home* to *house*, of *place* to *space*, of experiential meaning to tangible, fungible, commoditized value.

It can be argued that this development is a necessary feature of a modern, commercialized system of land law, in which both commercial property transactions and the expanded owner-occupied sector depend on a system which prioritizes speed, security and ease and affordability of conveyancing. Those interests trump the protection of informal interests or sensitivity to the emotional attachments that users hold for their land. In the US, for example, where registration of title has not taken hold in a mainstream way,[80] the insurance function performed by the Land Registry in England and Wales has taken the form of private title insurance: a form of indemnity insurance against financial loss from defects in the title to real property taken out at the consumer's (purchaser's) or lender's expense to mitigate the relative inadequacy of the US title system.[81] While it is possible to take out title insurance in England and Wales to protect against losses in particularly complex or high-risk transactions, or where there is an evident defect in title, it is not routinely used in normal residential or commercial transactions. Registration of title has virtually eliminated this expensive adjunct to secure transactions, by deflecting the insurance function onto the state through the Land Registry[82] and introducing a measure of certainty to supplement the simplification strategy of the 1925 legislation.[83]

While there is undoubtedly merit in the arguments in favour of registration of title *per se*, what is less convincingly established is the necessity of eroding the status of informal interests to the extent that the LRA 2002 has done. One area in which this has been particularly notable is the LRA 2002's reform of adverse

---

[78] K. Dovey, 'Home and Homelessness' in I. Altman and C. Werner (eds.), *Home Environments* (Plenum Press, 1985) p. 55.

[79] M. Weber, 'Essay on Bureaucracy' in F. Rourke (ed.), *Bureaucratic Power in National Politics* (Little, Brown & Co, 1978) p. 90.

[80] Only a very few, small US jurisdictions have versions of title registration.

[81] B. Burke, *Law of Title Insurance* (Aspen Publishers, 3rd edn., 2000).

[82] This insurance function is also shared by (and in most unregistered land transactions, assumed by) solicitors' professional indemnity insurance.

[83] Pottage, n.41, 390.

possession law – which Dixon described as: 'an unnecessary and economically unjustified "bolt on" to the reform of registered land'.[84]

While there can be little doubt that many of the reforms set out in the 2002 Act are instrumental in enhancing the maturity of the English system of landowner-ship, the move towards greater rationality also gives effect to a particular political ideology and approach to ownership. Gray and Gray have argued that:

> ... the ultimate achievement of the Land Registration Act 2002 is its ruthless maxi-misation of rational legal order, an aim which is symbolised by the statutory vision of an electronic register of virtually indefeasible titles, transactable by automated dealings and guaranteed by the state. Under this tightly organised regime, estate ownership, as constituted by the register record, becomes a heavily protected phenomenon, leaving little room for the operation 'off the record' of some ancient and pragmatic principle of long possession.[85]

This bureaucratic system favours those who are well-informed as to how to protect their rights – the kind of property subject who leads a 'tidy life' (see Chap-ter 11) – over right-holders who have acquired informal rights, and may be less capable or aware of the steps they need to take to sustain their interest in the land. The practical effect of the philosophical commitments underpinning the LRA 2002 has been a fairly relentless tide in favour of protecting legal title holders and purchasers (the capital interest or 'monied might' of property relationships) against informal claims such as those brought by squatters or the off-title interests of people in occupation of the land.

To the extent that such informal interests might have been accepted as carrying some claim to protection, the philosophy of the LRA 2002 overrode such claims on the basis that the reforms set out in the Act were necessary to develop the register in preparation for the commercial behemoth of e-conveyancing. It was perhaps surprising that, following the very slow development of registered land in England and Wales throughout the twentieth century, the LRA 2002 has, in its absolute commitment to perfecting the register, leap-frogged the English system beyond even the mature Torrens jurisdictions of some Australian states.[86] Burns has suggested that this can be explained by the origins of the Australian Torrens systems in the nineteenth-century goal of implementing 'a system for common land transactions which was cheap and simple', but which could accommodate 'long-established de facto enjoyment ... in some way within the system'.[87] The LRA 2002 had the distinct objective of preparing for e-conveyancing, making the driver for a hard-edged system much more powerful. As we wait to discover whether, and to what extent, the latest attempt to re-launch the e-conveyancing project will be deemed a success, it is important to keep in view the trade-offs

---

[84] M. Dixon, 'Adverse Possession and Human Rights' [2005] *Conv* 345, 351.
[85] Gray and Gray, n.33, 364.
[86] Which continue to allow title based on possession without registration: Victoria and Western Australia.
[87] F. Burns, 'The Future of Prescriptive Easements in Australia and England' [2007] *Melbourne Univ LR* 3, 29.

we make between competing values, and the extent to which we favour some kinds of people (see Chapter 1 for discussion of property insiders and outsiders), when we place all our effort in pursuing a single-value (alienation) driven land law system.

Further Reading

B. Boguzs, 'Defining the Scope of Actual Occupation Under the LRA 2002: Some Recent Judicial Clarification' (2011) *Conv* 268.

M. Dixon, 'The Reform of Property Law and the Land Registration Act 2002: A Risk Assessment', (2003) *Conv* 136.

C. Harpum, 'Property in an Electronic Age', in E. Cooke (ed.), *Modern Studies in Property Law* (Hart Publishing, 2007).

N. Jackson, 'Title by Registration and Concealed Overriding Interests: The Cause and Effect of Antipathy to Documentary Proof' (2003) 119 *LQR* 660.

A. Nair, 'Morality and the Mirror: the Normative Limits of the Principles of Land Registration' In S. Bright (ed.), *Modern Studies in Property Law, vol 6* (Hart Publishing, 2011).

6

UNLAWFUL OCCUPATION OF LAND: SQUATTING AND ADVERSE POSSESSION

INTRODUCTION

The philosophy and policies of the Land Registration Act 2002 – considered in the previous chapter – are sharpened by the issues surrounding the unlawful *use* of land by 'squatters'. Squatting can be described as the unauthorized occupation of land belonging to another, and 'a squatter ... [as] one who, without colour of right, enters on an unoccupied house or land, intending to stay there as long as he can'.[1] When such unlawful occupation extended over a sufficiently long period of time (in England and Wales, 12 years),[2] the traditional doctrine of adverse possession enabled such an occupier – through a combination of the limitation principle (which extinguished the displaced owner's right to bring an action to recover the land after 12 years)[3] and the doctrine of relativity of title (by which law protects the relatively stronger claim in any bilateral contest) – to acquire a status of irremovability when it came to defending their occupation of the land. Furthermore, in unregistered land – where possession provides the root of title – the squatter was the holder of a new common law estate in the land derived from her own possession; while in registered land – prior to the LRA 2002 – the squatter acquired *beneficial* ownership of the property automatically, under a statutory trust, and completion of the legal title to the land (by closing the registered proprietor's title and opening a new title held by the squatter)[4] was simply a matter of making an application to the Land Registry. Following the LRA 2002 the squatter of registered land obtains a freehold title by virtue of adverse possession but this title is extinguished if the squatter succeeds in an application to be registered under the legislation as proprietor of an estate in land.[5]

---

[1] *McPhail* v. *Persons Unknown* [1973] Ch 447, 456B.
[2] Where land is unregistered, and prior to the Land Registration Act 2002 for registered land.
[3] Limitation Act 1980, s. 15.
[4] *Spectrum Investment* v. *Holmes* [1981] 1 WLR 221; *Central London Commercial Estates Ltd* v. *Kato Kagaku Ltd* [1998] 4 All ER 948.
[5] LRA 2002, sch. 9, para. 1.

However, in a move that exemplifies the approach of the LRA 2002, Schedule 6 effectively limits the circumstances in which a squatter can claim title to registered land to cases in which the squatter has an estoppel in his or her favour; where the squatter has some other entitlement to be registered (e.g. an estate contract, inheritance); where the dispute concerns a mistake in good faith concerning a boundary;[6] or where the registered proprietor makes no objection to the squatter's claim.[7] Yet, while the reform of adverse possession in the 2002 Act was presented (and largely accepted)[8] as rooted in strategies linked to registration, it also implemented a specific moral agenda against the unlawful occupation of land.[9] This anti-squatting agenda is particularly evident in the previous Coalition Government's recent consultation on the criminalization of squatting, and the enactment of the new offence of squatting in residential buildings now found in section 144 of the Legal Aid, Sentencing and Punishment of Offenders Act 2012.[10]

Both the legal response to the phenomenon of squatting as a social fact and property law's doctrine of adverse possession invoke debates concerning the appropriate balance between the rights of a landowner (particularly when that landowner does not make use of their land)[11] and the interests of the squatter (who is making use of the land, usually – in the case of urban squatting in particular – for occupation as a home). To suggest that such a balance can be struck according to a morally neutral, rights-based approach does little justice to the reality of the contest at stake here.[12] Historically, the place of adverse possession within the framework of property law was supported by a range of justifications, including: the avoidance of stale claims; preventing hardship to a squatter who has been in occupation for a long time; promoting effective land use; and resolving conveyancing problems. The combined effect of the LRA 2002 and calls for the criminalization of the activity of squatting have progressively eroded these justifications, so that what is left is a contest between a landowner – whose proprietary claim is undergirded by a deeply embedded political and economic agenda in support of (formal) property rights – and a squatter – whose act of squatting has been designated as a wrongful and (in certain cases) a criminal act. This chapter

---

[6] LRA 2002, sch. 6, para. 5.

[7] LRA 2002, sch. 6, paras 2–3.

[8] For contrasting views, see M. Dixon, 'Adverse Possession and Human Rights' [2005] *Conv* 345; M. Dixon, 'Adverse Possession in Three Jurisdictions' [2006] *Conv* 179; N. Cobb and L. Fox, 'Living Outside the System? The (Im)Morality of Urban Squatting' (2007) 27(2) *Legal Studies* 236.

[9] Cobb and Fox, n.8.

[10] For further discussion of the new offence see N. Cobb, 'Property's Outlaws: Squatting, Land Use and Criminal Trespass' [2012] Crim LR 114; see also Ministry of Justice, *Options for Dealing with Squatting* (Home Office, 2011); Ministry of Justice, *Options for Dealing with Squatting: Response to Consultation CP12/2011* (Home Office 2011).

[11] The remoteness of such a landowner from the material reality of the land itself is reflected in the moniker sometimes used in this context of 'paper-title holder'.

[12] Although this 'rights' debate has become explicit and 'juridified' in the wake of the recent use of Article 8 ECHR in relation to claims for possession against trespassers on land: see, most recently, *Malik v. Fassenfelt* [2013] EWCA Civ 798 and more detailed discussion in Chapter 8.

considers these developments against the backdrop of the ideas developed in this book, including: the elevation of formal title over material physical occupation in conceptions of landownership; the selective application of norms of responsibility to property law's neoliberal subjects; the elevation of individual interests over social and community considerations in private property disputes; and the pursuit of economic security over social need in laws and policies concerning the ownership and regulation of land.

We discuss three great debates in this chapter. We begin with a discussion of whether squatting should be criminalized. We then move on to discuss the balance between private rights and public obligations, drawing attention to the ethic of stewardship. Finally, we discuss squatters' acquisition of title to land.

Debate 1

Should squatting be criminalized?

When demobilized soldiers returned to London following the Second World War to find their homes destroyed by the Blitz, up to 40,000 of them took up occupation with their families in empty homes, hospitals and military camps. To modern eyes, the response of the media to this, the first organized post-war urban squatting movement – and the systematic trespass to land it entailed – seems unusually accommodating; perhaps most intriguingly, the *Daily Mail* 'laud[ed] what it saw as "the robust common sense of ordinary men and women"' in taking steps to secure homes for themselves.[13] However, by the late 1960s and early 1970s, at a time when another housing crisis was attracting a new generation of urban squatters, the response of the media to the phenomenon had radically changed, as an editorial from the *Daily Telegraph* in July 1975 demonstrates:

> Of the many strange and frightening features of contemporary British life, none carries a more obvious and direct threat to society's survival than the growing phenomenon of squatting. Innumerable houses up and down the country are now in illegal occupation by organized gangs of thugs, layabouts and revolutionary fanatics. Costly and irrecoverable damage is continually being done to private property from sheer malice ... In reality the motive for most of this squatting is either political – a settled purpose of subverting public order – or simple greed and aggression.[14]

Previously, a consensus of sorts had settled in England and Wales, by which trespass to land was accepted to be a civil matter, with possession orders, injunctions and damages the appropriate tools to address unauthorized occupation.[15] Yet, in

---

[13] M. Whitaker, 'People Power', *Roof*, 2 January 2007, last accessed 18 September 2015.

[14] M. Brake and C. Hale, *Public Order and Private Lives: the Politics of Law and Order: A Critique of Conservative Criminology* (Routledge, 1991) p. 43.

[15] However, criminalization of squatting has a longer history in Scotland: see further B. Holligan, 'Criminalisation of squatting: Scottish lessons' in L. Fox O'Mahony, D. O'Mahony and R. Hickey, *Moral Rhetoric and the Criminalisation of Squatting: Vulnerable Demons?* (Routledge, 2015).

addition to the steps that have been taken to speed up and strengthen the process by which owners or legal occupiers secure and enforce possession,[16] an increasing momentum has emerged on the part of the state and in public opinion favouring the ethics and efficacy of criminal sanction to address the 'problem' of squatting.

In 1974, the Law Commission was instructed by government 'to consider in what circumstances entering and remaining on property should constitute a criminal offence'.[17] The legislation eventually enacted – the Criminal Law Act 1977 – entirely reworked the structure of criminal liability around trespass in buildings, with an explicit focus on the phenomenon of squatting. Two new offences set out in the 1977 Act continue to govern criminal liability in respect of squatting, subject to limited but significant amendments introduced in 1994.[18] On one hand, section 6 created a new offence of using or threatening violence to gain entry to property in occupation by someone opposed to that entry.[19] The main purpose of the offence was to prevent breaches of the peace, rather than shoring up property rights;[20] and as such, the law's protection of *anyone* in occupation of property at the time of entry extended the ambit of the criminal offence in principle not only to someone who entered into property against the wishes of the owner or legal occupier, but also to owners and legal occupiers if they took steps to retrieve property from squatters using violence or the threat of violence. However, section 6 was also subject to two further important exceptions permitting violent removal of occupiers from property in certain limited circumstances, which reveal the influence on the structure of the 1977 Act of growing political concerns with the negative impact of squatting on legitimate owners and occupiers. These exceptions ensured that the offence would not apply to owners or legal occupiers who deploy or threaten violence against an occupier if they fell within the category of 'displaced residential occupiers', or occupiers who were using the premises as a home at the time it was occupied by squatters, nor to so-called 'protected intending occupiers' or those who, while not in occupation at the time property was squatted, had an immediate need to use the premises as a home.[21]

This residual power of self-help against squatters who occupy property required as a home would be reinforced by the creation of another new criminal offence of 'adverse occupation of residential premises', contained in section 7 of the 1977

---

[16] See *McPhail v. Persons, Names Unknown* [1973] Ch 447, which permits summary eviction for trespassers, and more recently the system of Interim Possession Orders, backed by criminal sanctions for breach: Criminal Justice and Public Order Act 1994, s. 76.

[17] Law Commission Working Paper No 54, *Criminal Law: Offences of Entering and Remaining on Property* (TSO, 1974); Law Commission Report 76, *Criminal Law: Report on Conspiracy and Criminal Law Reform* (TSO, 1974).

[18] Criminal Justice and Public Order Act 1994; Home Office, *Squatting: A Consultation Paper* (1991).

[19] This offence replaced the Forcible Entry Acts, medieval statutes which had previously formed the basis for 'squatter's rights' prior to the enactment of the Criminal Law Act 1977.

[20] Law Commission Report, n.17, para. 2.49.

[21] The Law Commission proposed that owners or legal occupiers should not be granted a power of self-help against occupiers as protected intending occupiers, but only if they were displaced residential occupiers. The 1977 Act implemented the Commission's recommendation. However, the Major government extended the protection of self-help to protected intending occupiers in 1994.

Act. This offence prohibited 'failing to leave' property entered as a trespasser, when asked to do so by either a displaced residential occupier[22] or a protected intending occupier.[23] In this way, the offence extended only to those squatters who occupied property needed immediately as a home, and only after they resisted requests to leave the property by those so needing it. Nevertheless, the introduction of the offence again demonstrated a new perspective on unlawful occupation, in which, in certain limited circumstances, the imposition of criminal rather than civil liability was deemed a suitable response to the occupation of buildings by squatters. Working in parallel with the power of self-help for owners and legal occupiers reserved by section 6, the offence under section 7 significantly strengthened the protection for owners and legal occupiers who required immediate use of property occupied by squatters as a home.

For several decades, the 1977 Act appeared to provide a relatively resilient settlement on the role of criminal law in addressing squatting. Amended only once, in 1994, it ushered in a seemingly stable system of limited criminal liability for certain forms of squatting as well as bolstering the powers of owners and legal occupiers to self-help when seeking to recover property from squatters. However, in 2011, this settlement came under scrutiny once again. After the formation of the Coalition Government in May 2010, the legal regulation of squatting took on a renewed political significance. This followed, predictably, a raft of stories about squatters in the media, and seems to have been shaped by previous Conservative policy in the area.[24] In March 2011, the Department of Communities and Local Government and the Ministry of Justice issued joint guidelines explaining the legal measures available to deal with squatters in buildings.[25]

They also announced that the government was conducting a review to consider the need for a new criminal offence of squatting in buildings. A consultation paper followed in June 2011, which put forward several proposals to address 'the distress and misery that squatters can cause'.[26] The explicit agenda of these proposals, which were concerned solely with the role of criminal law in responding to squatting,[27] was to afford the protection of the criminal law not only to those owners and legal occupiers who require immediate use as a home of property occupied by squatters (the settlement under the 1977 Act) but *all owners and legal occupiers*. The consultation paper proposed two alternative approaches. On one

---

22. CLA 1977, s. 7(3).
23. Section 12A of the CLA 1977, as amended by Criminal Justice and Public Order Act 1994. The Law Commission opposed the extension of this offence to protected intending occupiers, but the 1977 Act included them.
24. Before the coalition, the Conservatives in opposition had previously announced plans to introduce an offence of 'intentional trespass'. Its concern was the need for strengthening even further the criminal sanctions to deter Gypsies, travellers and squatters (and others) from occupying both open land and buildings: R. Prince, 'Conservatives to Unveil Plans to Stop Illegal Gypsy Encampments' *Daily Telegraph*, 12 February 2010.
25. M. Hickman, 'Clarke Cracks Down on Wave of Squatters' *Independent*, 19 March 2011.
26. Ministry of Justice, n.10, Foreword.
27. Although the Legal Aid, Sentencing and Punishment of Offenders Act now also removes access to legal aid for squatter trespassers: see section 9, and sch. 1, subpara. 33(10).

hand, the paper suggested the option of strengthening the protections afforded against squatters by sections 6 and 7 of the 1977 Act. The paper put forward the possibility of repealing section 6 altogether, or else exempting all owners and legal occupiers of property from its ambit, expanding the powers of self-help available to retrieve property from squatters. It also proposed to extend the 'failing to leave' offence under section 7 to empower any and all owners and legal occupiers to order squatters to leave their property, with criminal liability attaching to the failure to take reasonable steps to comply with the order.

Alternatively, the consultation paper set out a more wide-ranging and radical approach to the criminalization of squatting. It suggested the creation of a new offence of 'entering and occupying premises as a trespasser'.[28] This option would significantly extend criminal liability for squatting: as with the government's proposed expansion of the 'failure to leave' offence under section 7 of the Act, the new offence would apply to all types of premises, even if they were not required by the owner or legal occupier for immediate use as a home.[29] However, the proposed offence also departed significantly from the approach adopted under section 7 by imposing liability (and empowering police to effect arrest) as soon as a squatter enters and occupies, rather than at the (later) point at which he or she fails to leave when asked to do so by the owner or legal occupier. The offence would therefore impose liability (and permit enforcement) even where the owner or legal occupier cannot be identified or located. It is this path which was eventually taken by the Coalition Government, with respect to residential buildings, through section 144 of the Legal Aid, Sentencing and Punishment of Offenders Act.[30]

The criminalization of squatting in England and Wales has been shaped by wider constructions of squatting and the squatter within popular discourse.[31] The perceived validity of criminal law relies on popular (or populist) conceptions of individual wrongdoing and blame, and media representations of squatting are replete with stories that present squatting as a lifestyle choice (rather than driven by need), and construct squatters as irresponsible, feckless and perpetrators of crime and anti-social behaviour.[32] There is, however, a counterpoint to this rhetoric of moral indignation and culpability.[33] Research has shown that for many squatting is not a lifestyle choice but a necessity brought about by the lack of decent and affordable housing, particularly in areas such as London with high demand and limited supplies of low-cost privately rented homes as well as social

---

[28] Ministry of Justice, n.10, para. 21.
[29] Although the government asked consultees if some types of building (including long-term empty buildings) should be excluded from the ambit of any new criminal offence: Ministry of Justice, n.10 p. 9.
[30] Ministry of Justice, n.10.
[31] It is a recurring criticism of the measures adopted by the state to address squatting that they are often introduced in the absence of reliable data about the nature and extent of the practice: see House of Commons Research Paper, *Squatting* (House of Commons, 1991).
[32] Cobb and Fox, n.8. See also T. Middleton, 'The role of rhetoric in the criminalisation of squatting' in Fox O'Mahony, O'Mahony and Hickey, n.15.
[33] Ibid..

housing.[34] These squatters have been described as part of the 'hidden homeless', and it has been noted that squatting attracts some of the most vulnerable, with often the greatest housing need as well as ancillary needs (mental illness, drug or alcohol dependency, recent release from prison) which can make it especially difficult for them to access mainstream housing support.[35]

Recognizing the role of housing need and homelessness in decisions to squat adds a new layer of complexity to the debates around the criminalization of squatters. Several questions might usefully be asked about the urge to criminalize in light of this alternative conception of the squatter's motivation. Is the use of criminal law an inappropriately severe response to what is sometimes a response grounded in necessity rather than choice? Is it acceptable to label and stigmatize as criminals people who are among the most vulnerable in our society? And does the individualized conception of the problem of squatting draw our attention away from (and allow the state to ignore its own responsibilities for) the structural problems of the current housing market, which have created the conditions that have encouraged, or necessitated, squatting?[36] When the Government set out to extend the reach of the criminal law to squatters, such arguments were given short shrift, as the Coalition's consultation paper clearly illustrates:

> [T]he Government does not accept the claim that is sometimes made that squatting is a reasonable recourse of the homeless resulting from social deprivation. There are avenues open to those who are genuinely destitute and who need shelter which do not involve occupying somebody else's property without authority. No matter how compelling or difficult the squatter's own circumstances, it is wrong that legitimate occupants should be deprived of the use of their property.[37]

Whether the mere existence of a bureaucratic system of housing allocation is sufficient to justify criminalizing those who squat due to housing need and homelessness remains contentious without linking this statement to proper evaluation of the performance of the system in practice, including the proposition that some squatters – arguably the most vulnerable amongst this diverse population – may struggle to engage with that system as a consequence of these vulnerabilities.

Is there more mileage in the claim that, regardless of the squatter's circumstances, the criminal law is an appropriate vehicle by which to protect the owner or legal occupier against 'deprivation of the use of property'? At first glance, this is a much more powerful argument in support of criminalization, drawing attention away from a squatter's motivation and instead towards the harm caused by his or her occupation of property contrary to the rights and entitlements of another.

---

[34] Crisis, *Life on the Margins: The Experiences of Homeless People Living in Squats* (Crisis, 2004). See also K. Reeve, 'Criminalising the poor: squatting, homelessness and social welfare' in Fox O'Mahony, O'Mahony and R. Hickey, n.15.

[35] Crisis, *The Hidden Truth about Homelessness* (Crisis, 2011).

[36] For one alternative perspective in this regard, see N. Cobb, 'The political economy of trespass: revisiting Marxist analysis of the law's response to squatting' in Fox O'Mahony, O'Mahony and R. Hickey, n.15.

[37] Ministry of Justice, n.10, p. 1. See also Home Office, *Squatting* (Home Office, 1991).

Irrespective of the *reasons* for squatting, it might be argued, the *impact* of squatting on owners or legal occupiers justifies a more punitive response. The consultation paper develops this line of argument further:

> [M]ost people would agree that the act of occupying somebody else's property without permission is wrong, *particularly when the occupation causes the property owner to become homeless or impacts negatively on the owner's business*.[38]

This concern – that owners will be deprived of the use value of their properties, whether residential or commercial, is a well-established trope in contemporary debates around squatting and its control.

One popular representation responding to the deprivation of use value by squatting is what Vincent-Jones has described as the 'moral panic' surrounding 'the stereotype of the invasive squatter', assaulting the homes or businesses of those who temporarily leave occupied premises unattended.[39] However, although scenarios of this type may sometimes occur,[40] the vast majority of squatters occupy long-term empty properties, or those planned for future occupation, left empty deliberately to maximize their future resale value,[41] or, in some cases, 'lost' by their owners. Indeed, 'spikes' in the prevalence of squatting depend as much on the availability of empty properties as they do on the absence of affordable and decent housing. It is therefore unlikely that owners or legal occupiers will be deprived of the immediate use value of premises of which they were previously in occupation; although, so long as squatted long-term empty properties are not 'lost' in the sense that the owner is unaware of their ownership,[42] the owners, or those to whom they later grant rights of occupation, may in the future have an immediate need to use those premises.

The Coalition Government's stated concern with protecting owners and legal occupiers made homeless by squatters belies the fact that the government's purported concern with the deprivations caused to owners or legal occupiers who need property as a home are dealt with more than adequately by the law as it stands. Where the criminal law may fall short is in those circumstances in which squatted premises are required for immediate *commercial* use, either because the owner or legal occupier has been displaced by the squatters, or has an immediate future need for the property for business purposes. That type of property, at present, is not affected by section 144, which extends instead to residential

---

[38] Ministry of Justice, n.10, para. 19 (emphasis added).

[39] P. Vincent-Jones, 'Private Property and Public Order: the Hippy Convoy and Criminal Trespass' (1986) 13(3) *Journal of Law and Society* 343, 351.

[40] For an (deliberately provocative) illustration, see R. Kisiel, 'Knife-Wielding Lithuanian Squatters Who Move in when Residents Go Out' *Daily Mail*, 24 September 2010.

[41] For an indication of the interest of squatters in these properties, consider the successful Freedom of Information request submitted by the Advisory Service for Squatters, requiring Camden Council to release information about void residential properties owned by the council and private organizations in the area: *Voyias v. Information Commissioner & London Borough of Camden* [2011] EA/2011/0007, 2 September 2011.

[42] As was sometimes the case in relation to local authority properties in the 1980s; see Cobb and Fox, n.8.

property alone. This restriction was motivated primarily by the government's concern that an offence applying to commercial property would curtail the right to peaceful protest, such as university sit-ins and occupations of business premises in support of industrial action.[43] However, it is still possible we may see further expansion of criminal liability to squatting in commercial property. Indeed, the need for protections for commercial landowners was mooted by Conservative Members of Parliament almost immediately after section 144's enactment, in light of the apparent movement of squatters from residential premises to commercial land as a consequence of the criminalization of squatting in section 144.[44]

Whatever one's view on the justifiability of criminal liability for squatters who deprive owners or legal occupiers of the immediate use value of their premises, it is clear that the government's purported concern with the deprivation of use value is not reflected in the scope and scale of the new offence of squatting in residential buildings created by section 144. Notably, the offence is not restricted in practice to premises required for immediate use. Instead, the offence will empower the police to take action against squatters whether or not the owner or legal occupier requires the property for any future purpose at all. In short, even though the harm of squatting is presented as a deprivation of the owner's use value, in reality, section 144 protects the title holder's bare proprietary or capital interest – over and above, and so excluding from the debate any consideration about land use, need, responsibility or empty homes. This represents a significant departure from the balance struck by the Law Commission and the legislators of the Criminal Law Act 1977, all of whom saw the need for immediate use for property, whether as a displaced or intending occupier, as the *sine qua non* of criminal liability.

AUTOBIOGRAPHICAL NOTE

Neil and Dave on the (legal) politics of squatting

Neil writes:

I was compelled by frustration to respond to the government's consultation on the new offence of squatting in buildings. The demonization of squatters in recent years, especially by the media, has always jarred with my own experience of squats. The few I came across as a student in Bristol were long-term empty properties that, in the hands of their new occupiers, were tended well and used creatively. For poorer students they were godsends. I can only imagine the housing pressures now faced by many students at university today in the wake of the increase in fees.

What also leaves me cold is the crude attempt to respond to the complexities of the deepening housing crisis by punishing the most marginalized, and diverting policing resources to protect the interests of wealthy absent property owners, who

---

[43] Ministry of Justice, n.10, pp. 37–38.
[44] O. Bowcott, 'Criminalise squatting in commercial premises, say Tory MPs' *The Guardian* 30 November 2012.

remain primarily responsible for the serious problem of long-term empty homes. It is no surprise that the state's response to squatting remains such a potent political fault line, when it divides right from left so successfully.

But it's my experience of the consultation process that makes me particularly angry. Out of 2217 responses to the consultation 2126 were received from members of the public concerned about the adverse impact of criminalizing squatting. Only 25 responses were from members of the public concerned about the harm squatting can cause. As such, the government's conclusion that it was right to press ahead with the new offence 'given the level of public concern about this issue' raises questions about its commitment to evidence-led policy-making. It took just three weeks for the Ministry of Justice to publish its response to the consultation, just in time for the new offence to be added to the Legal Aid Bill as a last-minute amendment, with minimal debate, before it left the Commons for the Lords. Which indicates that the government's mind was made up long before the consultation began, and in turn leaves one wondering what the point of the process was.

Dave writes:

Before and after the consultation document to which Neil responded, I was one of many who became concerned by the Coalition Government's representation of the current law. The question should have been whether the then current law was sufficient and whether it was enforced appropriately. The answer to the former question was probably that it could have been 'tweaked'; the answer to the latter was that it appeared to be poorly understood by the police and not enforced. All of the media-produced examples of the terrible effects squatting had on the owners of the properties were not the 'fault' of the law *per se* (in fact, they could have been dealt with relatively quickly through a combination of police enforcement and interim possession orders) but its inadequate understanding and enforcement. 'Nearly Legal', who authors a brilliant and highly recommended housing and property law blog, organized over 160 housing and property lawyers (there were 169 personal signatories and one organization – Housing Law Practitioners Association) to sign a letter which stated our (I was a signatory) concerns about '... such repeated inaccurate reporting of this issue [which] has created fear for homeowners, confusion for the police and ill informed debate among both the public and politicians on reforming the law'. The letter went on to clarify the precise extent of the then law (www.guardian.co.uk/society/2011/sep/25/squatting-law-media-politicians).

Mike Weatherley MP, a Conservative MP in favour of criminalizing squatting, sent a letter to the *Guardian* in response (www.guardian.co.uk/society/2011/sep/29/lawyers-interest-in-squatting-law). In it he wrote 'The self-proclaimed experts who signed the letter, sheep-like, have a huge vested interest when it comes to fees after all'; and, with a final flourish, he added:

> The police will not assist with an eviction in most cases without the backing of a
> magistrate's order. This takes sometimes a few hours, sometimes it's the next day. In

the meantime, the unlawful occupiers will have been damaging your home, using your electricity, drinking your wine and sleeping in your beds. The police should be able to act immediately. Squatters need the threat of a criminal conviction to stop them. If any of those who signed the letter doubt this, then let me throw down the gauntlet – vacate your house for a few days and advertise its emptiness on the appropriate squatter sites. We will see how quickly you can get them out and just how distressed you are at the lack of justice. Maybe then you will think twice before defending squatters. It's no wonder that the public have lost faith in our legal system.

Nearly Legal contained two blog entries in response to that letter. The first was by David Smith, an eminent, knowledgeable contributor, who wrote in careful, measured tones a brilliant response (http://nearlylegal.co.uk/blog/2011/09/squatting-a-reply-to-mike-weatherley-mp/). Quite different in tone, although equally brilliant, was the response from a person called 'the Chief', who savagely and wittily countered Mr Weatherley's arguments (http://nearlylegal.co.uk/blog/2011/09/pass-me-down-the-wine/). But, while those responses gave me fresh heart, the government continued with its reforming zeal. It is appropriate, as he organized and wrote the original multi-signatory letter, to leave the last word on this subject to Nearly Legal himself who, in a blog entry entitled 'Forward to the 18th Century', wrote:

> The consultation response, which is supposed to justify this amendment, is a confused affair, right from Crispin Blunt's foreword, where after noting that it is already an offence to continue to occupy someone's home, he promotes the amendment in these terms 'But the offence will provide greater protection in circumstances where the harm caused is the greatest – squatting in someone's home. This behaviour is unacceptable and must be stopped'. Mr Blunt should perhaps have read the response first. In particular the parts pointing out that failure to enforce existing powers by the police was a problem reported in landlords/property owners responses, see Q.19. In addition delays in court timetables and in bailiffs' appointments were raised by these respondents. This is, of course, a funding issue that is only going to get worse.

> The Metropolitan Police, on behalf of ACPO [Association of Chief Police Officers], opposed any change to the current law, while admitting that, well, maybe a bit of training on CLA 1977 wouldn't go amiss for officers.

> The equality impact assessment accompanying the consultation response also concedes that, even after this whole exercise, the MoJ have no real idea about the scale of the problem, or how far it is a problem. They estimate between '200 to 2100 criminal squatting cases in residential property' per annum. That is a broad range, equating to 'dunno'.

> The equality impact assessment notes that, on the basis of the reports prepared for Crisis and others, the proposal would impact disproportionately on the young and the disabled. But, well, tough. (http://nearlylegal.co.uk/blog/2011/10/forward-to-the-18th-century/)

Plus ça change.

Debate 2

Private rights versus public responsibilities: do owners bear an ethical responsibility to effectively steward their land?

The government's proposals to criminalize squatting, even in situations in which there is no deprivation of immediate use value of property, suggest it is concerned less with the deprivation of use value and more with protecting the rights of property owners. Thus, the present rhetoric of criminalization implies that squatting is intrinsically problematic simply because it constitutes an infringement of proprietary rights, regardless of the material effect of unauthorized occupation on owners or legal occupiers (whether loss of immediate use as a home, as commercial premises, or otherwise). The overall effect is to treat the squatter and squatting as 'immoral', while the use (or not) made by the owner or legal occupier of property is deemed morally irrelevant to the scope of criminal liability. This can be contrasted with the position under the 1977 Act, which placed an implicit moral value on the deprivation of an owner or legal occupier's use of premises as a home. In this way, contemporary debates regarding the criminalization of squatting also help to draw our attention conveniently away from the responsibility which might be apportioned to property owners (and the state) for allowing property to be used in ways which create the conditions in which squatting thrives.

Understanding squatting as (at least to some extent) a symptom of housing need and homelessness highlights the causal role played not only by an inadequate supply of decent and affordable housing, but also by the availability of long-term empty properties, which remain the most attractive option for squatters seeking stable residential accommodation. Empty properties of this kind have been identified as a problem not only because they encourage squatting, but because bringing empty homes into residential use potentially helps to meet demand for residential accommodation.[45] There is at least some passing recognition of the role played by empty properties in encouraging squatting, and the shared responsibility of the state and owners in failing to tackle this problem, in the Coalition consultation, where a review of what steps might be taken to bring more empty properties into residential use was also announced.[46]

That the government has pressed ahead first with proposals to criminalize squatters suggests, though, that squatters are more easily subject to blame than owners of empty properties or the state. Nevertheless, focusing for the moment on the responsibilities that might be understood to fall on the owner of empty property to bring those premises back into use, to what extent can squatting be constructed as a problem which implicates not only the moral failure of the squatter (if at all) but also the moral failure of the owner of squatted property to satisfy

---

[45] See, for example, Office of the Deputy Prime Minister, *Empty Homes: Temporary Management, Lasting Solutions: A Consultation Paper* (TSO, 2003); Office of the Deputy Prime Minister, *Empty Property: Unlocking the Potential – A Case for Action* (TSO, 2003).
[46] Ministry of Justice, n.10, Foreword.

the ethics of effective stewardship of land? And how might this affect how we think about the appropriate response of the state (and so law) to the phenomenon of squatting?

The ethical argument that landownership imposes a duty of effective stewardship is based on the public interest in effective land use[47] and the view that '[t]he quest to protect the privileges of private property against all intruders regardless of the price or need ... is an unholy one'.[48] The stewardship perspective posits that private landowners are the bearers not only of rights in respect of land, but are also subject to a corresponding duty or responsibility to ensure that the limited and vital resource of land is managed fairly on behalf of the community as a whole. Yet, this perspective does not sit easily within the traditional common law framework of property law. The common law typically conceived of property interests as vested in individuals (or groups of individuals), rather than the interests of the community or the public interest.

The shift from an idea that landowners have a responsibility to 'steward' their land effectively to a moral agenda against both the activity of squatting and the loss of title through adverse possession reflects a particular set of political priorities (underpinned by economic rationality) that has only emerged and achieved dominance in England and Wales in recent decades. Yet, in other contexts – whether in other jurisdictions, other disciplines, or even simply outside the realm of real property within English law – the philosophy of stewardship has continued to attract support (in some cases, increasingly) on the basis that it provides a defensible basis on which to develop strategies for the allocation or protection of scarce resources. For example, Gray has identified what he described as a form of 'equitable property' in 'the quality and conservation of the natural environment'.[49] He argued that this formed the basis of a new type of property claim – not concerned with merely empowering exclusion but with empowering reasonable shared access to valued resources for all citizens. Gray emphasized the prominence of *responsibility* – rather than merely rights – in this conception of property; a responsibility that is rooted in 'an overriding duty to "look after [sic] country"'.[50] Indeed, Gray claimed that there had been a marked resurgence of civic reciprocity as a key concept in property law discourse,[51] at least in relation to significant public issues, for example, relating to the environmental quality of life we enjoy, invariably in common with our fellow citizens.

This concept of responsibility can be discerned in a range of property contexts, particularly in the contexts of planning law or environmental protection: for

---

[47] See, for example, J. Karp, 'A Private Property Duty of Stewardship: Changing Our Land Ethic' (1993) 23(3) *Environmental Law* 737; L. Caldwell and K. Shrader-Frechette, *Policy for Land: Law and Ethics* (Rowman & Littlefield, 1993) ch. 7.
[48] Karp, n.47.
[49] K. Gray, 'Equitable Property' (1994) 47 *Current Legal Problems* 137, 188.
[50] Ibid., 189.
[51] See also K. Gray and S. Gray, 'The Rhetoric of Realty' in J. Getzler (ed.), *Rationalizing Property, Equity and Trusts: Essays in Honour of Edward Burn* (LexisNexis Butterworth, 2003) pp. 265–78.

example, the categories of 'listed buildings'[52] and 'ancient monuments' identify specific properties which have been designated as part of the built historic environment, so that their preservation is deemed to be in the public interest. They cannot be altered, extended or demolished without express permission from the local planning authority.[53] The concept of stewardship has also emerged in the context of indigenous rights to land, and rights to natural resources based on patterns of use and occupancy[54] have been a central part of the indigenous peoples' rights movements in the Americas, Australia, New Zealand and other parts of the world.[55] The indigenous rights movements emphasize the centrality of traditional land use to the cultural survival and physical well-being of indigenous communities, as well as the beliefs of many indigenous peoples that they bear a collective responsibility to steward the land. For example, in *Begay* v. *Keedah*,[56] the Navajo Supreme Court described the differences between the Navajo concept of landownership and land tenure under the English common law:

> Traditional Navajo land tenure is not the same as English common law tenure ... Navajos have always occupied land in family units, using the land for subsistence. Families and subsistence residential units (as they are sometimes called) hold land in a form of communal ownership.

Land and its resources are not viewed as primarily economic assets for exchange, but as a resource for use which imparts a sacred trust:

> Our lands are a sacred gift. The land is provided for the continued use, benefit and enjoyment of our people, and it is our ultimate obligation to the Great Spirit to care for and protect it.[57]

The concept of indigenous sovereignty thus includes the right *and responsibility* of indigenous nations to care for and protect traditional lands and resources.

This concept of responsibility for land as a valuable resource is also inherent to the Islamic conception of property rights, which '... conceives of land as a sacred trust',[58] supporting a duty of stewardship on the basis that '[p]roperty and land vest in God, but are temporarily enjoyed by men and women through responsibility or trust ... conditional on the requirement that property not be used wastefully ...'.[59]

---

[52] Structures which have been placed on the Statutory List of Buildings of Special Architectural or Historic Interest.

[53] See, for example, the Town and Country Planning Act 1947.

[54] See, for example, provisions of the American Declaration on the Rights and Duties of Man and the American Convention on Human Rights that affirm rights of indigenous peoples to lands and natural resources on the basis of traditional patterns of use and occupancy. McEvoy discusses the clash between common law conceptions of private property and indigenous practices of land holding: A. McEvoy, 'Markets and Ethics in US Property Law' in H. Jacobs (ed.), *Who Owns America? Social Conflict over Property Rights* (University of Wisconsin Press, 1998).

[55] S. Anaya and R. Williams Jr, 'The Protection of Indigenous Peoples' Rights Over Lands and Natural Resources Under the Inter-American Human Rights System' (2001) 14(1) *Harvard Human Rights Journal* 33.

[56] 19 *Indian L Rep* 6021, 6022 (Navajo 1991).

[57] Union of British Colombia Indian Chiefs, *Aboriginal Title and Rights Position Paper* (1978).

[58] UN-HABITAT, Islam, Land & Property Research Series, Paper 1: Islamic Land Theories and Their Application (UN-HABITAT, 2005) p. 8.

[59] Ibid., 10.

This perspective is also supported by the concept of property rights in Islamic economics, which 'has implications far beyond the material domain as it lays stress on responsibility, poverty alleviation and redistribution',[60] and seeks to work from 'a holistic, authentic, moral, ethical and legal land rights code'.[61] The relevance of this approach to squatters and unsupervised land is most clearly illustrated by the Islamic concept of *mewat* or 'dead land', which allows individuals to claim for their own use land that is empty and uncultivated or undeveloped.[62]

The concept of an ethic of care has been a significant theme in recent scholarship across the social sciences, notably in feminist theory,[63] and has been applied to a range of contemporary moral dilemmas, including the role of the dispassionate workings of market institutions, 'infused with an individualised competitive imperative',[64] compared to the responsibilities of the state in respect of social justice and inequality in housing. Whereas the ethic of rights and justice values individualized, commoditized rights to exclusion and control, an ethic of care and responsibility values interpersonal, intergenerational community interests. Yet, while the ethic of care invokes moral responsibilities, in the legal domain it is usually trumped by the rights-and-entitlements discourse of ownership. For example, even in the context of cultural property, where the concepts of stewardship and the ethic of care are clearly present, they take second place to the discourse of property rights.[65] It is only where specific public law protections are layered on top of the common law – for example, in relation to planning or environmental law, or land explicitly designated as commons land[66] – that the community interest in stewardship and the values of access and use (rather than exclusion and exchange) can play a role in the mediation of property claims.[67] Even in the context of commons land and public rights of access to the countryside, it has been argued that public rights created by legislation are 'subverted by vested interests and the ideological power of private property'.[68]

---

[60] Ibid., 14.

[61] Ibid..

[62] See S. Sait and H. Lim, *Land, Law & Islam: Property & Human Rights in the Muslim World* (Zed, 2006) p. 61.

[63] See for example, C. Gilligan, *In a Different Voice* (Harvard University Press, 1982), identifying a gendered distinction between 'masculine' (associated with an 'ethic of rights and justice') and 'feminine' (associated with an 'ethic of care and responsibility') moralities.

[64] S. Smith, 'States, Markets and An Ethic of Care' (2005) 24(1) *Political Geography* 1.

[65] See, for example, J. Sax, *Playing Darts with a Rembrandt: Public and Private Rights in Cultural Treasures* (University of Michigan Press, 1999), discussing the rights of the private owner of a work of art to destroy his property.

[66] See the Commons Act 2006, which allowed for the registration of common land or town or village greens. The concept underlying commons land is that it belongs to no-one and everyone; it can be used by all but appropriated by none.

[67] In the US, Alexander has challenged the idea that exclusion is the core of property, arguing instead that there is a competing tradition within property law which recognizes the communitarian nature of property ownership: see, for example, G. Alexander, 'Takings and the Post-Modern Dialectic of Property' (1992) 9 *Const Comment* 259. More recently, Alexander has identified this civic vision of property as the 'social-obligation' norm: see, for example, G. Alexander, 'The Social-Obligation Norm in American Property Law' (2009) 94 *Cornell L Rev* 745.

[68] J. Mitchell, 'What Public Presence? Access, Commons and Property Rights' (2008) 17(3) *Social and Legal Studies* 351, 352.

Yet, as with so many of the debates we consider in this book, this is not an inevitable feature of property law: the roots of a concept of stewardship within the English common law doctrines governing property were very much present in feudal structures and pre-1925.[69] Rather, it is the ideological framework of property law since 1925, and even more so since the LRA 2002, that is averse to restrictions on, or threats to the security of, formal landownership rights. Indeed, the idea of communal or collective land rights has been so divorced from conventional models of ownership that it is constructed as a form of resistance to the political ideology of private property.[70] For example, the criminalization of squatting has re-cast the debate concerning homeless squatters in empty properties so that the utilitarian argument that the landowner (who is neither using the property nor adequately fulfilling the duty of stewardship over their land) in fact has a morally weaker claim to that property compared to a squatter (who is making effective use of the property, and who is in desperate and pressing need of shelter) is excluded from the dominant discourse oriented around the idea that the squatter *is* the social problem.

The extent to which English law allows for the possibility of resistance to private ownership as exclusion, including by those who are marginalized under current property arrangements, has also been dramatically curtailed by the reform of adverse possession in the LRA 2002. As the discussion in the next section will demonstrate, this has fundamentally altered the matrix of rights and duties attendant on landownership in England and Wales. In the great debate between the private, individualized, capitalized interests of the landowner (the property 'insider' discussed in Chapter 1) and the public, community, socialized interests of the land user (sometimes, as in the case of squatting and adverse possession, a property 'outsider'),[71] the LRA 2002 provides one example of the more generally acknowledged pre-eminence afforded to private, 'insider' interests in land by the evolving legal system.

Debate 3

Owners versus squatters: how has the doctrine of adverse possession been effected by changing political values concerning ownership and acquisition of title to land by property insiders and outsiders?

The LRA 2002 adopted a strong policy position against adverse possession, effectively limiting the circumstances in which a squatter could claim title to registered land to either the three narrow 'special cases' exemptions, which were designed

---

[69] For example, the strict settlement, which explicitly preserved interests in land for future generations.

[70] J. Holder and T. Flessas, 'Emerging Commons' (2008) 17(3) *Social and Legal Studies* 299.

[71] Although an individual person in adverse possession (the 'squatter') is not 'the public' as such, in cases involving homeless squatters, the individual is representative of a social responsibility on the part of the community as a whole to respond to the needs of marginalized and vulnerable populations.

more to enhance the technocratic system than to facilitate a social and/or political objective; or to those (very unlikely) circumstances in which the registered proprietor makes no objection to the squatter's claim once notified. The erosion of traditional principles of adverse possession by the LRA 2002, together with the decision of the Grand Chamber of the European Court of Human Rights in *Pye* v. *The United Kingdom*[72] have embedded a new legal order for the regulation of title by adverse possession, underpinned by a set of taken-for-granted moral perspectives which reflect a wholly negative view of the activity of squatting.[73] These changes have taken place in parallel to a discourse of moral outrage towards squatters *per se*. From that perspective, it is unsurprising that English law has rejected the doctrine which allowed trespassers to land to secure a title interest against the registered proprietor.[74] The erosion of adverse possession in England and Wales was presented by the Law Commission and Land Registry as a necessary adjunct to the ever-tighter principles of registration implemented in the 2002 Act; although this perspective has been questioned by some scholars,[75] and is arguably at odds with the continued existence of traditional principles of adverse possession in many mature Torrens-style land registration systems.[76]

The erosion of the traditional doctrine of adverse possession in the LRA 2002 is certainly consistent with the principles of title registration advanced in that Act. However, there was clearly another agenda at work here, which went beyond the technicalities of land registration to the values that underpin the English system of landownership and property rights. This agenda, which has also been advanced through judicial dicta, reflects the ethic of justice and rights (for property owners) discussed in the previous section. For example, Lord Bingham described the operation of the pre-2002 principles of adverse possession as 'apparently unjust',[77] while Neuberger J claimed that it was: '... hard to see what principle of justice entitles the trespasser to acquire the land for nothing from the owner simply because he has been permitted to remain there for 12 years'; such a conclusion '... does not accord with justice, and cannot be justified by practical considerations, [is] draconian to the owner and a windfall for the squatter'.[78] Indeed, the House of Lords explicitly articulated an anti-stewardship ethic when expressing regret that the pre-2002 principles required that it find in favour of the squatter. In Lord Hope's opinion, the unfairness of the traditional doctrine of adverse possession was not 'the absence of compensation, although that is an

[72] (2008) 46 EHRR 45.
[73] See Cobb and Fox, n.8.
[74] Ibid., fn 4.
[75] Dixon described 'the reform of the process of adverse possession by the 2002 Act as an unnecessary and economically unjustified "bolt on" to the reform of registered land': Dixon (2005), n.8, 351.
[76] See *Adverse Possession*, a Report by the British Institution of International and Comparative Law for Her Majesty's Court Service (September 2006), which outlines the key principles of adverse possession across a range of ECHR and common law jurisdictions.
[77] *JA Pye (Oxford) Ltd* v. *Graham* [2003] 1 AC 419, [2], *per* Lord Bingham.
[78] *JA Pye (Oxford) Ltd* v. *Graham* [2000] Ch 676, 709–10.

important factor, but ... the lack of safeguards against oversight or inadvertence on the part of the registered proprietor'.[79]

While the human rights dimension of the English adverse possession debate was forestalled by the extended litigation in *Pye* v. *Graham*,[80] and subsequently, in the European Court of Human Rights in *Pye* v. *UK*[81] – decisions which themselves were shaped by England's domestic property politics[82] – these very decisions have re-invigorated the debate between possession and registration, and their respective underlying values of social use and economic efficiency, in other jurisdictions.[83] These values, in turn, come back to the debate about what we think it means to own land, and what weight we attach to the possession or use of the land. The curtailment of adverse possession clearly demonstrates a preference for rights of exclusion over rights of access in our conception of property ownership, for the abstract rights of title over what is in fact occurring on the land.

The political nature of the LRA 2002, and the importance of perspective, was illustrated in interesting ways by the approach to adverse possession taken by the Northern Ireland Law Commission in its report on Land Law.[84] While the Commission made extensive reference to the approach adopted by its English counterpart, its search for local solutions led to a rejection of the decisive policy departure taken by the English law in the LRA 2002. The Northern Ireland analysis explicitly recognized that the question of reform in this area required a careful consideration of the values and ethics that underpin the doctrine as well as its practical effects. Perhaps most significantly in comparison with the English experience, the political and moral agenda against squatting has not been a prominent feature in the Northern Ireland context. The result was that, when balancing the interests at stake, it was possible to talk in terms of the traditional justifications for the doctrine.[85] While the Commission's analysis of these traditional bases for the squatter's claim were not deemed sufficiently decisive to resolve the debate, the complexities of the social and economic issues that lie behind the law of adverse possession were clearly acknowledged.

---

[79] *Pye*, HL, n.77, [73].

[80] Ibid../

[81] *JA Pye (Oxford) Ltd* v. *United Kingdom* (2006) 43 EHRR 3 (Chamber judgment); *Case of J.A. Pye (Oxford) Ltd and JA Pye (Oxford) Land Ltd* v. *The United Kingdom (2008)* 46 EHRR 45 (Grand Chamber judgment).

[82] L. Fox O'Mahony and N. Cobb, 'Taxonomies of Squatting: Unlawful Occupation in a New Legal Order' (2008) 71(6) *MLR* 878.

[83] For example, Griggs has defined the debate underlying contemporary adverse possession discourse in Australia as between the 'economic imperatives' of the Torrens system and the traditional importance of possession to landownership: L. Griggs, 'Possession, Indefeasibility and Human Rights' (2008) 8(2) *Queensland University of Technology Law and Justice Journal* 286.

[84] Northern Ireland Law Commission, *Report: Land Law*, NILC 8 (TSO, 2010); the report followed a detailed discussion of adverse possession in Northern Ireland Law Commission, *Supplementary Consultation Paper, Land Law*, NILC No 3 (Northern Ireland Law Commission, 2010).

[85] For example, the avoidance of stale claims, or owners sleeping on their rights, the hardship arguments on the side of both the squatter and the landowner, the claim that adverse possession in fact promotes effective land use and the ethical argument that landownership imposes a moral duty of effective stewardship on the owner to look beyond their own selfish interests to ensure that this limited and vital commodity is managed fairly on behalf of the community as a whole

While the English approach to adverse possession was heavily influenced by the context of land registration, it was also clearly shaped by the political and moral agenda against trespass to land and squatting (now designated land theft). Indeed, the Northern Ireland Law Commission explicitly stated that it did not wish to adopt an ethical stance on adverse possession,[86] and rejected the moral agenda (referred to as the ethical element) introduced by the LRA 2002 through the good faith requirement attached to the exception for boundary mistakes.[87] The Commission also expressed 'considerable reservations' about the ethical implications of the shift in balance between landowner and squatter in the LRA 2002, which 'greatly increases the protection of the owner from a failure to keep an eye on the property'.[88] It is, of course, arguable that one cannot avoid moral judgments in this context, as they are implicit (one way or the other) to both an acceptance of the justifications for the doctrine, and also the rejection of those justifications (as has occurred in England and Wales in respect of registered land). Furthermore, at the time of writing (2015), the Northern Ireland Law Commission's 2010 report remains unimplemented – but that is another political story...

Meanwhile, in England and Wales renewed attention has been drawn to the obvious – but largely overlooked – philosophical and doctrinal tension between the residual property law right of acquisition through adverse possession and the new offence of squatting in residential buildings. Following the enactment of section 144, it had been assumed by the Land Registry that where adverse possession was found to constitute an offence under the section it could not form the basis for an act of possession for the purposes of the adverse possession doctrine. This was on the basis of earlier precedent, *R (Smith)* v. *Land Registry*, in which acquisition by adverse possession had been rejected where it also constituted an offence under the Highways Act 1980.[89]

In R *(Best)* v. *Chief Land Registrar*,[90] the claimant, Kevin Best, a squatter of residential premises since 2001, sought judicial view of the Chief Land Registrar's decision to reject his application to be registered as proprietor pursuit to the adverse possession provisions of the LRA 2002 on the basis that he had been committing a criminal offence since the coming into force of section 144. However, the Court of Appeal, upholding the decision of Ouseley J in the High Court, rejected the arguments of the Chief Registrar, and held instead, distinguishing *Smith*, that section 144 did not have the effect of curtailing the operation of the law of adverse possession.

The Court found that Parliament could not have intended the new offence to affect the system of adverse possession, and if it had wanted to do so it would

---

[86] '... partly because it would require the courts to consider the motives, intentions and beliefs of the parties. It would be likely to make the law much more complicated and thereby run counter to the Commission's primary aim of simplicity, clarity and certainty': Supplementary Paper, para. 2.42.

[87] LRA 2002, sch. 6, para. 5(4)(c).

[88] Supplementary Paper, para. 2.50.

[89] [2009] EWHC 328 (Admin).

[90] [2014] EWHC 1370 (Admin); [2015] EWCA Civ 17.

have made it plain on the face of the legislation. More importantly, the Court in reaching its decision also emphasized the public policy implications of allowing the offence to preclude the adverse possession doctrine. Not only would such an approach entirely undermine the role of the doctrine as a method of settling title to unregistered land in the absence of deeds; it would also arbitrarily distinguish between squatters who lived in buildings and squatters who secured adverse possession through other means, and it would ultimately defeat the overarching policy goal of the adverse possession doctrine to prevent land becoming sterile where the true owner could not be found.

In this way, the Court of Appeal succeeded in protecting the system of adverse possession from the destabilizing effects of section 144, but at a cost; as Hickey has noted, its approach, while understandable, has left the law looking increasingly incoherent:

> [I]t involves the troubling general proposition that different branches of the legal system (criminal law and the law of property) hold diametrically opposing views on the significance of living in a residential building as a trespasser; but a more specific difficulty is produced in this context, insofar as section 144 effectively operates as a gateway to adverse possession of residential premises. While the legitimacy of an adverse title will be recognized if 10 or 12 years are allowed to pass, a squatter ... will now need to run the risk of criminal prosecution. Whatever the broader merits or demerits of the enactment of criminal justice provisions in this context, it seems strange to reward criminal behaviour provided only that the criminal gets away with it. Conversely, if it is worth having a law of adverse possession, that is to say, if we are committed to the policy advantages it brings even in the context of registered land titles, it seems disproportionate, and perhaps even illogical, to impose a criminal deterrent at the point of entry to the LRA 2002's 'carefully balanced' regulation of the property position of squatters.[91]

Indeed, as Hickey concludes, this widening gulf between the objectives of the criminal and civil law with regard to the residential squatter may well fuel renewed debates about the appropriateness of criminalization in the area.

CONCLUSION

Both the agenda for criminalization of squatting and the erosion of the traditional doctrine of adverse possession in the LRA 2002 are clearly embedded within a broader commitment to the protection of property/capital ownership interests, the commodification of real property and the pursuit of economic security for those who hold formal rights in land. This agenda is neoliberal in the sense that it protects and prioritizes the market; but paradoxically it also reveals a tension

---

[91] R. Hickey, 'A Property Law Critique of the Criminalisation of Squatting' in Fox O'Mahony, O'Mahony and Hickey, above n.15.

within the neoliberal agenda. While neoliberalism is associated with ideas of self-responsibility and self-provision, the criminalization of squatting would bring what has historically been a civil law dispute for the recovery of land between two private individuals – with the landowner held responsible for protecting her own interests by discovering and acting to remove the squatter – into the realm of public protection, so empowering the police – without any intervening judicial process to adjudicate the parties' respective claims – to enforce the landowner's paper title.

This potential use of the criminal law to protect landowners who have failed to discharge their duty of stewardship inverts the neoliberal ideas of individual self-responsibility and non-intervention in private law. Similarly, the LRA 2002 rejects both the self-help activity of squatting by homeless populations (a practice widely recognized in many other jurisdictions) and the proposition that landowners are responsible for stewarding their own land. Rather, property law – through the agency of the Land Registry – has stepped into what was once regarded as a private dispute to safeguard the proprietary rights and entitlements of landowners who, it must be assumed, can no longer be held responsible (on pain of losing their investment in the land) for discovering and taking steps to remove unlawful occupiers within the traditional 12-year window. Indeed, it is arguable that both developments support the argument that the concept of individual responsibility underpinning neoliberal policies is both geared towards – and sometimes conveniently forgotten if that is what is needed to facilitate – the interests of a particular type of status- and capital-owning individual – the property insider.

Further Reading

N. Cobb and L. Fox, 'Living Outside the System? The (Im)Morality of Urban Squatting' (2007) 27(2) *Legal Studies* 236.

N. Cobb, 'Property's Outlaws: Squatting, Land Use and Criminal Trespass' [2012] *Crim LR* 114.

L. Fox O'Mahony and N. Cobb, 'Taxonomies of Squatting: Unlawful Occupation in a New Legal Order' (2008) 71(6) *MLR* 878.

L. Fox O'Mahony, D. O'Mahony and R. Hickey, *Moral Rhetoric and the Criminalisation of Squatting: Vulnerable Demons?* (Routledge, 2015).

K. Reeve with E. Batty, *The Hidden Truth about Homelessness: Experiences of Single Homelessness in England* (Crisis, 2011), http://www.crisis.org.uk/data/files/publications/HiddenTruthAboutHomelessness_web.pdf

P. Vincent-Jones, 'Private Property and Public Order: The Hippy Convoy and Criminal Trespass' (1986) 13(3) *Journal of Law and Society* 343.

7

THIRD-PARTY INTERESTS IN THE USE AND CONTROL OF LAND

INTRODUCTION

This chapter focuses on two categories of burden on land: easements (obligations that benefit and burden two separate pieces of land) and restrictive freehold and commonhold covenants (promises restricting the use of freehold land). Our approach in this chapter reflects our view that these private law obligations cannot be fully understood without also considering the broader context of public law obligations that relate to the use of land. Consequently, this chapter explores the nature and development of easements and restrictive covenants in the context of the social, economic and political arguments for permitting third parties to control use of land by private owners, as well as the control and regulation of land use as a public function.

This chapter also considers the historical context in which the legal framework for the regulation of third-party interests in the use of land has evolved. While easements have been recognized since time immemorial (originally in response to agricultural needs), restrictive freehold covenants are a relatively modern invention, triggered by a specific social need. The restrictive freehold covenant was first recognized in English courts at the height of the Second Industrial Revolution, in the landmark case of *Tulk* v. *Moxhay*.[1] The industrial revolutions had a huge impact on urbanization of England, which, in turn, raised major issues for land use control. Increased population density and the proliferation of land uses required 'effective techniques to control the manner in which land was used so as to avoid one landowner's interfering with the interests of his neighbour'.[2] The impact of these changes in land use patterns, as well as more recent demands for the commercialization and commodification of interests in land, alongside the growing emphasis on registration and discoverability as the requirements for enforceability, have put in play a series of debates which are explored in this chapter.

Each of these debates is linked to the tension between the private property owner's right to exclude all others from his land and the general public interest

---

[1] (1848) 2 Ph 774; (1848) 47 ER 1345.
[2] P. McCarthy, 'The Enforcement of Restrictive Covenants in France and Belgium: Judicial Discretion and Urban Planning' (1973) 73(1) *Colum L Rev* 1.

in the use of land as a valuable resource. This tension can be seen in the overlaps between strategies developed by private law and (latterly in the UK) public law to enable the control of a private owner's use of their land, as well as in the principles by which conflicts of interest between landowner and neighbours are resolved. While Gray and Gray described land transactions between strangers (for example, sale or mortgage of land) as characterized by meta-norms of heightened rationality,[3] in which the land is valued, perhaps even exclusively, according to its exchange value,[4] in cases involving neighbours they described the legal framework as shaped by a norm of 'reasonableness'. As neighbours, the parties have entered into voluntarily assumed relationships of 'medium-term proximity', giving them an extended timescale against which they will need to co-operate: 'with the result that neighbours tend to enjoy a longer line of social credit than is possible in random commercial interactions between strangers'.[5] Gray and Gray described these relationships as having 'an on-going, interactive and quasi-public quality', within a community domain shaped by shared and mutual interests, which 'tempers the aggressive pursuit of individual self-interest' which has come to be associated with land purchases and mortgage transactions.

Gray and Gray concluded that when it comes to third-party burdens on land, the ways that we think and debate about rights and interests 'within the forum of the neighbourhood' emphasize the *use value* of the land, rather than its exchange value (see Chapter 3); the *reasonableness* of actions rather than economic rationality; *social co-operation* rather than self-interest; and *duties and responsibilities* rather than simply rights.[6] This 'neighbourhood' principle is manifest in a number of ways that create burdens on the private owner's absolute dominion over her land. While the common law created the easement and the *profit à prendre*, and the Court of Chancery conjured up the restrictive freehold covenant, Parliament has also frequently intervened to recognize specific policy-driven burdens on private ownership – for example, through the Countryside and Rights of Way Act 2000, which limited private ownership over open countryside by creating public rights of way (a right to roam) with a view to giving people greater freedom to explore and to enjoy the health benefits of fresh air and exercise. There is also a relationship between the emergence and application of private rights controlling the use of land (initially through leasehold covenants, and from 1848 through restrictive freehold covenants) and the development of public planning law.

In this chapter, we frame these questions in terms of four great debates. First, we consider whether positive covenants should be enforceable against successors in title; second, we consider whether controls are better accomplished through private or public law; third, we ask about the impacts of the legal frameworks

---

[3] See K. Gray and S. Gray, 'The Rhetoric of Realty' in J. Getzler (ed.), *Rationalising Property, Equity and Trusts: Essays in Honour of Edward Burn* (LexisNexis UK, 2003) esp. pp. 253–65.
[4] Gray and Gray, n.3, p. 241.
[5] Ibid., p. 242.
[6] Ibid., p. 256.

enabling governance of use rights; and finally, whether property law should control the permissible content of easements and freehold covenants.

Debate 1

Should positive freehold covenants be enforceable against successors in title?

Prior to the decision in *Tulk* v. *Moxhay*,[7] promises relating to the use of land were mere contracts, personal obligations which were not generally assignable to third parties. At common law, while the benefit of the full range of freehold covenants could be enforced by a successor in title so long as the requirements set out in *Smith & Snipes Hall Farm* v. *River Douglas Catchment Board*[8] were satisfied, the burden of freehold covenants could not (directly) pass to a successor in title.[9] It was the reluctance of common law courts to accept that the burden of covenants might run – in light of the implications this would have in allowing private property ownership of freehold land to be burdened by promises made by another – which led to equitable intervention in 1848.[10] The decision to allow a restrictive freehold covenant to bind successors in title in equity coincided with the urban growth in development, as well as the emergence of concerns about the quality of amenities for residential occupiers. Urbanization increased the demand for private living space, and growing crime rates heightened concerns about security, privacy and exclusivity.[11] A demand emerged for a technique to enable vendors of freehold land to control the subsequent use of the land in a similar way to lessors of leasehold land, under the more readily enforceable leasehold covenant.

The emergence of the restrictive covenant as a potentially binding obligation was well aligned with the *laissez-faire* policies of the time, as they could be justified by their origins in the voluntary agreement of the parties. Yet, while the popular story suggests that – under careful judicial development – these private agreements became useful tools to control the use of land[12] (with the archetypal example of Leicester Square, the location of the dispute in *Tulk*, often offered to illustrate the power of the newly binding freehold covenant) it is important to recognize that, in the end, the maintenance of Leicester Square as an open space resulted not from the freehold covenant applied to it, but from the subsequent

---

[7] (1848) 2 Ph 774; (1848) 47 ER 1345.

[8] [1949] 2 KB 500.

[9] 'English common law dogmatically insists that only the benefit, and not the burden, of a freehold covenant may run with the land': K. Gray and S. Gray, *Elements of Land Law* (Oxford University Press, 5th edn., 2009), para. 3.3.24.

[10] That having been said, the reasoning in *Tulk* was circular – the right was binding because the stranger had notice of it. It was only subsequent authorities which rationalized and narrowed the jurisdiction – see, in particular, *Haywood* v. *Brunswick Permanent Benefit BS* (1881) 8 QBD 403.

[11] S. Blandy, 'Gated Communities in England: Historical Perspectives and Current Developments' (2006) 66(1) *Geojournal* 15, 18.

[12] McCarthy, n.2, 2.

public governance of land use. In fact, the restrictive covenant regime offered limited scope to maintain a high-functioning open space arrangement on the square, and thirty years after the decision the land was philanthropically donated to the local government authority, to be used as a public square.[13] It is therefore the power of the public authority, not the private covenant, which is responsible for today's Leicester Square.

Yet, while the judicial development of the restrictive freehold covenant has enabled certain covenants, which comply with the relevant conditions (restrictive in nature, intended to bind third parties, protected as necessary on the register), to have durable effect, courts have been reluctant to allow positive covenants to have similar effects. Judicial resistance to the general enforceability of positive freehold covenants according to the principles developed from *Tulk* v. *Moxhay* has been linked to the doctrine of *privity of contract*. At least, this is what seems to lie behind Lord Templeman's position in *Rhone* v. *Stephens,* expressed in this circular reasoning: 'Enforcement of a positive covenant lies in contract; a positive covenant compels an owner to exercise his rights. Enforcement of a negative covenant lies in property; a negative covenant deprives the owner of a right over property.'[14] Perhaps recognizing that this reasoning did not, in itself, offer a strong basis on which to reject the enforceability of positive freehold covenants, Lord Templeman also concluded that, by the time he was called to give judgment in *Rhone* v. *Stephens,* it was too late to overturn a rule of such elementary principle, which had guided behaviour since its inception.[15] In fact, the original basis for the rule, as suggested by Cotton LJ in *Austerberry* v. *Oldham Corporation,* was that to require owners to incur expenditure based on the promises of their predecessors would have been a new departure for a court of equity: '... a court of equity does not and ought not to enforce a covenant binding only in equity in such a way as to require the successors of the covenantor himself, they having entered into no covenant, to expend sums of money in accordance with what the original covenantor bound himself to do'.[16] Yet, as Dixon has noted, in the modern era of land registration any such burden would have to be registered to have binding effect on the purchaser, so that the purchaser would be well warned of the liability and could act accordingly – to walk away, to negotiate a lower price or to take out insurance.[17]

There is some basis for suggesting that the rule is not as strict as it might have been thought to be. Conveyancers have developed techniques to circumvent its strict application, including a chain of indemnity covenants, executing an artificial long lease, and most particularly through the doctrine of mutual benefit and

---

[13] J. Smith, '*Tulk v Moxhay*: The Fight to Develop Leicester Square' in G. Korngold and A. Morriss (eds.) *Property Stories* (Foundation Press, 2nd edn., 2009).

[14] [1994] 2 AC 310, 318.

[15] At 321.

[16] (1885) 29 CH D 750, 774.

[17] M Dixon, *Modern Land Law* (9th edn., 2014), pp. 361–62.

burden, as demonstrated in *Halsall* v. *Brizell*.[18] However, one result of the decision in *Rhone* is that the scope for enforcing a positive freehold covenant against a successor in title has been narrowed considerably.[19] We return to this question in Debate 4, when we reflect on the Law Commission's 2011 recommendations concerning the permissible content of third party obligations affecting land.

Debate 2

Should controls on land use be achieved through public law or private law?

The law governing burdens on land can be positioned within a broader set of laws and policies concerned with the regulation of land use. We typically tend to think of controls over land use as being primarily public, administered (in the public interest) through planning law and environmental law. Yet private law (in the form of property law's easement and restrictive covenant, and tort's doctrine of nuisance[20]) has also played its part in both the historical development of land use policies and in the matrix of controls that regulate the uses that contemporary private landowners can make of their land.

The idea that law places limits on the use of privately held land by an absolute owner raises important debates relating to popular conceptions of private ownership, on the one hand, and community ethics concerning land as a valued resource, on the other. Just how private is – or should be – ownership of land? Popular ethics concerning land use shift in response to political ideologies and socio-economic conditions: for example, the dramatic growth in owner-occupation in the twentieth century popularized the view that 'an Englishman's home is his castle'; but this came under challenge when Madonna (largely successfully) opposed the claim that the 'right to roam' in the Countryside and Rights of Way Act 2000 created public rights to enter onto her English country estate.[21] The issue of third-party rights to control the use of privately owned land usually invokes quality of life and environmental considerations, whether on the part of the community at large (the 'public interest'), or one or more private individuals who own or occupy proximate land. While this chapter primarily explores the principles that have informed the development of these private rights to control land use, both public and private actions concerning land use are (explicitly or, in the case of private claims, sometimes implicitly) potentially

---

[18] [1957] Ch 169.

[19] *Thamesmead Town Ltd* v. *Allotey* (1998) 30 HLR 1052.

[20] See J. Penner, 'Nuisance and the Character of the Neighbourhood' (1993) 5(1) *Journal of Environmental Law* 1, for discussion of how the concern with the 'character of the neighbourhood' cuts across the tort of nuisance and property law doctrines.

[21] The planning hearing determined that only 2 out of 17 parcels of land initially identified by the Countryside Agency would be deemed 'open countryside' and so accessible to the public – see www.independent.co.uk/environment/madonna-wins-battle-over-right-to-roam-732731.html.

informed by a broad range of ethical, aesthetic, ecological and socio-economic values concerning land use.[22]

Although questions concerning the permissible limits within which private landowners may exploit their land are now mostly addressed through planning law and environmental law, both of these branches of law are of relatively recent vintage in England and Wales. Indeed, historically, it was private property law which played the primary role in regulating how occupiers of land shared space as neighbours. The English planning system did not reach maturity until 1947, when local authorities were empowered to grant or refuse permission for development on land.[23] Indeed, the modern planning regime evolved from the control of building under the Public Health Acts, which in turn had emerged from the private exercise of building controls through property law.[24] Consider, again, the starting point of the landmark restrictive covenants case, *Tulk* v. *Moxhay*,[25] in which an agreement between private freeholders to keep an area of square garden and pleasure ground in Leicester Square, London 'in an open state, uncovered with any buildings, in neat and ornamental order' was enforced to prevent building on the open space that is now (a century and a half after it passed into local authority ownership) a central landmark in London's West End.[26]

The decision of the Chancery Court that the burden of freehold covenants should be enforceable in equity was timely and pre-empted the socio-economic shift in emphasis from leasehold to freehold ownership.[27] In the early phase of the Industrial Revolution, from the late eighteenth century, the existence of enforceable leasehold covenants had,

> prove[n] to be enormously effective in both releasing land for urban development and in controlling the form of that development. Such restrictive covenants could apply both to the form and construction of the buildings and to the use to which they were put. Covenants regularly excluded commercial uses in residential areas or prevented the opening of pubs or taverns ... Public control, by contrast, was rudimentary.[28]

---

[22] See L. Caldwell and K. Shrader-Frechette, *Policy for Land: Law and Ethics* (Rowman & Littlefield Publishers Inc., 1993).

[23] Town and Country Planning Act 1947; although the fundamentals of a planning system that involved plan making or zoning was put in place by the Housing, Town Planning, etc. Act 1909, and developed in the Housing and Town Planning Act 1919 as well as the Town and Country Planning Act 1932.

[24] P. Booth, 'From Regulation to Discretion: The Evolution of Development Control in the British Planning System, 1909–1947' (1999) 14(3) *Planning Perspectives* 277. Booth specifically points to building leases as a source of private control, although restrictive freehold covenants also performed this function.

[25] (1848) 2 Ph 774; (1848) 47 ER 1345.

[26] It is to be noted, of course, that the covenant was, at least in part, positive in nature, in requiring the 'neat and ornamental order'.

[27] Right up until the First World War, most people, regardless of income, rented their homes from private landlords; see M. Ball, *Housing Policy and Economic Power: The Political Economy of Owner Occupation* (Methuen, 1983).

[28] Booth, n.24, 281.

The private leasehold system regulated matters relating to the amenity value of the property, the character of the neighbourhood for other property owners and the function of these private rights in enabling control over land use. By the early twentieth century, however – and even with the added facility to enforce restrictive covenants against freehold owners – the limitations of this private system to achieve what was increasingly recognized as a public interest became clear. For one thing, it depended on private owners taking the initiative to insert appropriate covenants into their transactions. The extent to which private owners conceived of their role as including such a responsibility was attenuated by the early twentieth century, so that 'while in the past landowners had acted in enlightened self-interest "to promote the amenities of the neighbourhood", newer types of landowner just dealt with land as a commodity'.[29] The private system was also limited as it simply addressed issues such as 'amenity' or the 'character of the neighbourhood' in the interests of the property owner rather than the non-owner. Thus, Booth noted that: 'The system worked well where economic advantage was to be gained by targeting a well-to-do clientele who would expect their amenities to be protected, but landlords did not care to take special measures in areas destined for the working classes, where standards of building might well be much lower.'[30]

A further distinction can be drawn, within the categories of private control, between the tortious claim in nuisance and the proprietary or quasi-proprietary rights conferred by easements and restrictive covenants. If the tort of nuisance is an 'unlawful interference with a person's use or enjoyment of land, or some right over, or in connection with it',[31] then the existence of a (quasi-) proprietary burden on land creates the lawful basis for an interference with the landowner's use or enjoyment of her own land. In both cases, the claim is private in the sense that it arises between two private parties, each of whom has an interest in a parcel of neighbouring land. Penner has explained the existence of these types of obligation between neighbours on the basis that: 'Land is not the sort of property over which dominion can be exercised in disregard of the fact that land is situated in a particular place, and thus is by nature bound to the property of others.'[32] It has been argued that nuisance law can be regarded as part of the law of servitudes,[33] as it deals with how one land occupier's use of land may interfere with that of another, neighbouring, landowner. Indeed, in US law schools, courses on land use generally cover both public regulation of growth and development controls on land and private land use arrangements,[34] which may both reinforce public regulation and achieve forms and levels of control that public actions cannot.

---

[29] Ibid., 282.

[30] Ibid., 282.

[31] W. Rogers, *Winfield and Jolowicz on Tort* (Sweet & Maxwell, 13th edn., 1989) p. 378.

[32] Penner, n.20, 5.

[33] A.W.B. Simpson, *An Introduction to the History of Land Law* (Oxford University Press, 1961) pp. 245–46.

[34] See, for example, course texts such as R. Ellickson and V. Been, *Land Use Controls: Cases and Materials* (Aspen Law and Business, 3rd edn., 2005).

Debate 3

What are the impacts of legal frameworks enabling private governance of use rights in land?

The judicial rule that positive freehold covenants do not run with the land (discussed above, debate 1) has been hugely inconvenient to certain developments. The difficulties this generated in enforcing common obligations (for example, to maintain common areas of the building) in apartment buildings where title to the individual units is held on freehold rather than leasehold title prompted the rare event of statutory creation of a new form of tenure: 'commonhold'. The Commonhold and Leasehold Reform Act 2002 created a new type of freehold title which allows for the enforcement of community obligations through a 'commonhold association', where the nature of the property is truly interdependent, and includes the sharing of common parts. The commonhold association acts as a micro-government, making decisions for the members.[35] Indeed, it is this type of private governance – rather than a physical obstruction, a gate – that is the defining feature of the 'gated community'.[36]

The development of commonhold title has opened up new opportunities for privately managed local planning and neighbourhood management schemes in England and Wales. Beyond the basics of maintaining communal areas in a block of flats, commonhold allows the possibility of freehold ownership of land, combined with the provision of a 'bespoke package of paid-for neighbourhood facilities and services [making] it possible for middle- and higher-income people to move back into the city. The amenities bundled into the schemes by developers include secure access, uncongested parking and good quality, uncongested on-site facilities.'[37] This can be viewed as the ultimate privatization of housing: what would previously have been viewed as public neighbourhood amenities are re-created as private goods exclusive to the commonhold owners within the development,[38] so enabling the residents of such a community to opt out of using the public system.[39] While this type of scheme involves the exercise of private law rights to control the use of land, it can be regarded as an 'opt-in' scheme, to the extent that buyers of properties within commonhold developments should typically receive very clear information about the nature of the rights and responsibilities (usually financial) to which they will be subject; and the commonhold association itself functions as a kind of representative democracy within this micro-state.

---

[35] C. Webster and R. Le Goix, 'Planning by Commonhold' (2005) 25(4) *Economic Affairs* 19.

[36] Ibid..

[37] Ibid., 20.

[38] For discussion of the tradition of private amenities associated with affluent housing in England, see Blandy, n.11.

[39] G. Alexander, 'The Publicness of Private Land Use Controls' (1999) 3(2) *Edinburgh L Rev* 176, 181.

Lee and Webster have described the worldwide growth in gated communities as a 'general enclosure of the urban commons',[40] with potential implications for the availability of amenities and neighbourhood goods on a social (rather than private) basis. This raises a new set of policy issues: while there are clearly personal benefits for those who buy in to this type of property ownership, there are also potentially negative spill-over effects for those who are outside, particularly if the concentration of wealth within the private community has an adverse impact on the viability of amenities in the public neighbourhood. Other risks of privately controlled neighbourhoods include spatial-social segregation and homogenization of neighbourhoods; and political fragmentation, which disrupts the processes of redistributive taxation.[41] While there is little evidence as yet to indicate that the advent of commonhold has resulted in a significant upsurge in gated communities in England and Wales, developers and local authorities have predicted significant growth in the market in the coming decades.[42] Austerity-era welfare reforms – particularly housing benefit reform – have highlighted the impacts of spatial segregation, with concerns that lower-income households are being pushed out of London. This serves as an important reminder of the social consequences of privatized communities-within-a-community.

Gated communities are communities of exclusivity, in the sense that residents lead separated or segregated lives. This does not always mean luxury or elite life-styles: it can also be used to describe the refugee camp, or the ghetto.[43] Not all instances of gated living are chosen by the residents: the decision to separate a sub-population may be made by the residents themselves or by the wider community – although those gated communities which are not chosen by residents through the exercise of private property rights are less likely to be governed by formal (as opposed to informal) rules set out in legally binding covenants. What they have in common, however, is that as spaces and places they represent worlds of exclusion rather than worlds of inclusion. In the case of intentional communities governed by private rules, they employ a concept of property as a tool of exclusion rather than access, to enable them to live lives that are not fully integrated in their society. To the extent that private property law allows these limitations on the spatial rights of the community, as well as empowering residents to create domains of self-governance, it enables us to think about our communities in ways that are territorially bounded.

The rise of privatized space is challenged by the urban commons movement, which works to identify possibilities for recognizing shared public interests in urban space through alternative property rights models.[44] The idea of the urban

---

[40] S. Lee and C. Webster, 'Enclosure of the Urban Commons' (2006) 66(1) *GeoJournal* 27.

[41] Webster and Le Goix, n.35, 21–22.

[42] R. Atkinson, S. Blandy, J. Flint and D. Lister, 'Gated Cities of Today: Barricaded Residential Developments in England', Glasgow University Centre for Neighbourhood Research Paper 21, (2004).

[43] S. Brunn, 'Gated Minds and Gated Lives as Worlds of Exclusion and Fear' (2006) 66(1) *GeoJournal* 5.

[44] As evidenced, for example, in the Commons Act 2006; see also Lee and Webster, n.40.

commons is based on the historic English rural commons, where designated rural space was treated as subject to common ownership rights (i.e. belonging to everyone and no one). From the sixteenth century onwards,[45] these rural commons were enclosed or brought under private ownership (with a specific emphasis on the property right to extract economic benefit from the land), in a process triggered by what has been labelled 'the tragedy of the commons'.[46] As rights to land become increasingly valuable, so the argument goes, each person with access to the land seeks to maximize their gain from it (for example, by over-grazing their herd). This then supports a movement towards privatization (the enclosure of the commons) to restrain competition and protect the resource against depletion by overuse. It has been argued that this rationale can also be applied to contemporary urban resources or public goods (for example, parks and gardens, leisure facilities, playgrounds) whose overuse by the public tends to deplete the value of these resources. The tendency towards enclosure (or privatization) of land that serves as a public or civic good has been described as an 'inescapable consequence of economic progress',[47] so that the continued existence of a community's public goods thus depends on the existence of a legal mechanism to protect the community's property interest over the shared goods.

The rural enclosures of the eighteenth and nineteenth centuries were driven by the political power of the landowners, who were in an ideal position to push legislation which protected their economic and trade interests in land through Parliament.[48] While the landowners enjoyed the economic benefits of enclosure, critics have noted that: 'the social costs associated with the adversely affected welfare of the landless, although significant, were not born [sic] by most landowners, who tended to ignore them in the face of such substantial economic opportunity'.[49] The rural enclosures marked a decisive shift in English property rights, through which centuries of common ownership evaporated into a new culture of private ownership, justified by reference to the value of the land for trade and commerce. In the case of urban enclosure, Lee and Webster have argued that 'exclusion is an unavoidable and inevitable accompanying component to urban and economic development. Boundaries are necessary to delineate property rights amongst competing demands for land and all manner of scarce resources'.[50] This is, in effect, the fundamental principle of the institution of private property,

---

[45] When the value of agricultural land increased dramatically with the rising commercial demand for wool and cloth.

[46] G. Hardin, 'The Tragedy of the Commons' (1968) 162 *Science* 1243; and see further the Special Issue of *Social and Legal Studies* (2008) 17(3), dedicated to this issue.

[47] Lee and Webster, n.40, 29; see also C. Webster, 'Property Rights and the Public Realm: Gates, Green Belts and Gemeinschaft' (2002) 29 *Environment and Planning B* 397; C. Webster, 'The Nature of the Neighbourhood' (2003) 40 *Urban Studies* 2591; C. Webster and L. Lai, *Property Rights, Planning and Markets: Managing Spontaneous Cities* (Edward Elgar, 2003).

[48] Lee and Webster, n.40, 31.

[49] Ibid..

[50] Ibid., 32.

so it is hardly surprising that it has played a major role in the development of property law's arrangements for governing access to, and exclusion from, land.

In the last decade or two English property legislation has balanced debates between access to land (as urban or rural commons, for example, through the Commons Act 2006, or the protection of the right to roam in the Countryside and Rights of Way Act 2000) and exclusion (through the facility to create privately governed commonhold communities under the Commonhold and Leasehold Reform Act 2002). Findings to date suggest that large-scale gated communities in England and Wales remain relatively scarce.[51] Now that the legal structures are in place to support the development of urban enclosure, their development is likely to be determined by user demand and the dynamics of the market, rather than by public policy.

AUTOBIOGRAPHICAL NOTE

Public rights of way and private *profits à prendre*

Every evening, unless it's raining, we take a family walk along the river beside our house, up through the orchard and around by the farm. Our 21-month-old son looks forward to – and starts to talk about – this walk from the moment we leave the nursery. We talk about the fish and the ducks in the river, the cows and the rabbits in the field, and the barn where the cows will go to bed at night. We climb over stiles, look at the yellow flowers and learn not to touch the nettles. The land across which we walk is private property: there are signs along the riverside indicating that it is private land and that (the profit of) fishing in the river is restricted to members of Durham Anglers Club. But the paths we follow are ancient public rights of way. These days, the farm land is the edge of a conservation area, and the paths don't really 'go' anywhere, in the modern directive sense. But along the way we walk under the arch of an old gate house, built in 1112, which (situated out on the edge of the city) was at one time the fever hospital; and past the ruins of what our local history books tell us was once a medieval pub. The landscape bears the remnants of the various uses which the land has had over centuries, and provides welcome amenities of fresh air, exercise and nature trail. Before we moved here, I didn't really appreciate the value of public rights of way other than for access to a destination. In fact, as an ancient city, Durham is full of vennels and alleyways that have long been used as short-cuts to access parts of the city, as well as long-used pathways across the more rural outskirts of the city. But it is the amenity value of these public footpaths – rather than their access function – that has turned out to have real value. Of course, while this amenity is free at the point of use, it forms part and parcel of the market value of neighbouring property, so that access to such spaces may not be random but can become a selling point for middle-class family homes in desirable locations.

---

[51] Atkinson, Blandy, Flint and Lister, n.42.

THE CATEGORIES OF EASEMENT AND RESTRICTIVE FREEHOLD COVENANT

The development of statutory schemes such as the commonhold interest was a direct response to the limited scope and reach of the common law principles of easements and restrictive freehold covenants.[52] For one thing, there are carefully guarded restrictions on the permitted content of both types of servitude, in recognition of the burden which the existence of proprietary third-party interests imposes on private ownership of land. Second, there are strict rules concerning the circumstances in which such obligations are created, and the requirements that must be followed if they are to bind third parties and successors in title. In both cases, the Land Registration Act (LRA) 2002 has attempted to tighten up the registration requirement as a condition of enforceability for burdens on land, with discoverability emerging as the watchword to ensure priority against purchasers. The formalities surrounding the creation of these rights, their limited scope, and the strict rules governing their enforceability reflect the perception within English land law that third-party rights in the form of such servitudes represent a major incursion on the freedom of the private property owner,[53] and so should not readily be acceded to without clear justification.

Each category of burden has – both separately and concurrently – attracted the attention of the Law Commission on several occasions over the last few decades.[54] A number of reform attempts have been made in relation to both easements (often with an emphasis on easements created by prescription) and freehold covenants (mostly in relation to positive covenants) but with only limited results to date. In 1971, the Law Commission published a working paper on *Transfer of Land: Appurtenant Rights*[55] which proposed a statutory scheme to regulate both forms of interest, but remained unimplemented and was subsequently deemed too ambitious.[56] The 1984 report was confined to covenants, and set out proposals for a new land obligation, which would enable both positive and negative obligations, once registered, to be enforceable as an interest in land. The 1991 report, *Transfer of Land: Obsolete Restrictive Covenants*,[57] recommended that covenants automatically expire after 80 years, subject to a right of appeal by the owner of the right, and the consultation paper preceding the Land

---

[52] See D. Clarke, 'Occupying "Cheek by Jowl": Property Issues Arising from Communal Living' in S. Bright and J. Dewar (eds.) *Land Law: Themes and Perspectives* (Oxford University Press, 1998).

[53] Which, once recognized and registered, are not readily extinguished.

[54] Indeed, on the eve of the creation of the Law Commission, its predecessor, the Law Reform Committee, published its 14th Report on *Acquisition of Easements and Profits by Prescription* (Cmnd 3100); Law Commission publications concerning burdens on land have included Law Commission, *Transfer of Land: Appurtenant Rights*, Law Commission Working Paper No 36 (HMSO, 1971); Law Commission, *Transfer of Land: The Law of Positive and Restrictive Covenants*, Law Commission Report No 127 (HMSO, 1984); Law Commission, *Making Land Work: Easements, Covenants and Profits à Prendre*, Law Commission Report No 327 (TSO, 2011).

[55] Law Commission Working Paper No 36 (HMSO, 1971).

[56] Law Commission (1984), n.54, para. 1.6.

[57] Law Com No 201.

Registration Act 2002 identified a range of concerns relating to easements, including the inappropriateness of lost modern grant in relation to registered title; the problem of three methods of prescription (suggesting that common law prescription and lost modern grant should be abolished, leaving only statutory prescription, although not in its existing form).[58] These provisional recommendations were abandoned in the Final Report on Land Registration.[59]

In the 2002 edition of *Gale on Easements*, the author noted that: 'The Law Commission has ducked the law of easements more than once. We understand that it may now be girding its loins for the task of cleansing this particular Augean stable.'[60] Following the enactment of the LRA 2002, a new reform initiative focused on land obligations (easements, *profits à prendre* and freehold covenants) was launched, with a final report published in 2011.[61] The recommendations set out in this report and discussed below are wide-ranging, with identified goals of simplification, fairness and efficiency.[62]

Debate 4

Should property law control the permissible content of easements and freehold covenants?

The category of easements as recognized in English law has developed gradually through judicial reasoning. There is no definition or closed list (as there is in some other jurisdictions), although there are guidelines concerning the nature of an easement. For a claim to come within the category of easements, the following elements are required:[63] (1) a dominant and servient tenement;[64] (2) that the easement accommodate the dominant tenement;[65] (3) that the dominant and servient tenements are owned or occupied by different people; and (4) that the right is capable of forming the subject matter of a grant. This final requirement has its origins in the fallacy that all easements were originally granted, and demands that

---

[58] Law Com No 254.

[59] Law Com No 271, para. 1.19.

[60] J. Gaunt and P. Morgan, *Gale on Easements* (Sweet & Maxwell, 17th edn., 2002) p. vi.

[61] Law Commission, *Making Land Work: Easements, Covenants and Profits à Prendre*, Law Com No 327, HC 1067 (TSO, 2011).

[62] Ibid., para. 1.26.

[63] *Re Ellenborough Park* [1956] Ch 131.

[64] In *London & Blenheim Estates* v. *Ladbroke Retail Park* [1994] 1 WLR 31, it was held that there could be no easement of parking cars on a piece of land, because at the time the easement was allegedly created, there was no dominant and servient tenement.

[65] The easement must benefit the land, not confer a personal benefit on the holder of the land: for example, in *Hill* v. *Tupper* (1863) 2 H & C 121, an alleged right over land adjoining a canal, which was enjoyed in conjunction with the right to hire out pleasure boats on the canal was held not to be an easement, since the right to hire out boats was more important than the easement, so that the personal benefit associated with the claim outweighed the benefit to the land. While they need not be contiguous, the dominant and servient tenements must also be of sufficient proximity to each other for the benefit to be real: in *Bailey* v. *Stephens* (1862) 12 CB(NS) 91 the court held that land in Northumberland could not benefit land in Kent.

the easement is (a) sufficiently certain; and (b) within the general nature of rights recognized as easements.

The courts have exercised caution in extending this category of rights, in light of the substantial nature of the burden that an easement may entail. For example, while easements may be either *permissive* (allowing the dominant landowner to carry out some activity on the servient land, for example, a right of way, the right to park a car on neighbouring land, rights to lay gas mains or electric cables and the right to go on the land to inspect and maintain them); or restrictive (a right to restrain activity on the servient land, and so exercise a degree of control over how the servient owner uses their own land), they should not be personal. There is also a reluctance to recognize easements that impose a positive obligation (i.e. one which incurs expenditure) on the servient land.[66] The category of restrictive easements is limited to: (1) the right to light – that is, that the light flowing to a window shall not be unreasonably obstructed;[67] (2) the right to the free flow of air through a defined aperture (e.g. a ventilation shaft);[68] (3) the right to support of buildings – that is, a right to restrain any use of the servient land or buildings on the servient land that will interfere with the support afforded by them to adjoining buildings on the dominant land;[69] (4) a right to continued flow of water through an artificial watercourse; and (5) the right to use space for storage.[70] Rights which have *not* been recognized as easements include the right to a view[71] and easements of privacy,[72] and there is no easement to uninterrupted receipt of a television signal.[73] Rights which involve expenditure cannot generally be regarded as easements, because the duty of a servient owner is negative (that is, not to interfere with the dominant owner's enjoyment) rather than positive, although (perhaps demonstrating the pragmatic development of the category of easements to meet needs to control land use) an exception to this principle is the easement of fencing to keep in livestock, recognized in *Crow* v. *Wood*.[74] Finally, rights which involve exclusive or joint use are also unlikely to be regarded as easements.[75]

---

[66] An exception is the 'spurious' easement of fencing: *Crowe* v. *Wood* [1971] 1 QB 77.

[67] The right to light has long been recognized as a special category of easement and is specially protected by statute; see Prescription Act 1832, Right to Light Act 1959.

[68] Although there is no right to an uninterrupted flow of air for chimneys, which was deemed to be too broad: *Bryant* v. *Lefever* (1879) 4 CPD 172.

[69] *Dalton* v. *Angus* (1881) 6 App Cas 740; note that this right is distinct from the natural right to support of land; it is not automatic and must be acquired as an easement. If such an easement is acquired (for example, by prescription), then the servient tenement owner cannot demolish buildings on his or her land that provide support for buildings on the dominant land. There is no easement of protection by one building of another from weather: *Phillips* v. *Pears* [1965] 1 QB 76.

[70] *Wright* v. *Macadam* [1949] 2 KB 744.

[71] Deemed too broad: *Aldred's Case* (1610) 9 Co Rep 57b.

[72] *Browne* v. *Flower* [1911] 1 Ch 219.

[73] *Hunter* v. *Canary Wharf Ltd* [1997] AC 655.

[74] [1971] 1 QB 77.

[75] In *Copeland* v. *Greenhalf* [1952] Ch 488 the right to park lorries on land was taking up most of the land, and the court held that joint or exclusive possession cannot be regarded as an easement. This is, however, a question of degree: see *London & Blenheim Estates* v. *Ladbroke Retail Parks Ltd* [1992] 1 WLR 1278; *Bachelor* v. *Marlow* (2001) 32 P&CR 36; *Hair* v. *Gillman* (2000) 80 P&CR 108. Indeed, the House of Lords in *Moncrieff* v. *Jamieson* [2007] 1 WLR 2620 seemed less than convinced by this bar.

The most significant restriction on the permissible content of freehold covenants at common law is that they must be negative in nature. While the parties to the original covenant may make positive promises towards one another, which are normally enforceable in *contract*, successors in title of the original parties to the agreement are only bound by the covenant if the principles of property law which have grown up around freehold covenants are satisfied. At common law, the benefit of a freehold covenant could pass to a successor in title, but not the burden,[76] and it was only with the decision in *Tulk* v. *Moxhay* in 1848,[77] as subsequently interpreted, that it became possible for the burden of restrictive covenants to pass to successors in title.

The Law Commission's 2011 proposals would relax the permissible content of both easements and freehold covenants. Specific proposals included a more relaxed approach to easements conferring rights to extensive or exclusive use,[78] and a scheme through which both positive and negative covenants would become land obligations. The latter extends the scope for the creation of covenants that are enforceable as interests in land from commonhold properties to all land.[79] Although the Commission acknowledged the arguments against allowing positive burdens to run (for example, in restricting or constraining choice), and noted that the economic case for enforceable positive covenants had not specifically been made,[80] it concluded that since it is already possible to achieve enforceable positive covenants by roundabout means (for example, indemnity contracts), 'the market has made its own case'.[81] These developments would allow considerably greater incursion on the freedoms of the freehold owner. As the next section will show, the Law Commission justified this approach through its emphasis on registration and information as the guardians of fairness in land transactions.[82]

Debate 5

When should easements and covenants bind third party purchasers?

The rules concerning the creation – and to some extent the enforcement – of easements and freehold covenants invoke what Epstein described as 'a theme persistent in all legal discourse: the tension between private volition and social

---

[76] There were methods by which this rule could be circumvented. The doctrine of mutual benefit and burden was discussed above. Other methods include where property was transferred by lease instead of conveying fee simple; or where successors in title were enabled to sue directly on the contract, for example, through the Contracts (Rights of Third Parties) Act 1999.

[77] (1848) 2 Ph 774; (1848) 47 ER 1345.

[78] Law Commission, *Making Land Work: Easements, Covenants and Profits à Prendre*, Law Com No 327, HC 1067 (TSO, 2011), para. 3.209.

[79] Ibid., para. 5.30.

[80] Ibid., para. 5.35.

[81] Ibid., para. 5.36.

[82] Ibid., para. 5.59–5.62.

control'.[83] In the context on burdens of land, this debate has been expressed as one between a 'strict contractarian ethic' (the argument that law should defer to the intentions of the parties, to avoid limiting freedom of action),[84] and concessions to a more 'regulatory or interventionist ideology',[85] in the interests of social justice or the wider community. Alexander has noted that in a private property regime that emphasizes the freedom of the private owner there is a 'strong presumption' in favour of the contractarian approach, emphasizing private volition. Through this lens, purchasers should only be bound by those burdens which they have chosen, either by direct consent or where the burden was listed on the register and so was clearly identified as part of the bargain when the land was acquired:

> The notion of a land-use obligation binding persons who did not make the promise presents something of an anomaly in the liberal conception of property. Indeed, the term 'servitude' embarrasses a property regime committed to the autonomy of private owners.[86]

The rationale which has been created to justify the possibility of burdens that bind successors in title is rooted in the purchaser's knowledge of the burden – or, at least, the discoverability of the obligation when the land is transferred. Table 7.1 demonstrates how the LRA 2002 has embedded the twin requirements of registration and discoverability in the rules governing both legal and equitable easements. Where land is unregistered, the old distinction between legal and equitable easements continued to determine whether they bind the world without registration (legal easements) or require registration as a land charge (equitable easements).

Similarly, in the case of restrictive freehold covenants (and alongside the other requirements for the burden to run in equity), it is necessary that the covenant was registered either as a Class D(ii) land charge,[87] or, in the case of registered land, protected by the entry of a notice against the title of the servient land.[88] The emphasis on registration in respect of both types of burden on land[89] is consistent with the nature of title registration after the LRA 2002, while the introduction of discoverability requirements in respect of informally created and equitable easements underlines the (alienation themed) bias towards prioritizing the protection of purchasers over those of subsidiary interest holders. It purports to give effect to the choices of the purchaser, as the decision to go ahead with the purchase of land subject to a registered or discoverable obligation is deemed to be tantamount to

---

[83] See, for example, R. Epstein, 'Notice and Freedom of Contract in the Law of Servitudes' (1982) 55 *S Cal L Rev* 1353.

[84] Ibid..

[85] G. Alexander, 'Freedom, Coercion, and the Law of Servitudes' (1987) 73 *Cornell L Rev* 883. Alexander argues that the distinctions within this dichotomy are in fact blurred, to the extent that 'choiceless' is often experienced by parties within nominally consensual land transactions.

[86] Ibid., 889.

[87] Land Charges Act 1972, s.2(5).

[88] LRA 2002.

[89] Although the method of registration varies, with expressly created legal easements substantively registrable as interests in land, and equitable easements and restrictive covenants registrable though a notice on the register.

Table 7.1 Easements and transmissibility to third parties: a short guide

When are third parties bound by the easement?	**UNREGISTERED LAND**
LEGAL EASEMENTS	Legal proprietary interests in unregistered land **bind all the world.**
EQUITABLE EASEMENTS	Equitable easements in unregistered land are interests capable of registration as a land charge if they were created on or after 1 January 1926, and so must be registered in accordance with the Land Charges Act 1972 if they are to bind third parties (LCA 1972, s2(2)).
When are third parties bound by the easement?	**REGISTERED LAND (easements created before 13 October 2003)**
LEGAL EASEMENTS	Legal easements created before 13 October 2003 are *overriding interests* and so they bind the purchaser of registered land without need for registration (LRA 1925, s70(1)(a)).
EQUITABLE EASEMENTS	Equitable easements created before 13 October 2003 are *overriding interests* so long as the easement is exercised openly (*Celsteel Ltd* v. *Alton House Holdings Ltd* [1985]1 WLR 204).
When are third parties bound by the easement?	**REGISTERED LAND (easements created from 13 October 2003)**
LEGAL EASEMENTS	**Some** legal easements remain overriding – depending on how they were created; others must be registered to bind third parties.
	Expressly created easements (grant or reservation) *must be registered;* they are *not* overriding interests (LRA 2002, s.27(2)(d) & (e)).
	Informally created easements *may be overriding interests;* that is, easements arising by: ▶ Section 62, LPA 1925 – (LRA 2002, s.27(7)). ▶ Implied easements (necessity, common intention, *Wheeldon* v. *Burrows (1879) 12 Ch D 31*) – (LRA 2002, sch. 3). However, note that for informally created legal easements to be overriding interests you must *also* show that the easement was within the knowledge or notice (obvious on reasonably careful inspection) of the purchaser, or that it has been exercised in the last year (LRA 2002, sch. 3, para. 3).
EQUITABLE EASEMENTS	*Never overriding;* must be registered as a burden on the registered title.

consent to be subject to the obligation. The emphasis on registration and discoverability as the guardians of fairness when creating, or enforcing, third-party rights in land was also a prominent theme in the Law Commission's most recent Report on *Land Obligations*. The reform initiative was embedded in recognition of the role of easements and covenants in enabling the effective use of land,[90] but subject to the principle that such obligations be registered if they are to bind third parties. This rationale for a strategy that justifies reliance on registration and discoverability for the protection of private property interests in land (as proxies for the purchaser's free choice in undertaking the burden) was challenged by Alexander. He argued that the use of the (false) dichotomy between free choice (as the guiding tenet of private law) and collective coercion (where public intervention is justified) serves to privilege private law regulation (designated as choice) over public regulation (deemed choicelessness) as a means of governing land use.[91] While this issue has been extensively debated in the US literature, it remains to be seen whether the Law Commission's report will prompt any home-grown challenges to what has become a deeply embedded belief in the philosophy of gearing private regulation of land use towards controls that are registered and/or discoverable.

CONCLUSIONS

While both the easement and the restrictive covenant perform important functions in English land law, each operates under strict conditions, designed to limit the nature and extent of the burdens imposed through private law on the owners of land. Yet, however one strikes the balance between private ordering and intervention, public law and private property law, in relation to third party interests in land, it is important to be aware that what, on the surface, are often presented as settled doctrinal rules with no political or policy agenda in fact conceal value-laden choices concerning access to, and exclusion from, the limited resource of land.

Further Reading

S. Blandy, 'Gated Communities in England: Historical Perspectives and Current Developments' (2006) 66(1) *Geojournal* 15.

A. Bottomley, 'A Trip to the Mall: Revisiting the Public/Private Divide' in H. Lim and A. Bottomley (eds.), *Feminist Perspectives on Land Law* (Routledge-Glasshouse, 2007).

R. Epstein, 'Notice and Freedom of Contract in the Law of Servitudes' (1982) 55(4) *S Cal L Rev* 1353.

S. Lee and C. Webster, 'Enclosure of the Urban Commons' (2006) 66(1) *Geojournal* 27.

---

[90] Law Commission, *Making Land Work: Easements, Covenants and Profits à Prendre*, Law Com No 327, HC 1067 (The Stationery Office, 2011), para. 1.4.

[91] Alexander, n.39.

8

HUMAN RIGHTS AND PROPERTY LAW

INTRODUCTION

Other chapters in this book have briefly mentioned human rights – in relation to the mortgagee's right to possession, the doctrine of overreaching, and the landlord's right to possession of the occupied property. This chapter faces the issue head on. The great debate which raged during the Noughties, and partly resolved as that decade ended, was the extent to which property rights and human rights intersect and interact. Although this chapter could range widely, its focus is on two elements: mandatory rights to possession (Debate 1); and peaceful enjoyment of possessions (Debate 2). The former concerns Article 8 of the European Convention on Human Rights (given effect in Schedule 1, Human Rights Act 1998 (HRA)); the latter concerns Article 1, First Protocol, ECHR (1998 Act, sch. 1 (A1P1)).

As regards the questions around Article 8, the issues are now well-advanced and clear, involving the balancing of cherished assumptions about absolute rights to property with 'home' rights. There is now a bank of case law on which we can draw. In Debate 1, which asks whether mandatory possession proceedings are really 'mandatory', we discuss the twists and turns in the development of the law and then discuss the principles that have emerged since 2011 when the Supreme Court accepted that Article 8 was relevant to this question.

As regards A1P1, our sense is that the issues have been less well-advanced, and we provide three examples: adverse possession; shared ownership; and the rule in *Hammersmith and Fulham LBC* v. *Monk*. As regards adverse possession, the controversy has been resolved; as regards shared ownership, interesting problems may arise; as regards the rule in *Monk*, the issues have been partly resolved. There may well be overlaps in certain cases, regarding certain issues,[1] but there is quite a lot of room for interesting thought here.[2]

---

[1] For example, in the case of shared ownership, where possession is sought by the landlord on a mandatory ground, as to which, see D. Cowan, 'A Ticking Time Bomb' (2011) 161(7467) *New Law Journal* 729.

[2] One only needs to consider the differences of opinion in the Supreme Court discussion of A1P1 in relation to the 'benefit cap' to appreciate the potential here: *R(SG)* v. *Secretary of State for Work and Pensions* [2015] UKSC 16.

Debate 1

Are mandatory rights to possession mandatory?

It is of the essence of superior property rights that the holder of those rights has better title to the property than the occupier. Unless otherwise protected, the holder of the superior property right is entitled to possession of the property as a matter of right against a range of interposers. Interposers is not a particularly helpful word, it is accepted, but it carries with it a certain meaning. The interposer is the household which occupies the property. They may do so with rights to do so – for example, a tenant is an interposer between the landlord and the property. Alternatively, they may do so without rights to do so, for example, a trespasser is an interposer between the person with superior rights and the property. Where the court has a *discretion* whether to grant possession against the interposer, properly no human rights issue arises.[3] It is where the court has no discretion – it *must* make the possession order – that the real rights-based issues arise.

There has been considerable litigation on this point, and that litigation is probably still incomplete. In this part, we begin with a brief analysis of Article 8. We then show how the pre-eminence given to property rights has withered under consistent battering from the European Court of Human Rights (ECtHR), leading to the acceptance by the UK Supreme Court that it must follow the approach taken by the ECtHR in perhaps the most significant case of our generation: *Manchester City Council* v. *Pinnock*.[4] We move on to consider how this new intervention has been interpreted in the senior courts. Finally, we isolate certain potential lines of future argument, where either the dividing lines are currently unclear or fresh issues arise.

THE ISSUE STATED

Article 8 provides:

Right to respect for private and family life:

1 Everyone has the right to respect for his private and family life, his home and his correspondence.
2 There shall be no interference by a public authority with the exercise of this right except such as is in accordance with the law and is necessary in a democratic society in the interests of national security, public safety or the economic

---

[3] One can see this best in those cases which have sought to challenge the jurisdiction of the court under Trust of Land Act 1996, s. 14 and Insolvency Act 1986 (as amended), s. 335A through the use of human rights-based arguments: *Barca* v. *Mears* [2004] EWHC 2170 (Ch); *Nicholls* v. *Lan* [2006] EWHC 1255 (Ch).
[4] [2010] 3 WLR 1441, described as follows: '... there is now a new giant on the scene, one judgment to rule them all and in its 9 strong constitution bind them', http://nearlylegal.co.uk/2010/11/brave-new-world-or-same-old-story/

well-being of the country, for the prevention of disorder or crime, for the protection of health or morals, or for the protection of the rights and freedoms of others.

Article 8 does not guarantee a home for each household or at all. It merely provides that we all have a 'right to respect' for our home (thus assuming that we already have one and, if we don't, then tough). In itself, that right to respect appears rather limited. Second, paragraph 2 clearly qualifies this right to respect. It is now trite to say that whether something is 'necessary' or not is a question of proportionality, a balance between the rights of the parties and the state. In essence, the question before the courts has been whether mandatory possession proceedings enable the judge to conduct that assessment; put another way, it is whether the property rights to possession are so significant that any assessment of the proportionality of the act is entirely irrelevant. Let us leave to one side, for now, the question about whether these rights are generally applicable between private and/or public actors – this is a significant question in its own right which will bother the Supreme Court again shortly.

There are two other preliminary matters. First, there is the way in which the court must approach the question when a principle or statutory provision of English law is out of step – incompatible – with the HRA. The court has one of two options: it can either 'read down' the provision, so as to make it compatible, or it can make a declaration of incompatibility, which is for Parliament (not the court) to resolve.[5] Second, there is the precedent value of ECtHR decisions. UK courts must 'take into account' any 'judgment, decision, declaration or advisory opinion' of the ECtHR.[6] They need not slavishly follow the ECtHR. This has led to the UK courts entering into what they have described as 'valuable dialogue' with the ECtHR in certain areas 'where [the Supreme Court] has concerns as to whether a decision of the Strasbourg Court sufficiently appreciates or accommodates particular aspects of our domestic process'.[7]

THE 'HOME'

The precondition for Article 8's operation in this context is that the property must be the household's 'home'. The notion of 'home' has been discussed elsewhere in this book, but there is one thing that is absolutely clear: 'home' is independent of, and not dependent on, any rights which the occupying household may or may not have in relation to the property. In *Qazi* v. *Harrow LBC*, Lord Scott seemed to suggest the contrary when he argued that:

Each home had been established on the basis of a proprietary interest in the premises obtained under the contractual tenancy granted by the landlord. How

---

[5] 1998 Act, ss. 3 and 4.
[6] 1998 Act, s. 2(1).
[7] *R* v. *Horncastle* [2009] UKSC 14, [11].

could the termination of that tenancy in a manner consistent with its contractual and proprietary incidents be held to constitute a lack of respect for the home that had been thus established? The home was always subject to those contractual and proprietary incidents. The contrary view seems to me to treat a 'home' as something ethereal, floating in the air, unconnected to bricks and mortar and land.[8]

This narrow view of 'home' is certainly not consonant with the approach taken by the ECtHR, nor with the jurisprudence in the UK.[9] It was arguably also inconsistent with the views of the majority in *Qazi*. The understanding of 'home' is, it seems, 'ethereal, floating in the air', for it seems to connote some sort of psychosocial attachment to place. As the ECtHR has put it, home connotes '... the existence of sufficient and continuous links with a specific place'.[10] This first denial of the significance of the interposer's property rights is significant because it simply unpicks the assumptions of property law – the contractual and proprietary incidents, which so engaged Lord Scott – in favour of a much broader, contextual approach to home.[11] As Lord Hope put it, in *Hounslow LBC* v. *Powell*, 'This issue is likely to be of concern only in cases where an order for possession is sought against a defendant who has only recently moved into accommodation on a temporary or precarious basis.'[12]

QAZI: THE ZENITH OF THE PROPERTY RIGHTS THESIS

It is fair to say that *Qazi v Harrow LBC*[13] offers the zenith of the supremacy of property rights over the interposer's human rights. Mr Qazi and his then wife occupied a property with their daughter. The then Mrs Qazi left the property and served a notice to quit, which determined the tenancy. Mr Qazi was refused a sole tenancy of the property but subsequently re-married and his new wife joined him in the property, after which they had two further children. Harrow claimed possession of the property, which Mr Qazi defended on the basis of his rights under Article 8. Now, the way the case progressed (in retrospect) was not ideal because there was no attack on the mechanism used by the first Mrs Qazi to determine the tenancy.[14]

---

[8] [2004] 1 AC 983, [145].
[9] See the critique by T. Allen, *Property and the Human Rights Act 1998* (Hart, 2005) p. 230.
[10] *Paulic v. Croatia* (App no 3572/06), 22 October 2009, at [33].
[11] Lord Scott's approach in the relevant litigation is considered in D. Cowan, 'Territory and human rights: Mandatory possession proceedings', in D. Cowan and D. Wincott (eds.), *Exploring the Legal in Socio-Legal Studies*, Palgrave, 2016.
[12] [2011] 2 WLR 287, [33], citing *Leeds CC v. Price* [2006] AC 465 in which the interposing occupiers had been on the land for two days.
[13] [2004] 1 AC 983.
[14] See, for example, para. [60], Lord Hope, 'It is to be noted that the respondent does not contend that there has been an interference with his right to respect for his private and family life or his correspondence. The argument is directed entirely to his right to respect for his home.' The mechanism was the rule in *Hammersmith LBC* v. *Monk* [1992] 1 AC 478, which was subsequently found by the ECtHR not to provide the requisite procedural protection to the remaining occupier/s in *McCann v. UK* (2008) 47 EHRR 40.

The question for the House of Lords was, in essence, whether Mr Qazi's Article 8 rights overrode Harrow's right to possession. The House of Lords, by a majority, said that they did not. The process of reasoning which informed the majority judgments prized property rights above all else. This comes across most clearly in the opinion of Lord Scott, who begins his discussion of this issue with the observation that 'The intention of these instruments was to enshrine fundamental rights and freedoms. It was not the intention to engage in social engineering in the housing field.'[15] He went on:

> If, on the other hand, the tenant has no right to remain in possession as against the landlord he cannot claim such right under article 8. To hold otherwise, to hold that article 8 can vest property rights in the tenant and diminish the landlord's contractual and property rights, would be to attribute to article 8 an effect that it was never intended to have. Article 8 was intended to deal with the arbitrary intrusion by state or public authorities into a citizen's home life. It was not intended to operate as an amendment or improvement of whatever social housing legislation the signatory state had chosen to enact. There is nothing in Strasbourg case law to suggest the contrary.[16]

And further:

> If Mr Qazi has no contractual or proprietary right under the ordinary law to resist the council's claim for possession, and it is accepted he has not, the acceptance by the court of a defence based on article 8 would give him a possessory right over [the property] that he would not otherwise have. It would deprive the council of its right under the ordinary law to immediate possession. It would constitute an amendment of the domestic social housing legislation. It would give article 8 an effect it was never intended to have and which it has never been given by the Strasbourg tribunals responsible for implementing the Convention.[17]

In the course of an outspoken, forthright attack on the decision of the majority, Lord Steyn noted that 'The basic fallacy in the approach is that it allows domestic notions of title, legal and equitable rights, and interests, to colour the interpretation of article 8(1). The decision of today does not fit into the new landscape created by the Human Rights Act 1998.'[18] This analysis was both prescient and, in retrospect, spot on. The approach taken by the majority in *Qazi* was soon superseded by an attempt to mediate, perhaps pragmatically, between the approach taken by the ECtHR and public law principles. The key point, however, is that the property rights thesis was forced to give way to a more Europeanized version through which the interposer could challenge the decisions of the public authority.

---

[15] At [123].
[16] At [125].
[17] At [151].
[18] At [27].

THE GATEWAYS

It soon became clear that *Qazi* v. *Harrow LBC*[19] was by no means the last word on the matter as the House of Lords had hoped. A succession of cases sought to engage Article 8 rights in a rather more sophisticated way, arguing that the basis for the decision to claim possession and the means by which possession could be obtained in English law was impeachable by reference to Article 8. In *Kay* v. *Lambeth LBC*,[20] the House of Lords returned to the issue in the context of occupiers having no more than a personal right of occupation. *Kay* is the successor to *Bruton*, considered in Chapter 4. London and Quadrant, after the adverse judgment in that matter, surrendered its interest in the property to Lambeth, a surrender which effectively undercut Mr Bruton's successful claim rendering him and the other residents no more than unauthorized occupiers of the property. In defence to the council's claim for possession, Mr Kay, another occupier, raised his Article 8 right. Before the House of Lords, *Kay* was joined with *Leeds CC* v. *Price*, a claim for possession against travellers who were the unauthorized occupiers of a site for two days by the time of the council's claim. Again, they raised an Article 8 defence to the claim and both were unsuccessful but the decision was again on a knife-edge (4–3).

In what has come to be seen as the ratio of the decision, Lord Hope identified two gateways which occupiers would have to open in order successfully to challenge the council's decision. The first, gateway (a), could be opened if the occupier was able to show that there was a seriously arguable case that the law enabling the court to make the possession order was incompatible with Article 8. If so, the county court judge hearing the possession claim had two options – either to read the provision in accordance with Article 8 (in so far as it was able to do so) or remit the matter to the High Court for a determination of the compatibility issue. The scope of gateway (a) was always regarded as narrow out of deference to Parliamentary intention and the 'margin of appreciation' given by the ECtHR to member states. As Lord Bingham, in the minority in *Kay* but summarizing also the opinion of all members of the House of Lords, put it, 'Our housing legislation strikes a balance between the competing claims to which scarcity gives rise, taking account, no doubt imperfectly but as well as may be, of the human, social and economic considerations involved. And it is, of course, to housing authorities such as the respondents that Parliament has entrusted the power of managing and allocating the local authority housing stock and the pitches on local authority gipsy sites.'[21]

The second gateway, gateway (b), simply re-envisioned the common law principles that an occupier can raise, by way of defence to a claim for possession

---

[19] [2004] 1 AC 983.
[20] [2006] 2 AC 465.
[21] *Kay*, at [33]; see also Lord Hope at [108], Lord Scott at [169], and Baroness Hale at [190], and see also *Blecic* v. *Croatia* (2004) 41 EHRR 185.

matters, of public law '... to challenge the decision of a public authority to recover possession as an improper exercise of its powers at common law on the ground that it was a decision that no reasonable person would consider justifiable'.[22] Again, the threshold was that such a defence must be 'seriously arguable'.

The acceptance that the interposer could raise such a defence led to further refinement by the House of Lords in *Birmingham CC v. Doherty*.[23] This case again involved the local authority seeking possession against travellers. The travellers occupied two local authority pitches under licences, which Birmingham determined by the service of notice terminating the licences. Birmingham wanted to redevelop the site so that it could be used for 'genuine' travellers as temporary accommodation. The Doherty extended family had occupied the site for 17 years. There was no allegation of misconduct against them and no allegation of breach of the licence agreement. The basis of the claim for possession was, simply, the council's right to determine the proper use of the site. The House of Lords held against the council in the sense that they remitted the matter back to the county court for consideration of the matter in light of the statement of principle by the House so that the county court was forced to re-visit the gateway (b) defence (indeed, *Doherty* is one of the few successful gateway (b) defences).[24]

Lord Hope gave the leading judgment, in which he said:

> I think that in this situation it would be unduly formalistic to confine the review strictly to traditional Wednesbury grounds. The considerations that can be brought into account in this case are wider. An examination of the question whether the respondent's decision was reasonable, having regard to the aim which it was pursuing and to the length of time that the appellant and his family have resided on the site, would be appropriate. But the requisite scrutiny would not involve the judge substituting his own opinion for that of the local authority. In my opinion the test of reasonableness should be, as I said in para 110 of Kay, whether the decision to recover possession was one which no reasonable person would consider justifiable. The further point to which Lord Brown referred will have a part to play in that assessment.[25]

Lord Brown had referred in *Kay* to the possibility that a *Wednesbury* unreasonableness argument could have been mounted successfully in *Connors v. UK* (which concerned a gypsy family which was served a notice to quit on the basis of unsubstantiated allegations of nuisance and which did not have an opportunity to rebut those allegations):

> ... having regard to the great length of time (most of the preceding 16 years) that that gipsy family had resided on the site, it was unreasonable, indeed grossly unfair, for the local authority to claim possession merely on the basis of a determined

[22] At [110], Lord Hope, referring to *Wandsworth LBC v. Winder* [1985] AC 461.
[23] [2009] 1 AC 367.
[24] Along with *McGlynn v. Welwyn Hatfield DC* [2009] EWCA Civ 285 and *Croydon LBC v. Barber* [2010] HLR 26.
[25] At [55].

licence without the need to make good any underlying reason for taking such precipitate action.[26]

Lord Hope's approach in *Doherty* was taken as 'narrow[ing] (without closing) the gap between HRA grounds and traditional judicial review grounds'.[27]

This dramatic set of developments in *Kay* and *Doherty* was entirely due to the incoming tide of judgments post-*Qazi* from the ECtHR, which indicated that the property rights thesis of *Qazi* was questionable (even though an application to the ECtHR in *Qazi* itself was deemed inadmissible). In a series of judgments, beginning with *Connors* v. *UK*,[28] the ECtHR clearly expressed a radically different interpretation of Article 8 from the House of Lords in *Qazi*. This interpretation appropriated to Article 8 both substantive and procedural protection, '... namely the requirement to establish proper justification for the serious interference with his rights and consequently cannot be regarded as justified by a "pressing social need" or proportionate to the legitimate aim being pursued'.[29] *Connors* gave rise to a substantial body of case law developed by the ECtHR under which standard paragraphs would be repeated again and again, as if to emphasize the lack of uniformity of UK law with Article 8:

> The loss of one's home is a most extreme form of interference with the right to respect for the home. Any person at risk of an interference of this magnitude should in principle be able to have the proportionality of the measure determined by an independent tribunal in the light of the relevant principles under Art.8 of the Convention, notwithstanding that, under domestic law, his right of occupation has come to an end.[30]

The ECtHR was clearly identifying the requirement for procedural protection in court proceedings for possession of the interposer's 'home'. That procedural protection was the requirement on the judge to consider the proportionality of the eviction. *Connors* preceded *Kay*, and the House of Lords in *Kay* believed that it had achieved a sufficient balance between the gateways and Article 8, as interpreted in *Connors*, to enable English law to be compatible with the approach taken by the ECtHR. In this context, Lord Brown's comment about the length of residence as a factor going to the gateway (b) challenge was significant.

In *McCann* v. *UK*,[31] though, the ECtHR seemed to indicate that the gateways were insufficient (Mr McCann had sought judicial review of the council's decision to proceed with the eviction but had not been given leave to make the claim by the High Court). *McCann* was a direct challenge to the rule in *Hammersmith and Fulham LBC* v. *Monk* that one joint tenant can determine the entire tenancy, including the other joint tenant/s interest, by serving a notice to quit on the

---

[26] At [210].
[27] At [116], Lord Walker.
[28] (2004) 40 EHRR 189.
[29] See *Connors* at [95].
[30] *McCann* v. *UK*, at [50].
[31] (2008) 47 EHRR 40.

landlord. Mrs McCann, who had been allegedly the subject of domestic violence, had served that notice at the request of the council. The ECtHR noted that:

> Had the local authority sought to evict the applicant in accordance with this statutory scheme, it would have been open to the applicant to ask the court to examine, for example, whether his wife had really left the family home because of domestic violence and whether in his personal circumstances, including his need to provide accommodation for his children during overnight visits several times a week, it was reasonable to grant the possession order.[32]

The point was that Mr McCann had never had the opportunity to dispute his wife's allegations and, indeed, never had the opportunity to have the court consider the proportionality of his eviction.[33] The court also noted that 'Judicial review procedure is not well-adapted for the resolution of sensitive factual questions which are better left to the County Court responsible for ordering possession.'[34]

The ECtHR judgment in *McCann* was given after the hearing of the argument in *Doherty* but before judgment. The House of Lords were faced, therefore, with a judgment which was a direct challenge even to the jurisdiction opened up in *Kay*. Worse, the ECtHR in *McCann* appeared to justify the reasoning of the minority in *Kay*, arguing that there would be no 'serious consequences' for the system of seeking possession as it would only be in 'very exceptional cases that an applicant would succeed in raising an arguable case which would require a court to examine the issue'.[35] The House of Lords in *Doherty* proceeded to seek to dismantle the reasoning in *McCann*, directly questioning its authority, practicality and legitimacy, with Lord Scott in particular deprecating the position adopted by the ECtHR in that case.[36] In more measured terms, Lord Hope expressed the view that the 'highly exceptional' test '... suffers from a fundamental defect which renders it almost useless in the domestic context. It lacks any firm objective criterion by which a judgment can be made as to which cases will achieve this standard and which will not'.[37]

Why did the House of Lords in *Doherty* stick to the *Kay* gateways, albeit slightly refined? Cowan et al. have identified two core propositions underpinning the approach taken, which explain the rigid adherence to the gateways at that time:

> The gateway metaphor is powerfully deployed in these cases to suggest a way in to challenge judicial decisions, but it is firmly slammed shut in most cases either as a matter of law or, just as significantly (because such case management is usually silenced, conducted underground in mysterious proceedings, often conducted by telephone, extremely rarely subject to appeal because based on absolute discretion

---

[32] *McCann* v. *UK*, at [51].
[33] At [53].
[34] At [53].
[35] At [54].
[36] At [82]–[87], describing the reasoning as 'quite astonishing' and arguing that any domestic judge would be bound to take the proportionality of the decision into account (at [86] and [87] respectively), a position which in itself seemed counter-intuitive if possession is mandatory.
[37] At [20].

of the District Judge, and thus rarely the subject of academic engagement), procedurally. Those internal logics appear to be two, interrelated objectives:

First, and most significantly, there is protection of the integrity of the process. Time and again in the cases, we are told that most gateway (b) claims can, and should, be disposed of summarily, presumably as part of the list. Even Lord Bingham, who was in the minority in *Kay*, was clear that this was '... an important aspect of these appeals, and one that has caused the House much concern' but was a concern which could be assuaged by the high standard (which all Counsel who appeared accepted) to be applied.[38] In *Stokes v Brent LBC*,[39] protection of the integrity of the possession process, and particularly distinguishing it from public law claims, created a procedural distinction which appears hard to justify. Protecting the process must be managed against the contrary proposition of allowing occupiers to give full vent to their challenges as a result of the procedural and legal checks at this stage.

Second, it follows from that first point certainly as an outcome but, we suggest, also as part of the internal logic of public law itself, that considerable latitude is to be given to social housing providers in their possession claims. Part of the rationality behind that principle is deference to the nature of mandatory possession proceedings, as developed by the courts and appears in statutory provisions. However, it is also, at least, implicit in the higher standard required (as indeed it is in the permission stage for judicial review). This suggests an empirical conclusion, which may not be warranted, that social housing providers make rational, lawful decisions which comply with their policies and procedures. Curtailing the defences of occupiers only makes sense when this internal logic of the process is applied.[40]

So, the tension was as much over the practical effect of accepting the ECtHR's adherence to requiring the proportionality of the eviction to be decided as on the basic doctrine.

The House of Lords' position in *Doherty* became untenable after further decisions of the ECtHR.[41] Those decisions reiterated and restated *Connors* so that, as one blog entry put it:

In Pulp Fiction, John Travolta's character explains to Samuel L Jackson's that it is the 'little differences' in Europe that make it interesting – they do things differently there. Because France has the metric system, the burger joint calls a 'quarter pounder' burger a 'Royale with cheese'. *Zehentner v Austria*, a judgement of the First Section of the European Court of Human Rights, demonstrates yet again that the ECHR has a different approach to mandatory rights to possession than the House of Lords has expressed in the trilogy of cases (*Buckley, Connors, McCann* and *Cosic* against *Qazi, Kay, Doherty*). It surely cannot be much longer before the

---

[38] At [27] and [39] esp. point (4).
[39] [2009] EWHC 1426 (QB); and [2010] EWCA Civ 626.
[40] D. Cowan, C. Hunter and H. Pawson, 'Jurisdiction and Scale: Mandatory Possession Proceedings, Social Housing, and Human Rights' *(2012) 39(2) Journal of Law and Society 269*, 280–81.
[41] See *Ćosić* v. *Croatia* (App no 28261/06); *Zehentner* v. *Austria* (App no 20082/02); *Paulić* v. *Croatia* (App no 3572/06); *Kryvitska and Kryvitskyy* v. *Ukraine* (App no 30856/03).

Supreme Court is required to revisit this issue. Should the Supreme Court now be dealing with Royales with (or without) cheese or remain wedded to their quarter pounders?[42]

Mr Kay's case, when before the ECtHR, fell for the same reasons as all the others, the court noting that his case had failed before the House of Lords because '… it was not possible at that time to challenge the decision of a local authority to seek a possession order on the basis of the alleged disproportionality of that decision in light of personal circumstances'.[43]

'ONE RING TO RULE THEM ALL …'[44]

In the canon of property law, there are some crucial cases which require digesting but none more crucial than *Manchester City Council* v. *Pinnock* and its successor *Hounslow LBC* v. *Powell*.[45] In these cases, the Supreme Court introduced and refined (to a certain extent) the proportionality defence to mandatory possession proceedings. The defence must be raised by the interposer and it must be 'seriously arguable'.[46] While recognizing that the court is not bound to follow every decision of the ECtHR, the Supreme Court in *Pinnock* said:

> Where … there is a clear and constant line of decisions whose effect is not inconsistent with some fundamental substantive or procedural aspect of our law, and whose reasoning does not appear to overlook or misunderstand some argument or point or principle, we consider that it would be wrong for this court not to follow the line.[47]

That point had now been reached in the ECtHR jurisprudence on Article 8 and possession. Thus the Supreme Court adopted the minority reasoning in *Kay* that:

> … where a court is asked to make an order for possession of a person's home at the suit of a local authority the court must have the power to assess the proportionality of making the order, and, in making that assessment, to resolve any relevant dispute of fact.[48]

Difficult questions remain,[49] but the property law thesis in *Qazi* v. *Harrow LBC*[50] has been re-balanced without being comprehensively defeated. In essence, the

---

[42] http://nearlylegal.co.uk/blog/2009/10/14-pounder-or-royale-with-cheese-zehentner-v-austria/

[43] *Kay* v. *United Kingdom* (37341.06) [2011] HLR 2, [74].

[44] As *Pinnock* was introduced: http://nearlylegal.co.uk/blog/2010/11/brave-new-world-or-same-old-story/

[45] Respectively: [2010] 3 WLR 1441; [2011] 2 WLR 287.

[46] See, for example, *Powell*, at [33], Lord Hope; note Lord Phillips' observation in *Powell*, at [92], as regards the introductory tenancy regime, that it would only be in 'very highly exceptional cases' that such a challenge could be mounted.

[47] *Pinnock*, at [48].

[48] *Pinnock*, at [49].

[49] See D. Cowan and C. Hunter, '"Yeah but, no but": *Pinnock* and *Powell* in the Supreme Court', (2012) 75(1) *MLR 78*.

[50] [2004] 1 AC 983.

question for the court in any claim to possession brought that is (at least) based on absolute right – a mandatory claim – is to consider the proportionality of the claim, but only if that question is raised by the occupier/s. The re-balancing of the property law thesis was, pragmatically, to regard it as not just one factor to be taken into consideration but a highly significant element of the balance implied by the proportionality jurisdiction in combination with the broader public law obligations of the landlord:

> Where a person has no right in domestic law to remain in occupation of his home, the proportionality of making an order for possession at the suit of the local authority will be supported not merely by the fact that it would serve to vindicate the authority's ownership rights. It will also, at least normally, be supported by the fact that it would enable the authority to comply with its duties in relation to the distribution and management of its housing stock, including, for example, the fair allocation of its housing, the redevelopment of the site, the refurbishing of sub-standard accommodation, the need to move people who are in accommodation that now exceeds their needs, and the need to move vulnerable people into sheltered or warden-assisted housing. Furthermore, in many cases (such as this appeal) other cogent reasons, such as the need to remove a source of nuisance to neighbours, may support the proportionality of dispossessing the occupiers.[51]

Further:

> Unencumbered property rights, even where they are enjoyed by a public body such as a local authority, are of real weight when it comes to proportionality. So, too, is the right – indeed the obligation – of a local authority to decide who should occupy its residential property.[52]

It must now be accepted that an absolute right to possession is, simply, insufficient on its own to meet the proportionality jurisdiction successfully; it is that right in combination with the other rights and obligations of the 'social' landlord which does the job.

The developing jurisprudence

In *Pinnock*, the Supreme Court, rather whimsically, said that they were happy to leave the parameters of proportionality to the good sense and experience of the county court judge.[53] Certain factors clearly require balancing, including any specific use which the landlord wishes for the property,[54] the personal circumstances and vulnerability of the interposer,[55] and the statutory basis under which the interposer occupies, or has occupied, the property.[56] The balancing is to be

---

[51] *Pinnock*, at [52]; see also *Powell*, at [37], Lord Hope, and [88], Lord Phillips.
[52] *Pinnock*, at [54].
[53] *Pinnock*, at [57].
[54] *Pinnock*, at [53], although such use must be expressly claimed and proved.
[55] See, in particular, *Pinnock*, at [64].
[56] This was particularly emphasized in both *Pinnock* and *Powell* because, where that regime provides substantive and/or procedural protections, such as a right for the interposer to request that the claimant reviews their decision, it may require greater scrutiny.

weighed on the basis of the facts as they emerge at the date of the hearing,[57] if indeed there is a hearing. Just because Article 8 exists does not mean that a court hearing is required in all cases.[58]

In *Pinnock*, the Supreme Court considered whether it was only an exceptional case which crossed the threshold for the proportionality defence. The Court said that exceptionality 'was an outcome and not a guide'.[59] That made sense because you don't really know an exceptional case until you see it. The key question is as to the balance. Nevertheless, as noted above, the Supreme Court added that unencumbered property rights are of real weight. In *Powell*, Lord Phillips seemed to raise the bar higher when he drew attention to the ECtHR in *McCann* accepting that it would only be 'in very exceptional cases that an applicant would succeed in raising an arguable case which would require the court to examine the issue and that in the great majority of cases it would be possible for possession orders to continue to be made in summary proceedings'.[60]

In *Corby BC v. Scott*, Lord Neuberger MR tried to make sense of this apparent difference of opinion, when he said (a little tortuously), 'it will only be in "very highly exceptional cases" that it will be appropriate for the court to consider a proportionality argument', although 'exceptionality is an outcome and not a guide'.[61] Further, exceptionality is 'a useful cross-check' but should not distract a judge from the question of relevance (that is, proportionality).[62]

However, exceptionality seems to have taken root in the jurisprudence – when Etherton LJ sought to set out principles for the jurisdiction, he said, '[I]t is nevertheless clear that the threshold for establishing an arguable case that a local authority is acting disproportionately and so in breach of Article 8 where re-possession would otherwise be lawful is a high one and will be met in only a small proportion of cases .... The circumstances will have to be exceptional to substantiate an Article 8 defence ....'[63] He went on to make clear, in line with the Supreme Court decision in *Powell*, that 'the reasons why the threshold is so high lie in the public policy and public benefit inherent in the functions of the housing authority in dealing with its housing stock, a precious and limited public resource. Local authorities, like other social landlords, hold their housing stock for the benefit of the whole community and they are best equipped, certainly better

---

[57] *Southend-on-Sea BC v. Armour* [2014] EWCA Civ 231; [2014] HLR 23.

[58] Most tenancies do require an eviction through due process of law, i.e. a court hearing, but some do not: see ss 3 & 3A, Protection from Eviction Act 1977. In those latter, limited cases, a court hearing may not be required provided there are procedural safeguards in place through which the proportionality of the eviction can be considered: *R(ZH and CN) v. Newham LBC* [2014] UKSC 62, [67]–[74]; 'There is no need for an additional procedural hurdle which would impose costs on an authority without any significant benefit to the applicant', [68], Lord Hodge.

[59] [51].

[60] [94].

[61] [2012] EWCA Civ 276, [18].

[62] [27].

[63] *Thurrock BC v. West* [2012] EWCA Civ 1435; [2013] HLR 5, [24]

equipped than the courts, to make management decisions about the way such stock should be administered.'[64]

It is hardly surprising then that, other than in *Powell*, there has only been one successful proportionality defence.[65] In itself, this case was very much at the margins and could have gone one way or the other – the crucial thing was that the county court judge found in favour of the occupier and, as a result, a higher court was only at liberty to overturn the decision if that decision was one which was 'not open to her'.[66] In essence, good behaviour for over a year meant that the council's mandatory claim to possession was overcome. But that was a specific case with a specific tenancy (an 'introductory tenancy', designed as a probationary period for a year).[67]

In other cases, the principal difficulty has been showing that the relevant factors prayed in the interloper's aid are related to that specific home. A murderous attack on an occupier, for example, was irrelevant as it did not render it particularly harmful to the occupier to be evicted (that is, it was not relevant to the occupier's occupation of that particular home).[68] The same is true of the future housing prospects of an occupier or that the occupier has maintained the obligation to pay rent.[69]

In *Birmingham CC* v. *Lloyd*,[70] the Court of Appeal considered the question of the applicability of Article 8 in relation to a possession claim against a trespasser. The Court was not impressed. Lord Neuberger MR said that, '... *such a person seeking to raise an Article 8 argument would face a very uphill task indeed*, and, *while exceptionality is rarely a helpful test, it seems to me that it would [...] require the most extraordinarily exceptional circumstances*'.[71] Subsequently, it has been said that references to degrees of exceptionality may unnecessarily complicate matters but that, in a trespasser case, the problem is really one of remedy – if the trespasser is successful, then the court would have to usurp the (public) landowner's role and grant some form of occupation right, which is constitutionally problematic let alone problematic in land law.[72] Nevertheless, the question of trespassers' rights does not go away. As Ward LJ put it, perhaps most elegiacally:

> The idea that an Englishman's home is his castle is firmly embedded in English folklore and it finds its counterpart in the common law of the realm which provides a remedy to enable the owner of the castle to secure the eviction of trespassers from it. But what if the invaders occupy for long enough to establish their home within the keep? Whose castle is it now? Whose home must the law now protect?[73]

---

[64] [25].
[65] *Southend-on-Sea BC* v. *Armour* [2014] EWCA Civ 231; [2014] HLR 23.
[66] [20].
[67] Housing Act 1996, Part 5.
[68] *Scott*, [24].
[69] Although payment of rent '...might provide a little support for a proportionality argument, based on other, much stronger points', *Scott*, [25].
[70] [2012] EWCA Civ 969; [2012] HLR 44.
[71] [18].
[72] *West*, [24].
[73] *Malik* v. *Fassenfelt & Ors* [2013] EWCA Civ 798, [1].

> **AUTOBIOGRAPHICAL NOTE**
>
> These are amazing times to be a land lawyer! The precepts of 'property' are being challenged (not just by academics) but through the implementation of human rights law. What had seemed such a given is now being challenged day in day out. My barrister friends (and I) are searching for *that* case; the one which really tests the boundaries of exceptionality, and, in that sense, we are all still playing it a little 'by ear'. However, as the cases in the senior courts have developed, it does appear that the search for *that* case is becoming a bit like threading through the eye of a needle, i.e. so small that it is difficult to achieve. Tactically, it is a poor decision in many cases simply to seek to persuade a judge that your Article 8 proportionality defence is seriously arguable; if that is all you have, you are unlikely to be success-ful. That may be a reason why cases like *Ackerman-Livingstone* (see Chapter 9 for discussion) come about as defences raise new issues which bite away at the manda-tory nature of possession proceedings.

The reach of human rights

For land lawyers, the key concern must be the reach of this new jurisdiction. It clearly affects all landlords that are exercising 'functions of a public nature' as opposed to 'where the nature of the act is private'.[74] The Court of Appeal has said, broadly, that the management of housing, including eviction, is a function of a public nature,[75] but this does not quite answer the more general question as to whether the identity of the landlord matters and, indeed, whether the jurisdiction extends beyond that to others, such as lenders and receivers exercising rights to possession and/or sale.[76]

Traditionally, one applies a factor-based approach to this question as exempli-fied by the House of Lords decision in *YL* v. *Birmingham City Council*.[77] Under that type of approach, factors such as the regulatory regime, the nature of the contract between the parties, the nature of the provider (whether, for example, they are a commercial organization or not) and direct receipt of public funding are all relevant to the decision. On that basis, it would be unlikely that this jurisdiction would extend beyond social housing landlords. However, it is to be noted that

---

[74] s. 6(3)(b) and (5) respectively.

[75] *Weaver* v. *London and Quadrant HT* [2009] HLR 40; see also *Eastland Homes Partnerships Ltd* v. *Whyte* [2010] EWHC 695 (QB) and *R(McIntyre)* v. *Gentoo Group Ltd* [2010] EWHC 5 (Admin).

[76] See *Ropaigealach* v. *Barclays Bank* [2000] QB 263 and *Horsham Properties* v. *Clark & Beech* [2008] EWHC 2327 (Ch); even where the provisions of the Mortgage Repossessions (Protection of Tenants etc.) Act 2010 give limited protection to the unauthorized tenant. *Horsham* proceeded on A1P1, discussed below, and so the Article 8 argument (which was said to fail if the argument on A1P1 failed) was not put to the court, but, at [49], Briggs J relied on *Qazi* in relation to the Article 8 argument, a reliance which can no longer hold good.

[77] [2008] 1 AC 95.

the question whether the 1998 Act caught a private landlord housing a homeless household was expressly left open in *YL* itself.[78]

Nevertheless, although the factor-based approach is now established as the test, its applicability in the range of cases in which proportionality would otherwise become relevant remains uncertain. The Supreme Court in *Pinnock* explicitly left this open, noting that there were arguments both ways.[79] The question is whether the 1998 Act has horizontal as well as vertical application, so as to be applicable between purely private parties; the answer hinges in part on the role of the court as a core public authority, which cannot act in a way which is incompatible with Convention rights.[80] Although the Supreme Court referred to *Belchikova v. Russia* (App No 2408/06, 25 March 2010) as an example of where, possibly, the ECtHR had considered a matter between two private parties in relation to the Article 8 right, the better decision on this (arguably) is *Zehentner v. Austria (App No 20082/02, 16 July 2009)* in which the ECtHR intervened in a forced judicial sale between two private parties (an occupier and her plumber and other creditors) over a small debt.[81] It was the act of the forced judicial sale, like the act of ordering possession against an assured shorthold tenant, which was significant.[82]

Less clear, however, are cases of possession without the interference of judicial process. In the *Horsham Properties* case (receiver selling property over the heads of the mortgagors), the 1998 Act was deployed without thought. A factor of potential significance in relation to mortgage lenders is the extent of public funding/ownership of the bank or building society – it may matter, for example, at least as a relevant factor, if your mortgage came from (say) the publicly owned part of Northern Rock as opposed to a lender without any public ownership or funding. On the flip side of that coin, though, is the fact that these institutions remain public companies, or mutuals, seeking and obtaining commercial rates of return by virtue of contracts. The owner/mortgagee also has their own right to their possessions, including property,[83] which balances against the Article 8 rights of the occupier.[84]

In *McDonald v. McDonald*, the Supreme Court will probably have to face this issue head on. Fiona McDonald occupied a property that was bought by her parents with the aid of a mortgage. They bought it for her because she suffers from a 'mental disorder which makes her particularly upset by changes in her environment'.[85] Her parents granted her an assured shorthold tenancy but without

---

[78] At [85], Lord Mance. Local authorities can use the private rented sector to discharge their obligations to homeless households (s. 193(5) & (7AA)) given the satisfaction of certain conditions; the Localism Act 2011 contains provisions to extend this right in certain circumstances.

[79] At [50].

[80] s. 6(3)(a).

[81] [2009] ECHR 1119.

[82] See also *Ghaidan v. Godin-Mendoza* [2004] 3 WLR 113, where the 1998 Act was deployed between two private parties.

[83] See below.

[84] A point also made by the Supreme Court in *Pinnock*, at [50].

[85] [2014] EWCA Civ 1049, [1]

the consent of the mortgage lender. The mortgage lender appointed a receiver who was seeking to determine the assured shorthold tenancy through a mandatory claim to possession. She defended the claim in part on the basis of Article 8. The Court of Appeal held that there was no 'clear and constant' jurisprudence of the ECtHR through which a private landlord was found to be bound to apply between private landlord and tenant. In fact, the ECtHR jurisprudence reflects '… an important principle, namely the principle that parties who have exercised their contractual freedom to agree terms should not be allowed to invoke Convention rights to relieve themselves of the terms of the bargain'.[86] Further, precisely because we are dealing with a private landlord, even if proportionality was relevant:

> … the balance is almost always going to be struck in the landlord's favour because the landlord is enforcing his property right to return of the property. Moreover, he may well have suffered loss (most obviously, arrears of rent) which he may not be able to recover if the tenant has few means and continues in possession. The position of the landlord may be even stronger if there are third parties who are directly concerned in the protection of the landlord's rights and who are liable to be prejudiced by the refusal to make a possession order, such as mortgagees of the property or other creditors of the landlord. The position of those third parties is no less relevant to the balancing exercise than the position of homeless persons who are interested in the enforcement by social landlords of their rights to recovery of their housing stock from tenants to whom they no longer owe any housing duty.[87]

In these circumstances, the question of the horizontal effect of Article 8 will have to be faced.

Debate 2

To what extent does A1P1 interfere with established principles?

PEACEFUL ENJOYMENT OF POSSESSIONS

Article 1 to the First Protocol (A1P1) to the European Convention contains the following rights:

> Article 1
>
> Every natural or legal person is entitled to the peaceful enjoyment of his possessions. No one shall be deprived of his possessions except in the public interest and subject to the conditions provided for by law and by the general principles of international law.
>
> The preceding provisions shall not, however, in any way impair the right of a State to enforce such laws as it deems necessary to control the use of property in accordance with the general interest or to secure the payment of taxes or other contributions or penalties.

---

86 [37].
87 [50].

Properly, this provision contains three rights, the first being general; the second sentence of the first paragraph and the second paragraph are particular instances of interference with the right to peaceful enjoyment of property; and the latter two are therefore construed in light of the general principle in the first sentence of the first paragraph.[88] There are two particular legal issues which are considered in this section in relation to this provision: adverse possession and shared ownership. They are both of some difficulty, although one has been resolved (adverse possession) and the other remains an open question (shared ownership). Before that discussion takes place, we provide a broad summary of the basic principles in this Article.

SUMMARY

A number of points can be made about this Article, both generally and specifically in this context:

a. The definition of 'possessions' is broad and includes rights flowing from the identification of an item as property (such as the right of alienation), assets and other claims, such as those based on a legitimate expectation.[89]

b. The ECtHR usually proceeds by examining whether there has been a breach of the second or third rights before considering the general right.[90]

c. As regards 'deprivation', the ECtHR appears to look at the substance of the matter – so, for example, a successful claim of adverse possession was not a 'deprivation' of ownership rights but regulated questions of title; rather, that system involved a 'control of use' and fell within the second paragraph.[91]

d. An interference with the peaceful enjoyment of possessions,

> ... must strike a 'fair balance' between the demands of the general interest of the community and the requirements of the protection of the individual's fundamental rights. ... in particular, there must be a reasonable relationship of proportionality between the means employed and the aim sought to be realised by any measure depriving a person of his possessions.
>
> In determining whether this requirement is met, the Court recognises that the State enjoys a wide margin of appreciation with regard both to choosing the means of enforcement and to ascertaining whether the consequences of enforcement are justified in the general interest for the purpose of achieving the object of the law in question.
>
> ...
>
> 94. Compensation terms under the relevant legislation are material to the assessment whether the contested measure respects the requisite fair balance and, notably, whether it imposes a disproportionate burden on the

---

[88] *Pye* v. *UK* (2008) 46 EHRR 1083, at [52]; *Sporrong & Lonnroth* v. *Sweden* (1982) Series A No 52, at [61].

[89] *Marckx* v. *Belgium* (1979) Series A No 31, at [63]; *Pye* v. *UK* (2008) 46 EHRR 1083, at [61].

[90] *Ibid.*.

[91] *Pye*, at [66].

applicants. In this connection, the Court has already found that the taking of property without payment of an amount reasonably related to its value will normally constitute a disproportionate interference and a total lack of compensation can be considered justifiable under Article 1 of Protocol No. 1 only in exceptional circumstances.[92]

e. A failure to offer compensation is not necessarily determinative that the rights have been breached.[93]

f. The 'margin of appreciation' is particularly wide in the context of the 'public interest' and in housing, when aimed at 'securing greater social justice in the sphere of people's homes, even where such legislation interferes with existing contractual relations between private parties and confers no direct benefit on the State or community at large'; indeed, the width of the margin is such that the ECtHR will respect the state's position on the public interest 'unless that judgment be manifestly without reasonable foundation'.[94]

g. Finally, it is significant to note that the ECtHR arrogates jurisdiction to itself even if the primary dispute is between two private parties, but where the proper application of the law engages the rights.[95]

ADVERSE POSSESSION

In Chapter 6, we considered the law on adverse possession. The question for the ECtHR in *Pye* v. *UK* was as to the compatibility of that law operating prior to the Land Registration Act 2002 with A1P1. Having accepted as 'inescapable' that Pye's loss of their beneficial interest in land was a possession for the purposes of A1P1, the question turned on whether the loss of that interest was disproportionate bearing in mind the failure to compensate them for that loss. In turn, this depended on whether the specific right engaged was the deprivation of user or the loss of control (the second sentence and the second paragraph, respectively). It was held that the Limitation Act 1980 was part of the regulation of property rights, which controlled the use of land, and was not intended to deprive Pye of their ownership.[96] That distinction was important because, as opposed to deprivation of use, where the matter is considered to be one of loss of control, compensation is not a relevant criterion to weigh in the balance:

> The Court would note, in agreement with the Government, that a requirement
> of compensation for the situation brought about by a party failing to observe a

---

[92] *Jahn* v. *Germany* [2004] ECHR 36 at [93]–[94], 'Recapitulation of the relevant principles'; see also *James* v. *UK* (1986) Series A No 98, esp. at [54], noting that compensation does not, however, guarantee a right to 'full' compensation.

[93] *Jahn* itself (context of reunification of Germany).

[94] *James*, at [46]–[47].

[95] See, in particular, the discussion in *Pye*, at [75].

[96] At [66]. For similar reasoning, see *Horsham*, n.76 above, the reasoning for which is unconvincing at best.

limitation period would sit uneasily alongside the very concept of limitation periods, whose aim is to further legal certainty by preventing a party from pursuing an action after a certain date.[97]

The question, then, was whether the law on adverse possession provided a 'fair balance' between the public interest and the individual's interests. They held that it did so. Their reasoning was, first, that the UK had a wide margin of appreciation; the limitation of action rules were 'logical and pragmatic'; the companies knew or ought to have known about the legislation; during the limitation period, they had procedural protection (after all, they could have brought a claim for possession based on the Grahams' occupation qua trespasser); although the financial loss to Pye was considerable and the benefit to the Grahams correspondingly considerable, this fell within the margin of appreciation; and that limitation periods must apply regardless of the amount of the loss/gain: 'The value of the land cannot therefore be of any consequence to the outcome of the present case.'[98]

In a sustained critique of the ECtHR's decision, Fox O'Mahony and Cobb argue that the court drew on '... a variety of jurisprudential techniques to reposition the doctrine of adverse possession within a less morally contentious framework than that found within UK political discourse ...'.[99] Their argument was that fault and hardship to the squatter was found by the court to be irrelevant; rather the court regarded Pye's failure to act as blameworthy so that their hardship was a necessary and not unreasonable consequence. The Court, on their analysis 'de-moralised' the issue, so that adverse possession was '... a mere bureaucratic tool and, as such, downplayed its redistributive implications'.[100] One might say, then, that the court actually reinforced the notion of possession as central to property law and that the 'de-moralization' was, in fact, the property lawyer's traditional analysis.[101]

SHARED OWNERSHIP

The position in respect of shared ownership is rather more difficult – for discussion about the models of shared ownership, readers are referred to Chapter 4. Absent Article 8, the question is whether a rigid insistence by the provider on a mandatory ground for possession, or (indeed) a discretionary ground, which gives rise to a court order for possession within a certain period, is incompatible with A1P1.[102]

Such a question might have arisen in *Midland Heart* v. *Richardson*,[103] but was not developed in that case. Its facts are nevertheless instructive. Ms Richardson

---

[97] At [79].

[98] At [84].

[99] L. Fox O'Mahony and N. Cobb, 'Taxonomies of Squatting: Unlawful Occupation in a New Legal Order' (2008) 71 *MLR* 878, 903.

[100] At 902.

[101] See R. Kerridge and A. Brierley, 'Adverse Possession, Human Rights and Land Registration: And They All Lived Happily Ever after?' (2007) *Conv* 552; and, subsequently, *Ofulue* v. *Bossert* [2009] Ch 1.

[102] See D. Cowan, 'A Ticking Time Bomb' (2011) 161 (7467) *NLJ* 729.

[103] Birmingham Civil Justice Centre (ChD), 12 November 2007.

bought a 50 per cent stake in the property on a conventional SO basis – long lease – without a mortgage. She paid £29,500. In 2003, her ex-partner was imprisoned and Ms Richardson was forced to leave the property having received threats. She moved in to a women's refuge. Rent arrears built up. By the time of the possession claim, there were about 16 months' rent arrears (approx. £1941), which increased to around £3000 at the date of the hearing. Ms Richardson tried unsuccessfully to sell the property (which had been vandalized in her absence). By that time, the property was worth approximately £151,000. In 2005, Midland Heart sought possession on the basis of a mandatory ground for possession based on rent arrears (Ground 8).

The arguments deployed for Ms Richardson to defeat the claim relied principally on property law devices – it was argued that there were two tenancies crafted out of the single formal long lease, an assured tenancy and a long lease; and that there was a trust of the freehold – but these devices were properly rejected by HHJ Gaunt QC in the Birmingham County Court.

Bright and Hopkins, in their discussion of this case, found alternative property law arguments, based on resulting and constructive trusts or proprietary estoppels, to be similarly wanting on the facts of this case at least.[104] The outcome, though, was that Ms Richardson lost not just her £29,500 but also her share of the increase in value of the property – she lost everything (although it is reported that Midland Heart offered an ex gratia payment of £29,500, less the rent arrears and costs of repair[105]). As HHJ Gaunt QC put it:

> That all said, I have found this case troubling. Miss Richardson has had a rough ride in life and has now lost what is probably her only capital asset. Moreover, she lost it in proceedings brought at a time when, to the knowledge of the housing association, she was actively seeking to sell the house to pay off her debts and the housing association was itself involved in that process. I must say that I find the stance taken by the housing association strange in the circumstances and I have not received any adequate explanation. There may, of course, be many facts and matters in the background that I know not of and so I do not intend to be unduly critical. I simply comment on the timing.[106]

The interference with the shared owner's possessions through the claimant's successful claim is not at issue under A1P1; what is at issue is whether that interference is disproportionate to the owner's financial stake in the property. It is the equivalent of forfeiture *without* relief (and the ECtHR has shown itself willing to interfere where a state's act stops short of expropriation[107]), but the framing of the issue is only about the expropriation of the buyer's financial stake and probably not about their interest in the property.

---

[104] S. Bright and N. Hopkins, 'Richardson v Midland Heart Ltd: Low Cost Home Ownership – Legal Issues of the Shared Ownership Lease' [2009] *Conveyancer and Property Lawyer* 337.

[105] At [24]; See http://nearlylegal.co.uk/blog/2008/09/shared-ownership-midland-heart-with-benefit-of-transcript/

[106] At [23].

[107] *Sporrong*, n.88.

That having been said, though, it is the combination of the failure of the state to regulate this point beyond the Housing Act 1988, combined with the lack of compensation to the buyer, which frames this issue within the terms of A1P1. There is perhaps here an issue around compatibility, which may well be resolved by a proportionality hearing, but, even so, if the possession claim results in the loss of possessions without compensation for no justifiable reason, then A1P1 must be at issue. It seems indisputable that, as opposed to the way in which the ECtHR considered the limitation rules in *Pye*, we are dealing with a deprivation of possessions in these cases. In any event, whether this argument is framed as deprivation or loss of control, the appropriate balance and justification needs to be made. While that is axiomatic in the 'normal' tenancy relationship, it is less clear in shared ownership cases where this form of forfeiture, in effect, operates.[108] Ms Richardson's case is instructive in this regard – she lost £29,500 (or £75,500, if you account for the uplift in the property market) because of rent arrears of around £3000. The rent arrears, on the facts of the case, arose because of the refusal of the housing benefit authority to pay both for her place in the refuge and for the shared ownership rent for more than 52 weeks. It was clear, on any reading of the case that she could not and would not return to the SO property because of her fears for her personal safety (and no doubt was cast on their genuineness).

In summary, then, shared ownership cases represent a potentially fruitful ground for the further consideration of A1P1.

Hammersmith and Fulham LBC v. Monk

We have already noted above that, in *McCann* v. *UK*, the ECtHR required a consideration of the proportionality of an eviction under Article 8 where one joint tenant had determined a tenancy by service of a notice to quit – i.e. the rule in *Monk*.

In *Dacorum BC* v. *Sims*,[109] it was argued that the rule in *Monk* required reconsideration in part because it interfered with the remaining joint tenant's possessions under A1P1. However, there was an express clause in the tenancy agreement, which was signed by Mr and Mrs Sims, to the effect that it would be lost if a notice to quit was served by one of the joint tenants. So, the rule in *Monk* was written in to the tenancy agreement itself. This was not a propitious starting point for the remaining joint tenant's argument because 'the loss of [Mr Sims's] property right is the result of a bargain that he himself made'.[110]

The Supreme Court went on to say that the clause itself (and, one might suppose, the rule as well) was not an unreasonable provision: 'If the result is not as decided in Monk, either the tenant who served the notice is forced to remain a tenant against her will, or the landlord is landed with one tenant instead of two,

---

[108] Although, see *James* v. *UK* (1986) Series A No 98, and the admissibility decision in *DiPalma* v. *UK* (1988) 10 EHRR 149.
[109] [2014] UKSC 63.
[110] [15].

which means less security - and, in a case such as the present, a family property occupied by a single person. Just as a joint tenant in Mr Sims's position can claim that the outcome determined as correct in Monk is harsh, so could a joint tenant in Mrs Sims's position or a landlord in Dacorum's position contend that either of the alternative outcomes is harsh.'[111]

This reflects an inherent weakness in the position of those arguing a human rights-based claim – the remedy. If successful, the remedy may fundamentally affect the balance between the parties. Mrs Sims wanted to leave the property and her obligations under the tenancy agreement; but, if Mr Sims had been successful, she would not have been able to do so and Dacorum would have to put up with the situation. The rule in *Monk* has been a particularly powerful device for land-lords where there is some form of domestic violence between the joint tenants. It can evict the perpetrator and provide new accommodation to the survivor free of the obligations of the joint tenancy.

CONCLUSIONS

This chapter demonstrates that certain cherished principles of property law require re-balancing in light of the direct implementation of the principles of the European Convention in UK law. It can no longer be said that unencumbered property rights, on their own, are sufficient to maintain a claim when the inter-poser occupies property as their home and raises a defence based on Article 8. The precise parameters of this new jurisdiction as yet are unclear and it may well be that purely private entities, such as private landlords and private tenants, mort-gage lenders and receivers, will be caught up in this new jurisdiction. Similarly, although A1P1 may well provide the basis for an assumption that property law is consonant with that Article, given the wide margin of appreciation the bounda-ries of that particular jurisdiction remain to be fully appreciated.

Further Reading

D. Cowan and C. Hunter, '"Yeah but, no but": *Pinnock* and *Powell* in the Supreme Court' (2012) 75(1) *MLR* 78.

R. Kerridge and A. Brierley, 'Adverse Possession, Human Rights and Land Registration: And They All Lived Happily Ever after?' [2007] *Conv* 552.

A. Latham, 'Talking without Speaking, Hearing without Listening? Evictions, the Law Lords and the European Court of Human Rights' [2011] *Public Law* 730.

I. Loveland, 'A Tale of Two Trespassers: Reconsidering the Impact of the Human rights Act on Rights of Residence in Rented Housing' [2009] *European Human rights Law Review* 148 (pt 1), 495 (pt 2).

---

[111] [17].

9

LAW, EQUALITY AND HOUSING

INTRODUCTION

In the previous chapter we explored the often complex interaction between the principles of the European Convention on Human Rights, the Human Rights Act 1998 and land law. Here, we build on this discussion by considering the relationship between property interests – especially access to housing – and 'equalities law', or the specific statutory protections against unlawful discrimination found in the Equalities Act 2010, which together form a further aspect of the UK's human rights framework.[1]

The 2010 Equality Act (hereinafter the 'EA') consolidated and expanded the various complex and fragmented Acts of Parliament, statutory instruments and case law produced since the 1960s as part of the institutional response to the problem of unfair discrimination and inequality in British society, in spheres including race, disability and sexual orientation. One of the most long-standing equalities law protections now found in the EA is the prohibition of unlawful discrimination in relation to housing access, although discrimination in the housing field has been relatively overlooked in legal scholarship compared, for example, to fields like employment.[2] Housing is generally accepted as a basic and universal human need, and so it is unsurprising that discrimination and inequality in the sale, rental or management of residential premises has been typically seen as fundamental to the socio-economic exclusions bound up with the characteristics protected by the EA. This chapter considers the role played by the protections against unlawful discrimination in the EA in responding to the problem of unequal access to housing.

---

[1] For recent Supreme Court analysis of the interaction between Article 8 of the European Convention and the Equality Act 2010 in relation to possession proceedings brought against a disabled tenant, see *Akerman-Livingstone* v. *Aster Communities Ltd* [2015] UKSC 15, discussed further below. Note also that the European Convention on Human Rights (ECHR) and Human Rights Act 1998 require equal treatment in the protection of the other Articles of the Convention under Article 14, which has had some influence on the approach to equality and housing in the UK: see e.g. *Ghaidan* v. *Godin-Mendoza* [2004] 2 AC 557. See also the discussion of Article 14 in Equality and Human Rights Commission, *Human Rights at Home: Guidance for Social Housing Providers* (EHRC, 2011).

[2] See, though, the following law-focused studies on race and housing: D. MacKay, *Housing and Race in Industrial Society: Civil Rights and Urban Policy in Britain and the United States* (Croom Helm, 1977); M. MacEwan, *Housing, Race and Law: The British Experience* (Routledge, 1991).

We acknowledge that some may perceive our discussion of the impact of equalities law on land and housing as stepping beyond the bounds of 'land law' as it is generally understood; of all the issues raised in this volume, it is perhaps the one most distant from the usual terrain of an undergraduate land law module or textbook. Indeed, to appreciate the significance of equalities law to housing access one must necessarily look beyond the typical concern of land law teaching with basic rights in land itself, to reflect on the broader role played by social policy legislation in addressing the structural barriers that make it more difficult for some marginalized communities to gain access to those basic rights. Including equalities law in this book is an attempt – in light of the typically narrow construction of land law as an academic discipline – to draw out the often underestimated significance of discrimination in land and housing, both to the history of equalities law, and to continuing debates over its legitimate role and scope. In this respect, and like our discussion of the implementation of the European Convention, the interaction between equalities law and the domains of land and housing lies at the heart of the conflict between the basic right of an owner to deal with property as they wish, and the importance of that land to the citizenship of others.

At present, the EA extends the principle of non-discrimination across the fields of work, education, service provision, public functions and premises. Part 4 prohibits:

> direct and indirect discrimination,[3] harassment and victimization,[4] in the disposal, withholding of permission to dispose, and management[5] of premises, on grounds of race, sex, sexual orientation, gender identity, disability, and religion and belief (although not all these characteristics are equally protected).[6]

Disposal includes sale, rental (whether the landlord is a private individual or organization, a local authority or a housing association) and the granting of any other right to occupy premises.[7] In relation to disability, the EA also prohibits 'disability-related' discrimination in the disposal, withholding of permission to dispose and management of premises, and requires landlords and property managers to make certain reasonable adjustments in relation to premises to avoid a disabled person being placed at a substantial disadvantage in the use of those premises.[8] Not all forms of accommodation fall within Part 4 of the EA. Short-stay,

---

[3] EA 2010, ss. 13 and 19.
[4] EA 2010, ss. 26 and 27.
[5] The concept of premises is left undefined by the EA. However, previous legislation has explicitly defined 'premises' to include 'land' more generally: see Race Relations Act 1976, s. 78(2). On the basis of this old definition the meaning of premises is likely to be interpreted to include both buildings and other types of land.
[6] Though note that these protections have not been afforded consistently across all the protected characteristics. One example is the lack of protection from harassment on grounds of sexual orientation and religion and belief in the fields of service provision or premises: EA 2010, ss. 29(8), 33(6), 34(4) and 35(4).
[7] EA 2010, s. 28(3) and (4).
[8] EA 2010, s. 20 and sch. 4.

non-residential arrangements, such as occupation of hotel rooms or B&B accommodation for travellers and holidaymakers, are classified instead as falling within Part 3, relating to services and public functions,[9] as is provision of accommodation for the purpose only of exercising a public function or providing a service.[10]

It would be a task beyond the scope of this chapter to comprehensively explore the often complex implications of discrimination and inequality in housing provision – and the role played by equalities law in response – across the full range of characteristics protected by the EA. Instead, the chapter considers four of the most critical contemporary debates that have arisen over the legitimate role of equalities law in tackling inequality and discrimination in the housing field.

For Debate 1, we return to an aspect of long-standing housing discrimination that formed the primary justification for the first equalities laws introduced to Britain – race discrimination laws targeting discrimination against new ethnic minority immigrants in the 1960s – by asking whether modern equalities law has successfully eradicated racial inequality in housing. In Debate 2 we consider if equalities law should be extended to prohibit discrimination in the 'private' sphere of the home, in light of exemptions to the EA that allow discrimination in such circumstances, while Debate 3 relates to unresolved questions about the legitimate scope of disability discrimination duties on social landlords in relation to the provision of rented housing. Debate 4 then considers what future role might be played in the housing field by the range of additional legal mechanisms found in the EA which move beyond the proscription on unlawful discrimination and encourage a more strategic, holistic approach to addressing structural disadvantages in the housing market – in particular, through the regulatory interventions of the Equality and Human Rights Commission (EHRC), the public sector Equality Duty, and the legal concept of 'positive action'.

Debate 1

Has equalities law successfully addressed racial inequality in housing?

The first equalities law in the UK was a response to the deeply divisive politics of immigration, race and housing in Britain that emerged after the Second World War.[11] When economic migrants, encouraged by the government, began to arrive in the 1950s from the 'New Commonwealth', especially the Caribbean, to alleviate the chronic post-war shortage of labour at that time, they were met in many instances by hostility, discrimination and even violence at the hands of the indigenous white population. Race, racism and race relations were prominent political

---

[9] EA 2010, s. 32(3)(a).

[10] EA 2010, s. 32(3)(b).

[11] P. Goulbourne, *Race Relations in Britain since 1945* (Macmillan, 1998); P. Sarre, D. Phillips and R. Skellington, *Ethnic Minority Housing: Explanations and Policies* (Avebury, 1989). Race is used here as it is in the Equality Act, which defines it to include race, ethnicity and nationality.

issues for successive governments, leading to state-led efforts to integrate the new arrivals, while strengthening immigration controls to placate the indigenous population. The use of legal measures to control discriminatory conduct was first mooted following the race riots that erupted in Notting Hill and Nottingham in 1958,[12] although it would take until 1965 before Parliament enacted the first Race Relations Act, which outlawed direct race discrimination in prescribed public accommodations, such as hotels, restaurants and public transport. However, the 1965 Act was generally perceived even at the time as a 'token venture',[13] not least because it did nothing to address the endemic problem of race discrimination in the provision of housing.[14]

Calls for further protections in the housing field continued to grow, especially following the publication of several empirical studies which offered ample evidence of the inequality and discrimination faced by ethnic minorities in the housing market.[15] This research showed that immigrants typically lived in the oldest and poorest quality private rented or owner-occupier housing, in the most deprived parts of the inner cities; few were housed by local authorities, and when they were it was often in pre-war stock rather than new-build council housing. While poverty and other factors contributed to the poor housing outcomes of immigrants within the private sector it was clear that discrimination also shaped racial inequalities. Unequal treatment on grounds of race was deliberate and overt across the sector. Landlords openly discriminated, with 'No Coloureds' or 'Whites Only' often added to advertisements for properties, estate agents enabled their clients' prejudices when vetting prospective tenants, racial stereotypes informed the financial assessments of mortgage providers, and property developers imposed colour bars on the assumption that white households would only buy homes in all-white estates.[16] In respect of council housing, often the primary difficulty faced by newly arrived immigrants was the inability to meet the length of residency requirements imposed by many council allocation policies,[17] illustrating that racial inequality in housing could be exacerbated as much by the disadvantages arising from the application of ostensibly neutral rules, as by racial prejudice, bias or stereotyping.

In 1968, a new Race Relations Act finally outlawed direct discrimination (or less favourable treatment of a person on grounds of their race) in the disposal and management of premises, whether publicly or privately owned, following recommendations of the Race Relations Board[18] and the independent Street Report.[19]

---

[12] P. Sooben, *The Origins of the Race Relations Acts* (Warwick Research Papers Series, 1991).

[13] H. Street, G. Howe and G. Bindman, *Anti-Discrimination Legislation* (PEP, 1967), 63.

[14] B. A. Hepple, 'Race Relations Act 1965' (1966) 29(2) *MLR* 306.

[15] E. Burney, *Housing on Trial: A Study of Immigrants and Local Government* (Cambridge University Press, 1967); J. Rex and R. Moore, *Race, Community and Conflict: A Study of Sparkbrook* (Oxford University Press, 1967); W. Daniel, *Racial Discrimination in England* (Penguin, 1968).

[16] Daniel, n.15.

[17] Rex and Moore, n.15.

[18] M. Bonham Carter, *Report of the Race Relations Board for 1966–67* (RRB, 1967).

[19] Street, Howe and Bindman, n.13.

However, although the Act successfully addressed the most blatant forms of race discrimination in the private sector,[20] the law still lacked teeth. In particular, it would take another eight years before the Race Relations Act of 1976 extended protection for the first time against indirect forms of discrimination, or those facially neutral rules which disproportionately affected ethnic minorities, and granted individuals the power to bring claims under the Act before the courts themselves, liberating them from the bureaucratic conciliatory mechanisms of the Race Relations Board. The 1976 Act also established the Commission for Racial Equality (CRE), which was designed to take a more strategic approach to race discrimination and inequality.

Over the course of the 1980s and 1990s the CRE carried out a series of formal investigations into housing providers and ancillary services such as estate agents, some involving specific, named organizations and others more general in scope. These investigations indicated that while some progress was being made towards race equality in housing, the 1976 Act had not, in and of itself, eliminated discrimination by providers. For example, one early named investigation by the CRE of Hackney Borough Council in 1984 revealed that black applicants were consistently allocated housing of inferior quality to white applicants, due in part to stereotyping by housing officers in their appraisals during home visits.[21] The CRE's further, non-named investigation into discrimination in the private rented sector in 1990 concluded that one in five accommodation agencies discriminated on grounds of race in the letting of residential properties through subtle processes such as racial steering.[22]

By the end of century, new evidence emerged of rapidly improving housing outcomes for certain ethnic minority communities, while at the same time, 'in all tenures ethnic minority groups remain[ed] in a worse situation than whites in relation to housing quality, over-crowding, concentration in disadvantaged areas and levels of segregation'.[23] One cause for this differentiation seems to have been a growing divide in socio-economic position between distinct minority groups. Recent research has found that upward mobility of more long-standing minority groups has enabled their entry in significant numbers into suburban homeownership in the past two decades. However, other, often more recent immigrant communities remain disproportionately poorer than white households, and so have found themselves concentrated, as before, in either the depleted housing

20 N. McIntosh and S. Smith, *The Extent of Racial Discrimination* (PEP, 1974).
21 Commission for Racial Equality, *Race and Council Housing in Hackney* (CRE, 1984); see further M. Bryan, 'Discrimination in the Public Provision of Housing: The CRE Report on Housing in Hackney' [1984] *Public Law* 194. See also the now classic academic study on housing officer discretion: J. Henderson and V. Karn, *Race, Class and State Housing: Inequality and the Allocation of Public Housing in Britain* (Gower, 1987).
22 Commission for Racial Equality, *Sorry, It's Gone: Testing for Racial Discrimination in the Private Rented Sector* (CRE, 1990).
23 V. Karn and D. Phillips, 'Race and Ethnicity in Housing: A Diversity of Experience' in P. Bhikhu, P. Sanders and T. Blackstone, *Race Relations in Britain: A Developing Agenda* (Routledge, 1998).

stock of an increasingly residualized social sector or, more often than not, poor quality private sector accommodation in the inner cities.[24]

It is less clear to what extent unlawful racial discrimination by housing providers continues to contribute to the poorer housing outcomes of ethnic minority households. One reason for this is that since the 1990s there has been a dearth of new empirical research specifically focused on the existence of discriminatory practices in the housing market, including investigations or inquiries by the CRE, and its successor the Equality and Human Rights Commission (EHRC). This makes it difficult to evaluate the extent of discriminatory practices in the sector today.[25] While social landlords are more aware than ever of the need to address inequality in housing provision, the complexity of 'institutional racism' means that direct and indirect discrimination are likely still to persist.[26] On this basis, it seems somewhat premature to conclude, as at least one set of researchers has in recent years, that as '[t]here is no recent research providing evidence of discriminatory practices [in the social sector] it is fair to assume that these practices have been eliminated'.[27] However, it is perhaps more reasonable to assume that today racial prejudice and stereotyping are more likely to result in unlawful race discrimination by private landlords rather than social landlords. Indeed, the growing imbalance between supply and demand for private rented housing in urban areas like London may be creating new opportunities for private landlords, sellers and agents to discriminate against minority ethnic groups.[28]

The potential for unlawful race-based discrimination in the private rented sector also seems set to increase as a consequence of the recent controversial Home Office policy known as the 'Right to Rent Scheme', currently being piloted in the West Midlands. Introduced by provisions in the UK Immigration Act 2014,[29] the Scheme, in the words of the government, 'imposes a prohibition on renting premises to adults who do not have a right to stay here for use as their only or main home [in order] to deter illegal immigration and prevent illegal immigrants from accessing our finite housing stock and displacing lawful residents'.[30] The civil penalty for non-compliance is set currently at £3000. The scheme is intended to ensure landlords of private rented housing carry out checks on the immigration status of all prospective tenants to establish a person's 'right to rent' before entering into a tenancy agreement. Only comprehensible in the context of broader

---

[24] C. Hamnett and T. Butler, 'The Changing Ethnic Structure of Housing Tenures in London, 1991–2001' (2010) 47(1) *Urban Studies* 55.

[25] See the specific criticisms levelled at the lack of research in Karn and Phillips, n.23, 130–31.

[26] D. Phillips, 'The Rhetoric of Anti-Racism in Public Housing Allocation' in P. Jackson (ed.), *Race and Racism: Essays in Social Geography* (Routledge, 1987), 213.

[27] D. Manley and M. van Ham, 'Choice-Based Letting, Ethnicity and Segregation in England' (2011) 48(8) *Urban Studies* 3125, 3129.

[28] Karn and Phillips, n.23, 144.

[29] Immigration Act 2014, ss.22–31.

[30] Home Office, *Code of Practice for Landlords: Avoiding unlawful discrimination when conducting 'right to rent' checks in the private rented residential sector* (October 2014), available at https://www.gov.uk/government/uploads/system/uploads/attachment_data/file/376789/Code_of_Practice_for_Landlords__web_.pdf, last accessed 15 September 2015.

political and media concerns with the social impact of immigration, the Right to Rent Scheme has been criticized by housing and immigration organizations as a 'Charter for Discrimination' because it creates a new incentive for landlords to discriminate on racial or ethnic grounds against those they suspect may be immigrants in order to avoid the possibility of penalties under the legislation. Indeed, these concerns led the Home Office to issue a specific Code of Practice on the Scheme for landlords in October 2014 setting out their obligations to avoid race-based discrimination under the EA. Preliminary assessments of the West Midlands pilot suggest it has not been as successful as hoped, with high levels of non-compliance with the policy, but only seven penalties for non-compliance issued against private landlords. More importantly, a separate investigation into the pilot, in which a 'mystery shopping' exercise was carried out by undercover investigators, found non-Britons were refused tenancies on 11 out of 27 occasions, indicating that initial fears that the policy will exacerbate race discrimination may be well-founded.[31]

And yet the government seems intent on strengthening still further legal deterrents against landlords renting premises to those disqualified from renting by their immigration status under the Rent to Right Scheme in the Immigration Act 2014. The latest Immigration Bill, introduced to the Commons in September 2015, if passed, will expand the Right to Rent Scheme by creating a new criminal offence in England where a private landlord or agent rents residential premises in circumstances where they know or have reasonable cause to believe that the premises are occupied by an adult disqualified as a result of their immigration status from occupying the premises under the terms of Right to Rent Scheme.[32] The proposed maximum sentence on indictment for the new criminal offence will be five years' imprisonment. The bill also makes provision for summary eviction from premises where occupiers are disqualified from occupation due to their immigration status. At the time of writing, the Labour opposition continues to raise concerns about the impact of the new criminal offence as the bill progresses through Parliament, drawing particular attention to the potential for an increase in discrimination against ethnic minorities as landlords seek to avoid the impact of the law. Most recently, Shadow Home Secretary Andy Burnham has argued that the new offences risk a return to 'everyday racism' by landlords, reminiscent of the discrimination faced by early immigrants in the 1960s.[33]

Whether equalities law is capable of preventing an increase in race discrimination as a result of these new immigration rules is debatable. The inevitable problem with effective enforcement of equalities law is that it is often difficult to

---

[31] D. Gayle, 'Pilot scheme forcing landlords to check tenants' immigration status "has failed"', *The Guardian*, 6 August 2015 available at http://www.theguardian.com/uk-news/2015/aug/06/pilot-scheme-forcing-landlords-check-tenants-immigration-status-failed, last accessed 15 September 2015.

[32] Note, though, that the government also seeks to retain the power to extend the new offences and eviction procedures by regulation to Wales, Northern Ireland and Scotland: s. 15.

[33] J. Merrick, 'Right to Rent scheme risks discriminating against immigrants, warns Andy Burnham' *Independent on Sunday*, 10 October 2015.

prove that a specific refusal of tenancy is the result of unlawful discrimination,[34] and so the possible discriminatory impact of the Right to Rent Scheme is likely to go unchallenged in most instances when the Scheme is implemented in full. More broadly, it is disheartening to think that long-standing efforts by successive governments to address the problem of unlawful race discrimination in the housing field may be set back as a result of increasingly punitive state policies on immigration.

Debate 2

Should equalities law still permit discrimination where it takes place in relation to the 'private' sphere of the home?

At present, the general proscriptions against unlawful discrimination on protected grounds in the disposal and management of premises under the EA are subject to two important but little known statutory exemptions. The first might be termed the "small premises exemption", which permits a person to discriminate against someone who shares any protected characteristic except for race, where this relates to the disposal, management or occupation of premises in which the person also lives, and which can house a maximum of two other households, or a maximum of six other individual occupants.[35] The second is the 'private disposal exemption'. This permits discrimination in the disposal of premises by an owner who occupies the premises as a home, on grounds of sexual orientation, or religion and belief, and in relation to permission to dispose of the premises,[36] so long as the disposal is carried out in private. 'Private' means that the owner does not use the services of an estate agent or publish an advertisement regarding the disposal.[37] Versions of both the exemptions also extend to the duty to make 'reasonable adjustments' for disabled people in relation to premises.[38] The small premises and private disposal exemptions have been included in UK equalities law since the first protections from discrimination in housing under the Race Relations Act 1968,[39] and were modelled on exemptions found in US civil rights law of the time.[40] Importantly, however, since 2003 both exemptions have been abolished in relation to race discrimination to comply with the 2000 EU Race Directive,[41] but not in relation to other protected characteristics such as sexual orientation, an inconsistency in approach considered in more detail below.

---

[34] Cf. S. Halliday, 'Institutional Racism in Bureaucratic Decision-Making: A Case Study in the Administration of Homelessness Law' (2000) 27(3), *Journal of Law and Society* 449.

[35] EA, sch. 5, para. 3.

[36] EA, sch. 4, para. 1(4).

[37] EA, sch. 5, para. 1(2).

[38] EA, sch. 4, paras 2 and 4.

[39] RRA 1968, s. 7.

[40] In fact, only the civil rights laws in Alaska and Minnesota included neither one of the exemptions: see Street, Howe and Bindman, n.13.

[41] Race Relations Act 1976 (Amendment) Regulations 2003/1626, regs 23(2)(b) and 24.

To better understand the basis for both exemptions, we must return once again to the origins of UK equalities law. In February 1965, the then Labour Home Secretary Sir Frank Soskice presented a memorandum to the Cabinet setting out his proposals for the first Race Relations Act. In it, he offered an important insight into early concerns over the possible impact of the legislation on personal and private freedoms:

> [D]iscrimination on grounds of race or colour should be penalised if it is practised in places to which the public have access – in particular in hotels, restaurants, public houses, places of entertainment or recreation and public transport vehicles. There is not much evidence of discrimination in such places now; but it is indefensible if it should occur and I think it is right to prohibit it. We cannot, I feel, go further and deal (for example) with the refusal of landladies to take coloured [sic] lodgers – which leads to a lot of complaint – without interfering unjustifiably with the rights of the individual.[42]

The paradigmatic 'live-in' landlady and her refusal to house ethnic minority lodgers personified the potentially problematic impact of anti-discrimination laws on private freedoms. The problem was implicitly constructed, in the words of the Street Report of 1967, as an issue of 'intimate personal proximity',[43] and the concern that a live-in landlady who offered rooms in her own home to lodgers would be forced to share her home with those towards whom she held deeply felt objections. It was also a scenario that seems to have formed the basis for the government's initial refusal to outlaw discrimination relating to premises until 1968, even after acknowledging that this form of discriminatory conduct had led to significantly more complaints in practice than discrimination in public accommodations, which were outlawed by the 1965 Act. In the end, as we have already seen, the government of the day was persuaded by the stark evidence of widespread race discrimination in the housing market to extend the scope of the Race Relations Acts to residential premises in 1968. However, while applying the law to housing, the government also introduced the first small premises exemption into the new legislation, to remove from the law's ambit the live-in landlady who refused to accommodate an ethnic minority lodger.[44]

The Race Relations Act of 1968 also introduced the first 'private disposal' exemption, which would reflect further concerns about the impact of the new law on private freedoms involved in prohibiting discrimination in the sale of owner-occupied homes to ethnic minority households.[45] In this regard, the Street Report notes two main criticisms levelled at the possibility that the principle of unlawful discrimination might extend to the sale of premises by owner-occupiers: on one hand 'that owner-occupiers fear ostracism by their

[42] Cabinet Office, *Memorandum from the Minister for Home Affairs: Racial Discrimination and Incitement to Racial Hatred*, C(65)23, 17 February 1965.
[43] Street, Howe and Bindman, n.13, 83.
[44] Ibid., 85.
[45] Cabinet Office, *Cabinet Conclusions*, CC(67)74, 21 December 1967, Minute 2.

neighbours who feel that house values will be lowered if coloured [sic] residents move into an area',[46] and second that 'the home is so fundamental an aspect of the citizen's financial and domestic arrangements that it should not be the subject of legal regulation'.[47]

In the end, the issue of the sale of owner-occupied premises vexed the Cabinet to such an extent that it was referred to the Parliamentary Home Affairs Committee in December 1967 for further consideration and recommendations.[48] In their report, the Home Affairs Committee recognized that sales by owner-occupiers were 'a highly sensitive area' noting in particular that 'public opinion might be affronted by complaints against white home-owners who were exercising a legitimate freedom to dispose of their own property and were not actuated by racial prejudice', but where the house owner had still chosen to sell in the end to a white rather than a black person. However, the Committee went on to conclude, by a clear majority, that sales by owner-occupiers should stay within the ambit of the legislation because of the impact permitting discrimination in this context would have on the effectiveness of the new law:

> From the point of view of the immigrant community housing is where discrimination hurts most. Nearly 50 per cent of houses in England and Wales are in the hands of owner-occupiers, and what we do here will be regarded as a touchstone of the Government's sincerity. The whole philosophy of the Bill and its educative effect would be greatly weakened if the owner-occupier were excluded.[49]

Given the Home Affairs Committee's outright rejection of the need for any exemption for home sales in the proposed legislation it is surprising, then, that when the new Race Relations Act 1968 was finally enacted the 'private disposal' exemption had found its way back into the statute. The form of the exemption was now, however, no longer a general exemption for sales of all owner-occupied homes but instead covered only those transactions taking place without the use of either advertising or estate agents. This narrow approach to the issue suggests a compromise was struck – at the eleventh hour – between the perceived need to protect the freedom to discriminate in the disposal of private property, and the need to ensure immigrant communities gained meaningful access to owner-occupation. The compromise position, in the end, was to allow race discrimination in the sale of housing while pushing these discriminatory sales behind closed doors, outside the visible mainstream marketplace, where one might assume it was thought discrimination would have less direct negative impact on race relations.

In summary, both the small premises and private disposal exemptions were included by the government in the Race Relations Act 1968 on the ground that the prohibition of race discrimination in relation to housing, as the Street

---

[46] Street, Howe and Bindman, n.13, 85.
[47] Ibid., 86.
[48] Cabinet Office, *Memorandum from the First Secretary of State. Race Relations Legislation.* C(68)12, 8 January 1968.
[49] Ibid., 1.

Report put it, 'should fall short of certain personal and private relationships'.[50] However, the Street Report also recognized that the line between what should count as 'public' or 'private' is inevitably blurred and that 'in the end the drawing of such a line will be governed by personal and political choice'.[51] In the case of the exemptions, the political choice made by the government was clear: the personal and private sphere in which discrimination should be seen as permissible was aligned more or less with the protected private domain of the home.

Of course, the small and private disposal exemptions were as much pragmatic as they were principled measures, designed to allay the broader antipathy of the public to the new legislation. To have rejected either exemption might arguably have jeopardized the Act as a whole at a time of significant anti-immigration sentiment and public hostility towards racial integration. However, it was a settlement that would have far-reaching consequences for the scope of equalities law over the next forty years. From 1968, the exemptions were incorporated automatically by drafters into each new raft of UK equalities legislation. Yet these exemptions remained contentious, as they seemed to demonstrate that the interest of the homeowner in treating another person less favourably on grounds of a protected characteristic was of greater importance than the interest of marginalized communities in securing equal access to housing provision.[52]

Indeed, in the first years of the twenty-first century both exemptions were revisited again in the course of the implementation of further anti-discrimination measures enacted by the European Union. In 2000, the Council of the EU issued a new Race Directive, which for the first time extended protections from discrimination on grounds of race under European law to include 'access to and supply of goods and services which are available to the public, including housing'.[53] One problem faced by the New Labour government in implementing the Race Directive, however, was that no exemption was recognized in the new law for race discrimination in relation to either small premises or private disposals. Initially, the government had suggested in consultation that while the private disposal exemption would have to be abandoned, a narrower small premises exemption would still meet the Directive's requirements.[54] In the end, however, it concluded

---

[50] Street, Howe and Bindman, n.13, 64.

[51] Ibid., 64.

[52] For criticism of the small premises exemption in the US context, see J. Walsh, 'Reaching Mrs. Murphy: A Call for Repeal of the Mrs. Murphy Exemption to the Fair Housing Act' (1999) 34 *Harv CR-CL L Rev* 605. We consider further recent criticisms of the small premises exemption as it applies to disability, when we evaluate the protections afforded to disabled people by the Equality Act in more detail, below.

[53] Council Directive 2000/43/EC of 29 June 2000, implementing the principle of equal treatment between persons irrespective of racial or ethnic origin.

[54] Department of Trade and Industry, *Towards Equality and Diversity – Implementing the Employment and Race Directives* (DTI, 2003), 31; Department of Trade and Industry, *Equality and Diversity: The Way Ahead* (DTI, 2003), 43 (limiting small premises exemption to those premises where landlord shares facilities).

instead that it was in fact necessary to remove both exemptions altogether from the Race Relations Act to comply with the Directive.[55]

Today, the EA adopts the same approach to the two exemptions in relation to race discrimination but not for other protected characteristics such as sexual orientation, with the result that race, the characteristic which formed the basis for the earliest justifications for the exemptions, is now – ironically – the only protected characteristic excluded from both exemptions in modern equalities law. When the Joint Committee for Human Rights reviewed the Equality Bill in 2009, it concluded that the exemptions, as they are currently formulated, strike 'an appropriate balance between protecting the right to equality and the right to privacy and freedom of association'.[56] It gave no further justification for this view, nor did it grapple with the inconsistency that presently exists between race and other protected equality characteristics.[57] However, more recent debates over the scope of the principle of non-discrimination have raised new concerns about the legitimacy of the *status quo*.

For instance, during the passage of the EA the continued application of the small premises exemption to disability as a protected characteristic was criticized by the Disability Rights Taskforce, the government's consultative forum, on the basis that it struck an unfair balance between private freedoms of landlords and the needs of the disabled. This led to the incorporation of a power in the new legislation allowing the executive to amend or remove disability from the scope of the small premises exemption, although at the time of writing the government has not yet exercised it.[58]

In addition, it should be noted that in recent years the idea that the home constitutes a sphere legitimately protected from equalities law has been further challenged in relation to the problem of unlawful discrimination by Christian B&B owners against gay couples. Following proposals in 2007 to introduce the first protections against discrimination on grounds of sexual orientation in the provision of goods and services, a number of Christian B&B owners argued that

---

[55] Race Relations Act 1976 (Amendment) Regulations 2003/1626, regs 23(2)(b) and 24. Note that the government actually only removed the exemptions in relation to race, ethnic or national origins (which were grounds formally covered by the Directive) but not colour or nationality (which were further grounds under the RRA 1976 but were not covered by the Directive). The EA addressed the obvious irrationality of distinguishing between these different heads of discrimination by going on to outlaw the exemptions across the Act's extended umbrella concept of 'race'.

[56] Joint Committee on Human Rights, *Legislative Scrutiny: Equality Bill*, 26th Report of Session 2008–09 HL Paper 169 (HMSO, 2009).

[57] Perhaps once again change will be instigated by the EU, where proposals for a new Equal Treatment Directive are being debated: see European Commission, *Proposal for a Council Directive on Implementing the Principle of Equal Treatment between Persons Irrespective of Religion or Belief, Disability, Age or Sexual Orientation* (2 July 2008). If enacted, the directive will impose non-discrimination in the fields of goods, services and premises on grounds of sexual orientation, age, disability and religion and belief, and – like the Race Directive before it – may offer a future opportunity for the UK government to abolish the exemptions when transposing the law by regulation. However, governments are still stuck in negotiations over the directive after six years because of the resistance of a number of member states. See further, www.enar-eu.org/Joint-press-statement-EU-equal.

[58] EA, sch. 5, para. 5.

they should be protected from the new law on grounds of privacy because their B&Bs were also their homes (the small premises exemption did not apply as B&B owners are deemed by law to be service providers rather than disposers of premises). However, the government concluded instead that B&B owners should not be exempt from the legislation, asserting that when a B&B owner uses his or her home for business purposes, these purposes bring the property out from the otherwise protected private sphere of owner-occupation and into the public arena of commercial activity and profit-making.[59] The government took this view even though the arguments by B&B owners were the same in principle as those arguments accepted in relation to race and the small premises exemption in 1968.

The government's position was reaffirmed in a recent case challenging the application of equalities law in this area, *Preddy v. Hall*, in which the defendant B&B owners Mr and Mrs Bull argued that they should be able to refuse to allow gay couples to share double rooms on human rights grounds given their religious objection to homosexual relationships. In making this claim, the owners drew on the rhetoric of home and private property rights to defend their position using Article 8 of the European Convention, but the argument was rejected once again by both the Court of Appeal and Supreme Court.[60] This contemporary view of equalities law as protecting equal opportunity in the commercial market, while open to criticism for reducing the significance of non-commercial types of discrimination and inequalities,[61] raises questions about whether the value of 'private freedom' is still sufficient to vindicate the landlady or the private home seller when they discriminate for financial gain under the small premises or private disposal exemptions. Put another way, it casts further doubt on whether either of the exemptions has a place in modern equalities law.

AUTOBIOGRAPHICAL NOTE

Neil reflects on (safe) space and LGBT equality

The 'Pink Triangle' is home to Newcastle upon Tyne's gay scene. Like other scenes across the country, and the world, the Triangle developed away from the city centre proper, as a (relatively) safe space where gay men, lesbians, bisexual and transgender people could meet each other and socialize. Significantly and not uncontroversially, gay scenes are established on commercial terms, organized around bars, clubs and restaurants which serve a gay clientele.

As a gay man living in Newcastle I had a complicated relationship with the scene. Arriving for the first time in the city, and knowing practically no one, it was indispensable as a ready-made social hub which would not have been available

---

[59] Department of Communities and Local Government, *Getting Equal: Proposals to Outlaw Sexual Orientation Discrimination in the Provision of Goods and Services: Government Response to Consultation* (DCLG, 2007), 13.

[60] *Preddy v. Hall* [2013] UKSC 73.

[61] N. Cobb, '"Gay Couple's Break Like Fawlty Towers": Dangerous Representations of Lesbian and Gay Oppression in An Era of "Progressive" Law Reform' (2009) 18(3) *Social and Legal Studies* 333.

so straightforwardly to a straight person in the same predicament. However, I like others, am wary of the exclusions that operate invariably within a commercially orientated social space, in which income can dictate one's ability to participate.

Over my eight years in Newcastle I became aware of changes to the scene's demographics. As LGBT people have become more visible and accepted, the scene itself has become something of a tourist destination, with hen parties (particularly popular in Newcastle) descending on the Triangle in droves on Friday and Saturday nights.[62] The result is occasional gawping at best, and mockery or abuse at worst. My lesbian friends usually find things more difficult than me, as approaching a straight woman in the mistaken belief she is gay can lead sometimes to serious altercations.

I have a feeling that the increasing presence of straight people on the scene is partly to blame for its rapid contraction in recent years,[63] although responsibility must also go to the rise of the internet, punitive bar prices and the increasing acceptance of gay and lesbian people within Newcastle's mainstream night-time economy (transgender people still fare much less well).

One response to the problem of straight tourism has been to impose door policies barring straight people from entry (although I suspect that many gay establishments continue to encourage straight tourism for purely commercial ends). However, it was a surprise for many LGBT people to discover that the extension of equalities law to sexual orientation meant that it is now *prima facie* illegal discrimination on grounds of sexual orientation to operate LGBT-only venues.

Some flexibility remains: government guidance notes that 'a gay bar would still legitimately be able to turn away customers who they believed might be disruptive, or might wish to enter the bar to cause trouble.'[64] I have since wondered too whether it would be possible to justify LGBT-only door policies as positive action under the Equality Act, to support the need of LGBT people to have access to a safe space in which to express themselves without fear of judgement or ridicule.

Intuitively, though, I think it's probably right that it should not be possible to refuse entry to gay establishments simply on the ground that a person is (perceived to be) straight, not least because blanket rules of this kind lead inevitably to arbitrary door policies as bouncers are granted the authority to decide who is 'visibly' gay or not. But the wider debate from which this legal issue springs – the changing face of gay scenes like Newcastle's Pink Triangle and what it means to those who use them – highlights the complex relationship between (safe) space, commerce, equality and the power to exclude, at a time when LGBT people in Newcastle and elsewhere are emerging from the shadows of the ghetto.

---

[62] P. Hensher, 'Please Keep Out of Gay Bars and Clubs', *The Independent*, 25 June 2002.

[63] I. Herbert, 'Are Hen Nights to Blame for Hard Times in Manchester's Gay Village?' *The Independent*, 11 February 2006.

[64] B. Cohen, 'Government Tells Gay Bars to Let in Straights', http://www.pinknews.co.uk/2006/02/27/government-tells-gay-bars-to-let-in-straights/, 27 February 2006.

Debate **3**

What should be the scope of disability discrimination duties on landlords?

One further effect of the reforms introduced by the EA has been to consolidate and update the protections granted to disabled people by the Disability Discrimination Act 1995 (DDA) and amending legislation. The 'social model' of disability contends that the inequality experienced by disabled people is determined not by their condition but by the failure of society to accommodate the effects of that condition adequately.[65] For this reason, the EA – like the DDA before it – imposes more demanding duties to accommodate difference than the concept of 'indirect discrimination', which traditionally serves this purpose in relation to other characteristics. First, as well as direct and indirect discrimination, section 15 of the EA also prohibits 'disability-related' discrimination in relation to the disposal, permission to dispose or management of premises. This is defined as less favourable treatment of a disabled person where the other party 'knows or ought to know' of the disability, for a reason 'arising as a consequence' of the person's disability, unless it is a 'proportionate means to achieve a legitimate aim'.[66] Furthermore, under section 20, landlords (and property managers) are under a duty to make certain 'reasonable adjustments' when asked to do so by a disabled occupier if, without that adjustment being made, the occupier would be placed at a 'substantial disadvantage' in relation to the use of the premises when compared to a person without the relevant disability.

The protection from disability-related discrimination under section 15 of the EA has led to significant controversy and dispute in the housing field. In the years following the enactment of the original DDA, it became clear that the particular protection from disability-related discrimination granted by the DDA was creating important, and largely unforeseen, problems for social housing management.[67] The effects of disability can sometimes make it difficult, if not impossible, for a disabled person to adhere to the terms of a tenancy agreement. For example, a tenant may engage in conduct due to mental illness which negatively affects the quality of life of other residents, or the tenant might not be able to pay the rent because of physical or mental incapacity arising from disability. Landlords may wish to take steps to respond to that behaviour by evicting the tenant, or subjecting the tenant to other unwanted treatment, for example, by issuing an injunction or anti-social behaviour order. To do so may well also be in line with the landlord's published policies on tackling anti-social behaviour and its obligations to the tenant's neighbours, or required on the basis that the failure to pay rent poses a threat to the landlord's financial viability.

---

[65] M. Oliver, *Understanding Disability: From Theory to Practice* (Palgrave Macmillan, 1996).

[66] EA, s. 15.

[67] See, generally, N. Cobb, 'Patronising the Mentally Disordered? Social Landlords and the Control of "Anti-Social Behaviour" Under the Disability Discrimination Act 1995' (2006) 26(2) *Legal Studies* 238.

The difficulty faced by social housing managers, and the courts, was that the original concept of disability-related discrimination under the old DDA was significantly broader than the approach taken today by the EA, and was viewed by some as striking the balance too far in favour of the disabled person at the expense of the powers of social housing managers to tackle problem behaviour. The perceived issue with the old DDA was threefold. First, the old law was couched in terms that meant that *any* negative treatment, such as eviction, *relating to* a disability was *prima facie* illegal, even if a landlord would have evicted others without the disability for the same behaviour. This was because to establish less favourable treatment the old law required that the landlord's response to the disabled person should be compared with the response that would be given to someone who was not disabled, and did not behave in the same way.[68] The second problem was that disability-related discrimination had been found by the courts to be made out under the terms of the DDA even if the landlord did not know, and had no reasonable way of knowing, that the problematic behaviour was caused by a disability.[69]

In addition, once less favourable treatment was found under the DDA, it would only be justifiable if it fell within a narrow list of reasons for the treatment specified by the legislation: that the treatment was necessary in order not to endanger the health or safety of the disabled person or another; that the disabled person was incapable of entering into an enforceable agreement, or of giving informed consent; or, where the treatment related to the use of a benefit or facility, that the treatment was necessary in order for the disabled person or the occupiers of other premises in the building to make use of the benefit or facility.[70] If no such justification was established the landlord would be powerless to proceed with the less favourable treatment. The upshot was that, on the face of it, the DDA allowed social housing managers to evict mentally ill tenants who caused anti-social behaviour to neighbours only where this behaviour was significant enough to cause a threat to the 'health or safety' of others; and more importantly, the DDA seemed to offer no remedy at all to managers where a mentally or physically ill tenant was unable to pay rent as a result of their disability.

It was these concerns with the original DDA that led ultimately to the intervention of the House of Lords in the controversial decision in *Malcolm* v. *Lewisham London Borough Council*,[71] which overturned an earlier decision of the Court of Appeal that had held that the terms of the DDA prevented Lewisham Council from evicting Mr Malcolm, a mentally ill social tenant, in response to Mr Malcolm's decision to illegally sublet his flat, a decision it was accepted resulted in part from his disability.

---

[68] *Clark* v. *Novacold* [1999] IRLR 318.
[69] *Manchester City Council* v. *Romano and Sumari* [2005] 1 WLR 2775.
[70] DDA, s. 24(3).
[71] [2008] 1 AC 1399.

It is quite clear from the decision in *Malcolm* that the majority of the House of Lords were intent on recalibrating the protection from disability-related discrimination under the DDA to maximize the powers of social landlords to respond effectively to the types of problematic behaviour that might arise as a result of a tenant's disability. In doing so, however, the House effectively neutralized the protections granted by the concept of disability-related discrimination, reducing to almost vanishing point the protections under section 15. The House concluded that to establish less favourable treatment, the landlord's response to the disabled person's problematic behaviour must be compared with the response the landlord would have made to someone who was not disabled, but engaged in the same conduct (e.g. anti-social behaviour or non-payment of rent). The result of this reasoning was that punitive responses to behaviour arising from a disability would never be less favourable treatment if the landlord would have responded in the same way to the same behaviour if carried out by a non-disabled person. Thus, the majority concluded that to amount to discrimination, the claimant's disability must 'motivate' the actions of the landlord,[72] which by definition would also require the landlord to be fully aware of the existence of the disability when the negative treatment was carried out.

The decision in *Malcolm* illustrates the unresolved tensions behind the protection of the disabled from disability-related discrimination, in terms of the difficult balance that equalities law is expected to strike between the interests of disabled people and others. In the case of social housing management the question is whether, and if so when, a landlord should be entitled to take action to respond to conduct related to disability which has a negative impact on the landlord or other people, such as neighbours of the disabled tenant. The DDA was designed to limit the situations in which it would be permissible to subject a disabled person to less favourable treatment, in order to encourage society to accommodate the effects of disability as far as possible. For the majority of the House of Lords at least, however, the limited grounds on which less favourable treatment could be justified under the DDA were simply too inflexible to allow landlords (and others) to effectively balance the citizenship needs of disabled people with the interests of those affected by their disabilities. In addition, the majority clearly saw it as disproportionate and unfair that liability might accrue under the DDA even where a landlord was unaware of the existence of the disability and could not reasonably have been expected to identify it before taking action against a tenant.

The new concept of disability-related discrimination introduced by section 15 of the EA was formulated by government with one eye on tackling the problems with the DDA identified in *Malcolm*. However, rather than just replicating the *Malcolm* approach, the EA has rolled back some aspects of the decision in an effort to re-strengthen the rights of disabled tenants.

Most importantly, the new scheme under the EA imposes liability on landlords only if they knew *or ought to have known* about a disability at the time at which

---

[72] Ibid., [29].

they carried out activity otherwise prohibited by the Act.[73] This requirement protects landlords if they were unaware of the condition but, unlike *Malcolm*, requires them to take at least reasonable steps to find out whether conduct is disability-related. This new approach to the landlord's knowledge seems to have been designed to encourage landlords to more proactively investigate the possible links between problem behaviour and a disability before acting against a tenant.

The EA has also reinstated the pre-*Malcolm* approach by which any and all negative treatment arising from a disability must be justified before it can be permitted by law. However, unlike the previous approach taken to justifying discrimination by the DDA, the grounds for justification have now shifted from a prescribed, exhaustive list to a more broad-brush approach in which *prima facie* discriminatory acts must be found 'proportionate' in pursuit of a 'legitimate aim'.

In recent months, the Supreme Court in *Akerman-Livingstone* v. *Aster Communities Ltd* has had an opportunity to review the application of the new proportionality test used to justify disability-related discrimination under section 15 of the EA.[74] The case is important not only for its review of the operation of the proportionality approach, but also its reflections on the interaction in the disability discrimination context between equalities law and Article 8 of the European Convention (discussed in more detail in Chapter 8). Mr Akerman-Livingstone was housed by Aster Communities, a housing association, under the local authority's homelessness duty. He suffered from severe mental ill health caused by earlier childhood trauma, and his disability clearly fell within the terms of the EA. When the claimant housing association tried to evict Mr Akerman-Livingstone after he refused to accept their offer of rehousing in alternative properties, he challenged the possession proceedings brought against him on grounds of *both* Article 8 and disability-related discrimination under section 15 of the EA.

At preliminary hearing before the County Court, and later before the Court of Appeal, his claims on both grounds were rejected. More importantly, however, the Court expressly rejected his claim under section 15 on the basis that the test of 'proportionality' within the EA was exactly the same in scope and application as the very limited protections from otherwise permissible eviction offered to tenants by Article 8 in light of the decisions in *Pinnock* and *Powell*. In those decisions, of course, the Supreme Court held, as we have seen, that there will usually be a very strong case for granting possession under Article 8 where a social tenant has no other right to be in the property, given the 'twin aims' usually motivating possession by social landlords in most circumstances: (1) vindication of the landlord's property rights and (2) the need for landlords to comply with their statutory allocation duties to others.[75]

A unanimous Supreme Court, however, reversed the appeal court's conclusion on this point (while still dismissing the appeal on other grounds). It held instead that,

---

[73] The approach proposed by Baroness Hale in her dissenting judgment in *Malcolm*: [87].
[74] [2015] UKSC 125.
[75] *Manchester CC* v. *Pinnock* [2011] 2 AC 104; *Hounslow LBC* v. *Powell* [2011] 2 AC 186.

given the particular importance of legislative protection against disability discrimination in securing equal treatment for disabled people, the approach to proportionality under the EA should be seen as significantly different to that of Article 8, offering substantially stronger protections for disabled tenants from eviction than those granted under the European Convention.[76] As Baroness Hale concluded:

> When a disability discrimination defence is raised, the question is not simply whether the social landlord is entitled to recover the property in order to fulfil its or the local authority's public housing functions, but also whether the landlord or the local authority has done all that can reasonably be expected of it to accommodate the consequences of the disabled person's disability and whether, at the end of the day, the "twin aims" are sufficient to outweigh the effect upon the disabled person.[77]

In short, if possession proceedings are brought on grounds related to a disability, then the right approach is to ask whether any lesser action could be taken against the disabled tenant, and if not, whether the harm caused by evicting the tenant was outweighed by the benefit of eviction to the landlord and others affected by the decision not to evict (such as other homeless people, the general public and so on).

The Supreme Court's decision in *Akerman-Livingstone* makes clear that the proportionality test under section 15 of the EA is distinctive from, and more protective of the interests of disabled people than, the weak proportionality protections afforded by Article 8. This is surely right, as Baroness Hale acknowledged, given the far more ambitious aims behind the UK's equalities law compared to the European Convention. However, while the decision has strengthened the protections for tenants under the EA, it is less certain that it will protect the interests of disabled people sufficiently, given that the EA, even after *Akerman-Livingstone*, still grants a relatively broad discretion to courts to decide on the right balance between the interests of disabled people and wider society. The main difficulty is the lack of clarity the system still provides about the ambit of the protection from disability-related discrimination, and the inevitable concern that the courts will tend towards defending the interests of others (landlords, neighbours, etc.) over disabled tenants.

Indeed, there is perhaps still something to be said for the previous approach under the original DDA, by which specific justifications were specifically defined by statute and ancillary regulations. One dissenting voice in the original *Malcolm* decision was Baroness Hale, who indicated in her speech that the old DDA was not, in fact, as inflexible as appeared to the majority. This is because it already made statutory provision for the executive to enact further regulations setting out additional grounds on which disability-related discrimination would be justified, to enable the list of justifications to be modified where problems arose (such as

---

[76] Although note the Court of Appeal's approval of the view of the Equality and Human Rights Commission that proportionality under Article 8 was more likely to be relevant 'in respect of occupants who are vulnerable as a result of mental illness, physical or learning disability, poor health or frailty': [2014] EWCA Civ 1081 at [64].

[77] [2015] UKSC 125.

the dispute in the *Malcolm* case itself).[78] The strength of this system compared to the broad discretion now granted to the courts by the EA is that any further justifications would need to be formulated within a more democratic process, and after appropriate engagement with affected parties: an approach, one might argue, that is better suited to the complex policy questions that shape the scope of disability discrimination in the housing field.

Moving on from the question of 'disability-related' discrimination and its effect on housing access, it is also important to consider the further effect on the housing field of the additional legal duty on landlords under the EA to implement 'reasonable adjustments' for the benefit of disabled tenants. Like the DDA before it, the EA imposes a specific duty on landlords (including managers of property) to take reasonable steps to alter 'a provision, criterion or practice' or provide an 'auxiliary aid' if requested to do so by a disabled tenant, if the provision, criterion or practice, or the absence of the auxiliary aid, puts the disabled person at a 'substantial disadvantage' in their 'enjoyment' of the property or their 'use of a benefit or facility' related to the property.[79]

In much the same way as the concept of disability-related discrimination, the principle of reasonable adjustment raises difficult questions about the appropriate balance to be struck between the interests of the disabled tenant in having their disability accommodated in this way and the interests of others. For instance, where auxiliary aids are demanded, these may impose significant costs on a landlord (for example, where a tenant required a landlord to carry out interior decorating because a disabled person is unable to complete those works themselves),[80] and may also negatively impact on the tenant's neighbours (for instance, where a demand is made that a landlord allow a tenant to keep a noisy dog for disability-related reasons).[81]

Largely because of these potential problems, when the courts interpreted similar terms under the old DDA they typically adopted a cautious approach to the scope of the duty in the housing field. This led for instance to the Court of Appeal's conclusion in *Beedles* v. *Guinness Northern Counties* that 'enjoyment of premises' for the purposes of reasonable adjustment means only 'to live in the premises in an ordinary lawful way as any other typical tenant would live in them; enjoyment of premises does not mean deriving pleasure from them';[82] and in the case of *Ashley* v. *Drum Housing Association* that 'the right to enjoy the premises is dictated by the terms of the lease itself. That right cannot exceed what the letting entitles the tenant to do.'[83]

On the other hand, the EA appears in other ways to have strengthened the duty to make reasonable adjustments in favour of the disabled person, by now

---

[78] DDA, s. 24(5).
[79] EA, s. 20 and sch. 4.
[80] *Beedles* v. *Guinness Northern Counties* [2011] EWCA Civ 442.
[81] *Ashley* v. *Drum Housing Association* [2010] L&TR 117.
[82] [2011] EWCA Civ 442.
[83] [2010] L&TR 117.

requiring only that the occupier should be able to show they would experience 'substantial disadvantage' in the enjoyment of premises or use of a benefit or facility without a particular requested adjustment, rather than the more onerous requirement under the DDA that it should be 'impossible or unreasonably diffi- cult' to do so. As a result, in future, there is potential that cases like *Beedles* – in which the Court of Appeal found that poor interior decoration resulting from the inability of an epileptic tenant to carry out the decorating as required under his tenancy agreement did not make it 'impossible or unreasonably difficult' to enjoy the premises – could be decided more favourably for the disabled tenant under the broader 'substantial disadvantage' test.[84]

Overall, though, there is still strong evidence to suggest that the courts will continue to be more interested in protecting landlords over disabled tenants as they apply the reasonable adjustment duty under the EA. In particular, the Court of Appeal seems particularly attuned to the significant financial liabilities that could fall on landlords if the duty were to be interpreted too broadly, observing as a matter of *dicta* in *Beedles* that courts should legitimately be able to take into account the cost implications of a particular adjustment when evaluating what is 'reasonable' for the tenant to expect under the terms of duty.[85] This observation indicates not only that judges can be expected to apply the law with one eye on the economics of accommodating disability in housing, but also that the broader question of who should pay – the state, the landlord or the disabled person – is likely to be fiercely contested before the courts.

It is worth noting finally that a statutory power has been reserved by the execu- tive under the EA to make further regulations defining the scope of the reasonable adjustments duty in more detail if required.[86] Whether this statutory power is used (if at all) to challenge or support judicial attempts to reduce the burden on landlords under the duty will depend largely of course on the commitment of future govern- ments to accommodating the needs of disabled people living in rented homes.

Debate 4

What contribution can the Equality Act's 'equality work' provisions make in addressing unequal housing outcomes?

The primary focus of the debates in this chapter has been the principle of non- discrimination under the EA and the appropriate scope of that principle in the land and housing context. There is more to equalities law, however, than the protections against unlawful discrimination considered so far. It seems clear from our discussion of the long history of unequal access of ethnic minorities to hous- ing that the enforcement of the rules on non-discrimination against individual

---

84 [2011] EWCA Civ 442.
85 Ibid., at [27].
86 EA, s. 22.

landlords or owners is unlikely to eliminate inequality in housing outcomes. This is because housing inequality is as much about wider socio-economic structures – for instance, institutional racism – as it is about specific discriminatory acts or practices. For this reason, several measures under the EA increasingly move beyond the traditional concern of equalities law with negative prohibitions against unlawful discrimination and towards a more strategic interest in *equality work*, or administrative measures to encourage public and private bodies to promote equality in more positive ways.

This final section considers what role equality work might play in alleviating unequal housing outcomes in three areas: the work of the central coordinating responsibilities of the Equality and Human Rights Commission (EHRC) for promoting equality in housing (and other fields covered by the EA); the Public Sector Equality Duty imposed by section 149 of the EA; and the power granted by the EA to take positive steps to address the structural disadvantages of specific communities by discriminating in their favour.

Since it was established in October 2007, the EHRC has taken on the strategic remits of the Commission for Racial Equality, the Equal Opportunities Commission and the Disability Rights Commission, and has been given additional responsibilities regarding discrimination in the areas of age, sexual orientation, gender identity, and religion and belief.[87] Like its predecessors, the EHRC was designed to facilitate a more strategic approach to discrimination and inequality (together with its new remit for human rights promotion). It is empowered to support individual claims of discrimination, to act as an intervener in appellate cases on equalities law (but not to bring claims itself), and to carry out 'investigations' into alleged discriminatory practices by named persons and 'inquiries' focused more generally on non-named performance in fields or sectors. We have already seen there has been a long history of investigations and inquiries by the CRE into race discrimination and inequality in the housing market. Between 1980 and 1990, the CRE carried out several investigations into estate agencies, property developers, local housing authorities and housing associations, which shone a spotlight onto the problem of continued non-compliance with equalities law across the housing sector.[88] Over the last two decades, however, there have been no further investigations or inquiries carried out on the housing sector by either the previous commissions or the new EHRC. Instead, in recent years their equality work in this field has focused almost entirely on the release of guidance and codes of practice to housing providers.[89] This seems to suggest that the EHRC is likely to face the same criticisms in this area as previous commissions, who were

---

[87] For an overview and discussion, see C. O'Cinneide, 'The Commission for Equality and Human Rights: A New Institution for New and Uncertain Times' (2007) *ILJ* 141.

[88] See e.g. Commission for Racial Equality (1984), n.22.

[89] See, for example, Commission for Racial Equality, *Statutory Code of Practice on Racial Equality in Housing – England* (CRE, 2006). Equality-related guidance on housing (although in this case relating to Article 14 of the European Convention) has been issued recently by the Equality and Human Rights Commission: n.1.

consistently accused of being 'too timid in their enforcement work',[90] especially in relation to named investigations into the private rental sector.

It is worth remembering that this earlier timidity was the consequence in part at least of the 'cowing effect' of judicial controls on named investigations that followed a legal challenge to an early CRE named investigation into discrimination in the provision of council housing by Hillingdon Council in 1985.[91] Following that decision, the CRE and the other commissions 'tended to err on the side of extreme caution in deciding whether to launch formal investigations'.[92] Nevertheless, the legal controls on named investigations do not in themselves explain the reluctance of the EHRC to carry out new enforcement work in the housing field. On one hand, the EA has since strengthened considerably the EHRC's named investigation powers and yet the Commission still seems no more 'tough-minded' in its approach to enforcement in the housing sector compared to previous commissions, contrary to what many had hoped.[93] In addition, the 'political and judicial disquiet'[94] which effectively shut down previous efforts by the CRE to carry out named investigations cannot explain the apparent further institutional reluctance to carry out more general non-named (and thus less controversial) inquiries into the housing sector.[95] This suggests that initial fears the EHRC would adopt an even more 'excessively placatory and "soft touch" approach' to past commissions may be well-founded.[96] This reluctance of the EHRC to carry out named investigations or general inquiries into discrimination in housing is likely to be further reinforced by the significant cuts to the EHRC's budgets of 68 per cent imposed as part of the previous Coalition Government's austerity measures.[97]

The second aspect of equality work under the EA is the introduction of the new Public Sector Equality Duty. The aim of the Public Sector Duty is to encourage public bodies to 'mainstream' equality work throughout their core business by requiring these bodies to give 'due regard to the need to eliminate unlawful discrimination, harassment and victimisation; advance equality of opportunity between different groups; and foster good relations between different groups'.[98] Further specific duties were imposed recently by regulation to flesh out the General Duty in England, requiring public authorities 'to publish information' demonstrating compliance with the Duty, and prepare and publish 'one or more equality objectives' every four years, which are 'specific and measurable'.[99] In principle at

---

[90] O'Cinneide, n.87, 152.
[91] *R v. CRE*, Ex p *Hillingdon* LBC [1982] AC 779; see also *In re Prestige* [1984] ICR 473.
[92] O'Cinneide, n.87, 149.
[93] Ibid., 162.
[94] Ibid., 149.
[95] The last general housing inquiry was carried out in the private rented sector in 1990: CRE. n.22.
[96] O'Cinneide, n.87, 147.
[97] P. Curtis, 'Cuts Will Clobber Equality and Human Rights Commission, Claim Staff', *Guardian*, 8 February 2011.
[98] EA, s. 149.
[99] Equality Act 2010 (Specific Duties) Regulations 2011/2260.

least, the duties have the potential to encourage a more strategic and structural approach to discrimination and inequalities in housing. Both duties are imposed on the Department for Communities and Local Government, local authorities and the social housing regulator, while registered housing associations are subject to the general duty when carrying out public functions, as so-called 'hybrid' authorities. Each of these organizations will be expected therefore to integrate equality work when creating housing policy, or in the allocation, management and other regulation of all forms of housing.

For several reasons, however, it may again be more difficult in practice to realize the potential of the duties in the field of discrimination and inequality in housing. First, the scope of the duties suggests that in many cases it will be a struggle to keep housing outcomes at the forefront of the equality work of relevant authorities. With obligations owed across all protected characteristics, and an obligation under the specific duties recently released in England to formulate only 'one or more' equality objective every four years, national government departments and local authorities with their various other functions may not have the time or inclination to focus on housing (although this may be less of a problem for the social housing regulator, whose core business is oversight of all social renting). Second, while it remains possible to challenge specific policies and decision in the courts under the terms of the General Duty,[100] case law suggests that success in this area is likely to depend on evidence of inadequate consultation or a failure by an authority to consider the equality implications of the decision or policy at all: 'at best [section 149] will ensure public and hybrid authorities are willing to listen with an open mind'.[101] In law at least, no particular outcome will be required, and the authority will retain the final word. Much will depend instead on the capacity of individuals and organizations, including the EHRC, to hold authorities to account through the democratic process. For this reason, the specific duties require authorities to 'publish information' about how the duty is being met, and armed with this data it is expected that authorities will be held to account politically for their equality work. The problem with this approach is the lack of detail in the specific duties regarding the type and quality of information that must be published to satisfy the specific duties. The previous Coalition Government was worried that too much regulation would overburden authorities in a time of recession and on this basis ensured the regulations kept the demands of the specific duties to a minimum,[102] but without clear expectations on public bodies about what they must publish the possibility of accountability under the duty may prove illusory in practice.

---

[100] See, for example, in the housing context, but under the previous disability equality duty, *Pieretti* v. *Enfield LBC* [2010] EWCA Civ 1104.

[101] J. Halford and S. Khan, 'Equality Act Will Pressure Authorities to Listen' *Law Society Gazette*, 28 April 2011. See generally *R (Luton Borough Council)* v. *Secretary of State for Education* [2011] EWHC 217 (Admin).

[102] Compare the approach of the outgoing Labour government: Government Equalities Office, *Equality Bill: Making it Work: Policy Proposals for Specific Duties A Consultation* (GEO, 2009).

The final provision of the EA that could support a more far-reaching strategic approach to inequality in housing is the concept of 'positive action'. This concept now permits individuals and organizations to engage in what would otherwise be unlawful discrimination in the housing context if it is a proportionate way to address the structural disadvantage and inequality of particular communities or groups.[103] The CRE previously suggested in its *Guidance on Race Equality in Housing* that landlords might consider taking positive action under the terms of the race equality duty by, for example,

> developing temporary hostel accommodation catering especially for newly-arrived Somali refugees, who may have needs arising from shared traumatic experiences; or sheltered housing schemes for Chinese elders; or by providing wardens and carers who speak a particular Asian language; or by meeting certain dietary and religious requirements.[104]

There are obvious examples of specific housing needs across the range of disadvantaged groups now covered by the EA – such as social housing for young LGBT people, or supported accommodation for those with specific medical conditions like HIV/AIDS – which will almost certainly also be justifiable under the current terms of the positive action provisions.

Positive action is a power not a duty, unlike, for instance, the positive duty on landlords to make reasonable adjustments for disabled people. Permitting discrimination in order to address disadvantage is also politically sensitive, suggesting as it does the special treatment of certain groups. For these reasons, housing managers in the public sector may again be reluctant to engage in positive action for fear of possible public resistance. One need only consider the EHRC's recent commission of independent research into the allegation that immigrants receive preferable treatment compared to the indigenous white population in social housing allocation to recognize that social landlords may face a backlash if they use the discretionary power of positive action to provide services tailored to meet the needs of unpopular groups.[105] A further problem with positive action is that, as considered above, taking positive steps to meet specific group needs can be costly, and so – in a time of austerity – housing providers may be less able or willing than before to offer tailored housing services to particular groups. As such, the potential for positive action to challenge structural inequalities in a meaningful way will depend in large part on the resources invested in equality objectives across the housing sector. Like the future role of the EHRC, and the effectiveness of the equality duty, the success of positive action in challenging inequality will depend on the priority afforded by future governments to financial investment in equality work, in what is still a challenging economic climate.

---

[103] EA, s. 158.

[104] Commission for Racial Equality (2006), n.89, para. 2.41.

[105] J. Rutter and M. Lattore, *Social Housing Allocation and Immigrant Communities* (EHRC, 2009).

CONCLUSIONS

This brief survey of several key contemporary debates in the field of housing and equalities law has provided, we hope, an insight into the significance of rules – often located beyond the traditional boundaries of land law – to address the divisive and often highly damaging consequences of unequal treatment by property owners on the citizenship status of marginalized groups. What the chapter should also have demonstrated are some of the limitations of the current equalities law framework in addressing housing inequality, not only as a result of the law itself, but in terms of its enforcement, and the wider social, economic and political context in which it operates.

Further Reading

N. Cobb, 'Patronising the Mentally Disordered? Social Landlords and the Control of "Anti-Social Behaviour" under the Disability Discrimination Act 1995' (2006) 26(2) *Legal Studies* 238.

Commission for Racial Equality, *Statutory Code of Practice on Racial Equality in Housing – England* (CRE, 2006).

D. Cowan, 'State Support for Housing Ethnic Minority Households: Spatial Segregation and Ghettoisation?' in J. Murphy (ed.), *Ethnic Minorities, their Families and the Law* (Hart, 2000).

B. Hepple, *Equality: The New Legal Framework* (Hart, 2011).

V. Karn and D. Phillips, 'Race and Ethnicity in Housing: a Diversity of Experience' in P. Bhikhu, P. Sanders and T. Blackstone, *Race Relations in Britain: A Developing Agenda* (Routledge, 1998).

A. Lawson, *Disability and Equality Law in Britain: The role of Reasonable Adjustment* (Hart, 2008).

10

MORTGAGES AND SECURITY INTERESTS IN LAND

INTRODUCTION

One of the most familiar land transactions within the popular consciousness – and the most crucial for anyone who has bought their home with the support of a bank or building society loan – is the mortgage. From their origins as the last refuge of the necessitous borrower under the shadow of usury laws, mortgages evolved to become the enabler of capital investment to support industry and commerce from the Industrial Revolution. Indeed, it was only well into the twentieth century, when much of the mortgage law we would recognize today was well established, that the domestic mortgage emerged as a routine instrument by which building societies enabled the growth of owner-occupation in the UK. Today, alongside their commercial functions, mortgages are the bread-and-butter transactions which have enabled over 70 per cent of the UK's population to become homeowners.

In the period that has followed the latest global financial crisis (from 2007) – which began as a housing market crisis in the US when sub-prime borrowers were unable to discharge their loans – hundreds of thousands of UK homeowners have been unable to keep up repayments on their mortgages and have been threatened with – or experienced – repossession. Looking across a longer time frame, we can see the cyclical nature of spikes in mortgage repossession rates: the number of properties taken into possession rose from 43,900 in 1990 to 75,500 in 1991 (the high point of the previous housing crisis); then fell off to a low of 7013 in 2003, before beginning a gradual climb to 39,266 in 2008.[1] Since then, the number of mortgage possession actions in court has decreased (from a 2008 high of 142,741 to 41,151 in 2014, as have the total number of properties repossessed (4751 in 2014).[2]

This has coincided with lower interest rates, a proactive approach from lenders in managing consumers in financial difficulties and other interventions, including the

---

[1] For statistics, see Ministry of Justice website, Mortgage and landlord possession statistics, Possession data from 1990 to 2001; available online at www.justice.gov.uk/publications/statistics-and-data/civil-justice/mortgage-possession.htm.

[2] Mortgage and landlord possession statistics quarterly – Statistical Tables, Q2 2015, available online at https://www.gov.uk/government/collections/mortgage-and-landlord-possession-statistics.

Mortgage Rescue Scheme and the introduction of the Mortgage Pre-Action Protocol. At the same time, there has been a decrease in the proportion of owner-occupiers, following the credit crunch and the Financial Services Authority's Mortgage Market Review in 2011,[3] which implemented significant changes to the (new) Financial Conduct Authority's rules governing the selling and approval of mortgages to residential consumers. Key changes included the implementation of an affordability assessment, where income has to be verified in every mortgage application, and lenders must ensure that borrowers can afford the home loan, which includes stress-testing interest rate changes and considering major outgoings such as heating and council tax.

Of course, statistics on mortgage possession orders only tell part of the story of mortgage default. About half of mortgage orders throughout the period 1990 to 2011 were suspended,[4] although the percentage of orders suspended varies in inverse proportion to the number of possession orders made – from a low of 47 per cent in 1990 rising to around 60 per cent in the mid-1990s, and then falling again to 46 per cent in 2009. From 2010 to 2014, estimated proportions of claims leading to orders, warrants and repossessions have shown a steady decrease. Against a backdrop in which over-indebted owner-occupiers face heightened levels of risk in relation to default and repossession, the courts who administer these orders exercise a discretion to suspend the order (so allowing the borrower a further opportunity to resolve their own personal financial crisis). The proportion of orders suspended each year has remained relatively stable, ranging between 46 per cent and 50 per cent, from the benign pre-crisis climate of 2006 to the peak of the crisis and beyond.[5]

This chapter explores the key features of the mortgage market as it relates to property law by examining the core provisions of mortgage law, bankruptcy law and mortgage market regulation as they have been developed and applied in the contemporary context. This discussion will revolve around a core tension, between the use of domestic property as security and its function as an owner-occupied home. These competing uses (which echo the tensions discussed in Chapter 3) constitute the defining legal debate surrounding the use of property as security, which concerns how and where the balance should be struck between the protection of creditors' interests in mortgage land as security (with the implications that this is presumed to have for the availability of credit to homeowners) on the one hand, and the occupier's interest in the property as a home, on the other.

When the term 'occupier' is used in this context it usually refers to the owner-occupier, although mortgage repossessions often also affect private sector tenants. This dimension was notable in the most recent crisis, as growing numbers of

[3] FSA (2011), *Mortgage Market Review: Proposed Package of Reforms* (CP11/31); online at https://www. google.co.uk/url?sa=t&rct=j&q=&esrc=s&source=web&cd=1&cad=rja&uact=8&ved=0ahUKEwjQ6 quSlIHLAhVFOxQKHWQqCgAQFggcMAA&url=https%3A%2F%2Fwww.fca.org.uk%2Fstatic%2F documents%2Fconsultation-papers%2Ffsa-cp11-31.pdf&usg=AFQjCNGk2smvWjyaD2AO2WN5l FHt_E9TQ&bvm=bv.114733917,d.ZWU.
[4] Ibid..
[5] Mortgage and landlord possession statistics quarterly, Q2 2015; available online at https://www.gov. uk/government/collections/mortgage-and-landlord-possession-statistics.

private landlords defaulted on their mortgages, potentially leading to repossession for their tenants.[6] The position for these tenants depends on whether the lease is binding on the landlord's lender – this is usually the case where the landlord has a 'buy-to-let' mortgage, where the lender has given permission for the property to be let, or where the tenant's occupation pre-dates, and so takes priority over, the grant of the mortgage or the landlord's purchase of the property. At the peak of the crisis, Parliament intervened with the Mortgage Repossessions (Protection of Tenants etc.) Act 2010, which aimed to shore up the position of tenants in cases where the tenancy is not binding on the lender. This Act ensures that tenants are made aware of any repossession action at an earlier stage[7] and have the opportunity to apply to the court for a postponement of up to two months.[8] In exercising its discretion to order such a postponement, the factors to be considered by the court include the circumstances of the tenant, as well as any breach of terms by the tenant.[9]

While the recent mortgage crisis provides a useful frame through which to understand mortgage law, this chapter begins with the backdrop to Debate 1, by charting the development of the mortgage market, as it has been driven by the political ideology of homeownership and expansion of owner-occupation, including for low-income households. Debate 2 concerns access to mortgage finance and the appropriate level of consumer protection at the point of sale of the mortgage product, while Debate 3 focuses on the balance struck between mortgagees and mortgagors (and other occupiers of the mortgaged property) at the point of crisis. The terminology here is important because it reflects the different ways in which we think about the individual at different moments in their housing pathway: they are consumers at one point, occupiers at another. Furthermore, this is played out against an ideological backdrop that badges 'home buyers' (including the majority who buy subject to a mortgage) as 'homeowners' from the moment of sale, even though the reality of sustaining a mortgage can leave these 'owners' in a precarious legal position if they default on debt payments. Finally, it is worth noting that, post-global financial crisis, a key trend with respect to home finance mortgages has been the reduction in available mortgage credit for borrowers, a more cautious approach from lenders, lower levels of repossessions and the exclusion of many more householders (particularly first-time buyers, people with adverse credit histories, the self-employed, and older borrowers) from the mainstream mortgage credit market. One knock-on effect of the changing mortgage landscape is the increased pressure on the private rental market, discussed in Chapter 4.

---

[6] See Shelter, Citizens' Advice, Crisis, CIH, *A Private Matter? Private Tenants – the forgotten victims of the repossession crisis* (March 2009), available online at https://www.google.co.uk/url?sa=t&rct=j&q=&esrc=s&source=web&cd=1&cad=rja&uact=8&ved=0ahUKEwiMoKvKllHLAhUDThQKHXCACOUQFggdMAA&url=http%3A%2F%2Fengland.shelter.org.uk%2Fprofessional_resources%2Fpolicy_and_research%2Fpolicy_library%2Fpolicy_library_folder%2Fa_private_matter_-_private_tenants_the_forgotten_victims_of_the_repossessions_crisis&usg=AFQjCNGCL4PC-u5MwYsMyDg_0xoI_VWODw.

[7] The lender must send a notice to the tenant or occupier in advance of the possession hearing, followed by a second notice in advance of any eviction.

[8] Mortgage Repossessions (Protection of Tenants etc.) Act 2010, s. 1(2).

[9] Mortgage Repossessions (Protection of Tenants etc.) Act 2010, s. 1(5).

Debate 1

The functions of owner-occupied land: security interest or home?

One of the perennial great debates of property law, particularly brought to the fore in times of housing market crisis, is the inevitable tension between the use of property as security to leverage a loan (in some cases, the loan which has enabled the purchaser to acquire the property) and the function of the property as a home for the (owner-) occupier. Indeed, while this is the 'main story' of modern mortgage discourse, it is interesting to recall that the origins of the English mortgage – and the law by which it is governed – lie not in the domestic context, but in the world of commerce and industry. As policies promoting widespread owner-occupation – particularly from the second half of the twentieth century – anchored the mortgage more firmly within the domestic realm, it was transformed from a specialized instrument of industrialization and capital investment to become the primary vehicle through which the majority of the population access housing in the form of an 'owner-occupied' – subject to a mortgage to the building society – home. While some areas of mortgage law have recognized the importance of context in how we govern mortgages (for example, section 36 of the Administration of Justice Act 1970, which applies only to dwelling-houses; and the mortgage and home finance regulations administered by the Financial Conduct Authority (MCOB), which apply to transactions involving consumers), the default position is that – unless there have been specific interventions to make provision for the context in which the mortgage operates – the same principles apply across the spectrum from commercial to domestic mortgages.

Following the rapid expansion of homeownership, the deregulation of the UK's mortgage market in the 1980s triggered a further sea-change, with major implications for the meanings and functions of the domestic mortgage, as well as for the stability of the mortgage market and its ability to de-stabilize the wider economy. Mortgage market deregulation significantly broadened the range of situations in which borrowers may leverage their owned housing asset using not only conventional acquisition mortgages and second mortgages, but also 'flexible mortgages' and financial products which enable the release of equity (including equity release/reverse mortgages, home reversion plans for older owners, and sale and rentback).[10] This is important, when we think about the themes of alienation, rationality, citizenship, responsibility and place and space as they interact in mortgage law. For example, debates about the role and functions of owned housing echo the more general debate discussed in Chapter 3 about how we understand the balance between use value and exchange value in land.

---

[10] See L. Fox O'Mahony, *Home Equity and Ageing Owners: Between Risk and Regulation* (Hart Publishing, 2012). Note that although home reversion plans, and sale and rentback, are collectively categorized by the Financial Conduct Authority (with conventional mortgages and other forms of secured lending) as 'regulated home finance activities' (https://www.handbook.fca.org.uk/handbook/PERG/2/Annex2. html), they do not, in fact, involve using the property as security, but a sale of the property to the finance provider, with a lease back to the occupier on terms.

The upsurge in mortgage-based financial products which enable the use of the home as security, combined with government policies which not only facilitate but encourage and rely on such transactions in the neoliberal 'wealth-fare' state,[11] have heightened the tensions between the competing functions of owned property as security in financial transactions, on the one hand, and as the owner-occupier's home on the other. Susan Smith's description of owned homes as 'a hybrid of money, materials, and meanings'[12] highlights the tensions that the growth in financial transactions that use the owned home as security has created, changing the character of housing assets, the owned home and perhaps owner-occupiers themselves, as households shift towards deliberate strategies of 'banking on housing'. As property-holding citizens become asset-accumulating investors, Smith argues, the growing fungibility of housing wealth stimulates an 'ethically charged encounter between the governance of housing and the micropolitics of home'.[13]

AUTOBIOGRAPHICAL NOTE

On the power of the lender

One of my most brilliant friends reminded me the other day about the trick that property law plays on us. It makes us think that we are 'homeowners' when, in fact, we are nothing of the sort. My friend loves their home – it's funky and in a cool part of the city. They are about to go abroad for a couple of years and decided that they would rent out their home for that period so that they could come back to it. They wanted to do it properly and got in touch with their lender to tell it of their plan (although apparently some letting agents said that notification was unnecessary). Their lender said that the only way they would consent to the rental would be if my friend's mortgage (currently at a pretty good fixed rate) was moved to a different product at a much higher rate of interest (which would make renting it out effectively uneconomical). One possible outcome is that my friend will have to sell the much-cherished funky home.

As my friend remarked to me, 'it makes you realize, doesn't it?' Indeed, it does; if we go 'by the book', we find out just how disempowered we are in our own homes by the need for, and existence of, this thing called a mortgage. It's property law's most brilliant confidence trick because you only recognize it really when certain life-changing moments occur and you are, like my friend, stuck in the middle.

---

[11] The term 'wealth-fare state' reflects the shift from public provision of welfare to the neoliberal expectation that citizens, particularly owners, will self-provide for their own financial needs by leveraging their housing wealth: see S. Parkinson, B. Searle, S. Smith, A. Stokes and G. Wood, 'Mortgage Equity Withdrawal in Australia and Britain: Towards a Wealth-Fare State?' (2009) 9(3) *European Journal of Housing Policy* 363.

[12] S. Smith, 'Owner-Occupation: At Home with a Hybrid of Money and Materials' (2008) 40(5) *Environment and Planning A* 520, 521.

[13] Ibid..

The transformation of housing discourse in Britain in recent decades has been so significant that it is easy to forget that, until the 1970s, the paradigm of housing as home was clearly dominant.[14] To the extent that owned housing was also viewed as an investment asset, it was with a view to providing a resource for inheritance for the next generation. Financial deregulation set the scene for a fundamental change in the key purposes of owned housing: from providing a home and an asset that could be passed on as inheritance, to become an investment asset. The nature of the owned home was further changed by increased political expectations that owners will liquidate and spend their housing wealth, alongside the gradual normalization amongst owners of the idea that they could look to their owned home – using new financial products that enabled housing wealth to be released – as a pot of money to spend.

The first part of this story was the rise of the acquisition mortgage in enabling and supporting the expansion of owner-occupation as the tenure of choice for lower middle-class, and latterly low-income, households.[15] In the 1970s, Lord Diplock described the 'emergence of a property-owning, particularly a real-property-mortgaged-to-a-building-society-owning democracy',[16] which linked the availability of credit for homeownership with the idea of citizenship associated with owning property, discussed in Chapter 1. The expansion of ownership has many significant implications for the mortgage lending context, including the emergence of a line of argument that creditors must be protected and their interests afforded priority in legal contexts. The basis for that argument was that the expansion of homeownership was dependent on creditors' willingness to lend. A circuitous form of reasoning developed, maintaining that if creditors were not protected by the law in the event of debtor default, this would adversely affect the availability of credit, which would ultimately harm the consumer.[17] From a social perspective, the expansion of low-income ownership also exploded the myth that the status of owner could be viewed as providing a reliable indication of socio-economic wellbeing. In turn, that raised questions about the extent to which owners (or, more accurately, buyers, who remain subject to a mortgage, often for decades, before becoming unencumbered owners) could reasonably be viewed as a homogenous category of 'autonomous

---

[14] C. Hamnett, M. Harmer and P. Williams, *As Safe as Houses: Housing Inheritance in Britain* (Paul Chapman, 1991) p. 150.

[15] See R. Burrows and S. Wilcox, *Half the Poor: Home-owners with Low Incomes*, (Council of Mortgage Lenders Research Report, 2000), which demonstrated that half of the population categorized as 'living in poverty' in the UK were homeowners.

[16] *Pettitt* v. *Pettitt* [1970] AC 777, 824.

[17] In a Parliamentary debate concerning practices of pro-creditor priority in legal decision making, Lord Templeman claimed that: 'No one has great sympathy for lenders or banks ... [but] the point is that at the end of the day it is the borrower who pays, unless there is some speedy and efficient method of conveyancing': 437 HL Deb (5th Series) col 650 (15 December 1982). This reasoning is questioned in L. Fox, *Conceptualising Home: Theories, Laws and Policies* (Hart Publishing, 2006) p. 88ff.

consumers', free of the structural constraints that inhibit financial decision making concerning credit.[18]

Following on the heels of the increased availability of acquisition mortgages to expand the ownership sector, there was also, from the 1980s, a growing market in the use of the owned home as an asset to raise additional (non-acquisition) finance, often to fund business ventures and through the vehicle of the second mortgage. The reasons for taking a second mortgage (which generally ranks second in priority behind the first, acquisition, mortgage) vary, but can include repairs/maintenance/improvements to the property as well as securing business finance against the (often family) home. Interest rates on second mortgages are usually higher than those for acquisition mortgages, reflecting their second place in priority and so their greater riskiness. There has also been a long debate concerning the desirability of using the owned home – particularly a family home – to secure business liabilities. On the one hand, the owned home has been identified as a crucial source of finance for small business entrepreneurs; yet there has also been some debate surrounding the desirability of encouraging the use of the home – particularly a *family* home – as security against business debts.[19]

While the courts have appeared to support the use of the owner-occupied home as security for non-acquisition debts,[20] some commentators have argued that the risk involved in such a venture is too great, and that the interest of the family in preserving their home outweighs the arguments in support of facilitating credit transactions. Barlow, for example, argued that: '[w]hile restricting the availability of the family home as an easy means of securing business credit and reducing its attractiveness to lenders ... are consequences ... which commercial vested interests may oppose',[21] the use of the family home as security for non-acquisition credit should not be encouraged.[22] The paradigm of housing as investment to spend emerged from the 1980s as a result of the financial deregulation of the UK's mortgage market,[23] including the development of a new generation of flexible

---

[18] These constraints are linked to the reality of the choices that are available to any individual consumer, so that the freedom to make choices between options that are seen as 'bad', 'terrible' and 'disastrous' (A. Sen, 'Markets and Freedoms' in A. Sen (ed.), *Rationality and Freedom* [Belknap, 2002] p. 515) cannot be viewed as substantive freedom, but only 'process freedom'; J. Purdy, 'A Freedom-Promoting Approach to Property: A Renewed Tradition for New Debates' (2005) 72 *Univ Chicago L Rev* 1237, 1260.

[19] See, for example, A. Barlow, 'Rights in the Family Home – Time for a Conceptual Revolution?' in A. Hudson (ed.) *New Perspectives on Property Law, Human Rights and the Home* (Cavendish, 2003).

[20] For example, in *Barclay's Bank plc* v. *O'Brien* [1994] 1 AC 180, 188, Lord Browne Wilkinson described an 'important public interest *viz*, the need to ensure that the wealth currently tied up in the matrimonial home does not become economically sterile', to which Lord Oliver added that: 'If the rights secured to wives by the law render vulnerable loans granted on the security of matrimonial homes, institutions will be unwilling to accept such security, thereby reducing the flow of loan capital to business enterprises. It is therefore essential that a law designed to protect the vulnerable does not render the matrimonial home unacceptable as security to financial institutions': ibid..

[21] Barlow, n.19, 75.

[22] Ibid..

[23] S. Smith, 'Risky Business? The Challenge of Residential Mortgage Markets' (2005) *Housing Finance International* 3–8.

mortgage products.[24] This (dominant) paradigm supported a particular, politically driven, type of market in which housing wealth was viewed as 'fungible' (or spendable), and legal subjects (the borrowers) are presumed to fit an 'investor model' (as distinct from a consumer model) of legal rationality. This language matters, not least because of the different lenses we use in law to think about appropriate levels of protection for consumers (regarded as relatively vulnerable and less able to withstand high levels of risk),[25] compared to investors (able to take greater risks). Meanwhile, the growing use of flexible mortgages to enable owner-occupiers to have easy and ongoing access to their housing equity throughout the life of the mortgage led Smith to conclude – just before the global financial crisis – that wealth that was tied up in the owned home is not only a financial investment with a view to capital appreciation, but had also become 'more "spendable"... than it will ever be again'.[26]

These changing behaviours in the home-owner/mortgagee population were shaped by a political discourse which explicitly designated owned housing as an investment asset-to-spend, buffered by an expectation that this newly spendable wealth would be used to support welfare needs, both after retirement and throughout the life-course.[27] The practices that now surround the use of mortgaged residential land as security are intimately linked to the broader political discourse of the citizen-consumer. Neoliberal policies based on privatization and individual responsibility heighten expectations that older owners will take responsibility for their own lives (their biographies) by planning for the future, including strategies to ensure financial well-being after retirement and into old age. Meanwhile, private law typically characterizes its subject as an autonomous individual who takes responsibility for his own actions and choices and whose free and equal moral agency must be respected by holding him to those choices, no matter how bad they are;[28] while land law is geared around the presumptive priority of formally constituted rights and obligations. Modern citizen-consumers (to operate as full political and legal risk subjects) are expected to participate in financial transactions secured against their owned homes, to operate as informed consumers in the credit market, and to engage with the risks that are inherent to the deregulated mortgage market. Those who are successful in doing so are rewarded with capital growth, improved lifestyles and financial

[24] S. Smith, J. Ford and M. Munro with R. Davis, *A Review of Flexible Mortgages* (Council of Mortgage Lenders, 2002).

[25] See Financial Conduct Authority, *Consumer Vulnerability* – Occasional Paper No. 8, (London: FCA, 2015).

[26] S. Smith, 'Banking on Housing: Speculating on the Role and Relevance of Housing Wealth in Britain', Paper prepared for the Joseph Rowntree Foundation Inquiry into Home Ownership 2010 and Beyond (2005) 11; available online at http://dro.dur.ac.uk/71/1/Smith_speculating.pdf?DDD14, p2.

[27] 'Homes are not just places to live, they are also assets'; and the aims of widening homeownership include 'enabling more people to share in increasing asset wealth': Office of the Deputy Prime Minister, 'Homebuy: Expanding the Opportunity to Own', Consultation Paper (Office of the Deputy Prime Minister, 2005).

[28] See, for example, R. Dworkin, *Sovereign Virtue: The Theory and Practice of Equality* (Harvard University Press, 2000).

security; but those who are not are generally required to bear their own losses in this game of winners and losers.

This model of the homeowner as an autonomous consumer – and all the expectations that go with that in relation to their ability to make good financial decisions and the relative lack of protection they are afforded through property law, compared to creditors (and consistent with the alienation theme embedded in 1925) – is challenged by arguments that highlight the inequalities people face when it comes to opportunities to construct their own tidy, well-ordered and financially stable lives. Research has shown that the ability to be a self-responsible, autonomous consumer is limited by structural social factors (for example, education and access to information).[29] More recently, the global financial crisis and domestic recession provided a cogent reminder of the vulnerabilities of many homeowning consumers to default and repossession, as well as highlighting the link between individual, micro-level mortgage defaults and the macro-economic recession.

One consequence of the most recent housing market crisis is the shift in attitudes towards the idea of responsibility in mortgages and other secured lending transactions. While the neoliberal political landscape which established dominance in the UK from the late 1980s emphasized the individual self-responsibility of the owner-occupier as an autonomous consumer – including responsibility to bear the losses of default and repossession – following the global financial crisis, political and legal debates shifted towards greater lender responsibility. This can be seen in the emergence of the Mortgage Pre-Action Protocol (discussed below in Debate 3), as well as in more rigorous management of product risk and consumer risk under financial services regulation (discussed in Debate 2).[30] The Financial Conduct Authority (FCA) – which replaced the FSA from April 2014 – has implemented a post-GFC Mortgage Market Review. The main thrust of the review was the need to move from a 'light-touch' approach, regulating general standards of lender behaviour, to more prescriptive product regulation, increased lender responsibility for affordability and suitability, and a re-balancing of decision-making responsibilities between borrower and lender. Since then, changes to the rules and guidance applied to mortgage lenders have placed considerable emphasis on the lender's responsibility to test the affordability of the transaction

---

[29] See, for example, S. Lash, 'Reflexivity and Its Doubles: Structure, Aesthetics, Community' in U. Beck, A. Giddens and S. Lash (eds.), *Reflexive Modernisation: Politics, Tradition and Aesthetics in the Modern Social Order* (Sage, 1994), where he uses the example of a 'ghetto mother' to ask 'just how "reflexive" is it possible for a single mother in an urban ghetto to be? ... just how much freedom from the "necessity" of "structure" and structural poverty does this ghetto mother have to self-construct her own "life narratives"?'(p. 120).

[30] For a discussion of this shift, see S. Nield, 'Responsible Lending and Borrowing: Whereto Low-Cost Home Ownership?' (2010) 30(4) *Legal Studies* 610, for analysis of the concepts of responsible lending and borrowing in home finance and the impact of the 2009 Turner Review on the concept of lender responsibility (Lord Turner, *The Turner Review: A Regulatory Response to the Global Banking Crisis* (FSA, 2009); online at www.fsa.gov.uk/pubs/other/turner_review.pdf; the Turner Review was commissioned to look into the lessons from the financial crisis for the FSA).

for individual consumers. Sarah Nield described this shift as requiring lenders to: 'look beyond their own interests and take the mortgagor's interests into account. No longer can lenders be self-interested players within the neo-liberal market model.'[31]

In tracing the evolution of this debate through recent developments in mortgage law, this chapter considers the treatment of both creditors and borrowers under what might be termed conventional property law (the statutes and cases that determine when and why mortgages can be enforced by creditors) and the regulatory jurisdiction of the Financial Conduct Authority. The discussion is organized along the life-course of the mortgage: from the regulations surrounding creation of the mortgage at the point of sale, to provisions governing the point of crisis when a debtor defaults and the creditor seeks to realize the security.

Debate 2

What level of consumer protection is appropriate at the point of sale?

A conventional mortgage is primarily intended as a financial services contract, backed by proprietary securitization: in the normal course of events, the mortgagor will repay the loan to discharge the mortgage, and the securitization of the home provides an enforcement strategy which the creditor will only seek to use as a last resort in the event of default.[32] The validity of the mortgage transaction is determined according to conventional property law principles relating to enforceability: the core of the mortgage transaction is a valid contract between borrower and lender, with terms detailing the agreement relating to repayment, accompanied by the creation of a securitized interest over the property in favour of the mortgagor. The legal framework within which this transaction takes place is largely framed by the 1925 legislation, and its policy agenda in pursuit of alienability. In contrast to the pre-1925 position, the 1925 legislation set the scene for modern mortgage law by changing the legal structure of the mortgage transaction to recognize its function as a financial services contract with back-up securitization, rather than an outright transfer of the property.[33] This approach was further reinforced when the LRA 2002 provided that mortgages of registered land can

---

[31] Nield, n.30, 629.

[32] See L. Whitehouse, 'The Mortgage Arrears Pre-Action Protocol: An Opportunity Lost' (2009) 72(6) *Modern Law Review* 793, criticizing the Civil Justice Council's Pre-Action Protocol for merely encouraging, rather than compelling, lenders to view repossession as a last resort. The idea that repossession should be a last resort is also promoted by the FCA in its statement of policy and practice concerning possession actions under regulated mortgages: The Mortgages and Home Finance: Conduct of Business sourcebook (MCOB) 13.3.2E(1)(f) (available online at https://www.handbook.fca.org.uk/handbook/), as part of its policy of treating customers fairly.

[33] LPA 1925, s. 85(1).

now only be created by the use of a charge,[34] although the charge has the same effect as creation of a proprietary interest.[35]

While the conveyancing aspects of the mortgage transaction have been heavily influenced by the alienability agenda of the 1925 legislation (reinforced by the LRA 2002), equity historically intervened in the mortgage transaction to protect the mortgagor from unconscionable transactions. Equitable interventions to protect borrowers include the equitable right to redeem the mortgage and recover unencumbered title to the property;[36] a bar on clogs on the equity of redemption, when these make it prohibitively difficult to redeem the mortgage;[37] careful regulation of collateral advantages in favour of the mortgagee;[38] and the application of the historic unconscionable bargain doctrine, which offers relief against certain unfair transactions where the terms of the mortgage are oppressive.[39] These equitable doctrines ensure a minimal standard of fairness in the creation and terms of mortgage contracts, although – in the case of the unconscionable bargain doctrine – the fairness bar is set at a relatively low level.[40]

In additional to these equitable doctrines, mortgages fall under the jurisdiction of the Consumer Credit Act 1974 (as amended by the Consumer Credit Act 2006), which empowers the court to strike down a bargain where the credit relationship was 'unfair' due to the terms, the way the terms are exercised, or resulting from 'any other thing done (or not done) by, or on behalf of, the creditor (either before or after the making of the agreement or any related agreement)'. However, there is limited evidence that the courts are prepared to exercise this power except in the most exceptional circumstances.[41] Limited protection is also provided for borrowers under the Unfair Terms in Consumer Contracts Regulations 1999, which withdrew binding effect from any unfair term. Again, the standards of fairness applied by the courts under these consumer protection provisions still falls some

---

34 LRA 2002, s. 23(1).

35 LPA 1925, s. 87.

36 *Thornborough* v. *Baker* (1675) 3 Swans 628.

37 *Samuel* v. *Jarrah Timber* [1904] AC 323; *Jones* v. *Morgan* (2001) Lloyd's Rep 323.

38 *Bradley* v. *Carrit* [1903] AC 253; *Kregliner* v. *New Patagonia Meat Co* [1914] AC 25.

39 *Multiservice Bookbinding* v. *Marden* [1979] Ch 84; *Nash* v. *Paragon Finance* [2001] EWCA Civ 1466; *Paragon Finance* v. *Pender* [2005] EWCA 760.

40 It is not sufficient that the transaction is objectively harsh, unreasonable or foolish, and there must be misconduct on the part of the defendant – see for example, *Boustany* v. *Piggott* (1995) 69 P&CR 298, 303, Lord Templeman.

41 CCA 2006, s 140A(1). In *Khodari* v. *Al Tamimi* [2008] EWHC 3065, the court held that the high costs of the loan were balanced against the credit risk to the lender; while in *Nine Regions (T/A Logbook Loans)* v. *Sadeer*, Bromley County Court, 14 January 2009, the court held that since a last resort loan was of higher risk for the lender, it naturally attracted a higher interest rate (in this case, 384.4 per cent APR), and so did not give rise to an unfair relationship. Although the court did find an unfair relationship in *Barons Finance Ltd* v. *Olubisi*, Mayor's and City of London Court, 26 April 2010, Claim No: 7BB82089, the facts of that case were quite extreme – the agreement had not been properly executed, the interest rate on the loan was 3.5 per cent per month calculated on a day-to-day basis of the balance outstanding each month, and there had been flagrant breaches of the Consumer Credit Act and the 1983 Consumer Credit (Agreements) Regulations, and the loan was made in circumstances in which the borrower desperately needed to obtain the loan in order to stave off possession proceedings (the loan took place 2 days before the date fixed for the possession hearing).

way short of the standards expected by financial services regulator, the Financial Conduct Authority.[42]

More recently, the Financial Services Authority and Office of Fair Trading put in place regulatory systems (now under the single jurisdiction of the Financial Conduct Authority) to ensure that the creditor meets standards of (procedural) fairness at the point of sale. Conventional first mortgages are subject to a series of rules and guidance relating to the promotion of mortgages, advising and selling standards, disclosure rules (including the mortgage key facts information and health warning concerning the possible consequences of default), responsible lending practices, rules relating to charges and practices for dealing with customers in arrears and in repossession.[43] The UK's approach to financial services regulation – including, particularly, the regulation of the mortgage market – came under scrutiny following the global financial crisis and recession. The FSA conducted its own *Mortgage Market Review*[44] as well as a more general review of its approach to regulation (the Turner Review).[45] These reviews came at a moment when the global financial crisis challenged the paradigm of mortgage borrowers as 'self-responsible consumers',[46] under a neoliberal, market-led ideology which opposed stronger government intervention in macro-financial markets.[47] While much of the wider debate that followed the crisis in the UK focused on macro-prudential strategies to restore and maintain confidence in the stability of financial institutions,[48] the Turner Review, and the Mortgage Market Review, highlighted irresponsible lending as a key cause of the crisis. There followed a series of regulatory initiatives which suggest a stronger commitment towards lender responsibility in the conventional mortgage market, including affordability checks, better quality product information and arguments for minimum product standards.[49] This reflects a changing perspective on the capabilities of consumers as financial and legal subjects, and – under

---

[42] In a 2008 review of awareness of, and compliance with, the Unfair Terms in Consumer Contracts Regulations, and the use of the Regulations to secure an appropriate level of consumer protection, the FSA claimed that, while it expects firms to be proactive in reviewing all their contract terms and other firms' undertakings, firms need to do more to ensure that their terms are drafted fairly: FSA, *Fairness of Terms in Consumer Contracts: A Visible Factor in Firms Treating their Customers Fairly*, (FSA, 2008); para. 3.5.

[43] See FCA Handbook, Mortgages and Home Finance Conduct of Business Sourcebook (MCOB); online at https://www.handbook.fca.org.uk/handbook/MCOB/.

[44] FSA, *Mortgage Market Review* (FSA, 2009); online at www.fsa.gov.uk/pubs/discussion/dp09_03.pdf.

[45] Lord Turner, n.30.

[46] See Nield, n.30, for analysis of the concepts of responsible lending and borrowing in home finance and the impact of the Turner Review on the concept of lender responsibility.

[47] See R. Tomasic, 'Beyond "Light Touch" Regulation of British Banks after the Financial Crisis' in I. MacNeil and J. O'Brien (eds.), *The Future of Financial Regulation* (Hart Publishing, 2010).

[48] The Government's 2009 White Paper, HM Treasury, *Reforming Financial Markets*, Cm 7667, (London: TSO, 2009); online at http://news.bbc.co.uk/1/shared/bsp/hi/pdfs/08_07_09_markets.pdf, focused on four key objectives: dealing with firms deemed too big to fail; strengthening the UK's regulatory institutional framework; identifying and managing systemic risk at a macro-level; and learning and applying the lessons of the current financial crisis.

[49] See Nield, n.30.

the new Financial Conduct Authority (FCA)[50] – the 'autonomous consumer' model appears to have been tempered with a new awareness of consumer vulnerability.[51] It is still early days, and it remains to be seen how the FCA will apply the ideas of consumer vulnerability developed in its 2015 Occasional Paper under its mortgage regulation jurisdiction.

Debate 3

What level of occupier protection is appropriate at the point of crisis?

The crucial distinguishing factor between secured and unsecured credit is that, in the event of default on repayments, and in addition to the borrower's personal obligation to repay the loan,[52] a mortgagee may also seek to enforce its proprietary security over the property. Where the property is owner-occupied, this brings the property's dual functions as a securitizing asset and a home into conflict. The principal remedies available to the mortgagee in such circumstances are possession and sale of the property. This section will consider the balance struck by conventional property law between the roles of the property as security and as housing and home.

First, however, the conduct of the mortgagee in acting to recover possession of owner-occupied property has come under fresh scrutiny. In the past, the FSA has attempted to govern the arrears management practices of regulated mortgage lenders. In addition to the rules concerning the arrears management strategies of lenders, the creditor is required to market the property for sale as soon as possible, and obtain the best price that might reasonably be paid,[53] and to make reasonable efforts to re-negotiate with customers who are in financial difficulties,[54] including considering whether to extend the term of the mortgage.[55] In July 2010, the FSA fined one mortgage provider £630,000 for poor treatment of some customers facing mortgage arrears,[56] amid concern that sector-wide compliance remained exposed to the uneven uptake of guidance and good practice, and in some cases compliance with rules, across the industry. In 2014, the FCA conducted a thematic review of mortgage arrears management and forbearance, which concluded that while arrears management in firms had improved since the last review, mortgage lenders and administrators still need to place greater emphasis on delivering consistently

---

[50] The successor to the FSA – see FSA, *The Financial Conduct Authority: Approach to Regulation* (London: FSA, June 2011).
[51] FCA, *Consumer Vulnerability* – Occasional Paper No. 8, (London: FCA, 2015); see also the new style of regulation applied to pay-day loans, discussed in Andrea Fejős, 'Achieving Safety and Affordability in the UK Payday Loans Market' (2015) 38 *Journal of Consumer Policy* 181.
[52] *Bolton* v. *Buckenham* (1891) 1 QB 278.
[53] *FCA Handbook*, MCOB, 13.6.1; online at https://www.handbook.fca.org.uk/handbook/MCOB/13/6.html.
[54] MCOB 13.3.2A, online at https://www.handbook.fca.org.uk/handbook/MCOB/13/3.html.
[55] MCOB 13.3.4A.
[56] www.fsa.gov.uk/pages/Library/Communication/PR/2010/120.shtml.

fair outcomes for consumers based on their individual circumstances.[57] The FCA continues to work with the industry to help them improve their arrears-handling practices, emphasizing the importance of flexibility to support fair treatment of individual customers, based on their specific personal and financial circumstances. This review emphasized lenders' responsibilities to identify borrowers experiencing financial stress at an early stage, to engage appropriately with them and to tailor solutions to their individual personal and financial circumstances. The FCA also underlined the impact of the wider economic context, including potential interest rate rises, in exposing borrowers to the risk of over-indebtedness, as well as highlighting good practice in firms which had adopted pre-arrears strategies to identify early financial stress and offer proactive solutions.

The evolving culture of lender responsibility and contextualized sensitivity to borrower vulnerabilities was also influenced by the procedural guidelines set out in the Mortgage Arrears Pre-Action Protocol.[58] These sought to encourage greater communication between borrowers and lenders, to ensure that lenders act 'fairly and reasonably' in the event of arrears, and that they avoid repossession except as a last resort. Critics argued that the Pre-Action Protocol would be inadequate due to its reliance on good practice – which had, under the FSA's pre-crisis approach to regulation, proven ineffective in this context,[59] and which leaves borrowers 'vulnerable to inconsistent and potentially adverse treatment at the hands of lenders'.[60] A revised Pre-Action Protocol for Possession Claims based on Mortgage or Home Purchase Plan Arrears in Respect of Residential Property (referred to as the Possession Protocol) came into force on 6 April 2015. As well as making some specific provision concerning authorized tenants, the revised wording is stronger (for example, from stating that a possession action should 'normally' be a last resort, and lenders were to 'consider not' issuing proceedings in certain circumstances, to stating that lenders are 'not to consider' starting a claim unless litigation is really a last resort). It also states that possession claims should be postponed if a borrower can demonstrate that it requires time to seek free independent debt advice, has confirmed an appointment with a debt adviser or has a reasonable expectation of an improvement in their financial circumstances in the foreseeable future. This coincides with the broader shift towards a more customer-focused, proactive and preventative approach to arrears management, as reflected in the changing tide of financial services regulation. This includes greater emphasis on lender responsibility, on the impact (and potential impact) of the wider economic environment for vulnerable borrowers and on achieving good outcomes for consumers and firms. While the FCA has recognized that there is still more work to do in ensuring consistent good practice across the industry, there has been a notable change in the terms of this debate.

---

57 FCA, *Mortgage lenders' arrears management and forbearance* (TR14/3) (London: FCA, 2014).
58 Available at https://www.justice.gov.uk/courts/procedure-rules/civil/protocol/prot_mha.
59 L. Whitehouse, n.32.
60 Ibid., 812.

Where the FCA, and the Mortgages Pre-Action Protocol, have responded to the mortgage default crisis by encouraging – and latterly requiring – lenders to develop new strategies of forbearance, this sits in stark contrast to the exposure of the borrower according to the underlying land law. For example, while it is usual for a mortgagee to seek a court order for possession, this is not always strictly necessary[61] where the lender is able to take peaceful possession without a court order.[62] Although the practice of taking possession without a court order is uncommon in owner-occupied homes, it is more common in relation to buy-to-let properties (which are excluded from the Possession Protocol).[63] Some concerns have been expressed about the potential for lenders to make increasing use of the inherent right to possession as they become more aware of the possibility of avoiding section 36.[64] If the lender does apply to the court for an order for possession, the court has only limited discretion to intervene on behalf of the occupier who wishes to stay in their home. The court's inherent equitable jurisdiction to adjourn possession proceedings is limited to a very short time – probably no longer than 28 days – to allow the mortgagor to find the money to pay arrears. While the statutory power to delay repossession of property that includes a dwelling-house under section 36 of the Administration of Justice Act 1970 is considerably more significant, it is also limited to cases in which '... it appears to the court that in the event of its exercising the power the mortgagor is likely to be able within a reasonable period to pay any sums due under the mortgage ...'.[65]

The conditions for the exercise of this discretion are strict, based on the debtor's financial ability to make good on arrears within a 'reasonable time' – taking as a starting point the whole remaining term of the mortgage[66] – while continuing to meet instalments as they fall due.[67] The opportunity to spread the arrears over a longer period appeared to favour the owner-occupier's interests in the property as a home over the enforcement of the creditor's right to possession. This was tempered, however, by the strong emphasis placed on 'detailed analysis of present figures and future [budget] projections',[68] requiring the owner-occupier to establish their financial credibility if they are to persuade the court to adjourn the possession proceedings.[69] In any event, section 36 can provide no more than interim relief where temporary financial straits have led to the accrual of arrears; the owner-occupier must demonstrate their financial credibility to ensure such

---

[61] *Ropaigealach* v. *Barclay's Bank plc* [2000] QB 263; *Horsham Properties Group Ltd* v. *Clark* [2009] 1 WLR 1255.

[62] Both the Criminal Law Act 1977 and the Protection of Eviction Act 1977 impose criminal sanctions against the forcible eviction of residential occupiers.

[63] Council of Mortgage Lenders, *Mortgage Remedies (Possession and Sale) Review Response by the Council of Mortgage lenders to the Ministry of Justice's Initial Review* (14 January 2009), para. 3.

[64] S. Greer, 'Urgent Review' (2009) 159 *NLJ* 254.

[65] Administration of Justice Act 1970, s. 36(1).

[66] *Cheltenham & Gloucester Building Society* v. *Norgan* [1996] 1 WLR 343.

[67] Ibid..

[68] *Norgan*, above, Waite LJ; *Bristol & West Building Society* v. *Ellis* (1996) 73 P&CR 158 (CA).

[69] See also *Cheval Bridging Finance Ltd* v. *Bhasin* [2008] EWCA Civ 1613.

interim relief; and the courts have become progressively less likely to tolerate repeated applications for relief. The prospect of employment for the borrower is not necessarily to be equated with the prospect of payment of the mortgage instalments.[70] Thus, while the function of the property as housing and home is clearly recognized, the mortgagee's interest in recovering possession once the borrower is in default continues to dominate. It also remains somewhat arbitrary that access to the section 36 protection is dependent on whether the mortgagee has been able to recover possession without a court order.

Although the primary purpose of recovering possession is to facilitate sale of the property, capitalizing the financial asset represented by the home so that the mortgagee can recover the value of the loan, as the decision in *Horsham Properties* v. *Clark & Beech*[71] illustrated, it is not necessary for a lender to take possession in order to exercise the right to sale. The procedure to achieve sale depends on the method by which the mortgage was created, the nature of the mortgagor's default, and the nature of the ownership interest(s) in the property (sole ownership or jointly owned property). The most straightforward method for a mortgagee to achieve sale is through an out-of-court sale under sections 101–103 of the Law of Property Act 1925, which incorporates an automatic power of sale in the mortgagee for all mortgages created by deed.[72] Certain conditions must be satisfied before this power of sale arises (the legal date of redemption must have passed; this is set by the mortgage terms, usually a relatively short time after the mortgage is granted) and become exercisable (when *one* of the three conditions set out in section 103 of the Law of Property Act 1925 has been satisfied).[73] The ease with which a mortgagee can achieve sale through this route reflects the pro-purchaser policy of the 1925 legislation, and represents a powerful remedy for the mortgagee once the borrower is in default. Furthermore, in cases where the mortgagee is able to achieve possession without a court order, the out-of-court sale route presents an opportunity for the mortgagee to recover possession of mortgaged property and realize its capital value without the mortgagee having any opportunity to defend the action in court.

This potentially raises issues under the right to respect for home in Article 8 of the Human Rights Act 1996, as it enables the mortgagee to dispossess occupiers from their homes without any recourse to adjudication concerning the proportionality of the decision to take possession. While a successful Article 8 case is yet to be made in these circumstances, the court appears to have implicitly accepted that the private nature of the dispute does not preclude the raising of the human rights arguments in this context.[74] As the decisions of the Supreme Court

---

[70] *Halifax Plc* v. *Okin* [2007] EWCA Civ 567.

[71] [2008] EWHC 2327.

[72] Law of Property Act 1925, s. 101(1)(i).

[73] These conditions are that either (a) notice requiring payment has been served on the mortgagor and default has continued for three months after service of the notice; (b) interest is in arrears for two months or more; or (c) there has been a breach of any other mortgage provision or LPA provision, other than a covenant for payment of mortgage debt or interest.

[74] See *Horsham Properties Group Ltd* v. *Clark* [2009] 1 WLR 1255.

in *Manchester City Council* v. *Pinnock*[75] and *London Borough of Hounslow* v. *Powell*[76] have begun to embed the proportionality test under Article 8 within domestic UK law, and *Malik* v. *Fassenfelt*[77] indicated that the proportionality test must be applied in cases of horizontal (between private actors) as well as vertical (between the state and a private actor) effect, there is arguably greater scope for challenging procedures which allow an occupier to be evicted by a mortgagor without the due process of a court hearing.

Efforts to close the loopholes of out-of-court repossession and sale have also been brought through political avenues. For example, in 2009, Andrew Dismore MP (Chair of the Joint Committee on Human Rights) introduced a Ten-Minute Rule bill entitled 'Home Repossession (Protection) Bill', which proposed amending the Law of Property 1925 to require mortgagees to obtain the court's permission before exercising the power of sale, where the mortgaged land consists of or includes a dwelling-house. That Bill did not reach its second reading.[78] And in 2009, the Ministry of Justice published a Consultation Paper advancing a tentative proposal that the law should be amended so that a mortgagee of residential land would not be able to exercise the power of sale without the consent of the borrower or a court order (the court's power to make such an order to be framed by a discretionary jurisdiction echoing that in section 36 of the Administration of Justice Act 1970).[79]

The link between financial crises and initiatives to shift the balance of mortgage law towards the protection of the occupier is clear. An earlier attempt to close these loopholes dates back to the previous housing market crisis in 1991, when the Law Commission made recommendations (which were not implemented either) that the mortgagee's rights in respect of possession and sale should be exercised only in good faith and for the purposes of protecting or enforcing the security;[80] and that the artificiality of the two-stage test should be abandoned in favour of one test involving 'enforceable events' defined to allow sale only where the mortgagor has failed to keep to the original repayment bargain, or where the mortgagee's security is otherwise threatened.[81]

There are alternatives to out-of-court sale. Section 91 of the Law of Property Act allows the mortgagee to apply to the court for sale of mortgaged property, and the court may in its discretion direct that the mortgaged property be sold. When judicial sale is requested under section 91, the court has an unfettered discretion to order sale, notwithstanding the objections of any parties. It has been suggested

---

[75] [2010] 3 WLR 1441.

[76] [2011] 2 WLR 287.

[77] [2013] EWCA Civ 798.

[78] http://services.parliament.uk/bills/2008-09/homerepossessionprotection.html.

[79] Ministry of Justice, *Mortgages: Power of Sale and Residential Property* (Consultation Paper) (MoJ, 2009).

[80] Law Commission, *Transfer of Land: Land Mortgages*, Law Com No 204 (Law Commission, 1991), paras 3.4, 7.3.

[81] Ibid., paras 7.7, 7.8. These proposals were taken up by the Northern Ireland Law Commission in its 2010 Report on *Land Law* (NILC 8), available online at http://www.nilawcommission.gov.uk/report_on_land_law_nilc_8__2010.htm.

that 'in exercising its discretion the court is not limited to considering financial matters, but can also take into account social considerations',[82] although the case law supporting this proposition involved requests by occupiers to *proceed* with sale against the wishes of the banks, rather than to *prevent* sale of the property.[83] Finally, any creditor holding a security interest in co-owned land can apply for sale of the property under the Trusts of Land and Appointment of Trustees Act 1996 and, as demonstrated in Chapter 3, the courts have, to date, followed a strong pro-sale policy under sections 14 and 15. The overall picture, when it comes to mortgage enforcement, is that while the Financial Conduct Authority is working to encourage forbearance and resolution of mortgage disputes in the event of default, the background land law principles and provisions continue to strongly favour lenders and their rights over property as security, over borrowers and their claim to occupation of the property as housing and home.

CONCLUSIONS

The pro-creditor bias – which has its origins in a political and economic agenda in favour of alienability and support for the creditors whose financial backing has enabled the growth of owner-occupation – continues to come under fresh political challenges in the context of the financial crisis. This is hardly surprising, in light of evidence concerning the public (as well as private) costs when mortgage repossessions reach critical levels,[84] not only for borrowers and lenders but also for insurers, central government, local government, housing market institutions, labour market institutions and health services. Indeed, since the impact of widespread foreclosures in the US sub-prime mortgage market triggered the current global economic crisis, it is difficult to underestimate the economic, as well as political, social and personal effect of loss of the securitized home through mortgage repossession actions.

There was a history of government-sponsored mortgagor safety nets in the UK in the twentieth century, although these were significantly eroded under the Thatcher governments of the 1980s. Those safety nets were revived under subsequent Labour governments, but their provision became increasingly privatized within the neoliberal mantra of self-responsibility and self-provision. The provision of safety nets for homeowners facing payment problems, and legal policies that seek to value the occupier's interest in their home, perform similar functions as they attempt to ameliorate the risks that are inherent to market-led housing consumption. Historically, government-funded support for homeowners took two main forms: mortgage interest tax relief, and the safety-net provisions

---

[82] Fisher and Lightwood, *Law of Mortgages* (Elsevier, 11th edn., 2002) para. 21.8.

[83] *Polonski* v. *Lloyd's Bank Mortgages Ltd* (1997) 31 HLR 721; *Palk* v. *Mortgage Services Funding plc* [1993] Ch 330.

[84] See Fox, n.17 pp. 109–22.

which entitled mortgagors to claim assistance with their mortgage costs when their income level fell below a specified amount. Although provision for mortgage interest tax relief was established before World War II, the significance of this tax exemption grew as a result of the sheer volume of home owning households, and as house prices began to rise significantly, from the 1970s. It was just as the proportion of homeowners seeking to claim mortgage interest tax relief was beginning to turn it into a widespread and significant welfare support that the government took steps to limit its availability. The decline in mortgage interest tax relief provision began in 1974, when relief was withdrawn for mortgage debts over £25,000; further reductions were made in 1991, until this head of tax relief was finally abolished in 2000. The principal form of state safety-net provision for homeowners, introduced in Britain under the National Assistance Act 1948, was aimed at mortgagors who became unable to meet their repayments due to unexpected loss of income. However, in a significant policy departure from 1995, Income Support for Mortgage Interest (ISMI) was restricted in various ways, including restrictions in when assistance could be claimed and the total loan amount covered.

The privatization of safety nets for mortgage borrowers meant that debtors are now expected to protect themselves through private insurance policies, such as Mortgage Payment Protection Insurance (MPPI), Critical Illness Insurance (CI), Permanent Health Insurance (PHI) and Unemployment Insurance (UI), as well as drawing on personal savings, reserves through flexible mortgages or from employee benefits. It is only when these avenues of relief are exhausted that the residual role of Income Support for Mortgage Interest (ISMI) comes into play.[85] The decline in state-sponsored provision for homeowning households advances the neoliberal agenda and ideological commitments towards self-responsibility, although research has shown that take-up on these self-provided safety-nets has been low and does not provide a robust form of protection.[86] Having said that, though, steps were taken in 2008 to re-introduce ISMI, by way of recognition of the failure of MPPI (and its misselling).[87]

The links between welfare support and safety nets, on the one hand, and the legal frameworks governing the enforcement of mortgages in the event of default, on the other, were explicitly recognized in a House of Commons debate that followed the decision in *Williams and Glyn's Bank Ltd* v. *Boland*,[88] when one member rejected a proposal to strengthen the legal protection afforded to occupiers with the suggestion that: 'If the Government want to do something to help owner-occupiers in this regard ... they should withdraw their proposals to cut back

---

[85] J. Ford, D. Quilgars, R. Burrows and D. Rhodes, *Homeowners Risk and Safety-Nets: Mortgage Payment Protection Insurance (MPPI) and Beyond* (Office of the Deputy Prime Minister, 2004) p. 4.

[86] See J. Ford, R. Burrows and S. Nettleton, *Home Ownership in a Risk Society: A Social Analysis of Mortgage Arrears and Possessions* (Policy Press, 2001); Ford, Quilgars, Burrows and Rhodes.

[87] For discussion, see J. Ford, J. Bretherton, A. Jones and D. Rhodes, *Giving up Home Ownership: A Qualitative Study of Voluntary Possession and Selling because of Financial Difficulties* (DCLG, 2010), esp. para. 3.30–3.31.

[88] [1981] AC 487.

mortgage relief for those who are unemployed ....'[89] This underlines the implicit trade-off between welfare policies and legal policies, in the sense that the existence of welfare protections for occupiers might be regarded as mitigating the tendency to overlook such interests within the property law framework.

The role of government rescue schemes for mortgagors facing payment difficulties made a decisive return to the policy agenda following the most recent housing market crisis. The UK government set in place a number of such schemes following the 2008 downturn, including a Mortgage Rescue Scheme (MRS), designed to provide a structured exit from homeownership for vulnerable households who would otherwise have been entitled to homelessness assistance; and the Homeowners Mortgage Support (HMS), which provides support to lenders to encourage greater levels of forbearance for up to two years for borrowers unable to access other support. While initial evaluations suggest that the MRS has been deemed a qualified success, HMS has proven more problematic, although it has had an indirect benefit to the extent that it has encouraged lenders themselves to offer greater degrees of forbearance.[90]

Finally, there are some moves towards providing greater levels of mortgagor protection within the property law framework, although it remains too early to say whether these will be successful. In June 2010, a Secured Lending Reform Bill was presented to Parliament as a Private Members Bill, but lapsed on 30 March 2012. Proposals in this Bill included amendments to provide for the Secretary of State (by regulations) to abolish the right of a mortgagee to obtain peaceable re-entry of a property and to prescribe maximum penalties that may be imposed on a mortgagee who peaceably re-enters a property,[91] as well as provision for the Secretary of State to ensure that a possession order is not made by the court on the application of a mortgagee unless the court is satisfied that the mortgagor has received an adequate opportunity to raise any counterclaim, set-off or other defence that may be available against the mortgagee, and the court has determined the merits of any such defence.[92] Finally, it would have allowed for provision to confer on the court power to vary terms of the mortgage (the rate of interest, the schedule of payments, or the value of payments) where it appears just to do so.[93] These amendments were intended to aid *all* mortgagors in financial difficulty – not merely owner-occupiers; clause 4 would broaden the court's discretion under section 36 of the AJA to remove the restriction to 'dwelling houses'.

The Bill was designed to encourage a 'rescue culture' within the banking industry by embedding a framework to support forbearance and closing the loopholes that have allowed some mortgagees to enforce their security aggressively, without giving the mortgagor any opportunity to defend the proceedings in a court. This

---

89 Mr Nicholas Brown, MP, HC Standing Committee Official Report, Session 1985–6, Vol X, (21 May 1986), p. 3.
90 Ford, Bretherton, Jones and Rhodes, n.87 esp. para. 3.30–3.31.
91 Cl 2.
92 Cl 3.
93 Sch. 5.

move was consistent with the discourse of greater lender responsibility in the regulatory context. It may transpire that this most recent moment of 'crisis' in the housing market and wider economy will effect significant shifts in the philosophical orientation of property law;[94] as yet, any lasting impact remains to be seen.

Further Reading

J. Ford, J. Bretherton, A. Jones and D. Rhodes, *Giving up Home Ownership: A Qualitative Study of Voluntary Possession and Selling because of Financial Difficulties* (DCLG, 2010).

L. Fox, *Conceptualising Home: Theories, Laws and Policies* (Hart Publishing, 2006).

S. Nield, 'Responsible Lending and Borrowing: Whereto Low-Cost Home Ownership?' (2010) 30(4) *Legal Studies* 610.

L. Whitehouse, 'The Mortgage Arrears Pre-Action Protocol: An Opportunity Lost' (2009) 72(6) *MLR* 793.

L. Whitehouse, 'Making the Case for Socio-Legal Research in Land Law: Renner and the Law of Mortgage' (2010) 37(4) *Journal of Law and Society* 545.

---

[94] N. Davidson and R. Dyal-Chand, 'Property in Crisis' (2009) 78 *Fordham L Rev* 1607.

11

COHABITATION: RIGHTS TO THE HOME

INTRODUCTION

Nowhere in land law is the tension between the theme of rationality and the emotional dimensions of property more exposed than in the question of whether a non-owning cohabitant is entitled to a share of (or interest in) their co-lived property; and, if so, the quantification of that share or interest. Those are the fundamental debates tackled in this chapter, which focuses on the rights of cohabitants in their homes.[1] They are in many ways *the* Great Debates of our time, masking doctrinal, procedural, political and broad socio-legal issues.[2] Those issues highlight the problematic nature of land law's rational search for intention when the parties themselves may not have expressed it. The first flush of love leads people to do extraordinary things without thought; it is only when, inevitably, that love turns to bitterness and hatred, or, more mundanely, the cohabitants part company, that the issues for land law arise. It is at that latter point, the bitter end, that land law requires the re-construction – or, perhaps, the better word is translation – of events around the tools it provides: the constructive trust and proprietary estoppel.

That this is an *interdisciplinary* issue almost goes without saying, but it also highlights what we have referred to as the 'destination' nature of land law within the legal canon. It is where land law meets family law and trusts law, each vying for supremacy.[3] It is where socio-legal and feminist critique often meets land law, exposing its assumptions and monochrome understandings.[4] It is where empirical socio-legal research exposes the fallacies inherent in the assumptions of land law about why people might do certain things. It is where the uncertainty at the roots of the doctrines creates considerable practical problems and also exposes the

---

[1] We do not here deal with the rights of married couples and civil partners, which are governed by different legislative principles.

[2] See, L. Fox O'Mahony, 'The politics of *Lloyds Bank v Rosset*', in S. Douglas, R. Hickey and E. Waring (eds.), *Landmark Cases in Property Law* (Oxford: Hart, 2015).

[3] For an interesting discussion of the different ways of thinking and procedural interaction, see A. Bottomley, 'Production of a Text: *Hammond v Mitchell* [1991] 1 WLR 1127' (1994) 2(1) *Feminist Legal Studies* 83.

[4] See, for example, A. Bottomley, 'Self and Subjectivities: Languages of Claim in Property Law' (1993) 20(1) *Journal of Law and Society* 56.

fallacy of rationality in law. As Bettina Lange explains, law 'others' emotion in the pursuit of rationality:

> [E]motions are considered as potentially anarchic, unbounded, and associated with a lack of control. Therefore when lawyers have discussed the role of emotions in legal processes they have emphasized the importance of containing them. The 'messy individuality' of emotions is contrasted with hard and fast 'categorical rules'. Thus, lawyers' construction of emotion as 'other' distances emotion not just from cognition but also from normative processes. This again is different from sociologists' understanding of emotions.[5]

And, notwithstanding numerous Law Commission projects and proposals for reform, successive governments have failed to address these conflicts through legislation, not wanting to touch the 'hot potato' for fear of undermining the supposed naturalness and better associations of marriage and civil partnership. The blood that has been spilt – that may be hyperbole, but the area rouses strong emotions – by judges, academics and policy-makers, together with the trees that have been mercilessly cut down to enable them to develop their positions, could so easily have been resolved by Parliamentary intervention. Scotland has done so and the Law Commission made reform proposals which, to a certain extent, mirrored and extended the Scottish position.[6] However, the 2010 Coalition Government refused to implement the Law Commission's proposals,[7] and there is no sign that the 2015 Tory government intends to intervene.

It is no wonder, given the level of dissatisfaction amongst the experts with the current state of the law, that there is also considerable confusion in the public domain, including among members of the legal profession. Study after study has found that non-owning and part-owning cohabitants believe in a set of laws which have no foundation in *the* law. So, for example, the myth of common law marriage (that cohabitants somehow 'become' the equivalent to married couples over an unspecified period of time, and thus gain the same rights as married couples) remains prevalent – in one large-scale survey, just under six in ten of cohabiting couples believed in the common law marriage.[8] There is also consider-able evidence of *diversity* of practice amongst cohabitants as to how they arrange their finances and, at a qualitative level, the influence of interactional settings.[9]

---

[5] B. Lange, 'The Emotional Dimension in Legal Regulation' (2002) 29(1) *Journal of Law and Society* 197, 199.

[6] Family Law (Scotland) Act 2006; Law Commission, *The Financial Consequences of Relationship Breakdown*, Law Com No 307 (TSO, 2007). In addition, a Private Members' Bill introduced into the House of Lords by Lord Lester, the Cohabitation Bill, did not survive the Parliamentary process, but offered a further alternative vision.

[7] HL Deb, 6 September 2011, Col WS18; although, see s. 199, Equality Act 2010, which, when brought in to force, will abandon the outmoded 'presumption of advancement' in relation to the resulting trust.

[8] A. Barlow, C. Burgoyne, E. Clery and J. Smithson, 'Cohabitation and the Law: Myths, Money and the Media' in A. Park, J. Curtis, K. Thompson, M. Phillips, M. Johnson and E. Clery (eds.), *British Social Attitudes: The 24th Report* (Sage, 2008) p. 40.

[9] See, in particular, G. Douglas, J. Pearce and H. Woodward, *A Failure of Trust: Resolving Property Disputes on Cohabitation Breakdown*, Report of a Study Funded by the ESRC (Cardiff Law School, 2007).

In this chapter, we isolate four Great Debates. The first two are doctrinal. Debate 1 concerns the principles by which cohabitants can establish an interest in their home. Debate 2 concerns the principles by which, if a cohabitant has successfully established an interest in their home, the law assesses that interest. The purpose of our discussion of these debates is to isolate certain schemas of this doctrinal law – the way it thinks about why people do things and the sort of evidence by which the cohabitant can establish their interest and its extent. In those two debates, we draw attention also to the apparent differences and similarities between constructive trusts and proprietary estoppel. That leads into Debate 3: are constructive trusts and proprietary estoppel different and, more to the point, does it matter? Debate 4 takes a step back from that heavy-duty doctrinal law and draws on the broader literature in this field, theoretical and empirical, to demonstrate that law's rationality and assumptions have little empirical foundation. Although the development of the doctrinal law in this area was, in part, designed to come to terms with the empirical quantitative reality of large-scale cohabitation, it has done so through rational doctrines which cannot account for the qualitative lived experience.

AUTOBIOGRAPHICAL NOTE

On writing ...

I wrote what follows as a *cri de coeur* in the first edition of this book. I still feel the same way, but, this time, colleagues have pointed me in the direction of some post-first edition work, which has really helped me knuckle down! Anyway, here goes:

When one begins a book project like this with other people, the first thing we do is to split it up. Who is going to take primary responsibility for which chapter? We carved this book up in that way and, although each of us has edited the others' work, it is still pretty obvious (to us, at any rate) who wrote which bit. At the carve-up, I got lumbered with this chapter. At the time, I wasn't hugely bothered but subsequently I just couldn't get round to it. I procrastinated and, when the commissioning editor came asking, there was a great excuse: 'we're expecting *Jones* v. *Kernott* any day now'. But, by mid-November, I couldn't ignore it any longer: *Jones* was out. I'd blogged about it. The chapter had to be written, although my computer tells me that it took another month before it was done. But, well, the original draft was wobbly and the reviewer picked up on the uncertainty inherent in the chapter, as well as kindly pointing out how it could be fixed. The reviewer isn't responsible for this final version but they helped it on its way.

The thing is, I love writing and particularly about tricky inter- or multi-disciplinary things. Most of all, though, I need to care about something before I write about it. Writing is emotional and my style, if there is one, reflects that experience. But this chapter was just a step too far. The hesitation was not induced by the fact that there is so much written about this subject by incredibly clever people, with some of whom I disagree both expressly and by implication. It's just that, although I appreciated how the law had developed, I have absolutely no faith in it at all; in fact, I regarded it as intellectually moribund.

The starting point of the approach taken by law to human motivation seems so banal, monochrome, one-dimensional, irrelevant to lived experience and requires subjective opinion which merely exposes the prejudice/s of the speaker. It ignores the complicated narratives of the parties, fixes on certain matters which may have been an afterthought (if they gave any thought to it or its implication) and, despite the (sometimes) best intentions of the judges to do 'the right thing', the law just is plain stupid.

What finally galvanized me and made me care enough to write this chapter was its links with a parallel project concerning a focus on legal technique and technicality as a resource for socio-legal studies. I also found much rich literature that reflected on the law from the outside, with which I have far more empathy than that produced by those insiders. So, I cared again, and found that I passionately cared, and hope that some of that passion rubs off in this chapter.

Debate

What are the principles by which a cohabitant can establish an interest in their home?

This is the foundational doctrinal question. What parties should rationally do is to set out in writing at the outset what type of interest they each have in the property and (hopefully) the extent of that interest. That was the expectation and hope of the Law of Property Act 1925. If that is done, and done properly (in the sense that it complies with the formalities), that document will bind the parties subject to the application of limited equitable doctrines (such as rectification and mistake).[10] There are many examples of the most learned judges throwing their hands up in the air and wondering why people do not adopt this rationalist solution to avoid costly litigation. Perhaps the best example of this is the comment of Ward LJ:

> I ask in despair how often this court has to remind conveyancers that they would save their clients a great deal of later difficulty if only they would sit the purchasers down, explain the difference between a joint tenancy and tenancy in common, ascertain what they want and then expressly declare in the conveyance of transfer how the beneficial interest is to be held because that will be conclusive and save all argument. When are conveyancers going to do this as a matter of invariable standard practice? This court has urged that time after time. Perhaps conveyancers do not read the law reports. I will try one more time: ALWAYS TRY TO AGREE ON

---

[10] *Goodman* v. *Gallant* [1986] 2 WLR 236; the formalities are contained in LPA 1925, s. 53(1)(b).

AND THEN RECORD HOW THE BENEFICIAL INTEREST IS TO BE HELD. It is not very difficult to do.[11]

Since 1998, HM Land Registry has had a form TR1, which allows parties to express the nature of the trust by which they share the beneficial ownership. Box 10 enables parties to say how they hold the property and in what shares, but it is not compulsory to complete this box. Where it has been done, this simple process would avoid many subsequent legal disputes, although it may also leave the parties dissatisfied.

There are potentially two legal doctrines involved when disputes arise – the constructive trust and proprietary estoppel. These are similar but there are differences, at the very least terminological (holding off debate for now about their substantive and procedural assonance and/or dissonance). We will take each in turn.

But first, there is a preliminary question which we must clear out of the way. Why use the constructive trust, and not the resulting trust? Despite considerable evidence from some quarters of a desire to use the resulting trust[12] – which, in essence, entitles a paying party to the return of their money as a matter of rebuttable presumption and, in its absence, a property right – it is now crystal clear that the resulting trust has only a residual value where the parties are in some sort of commercial relationship with each other (as lovers and business partners or just business partners). That is because, in essence, the resulting trust is just too blunt an instrument because of its single-minded financial focus – as Baroness Hale pithily observed: 'The law has indeed moved on in response to changing social and economic conditions.'[13] In her joint judgment with Lord Walker in *Jones* v. *Kernott*,[14] they make clear that it is these social and economic conditions which make problematic the enquiry, inherent in the resulting trust, into who paid for what, and render inappropriate the discriminatory presumption of advancement which could be used to undermine the presumption of the resulting trust.[15] As Lord Hope put it in *Stack* v. *Dowden*:

> [C]ohabiting couples are in a different kind of relationship. The place where they live together is their home. Living together is an exercise in give and take, mutual co-operation and compromise. Who pays for what in regard to the home has to be seen in the wider context of their overall relationship. A more practical, down-to-earth, fact-based approach is called for in their case. The framework which the law provides should be simple, and it should be accessible.[16]

---

[11] *Carlton* v. *Goodman* [2002] EWCA Civ 545 at [44].

[12] See, for example, W. Swadling, 'The Common Intention Trust in the House of Lords: An Opportunity Missed' (2007) 123 *LQR* 511.

[13] *Stack* v. *Dowden* [2007] 2 AC 432, [60].

[14] [2011] UKSC 53, [24].

[15] The presumption of advancement was a method of rebutting the presumption of the resulting trust. In certain cases and in certain relationships (e.g. wife to husband but not vice versa), equity presumed a gift, as opposed to a resulting trust. The presumption of advancement is to be abolished by Equality Act 2010, s. 199.

[16] n. 13, [3].

Quite so, but one might remark that the framework we have been left with is anything but simple and accessible, and, according to one venerated author, historically inaccurate and technically incorrect.[17] In any event, we are left, in most cases, with the choice of the constructive trust or estoppel.

CONSTRUCTIVE TRUST

It is now established that the first question to be addressed is how legal title is held.[18] What this establishes is a presumption. Where legal title to the property is vested in one party, the presumption is that party has sole beneficial ownership as well. Where legal title is vested in both cohabitants, the presumption is that they intend that each of them is to have an interest in the property. To put these propositions another way, that vesting of legal title establishes a common intention. The question is how, in cases of sole ownership, that presumption or common intention can be rebutted to enable the non-legal owner to obtain such an interest.

That rebuttal can be demonstrated, in broad terms, by a common intention between the cohabitants that they hold the property differently from that initial presumption, and they acted in some way on that different common intention. Common intention on its own is never enough because that would be the equivalent of a mere promise; but common intention is an essential ingredient.

Common intention

On the question of common intention, the law divides into two or, possibly, three parts. Common intention may be express or inferred; the law is currently in a state of flux as to whether, at this stage of the inquiry, it is appropriate to impute a common intention. The significance of this inquiry and the basis for the common intention is that the quality of acts of detriment required by the non-owning cohabitant are, or are likely to be, different as a matter of law. It is, therefore, essential to get a handle on what is meant by these different types of intention. Again, the law is in a state of flux here, but there is some common ground.

EXPRESS COMMON INTENTION

The classic description of the express common intention was provided by the judgment of Lord Bridge in *Lloyds Bank* v. *Rosset*:[19]

> The first and fundamental question which must always be resolved is whether, independently of any inference to be drawn from the conduct of the parties in the

---

[17] P. Sparkes, 'Non-declaration of beneficial co-ownership', [2012] *Conv* 207, who '... retrace[s] the history of land registry transfers step by step in order to explain how the technically incorrect solution reached in *Stack* came to appear believable'.

[18] *Stack.*

[19] [1991] 1 AC 107, 132.

course of sharing the house as their home and managing their joint affairs, there has at any time prior to acquisition, or exceptionally at some later date, been any agreement, arrangement or understanding reached between them that the property is to be shared beneficially. The finding of an agreement or arrangement to share in this sense can only, I think, be based on evidence of express discussions between the partners, however imperfectly remembered and however imprecise their terms may have been.

There is no disagreement about this category, although there is an oddity. The oddity is that, in some cases, the courts derive an express common intention when clearly there was not one. In these cases, the owner partner generally provides a misleading explanation about why the non-owning partner is not on the title to the property – 'it will affect your divorce settlement', 'you are under age', 'it will affect your matrimonial dispute with your previous partner' or 'it will affect your taxation liability'.[20] On the face of it, there can be no meeting of minds between the parties; but the courts have constructed the common intention by making the point that, if the bar was gone, then the parties would have been joint owners; or to put the point another way, but for the excuse, the parties would have been joint owners.

That line of authority, however, was distinguished in *Curran* v. *Collins*.[21] Although there were a number of properties involved in this case, in relation to one property, a house in Feltham owned solely by Mr Collins, Ms Curran '... raised the subject of her having a share of the property with Mr Collins and he told her that it was too expensive for her name to be on the property because it would involve paying the premia for two life insurance policies ("the Excuse")'.[22] The judge had originally found that Mr Collins had made this statement to avoid the embarrassment of having to tell Ms Curran that he refused to make her a co-owner.

Actually, the trial judge had found Ms Curran to be both entirely honest but also unreliable, because she expressed herself without precision; Mr Collins, however, was described as 'intelligent and capable of being very calculating, and [the judge] approached his evidence with caution'.[23] The judge's view of the evidence is important because she is the only one who hears it 'live' and a subsequent court is always unwilling to overturn findings of fact.[24] That view of the evidence taken by the judge supported the construction of those facts – Mr Collins' character was one which was capable of making that calculation as to interest (assuming he was aware of what he was doing). It is also the only moment at which a party can influence the court proceedings – to escape from the bottle-neck of legal principle imposed on the parties' relationship – before they 'become

---

[20] Respectively *Eves* v. *Eves* [1975] 1 WLR 1338; *Grant v Edwards* [1986] Ch 638; *Hammond* v. *Mitchell* [1991] 1 WLR 1127.

[21] [2015] EWCA Civ 404.

[22] [3] (ii).

[23] [16]–[17].

[24] *Langsam* v. *Beachcroft LLP* [2012] EWCA Civ 1230; *Curran*, at [29]–[33].

almost entirely detached or "abstracted" from the proceedings both physically and emotionally'.[25]

The judge's view of the facts, however, meant that there was no express common intention. In a sense, that exposes the fundamental fallacy underlying this brand of express common intention – there would be no reason for an excuse if the intention was truly common. Arden LJ was able to distinguish this case from the others on relatively narrow grounds – the parties were not living together when the excuse was given and did not do so until many years later, as well as the fact that Ms Curran was said to have made no significant contribution to the property leading to the assertion that she placed no reliance on the excuse.[26] Lewison LJ faced up to the apparent conflict between this matter and previous authority. He drew a similar distinction to Arden LJ – unlike the other cases, the Feltham property was not bought as a family home – but also went on to say that the excuse in this matter was of a different order to those other cases. That is, the excuses in those cases were positive assertions that the property would have been acquired in joint names but for the excuse; the excuse here was a negative representation, i.e. the house will not be bought in joint names because of the expense of doing so. This appears to allow mere sophistry, the words and expressions that people use (and, of course, the excuses in the other cases could equally have been expressed negatively), to be allotted a formal force; in itself, that is an irony as we are dealing with doctrines designed to deal with informality. The case itself bears witness to Fox O'Mahony's argument that, although claimants are not explicitly portrayed as greedy or self-dealing, the doctrine '... does imply normative expectations about acquisitive-individualism over family-communitarianism, self-interest over trust, and the "tidy lives" of consent, private ordering, and capital investment over non-financial contributions and the messy realities of family life'.[27]

INFERRED AND IMPUTED COMMON INTENTION

However, the difference between the inference and the imputation is central. The starting point is the description of both provided by Lord Neuberger in *Stack* v. *Dowden*:

> An inferred intention is one which is objectively deduced to be the subjective actual intention of the parties, in the light of their actions and statements. An imputed intention is one which is attributed to the parties, even though no such actual intention can be deduced from their actions and statements, and even though they had no such intention. Imputation involves concluding what the parties would have intended, whereas inference involves concluding what they did intend.[28]

[25] D. Watkins, 'Recovering the lost human stories of law: Finding Mrs Burns', (2013)7(1) *Law and Humanities* 68, 77.

[26] [41].

[27] L. Fox O'Mahony, 'The politics of *Lloyds Bank v Rosset*', in S. Douglas, R. Hickey and E. Waring (eds.), *Landmark Cases in Property Law* (Oxford: Hart, 2015), 195.

[28] [2007] 2 AC 432, [126].

If we leave to one side for the moment the question of from what the inference is to be drawn, the distinction between these two types of intention appears to be essentially a difference of emphasis. An inference is derived from the facts and explains the actions of the parties only on the basis that the non-owner is to get a share in the property (or not). An imputation puts thoughts into the minds of the parties which were never there in the first place but, judged objectively, concluding what they would have intended had they given their minds to the question.

At the moment, it is settled law that a common intention can be inferred.[29] What remains unsettled is the fact-base from which one can infer that intention. In *Rosset*, Lord Bridge said that, as he read the authorities, it is at least doubtful whether anything other than direct contributions to the purchase price or mortgage payments would be sufficient.[30] We must, however, treat that comment with caution (as, indeed, it was expressed). In *Stack*, for example, Lord Walker noted that the comment was 'certainly consistent with many first-instance and Court of Appeal decisions, but I respectfully doubt whether it took full account of the views (conflicting though they were) expressed in *Gissing* [*v Gissing*]'.[31] And, as Baroness Hale put it in *Stack*, Lord Bridge's comment may well have 'set that hurdle rather too high in certain respects'.[32]

We must, therefore, turn to the case of *Burns* v. *Burns*, which has been treated as something of a *cause célèbre* in the clamour for reform.[33] As will be seen, we take rather different messages from the case. Mr and Mrs Burns were not married but lived together for 17 years. They had two children together. The home was bought by Mr Burns and in his name. Mrs Burns cared for the children and, only when they were old enough, did she start to earn any money (about £60 per week from her driving instructor business), which was combined with the housekeeping allowance paid to her by Mr Burns. She bought a few bits and pieces around the home and re-decorated it completely a couple of years before they split up. She paid some of the bills, but this was out of money given to her by Mr Burns.

The Court of Appeal was split on the outcome, but the majority were clear that there was insufficient evidence from which one could infer a common intention. They wrote off her non-financial contributions to the household as being irrelevant to the enquiry. However, the majority also seemed to be clear about the types of expenditure from which the common intention could be inferred. Fox LJ said:

> If there is a substantial contribution by the woman to family expenses, and the house was purchased on a mortgage, her contribution is, indirectly, referable to

---

[29] *Rosset*, 132–33.

[30] 133.

[31] [1971] AC 886 , [26], citing the speeches in *Gissing* of Lord Reid [1971] AC 886 at 896G–897B and Lord Diplock at 909 D-H.

[32] n. 13, [63].

[33] For discussion and critique, see A. Bottomley, 'From Mrs Burns to Mrs Oxley: Do Co-Habiting Women (Still) Need Marriage Law?' (2006) 14(2) *Feminist Legal Studies* 181.

the acquisition of the house since, in one way or another, it enables the family to pay the mortgage instalments. Thus, a payment could be said to be referable to the acquisition of the house if, for example, the payer either (a) pays part of the purchase price or (b) contributes regularly to the mortgage instalments or (c) pays off part of the mortgage or (d) makes a substantial financial contribution to the family expenses so as to enable the mortgage instalments to be paid.

But if a payment cannot be said to be, in a real sense, referable to the acquisition of the house it is difficult to see how, in such a case as the present, it can base a claim for an interest in the house.[34]

May LJ added that, for a common intention to be inferred, there needed to be some '"real" or "substantial" financial contribution towards either the purchase price, deposit or mortgage instalments by the means of which the family home was acquired'.[35] Whether that expression of real or substantial referred back to the earlier part of the paragraph in which that sentence appeared, where he had accepted the significance of indirect payments, is unclear.

Be that as it may, it is already clear that Lord Bridge's reading was narrow. Yet, if we take a moment to think about indirect payment, it does not seem to be the answer at all; in fact, it also seems quite perverse. Remember that Mrs Burns was given a housekeeping allowance into which she put her own income as well. Mr Burns did not really need her to pay the bills so that, in fact, her indirect contributions were neither here nor there. This is the fallacy of that debate – it only 'works' when there is already financial equality or the owning partner *needs* the resources of the non-owning partner. The indirect contribution line, then, misses the point in some cases.

The real point is the failure (or refusal) to accept the relevance of non-financial contributions. Dawn Watkins' empirical research allows us to 'recover' Ms Burns' narrative. Although she was portrayed as 'mistress', they were a 'typical married couple', he '… was the major breadwinner but she was also industrious, a good mother and homemaker, earning such money as she could by flower-arranging etc. and taking a driving-instructor's course'.[36] Ms Burns, in fact, worked all through their relationship (her training had been as a couturier), and she worked at Mr Burns' driving instructor office. She said:

So I got this money, and if he didn't want to pay the gas or the electricity he would say, "Oh, well you've done so many hours this week you can pay it." And so I would pay it … And if you look at all the … the utility bills, they were in my name and not his name, but when I brought that up in the court thing, saying I did that, they said, "Yes, but he could have still paid it, even if it was in your name" … sometimes he would say "Oh, I think you've earned enough this week. You better pay that, you know, or you do that and this, that and the other." I mean, I used

---

[34] [1984] 1 Ch 317, 329.

[35] At 345.

[36] D. Watkins, 'Recovering the lost human stories of law: Finding Mrs Burns', (2013) 7(1) *Law and Humanities* 68, 83.

to do stupid grandiose dinner parties for shop owners that he wanted to impress – anybody who he wanted to impress – and they used to come and I can remember one man said, "We're dying to meet this goddess at home."

One might say that this judicial refusal was doctrinally justified because these activities were not related to the actual purchase of the home or because one does such acts (such as childcare, housework, DIY) not out of a desire to obtain an interest in the property but out of love, affection and, perhaps, because it is the norm.[37] And, Bottomley asks, 'Should we support or defend the development of an area of law which allows the play of a figure of woman/victim and privileges women who can be ascribed within the wife/mother role?'[38]

IMPUTING COMMON INTENTION

And now we come to the question of whether one can impute a common intention at this stage. In the earliest House of Lords decision developing the application of the constructive trust in this context, *Pettitt* v. *Pettitt*,[39] the Law Lords divided on the question, and the majority seemed to settle uneasily on the proposition that the intention could not be imputed. In the subsequent case, *Gissing* v. *Gissing*, there was an uneasy truce. Lord Diplock, who in *Pettitt* had advocated the use of imputation, can be read as making the same point in his speech in *Gissing*, simply replacing the word 'impute' with 'infer'.[40]

The description by Baroness Hale and Lord Walker in *Jones* v. *Kernott*[41] of the different reasoning of the House of Lords in *Gissing* summarizes the general expression of dissatisfaction with that decision:

> ... It may be worth pointing out that their Lordships' speeches were singularly unresponsive to each other. The only reference to another speech is by Viscount Dilhorne (at p 900) where he agreed with Lord Diplock on a very general proposition as to the law of trusts. The law reporter has managed to find a ratio for the headnote (at p 886) only by putting these two propositions together with some remarks by Lord Reid (at p 896) which have a quite different flavour. We can only guess at the order in which the speeches were composed, but [certain passages from] Lord Reid's speech ... suggest that Lord Reid had read Lord Diplock's speech in draft, and thought that it was about 'an imputation of a deemed intention'.[42]

---

[37] See, for example, *Rosset*, n.27 127–28.
[38] A. Bottomley, 'Self and Subjectivities: Languages of Claim in Property Law', (1993) 20(1) *Journal of Law and Society* 56, 60. The question derives from Bottomley's reading of the text in *Eves* v. *Eves* [1971] 1 WLR 1338. The discussion of the ideology of the victim by Kristin Bumiller in *The Civil Rights Society: The Social Construction of Victims*, (Johns Hopkins Press, 1989) has particular power in this context.
[39] [1970] AC 777.
[40] Lord Walker, in *Stack*, makes this point: 'But for the substitution of the word 'infer' for 'impute' the substance of the reasoning is, it seems to me, essentially the same (although worked out in a good deal more detail) as Lord Diplock's reasoning in *Pettitt v Pettitt*, when he was in the minority' ([20]).
[41] [2011] UKSC 53.
[42] *Stack*, [28].

It is clear that Lord Walker and Baroness Hale believe that the time may well have come to roll back these decisions and accept that a common intention at this stage can be imputed. The groundwork has been laid for that development in *Stack*.[43]

It may well be that we are arguing over nothing. As we shall see, in *Jones* v. *Kernott*,[44] the majority of the Supreme Court argued that there was considerable overlap between the concepts. But the resistance to imputed intentions seems ingrained into the property lawyer's psyche. Furthermore, if accepted, difficult questions remain about what types of factors or acts can give rise to such an imputation and, indeed, whether an imputation would really remedy injustice.

Detriment

When it comes to proving detriment, inferred common intention cases are the easiest – the facts which give rise to the inference also provide the detriment. It is express common intention cases which are the most difficult. The test which seems most useful is that propounded by Nourse LJ in *Grant* v. *Edwards*, where he said that:

> The difficulty is caused, I think because although the common intention has been made plain, everything else remains a matter of inference. Let me illustrate it in this way. It would be possible to take the view that the mere moving into the house by the woman amounted to an acting upon the common intention. But that was evidently not the view of the majority in *Eves* v. *Eves* [1975] 1 WLR 1338. And the reason for that may be that, in the absence of evidence, the law is not so cynical as to infer that a woman will only go to live with a man to whom she is not married if she understands that she is to have an interest in their home. So what sort of conduct is required? In my judgment it must be conduct on which the woman could not reasonably have been expected to embark unless she was to have an interest in the house. If she was not to have such an interest, she could reasonably be expected to go and live with her lover, but not, for example, to wield a 14-lb. sledge hammer in the front garden. In adopting the latter kind of conduct she is seen to act to her detriment on the faith of the common intention.[45]

So, the type of conduct required is conduct out of the norm. The use of the '14-lb. sledge hammer' is because the Claimant in *Eves* did precisely that while pregnant. It does not really take too much thought to appreciate the inherent fallacy in this test. If one is looking for conduct outside the norm, then one needs to have an appreciation of the norm from which one can make that judgment. One needs to ask why the person did the act in question and, suspending reality for a moment, assume that there is one single motivation as, it seems, the courts do. So, in *Rosset*, even if there had been a common intention, Mrs Rosset had simply

---

[43] Lord Walker, [20]–[21]; Baroness Hale, [60].
[44] [2011] UKSC 53.
[45] [1986] Ch 638, 648.

not acted outside the norm. Her activities (assisting and managing builders) were constructed by Lord Bridge as follows:

> It was common ground that Mrs Rosset was extremely anxious that the new matrimonial home should be ready for occupation before Christmas if possible. In these circumstances it would seem the most natural thing in the world for any wife, in the absence of her husband abroad, to spend all the time she could spare and to employ any skills she might have, such as the ability to decorate a room, in doing all she could to accelerate progress of the work quite irrespective of any expectation she might have of enjoying a beneficial interest in the property. The judge's view that some of this work was work 'upon which she could not reasonably have been expected to embark unless she was to have an interest in the house' seems to me, with respect, quite untenable.[46]

Furthermore, and in any event, Lord Bridge said that Mrs Rosset's acts were 'so trifling as to be almost de minimis', and would not have supported any claim if there had been the clearest common intention.[47]

PROPRIETARY ESTOPPEL

By contrast with the contestation over constructive trusts, the principles in relation to proprietary estoppel seem relatively simple. In essence, what is required is an assurance by one party on which the other party relies to their detriment. Sometimes, instead of the assurance, that party simply stands back while the other acts to their detriment in reliance on facts which they believe.[48] That is something of a reduction of three rather different types of case, which all have an element of mistake underpinning them: imperfect gift (common mistake), standing by (unilateral mistake) and common expectation (a 'flavour' of mistake or misprediction).[49] Perhaps the unifying element is 'unconscionability' – as Lord Walker suggested, 'If the other elements appear to be present but the result does not shock the conscience of the court, the analysis needs to be looked at again.'[50]

The concepts are flexible, but within boundaries. As Lord Walker memorably put it in *Yeoman's Row* v. *Cobbe*:

> [E]quitable estoppel is a flexible doctrine which the court can use, in appropriate circumstances, to prevent injustice caused by the vagaries and inconstancy of

---

[46] At 131. As Bottomley aptly puts it, 'What is required is not only labour which can be valued, but labour which can be dissociated from any wifely role and in which it can be proved that the woman specifically directed the activity towards ownership rather than simply use of the property. We are drawn back to forms of specific thinking which seem at variance not only with women's socio-economic activities but with the very way in which they think them': A. Bottomley, n.33, 65; see also A. Bottomley, n.38, especially at 207.

[47] Ibid..

[48] *Ramsden* v. *Dyson* (1866) LR 1 HL 129.

[49] [2008] 1 WLR 1752, [63].

[50] [2008] 1 WLR 1752, [92]; see also M. Dixon, 'Confining and Defining Proprietary Estoppel: The Role of Unconscionability' (2010) 30(3) *Legal Studies* 408.

human nature. But is not a sort of joker or wild card to be used whenever a Court disapproves of the conduct of a litigant who seems to have the law on his side. Flexible though it is, the doctrine must be formulated and applied in a disciplined and principled way. Certainty is important in property transactions.[51]

The usual requirement is that the assurance must be 'clear and unambiguous', but this is context-specific – so, in *Thorner* v. *Major*, the representor was '... a very taciturn farmer, given to indirect statements, [who] made remarks obliquely referring to his intention with regard to his farm after his death'.[52] On the other hand, in *Yeoman's Row* v. *Cobbe*, the context of a commercial transaction between two experienced property business people, which was not properly formalized, was accepted as binding in honour only, and for which some of the terms remained to be negotiated, told against an estoppel arising. It now also seems to be the case that a representation about how property is to be left on death is sufficiently certain, even if the shape of the property changes. Thus, in *Thorner*, the apparent promise concerned a farm on the Mendips, but over time parts were sold and bought. That was neither here nor there for the House of Lords because the subject matter was the farm; it was, therefore, certain.[53] Finally, the criteria for raising the estoppel are interactive, so that a particularly clear representation will result in a lowering of the threshold for the detriment and reliance elements;[54] and, it should be added, the acts of detrimental reliance are for the representee to take from the representation (irrespective of whether the representor meant their words to be taken that way).[55]

Perhaps the classic example of the operation of proprietary estoppel occurred in *Crabb* v. *Arun DC*.[56] Crabb owned some land and the council owned a lane by the side of that land. Crabb needed another point of access to part of his land and negotiated an oral agreement with the council for that access point from their lane. No formal agreement was completed. Crabb nevertheless acted on that agreement, setting new gateposts in concrete next to the land, and sold off a part of the land. The council then uprooted the gatepost and refused rights of access from their lane, leaving Crabb's property effectively landlocked. The Court of Appeal held that it would be inequitable for the council to rely on their strict legal rights. In principle, of course, they could act in the way they did because no formal agreement had been signed and thus no title had passed to Crabb. However, the Court held that their conscience was affected and granted a right (the access point) to Crabb by way of a proprietary estoppel.

---

[51] [2008] 1 WLR 1752, [46].

[52] [2009] 1 WLR 776, [80], Lord Neuberger.

[53] [18], Lord Scott. He notes that, if the representor were to have sought to sell the farm before his death, it would have been possible for the representee to establish a claim through estoppel and to consequential relief, as in *Gillett* v. *Holt* [2001] Ch 210.

[54] *Gillett* v. *Holt* [2001] Ch 210.

[55] *Thorner*.

[56] [1976] Ch 179. Although the context of the case is non-domestic, it provides a useful example and examination of the key concepts involved in proprietary estoppel claims.

Debate 2

What principles does the law use to assess the remedy?

Once the Claimant has surmounted the first hurdle, the next question is the extent of the interest to which the Claimant is entitled. Once more, there is a degree of uncertainty, although recent cases have provided some clarification. The analysis is once again split between the constructive trust and proprietary estoppel.

CONSTRUCTIVE TRUST

The same two starting presumptions apply here, viz. if the property is held by one person, the assumption is that they are the sole beneficial owner; if the property is held jointly, the assumption is that they hold the property as joint owners, 50:50. The basis for that proposition is that 'equity follows the law',[57] although there are significant policy reasons for this outcome, most notably certainty.[58] The onus is on the Claimant to prove that they are entitled to more, and the principles regarding quantification are the same whether one is dealing with a joint names or a sole name case.[59] There are suggestions that it is only very rarely that that starting point is capable of being displaced. As Baroness Hale put it in *Stack* v. *Dowden*:

> This is not a task to be lightly embarked upon. In family disputes, strong feelings are aroused when couples split up. These often lead the parties, honestly but mistakenly, to reinterpret the past in self-exculpatory or vengeful terms. They also lead people to spend far more on the legal battle than is warranted by the sums actually at stake. A full examination of the facts is likely to involve disproportionate costs. In joint names cases it is also unlikely to lead to a different result unless the facts are very unusual.[60]

Yet, it is also the case that in both *Stack* and *Jones* v. *Kernott*[61] the Supreme Court did engage in that process, so that it remains unclear what facts are 'very unusual'. It is the plurality of relationships and individual decisions made which suggest that there is no particular norm, a point to which we return below.

It is now crystal clear that quantification depends on the common intention of the parties. That is the guiding principle. There is a degree of consensus as to the type of common intention: one can look to express, inferred *or* imputed common intention. That is the clear outcome of both *Stack* and *Jones*. The issue lies in how one operationalizes the difference between inferred and imputed intention,

---

[57] *Stack*, [54], Baroness Hale.
[58] *Jones*, [19], Baroness Hale/Lord Walker, where it was noted that this is not a 'slavish' application of that equitable maxim.
[59] [65].
[60] [2007] 2 AC 432, [68]; see also *Jones*, [19]–[22].
[61] [2011] UKSC 53.

and, indeed, whether it matters or not. Let us start with the conclusion, which is summarized by Baroness Hale and Lord Walker, and about which there can be no disagreement:

(1) The starting point is that equity follows the law and they are joint tenants both in law and in equity.

(2) That presumption can be displaced by showing (a) that the parties had a different common intention at the time when they acquired the home, or (b) that they later formed the common intention that their respective shares would change.

(3) Their common intention is to be deduced objectively from their conduct: 'the relevant intention of each party is the intention which was reasonably understood by the other party to be manifested by that party's words and conduct notwithstanding that he did not consciously formulate that intention in his own mind or even acted with some different intention which he did not communicate to the other party'.[62] Examples of the sort of evidence which might be relevant to drawing such inferences are given in *Stack* v. *Dowden*.[63]

(4) In those cases where it is clear either (a) that the parties did not intend joint tenancy at the outset, or (b) had changed their original intention, but where it is not possible to ascertain by direct evidence or by inference what their actual intention was as to the shares in which they would own the property, 'the answer is that each is entitled to that share which the court considers fair having regard to the whole course of dealing between them in relation to the property'.[64] In our judgment, 'the whole course of dealing ... in relation to the property' should be given a broad meaning, enabling a similar range of factors to be taken into account as may be relevant to ascertaining the parties' actual intentions.

(5) Each case will turn on its own facts. Financial contributions are relevant but there are many other factors which may enable the court to decide what shares were either intended (as in case (3)) or fair (as in case (4)).[65]

The same reasoning process should also apply in sole name cases.

The Supreme Court in *Jones* differed as to the breadth of inference. The facts of *Jones* are relatively simple. The parties were in a relationship in which they had two children. They bought a house in their joint names in 1985. In 1993, Mr Kernott left. At this stage, all parties agreed that the property was to be shared 50:50. After leaving, Mr Kernott stopped making payments to anything.[66] In 1995,

---

[62] *Gissing* v. *Gissing* [1971] AC 886, 906, Lord Diplock.

[63] at [69].

[64] *Oxley* v. *Hiscock* [2005] Fam 211, para. 69, Chadwick LJ.

[65] *Jones*, [52].

[66] At least, this is the judicial version of truth. Dawn Watkins' interview with Mr Kernott suggests that the judicial version was a 'misshapen identity' – by his own admission, he might have 'done more' but he did not have the resources, and he 'felt like a bit of a failure to my kids'; but that was translated as the case progressed through the court hierarchy, as Watkins puts it, 'Lack becomes little or nothing, and then nothing at all'; see. D. Watkins, 'The shaping and misshaping of identity through legal practice and process: (Re)discovering Mr Kernott', (2014) 8(2) *Law and Humanities* 192.

the parties cashed in a life insurance policy, which enabled Mr Kernott to buy another home to live in. In 2007, he asked for his half share of the former family home. In the meantime, Ms Jones had been making all payments for the home and children. There was no express agreement between the parties as to whether, after 1993, the parties had altered their intentions as to the shares in which they held the property. The question seemed to be whether, if one could not infer a common intention in these circumstances, one could impute such an intention.

For Lord Walker and Baroness Hale, however, this was a case of inference. They make the important point that an imputation is not such an unusual approach in law:

> Whenever a judge concludes that an individual 'intended, or must be taken to have intended,' or 'knew, or must be taken to have known,' there is an elision between what the judge can find as a fact (usually by inference) on consideration of the admissible evidence, and what the law may supply (to fill the evidential gap) by way of a presumption. The presumption of a resulting trust is a clear example of a rule by which the law *does* impute an intention, the rule being based on a very broad generalisation about human motivation.[67]

Furthermore, '... while the conceptual difference between inferring and imputing is clear, the difference in practice may not be so great. In this area, as in many others, the scope for inference is wide. The law recognizes that a legitimate inference may not correspond to an individual's subjective state of mind.'[68] This line of argument was followed by Lord Collins, who pointed out that 'what is one person's inference will be another person's imputation'.[69] On this point, there was a difference of opinion – Lords Kerr and Wilson found that the case depended on 'fairness', an imputation from the facts.[70] Both preferred a clear demarcation between an inference and imputation.

Nobody, however, disagreed on the outcome. Ms Jones was entitled to 90 per cent of the property. This could be inferred (Lord Walker/Baroness Hale, Lord Collins) from the sale of the life insurance policy in 1995, when 'a new plan was formed' by the parties.[71] That was not a finding of fact made by the judge, but one that would have been open for him to make. Lords Kerr and Wilson reached the same result on the basis of fairness/imputation. As Lord Kerr put it, '... the bare facts of his departure from the family home and acquisition of another property are a slender foundation on which to conclude that he had entirely abandoned whatever stake he had in the previously shared property'.[72]

This still leaves the question of when it will be appropriate to upset the starting presumption. The answer seems to be that it depends on the facts of the case. In *Stack*, the parties had been in a relationship for 27 years and had four

---

[67] [29].
[68] [34].
[69] [65].
[70] Although it is fair to say that Lord Kerr was not overly enamoured by the concept of 'imputation': [74].
[71] [48].
[72] [76].

children. Mr Stack had made direct and unquantifiable payments to the purchase of the home and had done work to it (he was a builder). They had both looked after the home and the children. The judge's original finding had been that they should share 50:50 in the proceeds. The House of Lords disagreed, awarding Ms Dowden 65 per cent. They upset the starting point by looking principally at the way the parties organized their finances – separately from each other and without joint savings[73] – and noted that Ms Dowden had paid the capital up front to the purchase so that Mr Stack had contributed to the mortgage payments. This was, therefore, a 'very unusual' case – as Baroness Hale put it, 'There cannot be many unmarried couples who have lived together for as long as this, who have had four children together, and whose affairs have been kept as rigidly separate as this couple's affairs were kept.'[74]

PROPRIETARY ESTOPPEL

The interest that the successful Claimant may obtain in the property through proprietary estoppel is extremely flexible. It might be said that, ordinarily, the remedy should follow the representation – the Claimant obtains their expectation loss. If the representation is that the Claimant will be 'given' the house, then that should ordinarily be the remedy.[75] This was the outcome in, for example, *Pascoe* v. *Turner*.[76] However, that analysis, while doctrinally appropriate in that equity perfects the gift through estoppel, does not reflect the authorities. Indeed, in *Pascoe* itself, the ratio for requiring the transfer of legal title to the representee was based on the Court of Appeal's view that '... the equity cannot here be satisfied without granting a remedy which assures to the respondent security of tenure, quiet enjoyment, and freedom of action in respect of repairs and improvements without interference from the appellant'.[77] The conduct of the representor had been ruthless, and the remedy was designed to protect her from future manifestations of that ruthlessness, as well as enable her to finance any major repairs by way of loan.[78] Similarly, in *Crabb* v. *Arun DC*,[79] Mr Crabb obtained his expected

---

[73] As Baroness Hale, at [90], said, 'This is not a case in which it can be said that the parties pooled their separate resources, even notionally, for the common good. The only things they ever had in their joint names were Chatsworth Road and the associated endowment policy. Everything else was kept strictly separate.'

[74] *Stack*, [92].

[75] See, for example, *Jennings* v. *Rice* [2003] 1 P & CR 8; *Yeoman's Row* v. *Cobbe*, at [4], Lord Scott; see also, S. Moriarty, 'Licences and Land Law: Legal Principles and Public Policy' (1984) 100(3) *LQR* 376; J. Dewar, 'Licences and Land Law: An Alternative View' (1986) 49(6) *MLR* 741; for further discussion, see S. Gardner, 'The Remedial Discretion in Proprietary Estoppel' (1999) 115(3) *LQR* 438; and S. Gardner, 'The Remedial Discretion in Proprietary Estoppel Again' (2006) 122(3) LQR 492.

[76] [1979] 1 WLR 431.

[77] At 438.

[78] At 438–39.

[79] [1976] Ch 179.

easement by way of proprietary estoppel, but the court's approach to the remedy was rather different.

Scarman LJ, in *Crabb*, analysed the grant of the easement as the 'minimum equity to do justice to the [Claimant]'.[80] It is that approach to remedy which seems to have characterized the development of the law in this area, although that approach also has considerable discretion and uncertainty attached to it. It is also not hugely helpful. It is sometimes framed, in more modern vein, as equity seeking a proportionate outcome.[81] The problems to which these approaches give rise are exemplified by *Gillett* v. *Holt*.[82] This was a case in which Mr Holt promised Mr Gillett his entire farming business on Holt's death. The relationship lasted an extended period. The underlying promise was simple; but the actual farming business was complicated, the acts of detriment in reliance took place over a lengthy period, and involved a number of separate properties, and also a series of transactions after the parties had fallen out. Robert Walker LJ set out to find the maximum extent of the equity so as to form a basis for identifying the minimum, with the observation that 'The court must look at all the circumstances, including the need to achieve a 'clean break' so far as possible and avoid or minimise future friction'.[83]

It seems that the courts have now moved to what might be described as a 'broad inquiry'. Following the lead in the constructive trusts jurisprudence, the Court of Appeal in *Southwell* v. *Blackburn* moved away from an 'exercise in financial accounting', recognizing that cohabitation involves '... a range of activities and mutual support which is simply incapable of financial quantification', so that it does not lend itself to such a mechanistic approach.[84] The judge, whose award was upheld by the Court of Appeal, made an award of £28,500, which, perhaps oddly, was related to what Ms Blackburn had spent on her previous property (a housing association tenancy) and what she had spent on setting up in the new house shared with her partner. That sum was also said to represent a quarter of her notional half share in the former cohabited home – the judge contented herself by saying that the figure 'should allow her to set herself up in much the same way as she was in 2002 before she moved in with the Defendant. That is the best I can do to quantify the measure of the prejudice to her by the Defendant's failure to honour his promise.'[85]

All of this seems unsatisfactory as it is not conducive to certainty or, indeed, a principled jurisdiction (as was the appellant's complaint in *Southwell*). It seems clear, however, that the remedy is tailored to the facts. The need for a clean break,

[80] At 198.

[81] E.g. *Sledmore* v. *Dalby* (1996) 72 P & CR 196, 208–9.

[82] [2001] Ch 210.

[83] At 237.

[84] [2014] EWCA Civ 1437, [17], [18].

[85] [14]. The promises had been that 'she would always have a home and be secure in this one'; 'he was taking on a "long-term commitment to provide her with a secure home"'; and 'he led her to believe that she would have the sort of security that a wife would have, in terms of accommodation at the house, and income.'

as best as possible, is clearly a relevant criterion. Equally, the remedy needs to be realistic. There is no point giving effect to a representation where the outcome is unachievable. It may well be, therefore, that a proprietary claim may give rise to a personal remedy (such as the payment of money to satisfy the equity), or, indeed, to no remedy at all (as the extent of the equity has already been satisfied).[86]

From *Sledmore* v. *Dalby*, Gardner identifies seven possible factors affecting the remedy if one has to pass over the expectation criterion: '(i) the claimant's expectation, but also proportionality with her detriment; (ii) the parties' conduct; (iii) the need for a clean break; (iv) alterations in the defendant's assets and circumstances; (v) the effect of taxation; (vi) other claims on the defendant or his or her estate; (vii) possible other factors'.[87] Gardner's position is that the role of this jurisdiction is to rectify unconscionability, which 'can be understood as the extent to which the defendant's role in the claimant's detrimental reliance upon her expectation makes it right to hold the defendant responsible for it. Addressing this is a reasonably well-defined aim, such that a judge can work to it as the law's agent.'[88]

Bright and McFarlane, by slight contrast, argue for a restrictive approach to a proprietary remedy, on the basis that the key ingredient should be the Claimant's reliance.[89] A proprietary remedy should only ensue, on this argument, if that protects the Claimant's reasonable reliance. As yet, there is no answer to this question. Our preference is for Gardner's proffered solution as this seems more in tune with an explanation of the *outcome* of most of the cases.

Debate 3

Are constructive trusts and proprietary estoppel different and, more to the point, does it matter?

Let us start with two propositions by way of answering the first part of this question. The first is that the constructive trust (or, at least the type considered above) arises as a result of the common intention regarding the *acquisition* of the property;[90] in principle, proprietary estoppel is not so limited and can arise at any stage. If you think in terms of venn diagrams, it is the fried egg one, with estoppel the whole egg and constructive trust the yolk bit. The second proposition is that a

---

[86] See, for example, *Burrows* v. *Sharp* (1993) 23 HLR 82; *Baker* v. *Baker* (1993) 23 HLR 408.

[87] Gardner, 2006, n.75, 494.

[88] At 506. He also notes certain problems in relation to the factors identified, not least that they are not necessarily related to detrimental reliance and also because different judges' 'positions remain unstated', at 507.

[89] S. Bright and B. McFarlane, 'Proprietary Estoppel and Property Rights' (2005) 64(2) *CLJ* 449.

[90] It is fair to say that this proposition is, on its own, controversial and liable to confusion. There can be no doubt that acquisition extends beyond the initial purchase – acquisition in most cases is an ongoing process as the mortgage is an ongoing expense through which parties acquire the property (although perhaps there are distinctions between interest only and other types of mortgage). The point is, though, that, in principle, the common intention must occur at the time of acquisition. It is the case, however, that some cases do not fit easily with this proposition – see, for example, *James* v. *Thomas* [2007] EWCA Civ 1212.

constructive trust arises by the acts of detrimental reliance, whatever they may be; the estoppel, however, in principle, only arises when a judge so pronounces.[91] As regards the latter point about estoppel, that seems to follow from the flexibility of the remedy – it may not give rise to a proprietary right at all. There is a legislative corrective in relation to registered land for the protection of the person claiming the right to estoppel 'for the avoidance of doubt' – the equity by estoppel 'has effect from the time the equity arises as an interest capable of binding successors in title ...'.[92] However, this legislative correction is a little eliptical and, as Lord Collins suggested in *Scott* v. *Southern Pacific Mortgages Ltd*, rather begs the question as to when the equity arises, '... and probably assumes that it first arises (as it usually does) as against the legal owner who is estopped or who is bound by the equity'.[93]

Lord Scott, in *Thorner*, suggests a third proposition, that the inheritance cases (like *Gillett*, for example) are better explained by way of constructive trust but this seems to have been based more on instinct than grounded doctrine.[94] However one frames it, then, there are (or seem to be) differences between the two doctrines.

Nevertheless, there is considerable discussion in the cases about the overlap. Browne-Wilkinson V-C, in *Grant* v. *Edwards*, suggested that they are 'closely akin' and 'they rest on the same foundation and have on all other matters reached the same conclusions'.[95] Lord Walker, who, in *Yaxley* v. *Gotts*,[96] had found similar crossovers, nevertheless resiled from the view that they should be unified in *Thorner*:

> Proprietary estoppel typically consists of asserting an equitable claim against the conscience of the 'true' owner. The claim is a 'mere equity'. It is to be satisfied by the minimum award necessary to do justice ... , which may sometimes lead to no more than a monetary award. A 'common intention' constructive trust, by contrast, is identifying the true beneficial owner or owners, and the size of their beneficial interests.[97]

Why the fuss? It seems that the principal problem, quite apart from the doctrinal differences, lies in section 2 of the Law of Property (Miscellaneous Provisions) Act 1989. That section expresses Parliamentary intention regarding the required formalities for the sale or disposition of an interest in land. Constructive trusts

---

[91] See P. Ferguson, 'Constructive Trusts – A Note of Caution' (1993) 109(1) *LQR* 114; cf. P. Matthews, 'The Words Which Are Not There: A Partial History of the Constructive Trust' in C. Mitchell (ed.), *Constructive and Resulting Trusts* (Hart, 2009) pp. 55–7; B. McFarlane, 'Proprietary Estoppel and Third Parties after the Land Registration Act 2002' (2003) 62(4) *CLJ* 661.

[92] LRA 2002, s. 116.

[93] [2014] UKSC 52, [58].

[94] [2009] 1 WLR 776, [20], and no other member of the House explicitly agreed with that proposition; see also *Re Basham* [1986] 1 WLR 1498, 1504.

[95] [1986] Ch 638, 656; see also *Yaxley* v. *Gotts* [2000] Ch 162, 177.

[96] *Yaxley* v. *Gotts* [2000] Ch 162, 177, Robert Walker LJ.

[97] *Stack*, [37].

(as well as resulting and implied trusts) are exempted from those strict requirements.[98] Estoppel is not so exempted. In *Yaxley* v. *Gotts*, where only proprietary estoppel was pleaded, it was argued that public policy prevented estoppel from getting round the section 2 formalities. As Robert Walker LJ put it in that case: 'If an estoppel would have the effect of enforcing a void contract and subverting Parliament's purpose it may have to yield to the statutory law which confronts it, except so far as the statute's saving for a constructive trust provides a means of reconciliation of the apparent conflict.'[99] On the facts, he was able to find a constructive trust as well, so there was no problem for him. Beldam LJ (who was the Law Commission Chair at the time the report which led to the 1989 Act was under consideration by that body) was less concerned and (naturally) referred to the Law Commission report which assumed the continued availability of proprietary estoppel to defeat a claim, even where there had been no compliance with the section 2 formalities.[100]

However, in *Yeoman's Row*, Lord Scott suggested:

> My present view, however, is that proprietary estoppel cannot be prayed in aid in order to render enforceable an agreement that statute has declared to be void. The proposition that an owner of land can be estopped from asserting that an agreement is void for want of compliance with the requirements of section 2 is, in my opinion, unacceptable. The assertion is no more than the statute provides. Equity can surely not contradict the statute.[101]

In *Thorner*, Lord Neuberger said:

> [A]t least as at present advised, I do not consider that section 2 has any impact on a claim such as the present, which is a straightforward estoppel claim without any contractual connection. It was no doubt for that reason that the respondents, rightly in my view, eschewed any argument based on section 2.[102]

In neither case was the point particularly argued. It leaves us with four possible solutions: estoppel cannot get round section 2 plain and simple; estoppel can where the same facts would give rise to a constructive trust; estoppel can where the parties are not seeking to create a 'contractual connection'; estoppel is unaffected by section 2.[103] In the only subsequent case to date, Bean J preferred the latter interpretation.[104] That probably is the best interpretation because of the second proposition above – until a judge formalizes the remedy, there is no estoppel and, therefore, nothing on which section 2 can 'bite'. It is to be noted that, if the first proposition is correct, then proprietary estoppel would, in most circumstances, be of extremely limited practical utility.

---

[98] s. 2(5).

[99] At 175; Clarke LJ agreed with him on this point, at 181.

[100] At 190–91.

[101] [29].

[102] [99]; see also *Anderson Antiques* v. *Anderson Wharf* [2007] EWHC 2086 (Ch).

[103] See generally, Dixon, n.50, who argues that unconscionability provides the answer.

[104] *Whittaker* v. *Kinnear* [2011] EWHC 1479 (QB), [30].

Debate 4

Do the foundations of the doctrinal law correlate with empirical findings?

It is easy to get caught up in hard, doctrinal law. Given that it is under-developed and there are many outstanding questions, it is both interesting and thought-provoking stuff. But we should also take a step back and consider whether the foundations of that law actually correlate with lived realities. As demonstrated above through the work of Dawn Watkins, the law probably did not correlate with the lived realities of two of the key players in the cases (Ms Burns and Mr Kernott).

Nevertheless, we are referring here to the empirical assumptions of the law – for example, Baroness Hale's assertion that the facts in *Stack* v. *Dowden* were very unusual.[105] The simple answer to the question is 'not really'. Indeed, the development of the law in this area is characterized by its inability to cope with the plurality of circumstances by which ordinary people live and manage their lives. The findings of qualitative studies in this regard are particularly illuminating. As Barlow and Smithson put it, 'our analysis [of their data] shows that there was often a surprising ability to separate off the emotional or social commitment from a sense of legal and financial commitment which might be expected to accompany it'.[106] More directly, Douglas, Pearce and Woodward directly attack the empirical basis for Baroness Hale's claim that the facts of *Stack* were very unusual – as they put it:

> ... there is little clear correlation between other features of relationships and the way the couple organised their finances. ... [their] study also found cohabitants to be more likely than not to keep their finances separate, with two-thirds of [their] sample only operating sole bank accounts. Even among couples who owned their home in joint names, fewer than half operated joint bank accounts. ... This all suggests that keeping money separate – or pooling it – does not necessarily provide reliable evidence of the parties' intentions, and it may not be at all easy for practitioners to identify cases which have sufficiently unusual financial arrangements to justify attempting to displace the heavy presumption emphasised in *Stack v Dowden* that equity follows the law in determining beneficial interests.[107]

The findings of Douglas, Pearce and Woodward provide particular pause for thought. Theirs was a small-scale qualitative study – which included cohabitants, conveyancers and family solicitors – but the findings demonstrate not just the

---

[105] [2007] 2 AC 432.

[106] A. Barlow and J. Smithson, 'Legal Assumptions, Cohabitants' Talk and the Rocky Road to Freedom' (2010) 22(3) *Child and Family Law Quarterly* 328.

[107] G. Douglas, J. Pearce and H. Woodward, 'Cohabitants, Property and the Law: A Study of Injustice' (2009) 72(1) *MLR* 24, 37–38; see also A. Barlow, C. Burgoyne and J. Smithson, *The Living Together Campaign – An Investigation of its Impact on the Legally Aware Cohabitants* (Ministry of Justice, 2007); R. Tennant, J. Taylor and J. Lewis, *Separating from Cohabitation: Making Arrangements for Finances and Parenting*, DCA 7/06 (DCA, 2007).

variety of different pressures involved when cohabitants buy or mortgage a home, but also the antipathy of different elements of the legal profession towards each other. It is particularly notable, for example, that cohabitant property issues are routed by firms to their family departments, which (by definition) are not as aware of the *civil* procedure applicable to these claims, which are different from family procedural rules including (most importantly) regarding costs.[108] Few of the couples in this study had made written agreements relating to their property, although most had made wills; but the agreements '... had as much potential to exacerbate as to clarify issues' and their understandings of ownership at the time of purchase were hazy.[109] Separate legal advice was generally not sought (or suggested).

But one of the key findings of the study concerns the power of the emotions, which led to many of their sample not questioning arrangements, and doing things (like ticking a box to indicate joint ownership) on the basis that it would otherwise be embarrassing (as one cohabitant participant put it, *'It was explained to me that I could protect my extra contribution – but she was pregnant, sitting there next to me – you just don't do that'*[110]). Conveyancing solicitors were generally complicit in these power issues. As the researchers put it, 'One conveyancer summed up the attitude of purchasing clients in a nutshell: *Normally they just want the keys and to know when they're moving in. The legal aspects of it, they don't really think about.'*[111] The cohabitants' views as to the types of principles which should be relevant to the resolution of their disputes (contribution/compensation, need, honesty/ honour, strict legal entitlement) were necessarily reflected by the law and practice. One conclusion expressed is damning:

> The legal construction of property ownership does not reflect any lay conception of cohabiting partnerships. The concepts used in property law do not reflect matters which are likely to appear relevant and important to clients, or the way they have lived their lives together. Furthermore, the law brings together and treats as the same issues which from a practical 'client' point of view are quite different, while conversely separating and treating differently issues which, as experienced practically, seem very similar to the lay person.[112]

Further, 'the way in which property is owned may not reflect the parties' understandings, what they feel to be fair, or what can practically be achieved'.[113] In any event, getting the evidence together to justify a claim was likely to be unrealistic.

One conclusion that one might draw is that the law has got some way to go before it catches up with everyday life. However, the research makes a number of more wide-ranging points about the organization of the profession: the lack of

---

[108] Paras 7.20–7.27.
[109] Paras 5.8–5.9.
[110] Para. 5.12.
[111] Para. 5.28.
[112] Para. 6.38.
[113] Para. 6.43.

knowledge of cohabitants about their entitlements (and, more so, the mis-knowledge[114]); the difficulty of knowing with any degree of certainty what principles are, so that bargaining in the shadow of the law becomes impossible; and the significance of everyday interactions, including the shame (or stigma) attached to claiming or acting contrary to expectations.

CONCLUSIONS

There is not much more to say than appears in the previous paragraph. The doctrinal law is confused and confusing, it lacks much by way of principle and application, and there are outstanding gaps. It is entirely ridiculous that some 40 years after the leading case of *Pettitt*, we are still searching for principle, but that is the doctrinal position. The lack of Parliamentary leadership in this area is also entirely lamentable – if it was apathetic, it would be perhaps more understandable – and there is a desperate need for somebody, anybody, to grapple with the really difficult issues.

Further Reading

A. Barlow, C. Burgoyne, E. Clery and J. Smithson, 'Cohabitation and the Law: Myths, Money and the Media' in A. Park, J. Curtis, K. Thompson, M. Phillips, M. Johnson and E. Clery (eds.), *British Social Attitudes: The 24th Report* (Sage, 2008).

A. Bottomley, 'Self and Subjectivities: Languages of Claim in Property Law' (1993) 20(1) *Journal of Law and Society* 56.

G. Douglas, J. Pearce and H. Woodward, 'Cohabitants, Property and the Law: A Study of Injustice' (2009) 72(1) *MLR* 24.

L. Fox O'Mahony, 'The politics of *Lloyds Bank v Rosset*', in S. Douglas, R. Hickey and E. Waring (eds.), *Landmark Cases in Property Law* (Oxford: Hart, 2015).

D. Watkins, 'Recovering the lost human stories of law: Finding Mrs Burns', (2013) 7(1) *Law and Humanities* 68.

---

[114] There is a reminder here of the analogy drawn by Ewick and Silbey of legal consciousness developing like whale song: P. Ewick and S. Silbey, *The Common Place of Law: Stories from Everyday Life* (University of Chicago Press, 1999) p. 44.

12

CONCLUSIONS: WHAT IS THE POINT OF PROPERTY?

We have spent some time in this book identifying some of the flaws in the conventional law of property, in particular through the lens of the six themes of property identified in Chapter 1: alienation, citizenship, exclusion, rationality, responsibility and space. In this conclusion, we reflect on our journey by way of extended observations on the limits of property in law. We do not seek to repeat our call to arms in the introduction here, and nor is what follows a manifesto or suchlike; what we offer here are merely some personal observations to which we collectively mostly sign up.

Our opening observation is significant for us as teachers. If this book has sought to do one thing, it is to exhort our colleagues and students to go beyond the doctrine, to see the real in real property, and not slavishly to follow others' agendas for conventional analysis. The simple thing, of course, is to stick with what we know, what we were taught, and to limit ourselves accordingly.[1] In doing so, we fear that we fall into the trap laid for us by our teachers and others, so that we end up subscribing to what we regard as the rationality errors of property law, its liberal emphases on alienation, its circuits of inclusion masquerading as citizenship, its assumptions about (and individualization of) responsibility and its carving up of space. It is the apparently mundane, taken-for-granted, everyday life of property law which, perhaps paradoxically, means that we miss the variety of experiences of the everyday – as Delaney observes, we need to investigate '... *how* unremarkableness (particularly the unremarkableness of mundane power) is produced and maintained'.[2]

We forget that there is a public dimension to private law (or, as Annelise Riles puts it, 'there is nothing inherently public or private about legal technicalities'), and we forget that the real in property is unreal, lacking in both empirical validity and credibility. Indeed, we see many parallels between our rather mundane book about land law and Riles' ethnographic study of collateral in global financial markets. Part of Riles' study concerned the use of legal techniques, which are means and not ends (although lawyers regard them as instrumental

---

[1] Dawn Watkins' work on Mrs Burns and Mr Kernott, discussed in Chapter 11, explodes such simplicities though.

[2] D. Delaney, *Nomospheric Investigations: The Spatial, The Legal and the Pragmatics of World-Making* (Routledge-Glasshouse, 2010) p. 48 (emphasis in original).

in achieving their desired ends), and she argues that law is seen as a tool in this process. She goes on:

> This deceptively simple cultural reality deserves a bit more attention. The notion of law as tool assumes that the user of the tool is completely in control of the purpose, process, and outcome of the tool's use. It assumes that the legal tool is really nothing but collateral knowledge, on the way to achieving certain stated objectives, defined in other terms. But legal tools … are more interesting than this. They sometimes, mysteriously, overtake their users. And the 'users' (perhaps we dare say 'collaborators with') of such tools are neither completely aware, nor completely unaware, of the agency of 'their' tools. Again, it is one of those collateral realities that lies under the radar, and yet in plain view for all to see. … [W]e are dealing with something more mysterious and profound: in the 'meantime', the means often occlude the ends and overtake the instrument's user. There are intriguing political possibilities in this too-often-unacknowledged technical reality.[3]

Our perspectives on land law, which in places appears fixed and barely changed, has similarly drawn attention to the agency of these tools and the truths which they expose. So, our point (like Riles) is not to throw the baby out with the bathwater, but that we should take legal technicality on, on its own terms, and seek to expose its truths and hidden assumptions. So, for example, if we think about the figure of Mrs Burns (see Chapter 11), our analysis of the injustice to her is that, on the facts and without an express common intention, the methods of inferring a common intention were of no use to her because of the financial imbalance between herself and Mr Burns. This is a slightly different way of telling that story, in which the public and private merge in legal technicality, the key point being not that we have no way of quantifying her contributions (which is, of course, true; it is the end of legal technicality) but that, even if we did, it would have been unlikely that she would have been able to demonstrate that inference. By way of further example, our analysis of the apparently paradigmatic shift from a trust for sale to a trust of land in Chapter 3 demonstrates that the shadow of the past bears heavily, and so the sub-title of that chapter might have been 'change but no change'.

Our second observation, linked to that, is that we often have a blinkered analysis where our focus remains within the conventional boundaries of land law. And our conventional focus on rights and entitlements to property – the metaphors of land law – make us miss a trick because we lose sight of the phenomena of land, and we miss out on seeing the thing or the asset itself (whether as home, security, profit-making, etc.).

In particular, we argue that the presentation of land law as apparently 'neutral' is wrong-headed. In our apparent need for conventional principle, we forget that there is a shared human need to *use* land. That use is the basis for all human

---

[3] A. Riles, *Collateral knowledge: Legal Reasoning in Global Financial Markets* (University of Chicago Press, 2011) p. 229.

activities, yet the principles by which this use is governed tend to be abstracted from the reality of human experience. The presentation of the subject of land as apparently neutral (which is, of course, a political statement in itself) suggests that the priorities of legislators and courts are not driven by values; or as if those values are incontestable. What this book has demonstrated is that the orientations of land law – and the patterns of land use and access to land that are shaped by that law – are not neutral but directed by specific (if sometimes unarticulated) policy goals. Those policy goals – especially a particular, pro-purchaser, commercialist ethos – live on despite apparent shifts in use and values (Chapter 3).

The particular policy driver which those goals have facilitated has been the shift towards 'homeownership', discussed in Chapter 2. This is regularly presented as the natural desire of the population, which is facilitated by housing policy.[4] However, the alternative story that might be told is of differentiated citizenship among such homeowners. In her extended analysis of the right of council tenants to buy the flat they rent on long leaseholds, Helen Carr makes this same point:

> [T]here seems to have been an assumption that home-ownership in whatever form and however extended would convey these inherent qualities [capital growth, independence, responsibility], offering them equally to all who acquired its status ... [T]he stratification that is inherent in private ownership [is demonstrated by] its limits as a mechanism of economic and social inclusion.[5]

She goes on to add a biting critique of the assumption of equivalence between citizenship and homeownership:

> What concerns me is that for the Right to Buy lessees, the citizenship that the democratization of home-ownership offers may be as conditional as the flawed welfare citizenship that it replaces, and that the risk of impoverishment appears disproportionately high. The stretching of home-ownership by extending it to those occupiers of inner-city tower blocks, whilst at the same time minimizing their autonomy, reveals what is frequently obscured, namely, that private ownership is stratified, a site 'where very unevenly distributed power is exercised'.[6]

Our point, as with Carr, is that the apparent neutrality of property law obscures this differentiated citizenship.

Our third observation is that, as we have argued, land law is a destination subject; it needs to remain flexible, perhaps normatively open, not siloed in some foundational subject backwater subject to professional demands. The study of the reception of the Article 8 proportionality defence to mandatory possession claims in Chapter 8 provides an example of the way in which a blinkered land law analysis (*Qazi*) was dragged, kicking and screaming, into a pragmatic compromise, in which land and human rights were balanced – with the edge firmly in favour of

---

[4] See HM Government, *Laying the Foundations: A Housing Strategy for England* (DCLG, 2011) esp. ch. 2.
[5] H. Carr, 'The Right to Buy, the Leaseholder, and the Impoverishment of Ownership' (2011) 38(4) *Journal of Law and Society* 519, 539–40.
[6] Ibid., 541.

property (*Pinnock* and *Powell*). The same analysis can be applied to equality issues, although here the fallout from *Akerman-Livingstone* remains an unknown. There is, in one sense, a natural inclination to avoid these issues in conventional land law, but, as we have demonstrated in Chapter 9, the interface between public and private in land is brought to the fore, in this case by reference to the 'paradigmatic landlady'.

The effect of placing rights and entitlements at the centre of land analysis is – as Kate Green memorably argued – that the 'needs of property owners, self-interested and rational individuals in the market place, override the needs of those who are different: weaker or poorer, or in a different way defined as Other'. In his analysis of South African cases in which residential occupiers were evicted by the state for the purposes of economic development, van der Walt observed that 'the hierarchical domination of ownership' prioritizes certain types of claim, rooted in contractual and proprietary rights, so that:

> [E]ven when contextual factors enter the equation, courts' professional tendency to enforce the law of eviction 'normally', 'neutrally' or 'objectively' will more often than not still privilege the protection of stronger rights and result in more or less mechanical eviction of unlawful or weak occupiers who are unable to prove legal occupation rights that are strong enough to trump the owner's right.[7]

Some property scholarship has challenged this emphasis on rights and entitle-ments from within: for example, the Cornell School of Progressive Property[8] argues for a re-distributive approach to property rights and entitlements on the basis that our shared commitment (as human beings) to the values of 'life and human flourishing, the protection of physical security, the ability to acquire knowledge and make choices, and the freedom to live one's own life on one's own terms',[9] implicates moral and political conceptions that require property law to promote that human flourishing. This type of 'strong property rights' stance[10] seeks to address issues of justice and equality through a more just allocation of rights and entitlements in property. We (the authors) might fall out over whether this is 'progressive' or, indeed, 'modern', but the important point is that we need to explore alternatives to the narrow doctrine.

Such approaches can be contrasted with alternative approaches which rely not on challenging capital/commercial agendas through property rights *per se*, but on non-property entitlement approaches (for example, by arguing for greater recognition of home interests, protection of occupation, giving content to the idea of a right to housing or other human rights strategies). This is the kind of

---

[7] A. van der Walt, *Property in the Margins* (Hart, 2009) p. 73.

[8] G. Alexander, E. Peñalver, J. Singer and L. Underkuffler, 'A Statement on Progressive Property' (2009) 94 *Cornell L Rev* 743.

[9] Ibid..

[10] For an extensive illustration of the insights to be gained through considering alternative perspectives to the 'strong property rights' paradigm, and arguing for a wider notion of what can be considered worthy of recognition as property interests, see van der Walt, n.7.

work on which some have embarked – Cooper and Keenan, for example, focusing on subverting property rights through an understanding of propriety and belonging; Fox, for example, by focusing on binaries between insiders and outsiders. Yet, as the discussion in Chapter 8 has shown, the application of human rights arguments to counter commercialist ideologies is not straightforward. Indeed, at a time when the human rights movement itself is at risk of being subverted by the recognition of 'human' rights for corporate and profit-making entities,[11] the reluctance of domestic English courts to give meaningful effect to the right to respect for home under Article 8 in domestic eviction cases provides a sharp contrast to the recognition of a corporation's right to 'home, family and private life' in the course of competition proceedings brought against it.[12]

Fourth, in our introduction to Chapter 2, we meandered a little, wondering what land law might look like if it was recast as a law of place or the law of the home. It would, of course, be forced to shed its rationality commercial cloth, and take the empirical as the starting point. It would also be more humanistic, more emotional, without denying the importance of other actors (like documents and other artefacts of the legal, reducing to objects on the land like trees and hedges[13]). This seems to be the direction of much land scholarship, which is both at the margins and at the cutting edge. It would require a reconfiguration of conventional understandings to allow for the significance of place and space; it would recognize that the public and the private merge, and emerge '... acknowledge[ing] that the site of regulation may shift from the national, local or individual level to a more amorphous scale, delineated on an ad hoc basis by developers, local authority officials or regulators'.[14] It would require us to think about belonging and propriety, and the ways in which law structures power relations, including resistance.[15]

Our final observation is that the effect of the narrow focus on rights and entitlements in land law is that the human context and consequences of the dispute are often excluded from the adjudicative process. Some interests or claims – for example, the (subjective, emotional) claim of the property-less to housing and/

---

[11] See M. Addo, 'The Corporation as a Victim of Human Rights Violations' in M. Addo (ed.) *Human Rights Standards and the Responsibility of Transnational Corporations* (Kluwer, 1999) p. 187 (supporting this development); M. Emberland, *The Human Rights of Companies: Exploring the Structure of ECHR Protection* (Oxford University Press, 2006); cf. A. Grear, 'Challenging Corporate "Humanity": Legal Disembodiment, Embodiment and Human Rights' (2007) 7(3) *Human Rights Law Review* 511.

[12] See *Société Colas Est and Others v. France* (2004) 39 EHRR 17, at [41] in particular, where the European Court held that, 'Building on its dynamic interpretation of the Convention, the Court considers that the time has come to hold that in certain circumstances the rights guaranteed by Article 8 of the Convention may be construed as including the right to respect for a company's registered office, branches or other business premises.'

[13] See, for example, the important work of I. Braverman, '"The Tree Is the Enemy Soldier": A Sociolegal Making of War Landscapes in the Occupied West Bank' (2008) 42(3) *Law and Society Review* 449; or the high hedge as actant in anti-social behaviour, as to which see the Anti-Social Behaviour Act 2003, pt 8.

[14] A. Layard, 'Shopping in the Public Realm: A Law of Place' (2010) 37(3) *Journal of Law and Society* 412, 414.

[15] For a classic such study, or series of studies, see D. Cooper, *Governing out of Order: Space, Law and the Politics of Belonging* (Rivers Oram Press, 1998).

or home – are not conceptually suited to the absolute standards required of legal frameworks of rights and entitlements. Even where the court expresses sympathy with the apparently weaker party – who does not have the benefit of strict legal rights to secure their claim to property – the rhetoric of rights and entitlements functions to suggest that property law (and those who apply it) lacks power to change the harsh realities of society, so placing the problems under adjudication beyond judicial power or jurisdiction.[16] A particular example of this can be found in the context of shared ownership and sale and rentback transactions, discussed in Chapter 2, where the court becomes literally powerless in the face of its own self-created doctrine.

The vocabulary with which we allow claims to be articulated within land law, and the centring of rights and entitlements in legal methodologies, determines whether we can even recognize an issue or outcome as a problem to be addressed. Furthermore, policy analysts recognize that 'facts are things that never speak for themselves, they require an interpreter'.[17] Land lawyers are the interpreters of the anecdotal experiences of everyday life but they also make worlds in their translations. This is a fairly basic legal method point, of course; it is how to answer a problem question in a way, but the practice of translation is to objectify, de-emotionalize and prescribe relevance to certain facts based on collages of various legal artefacts.[18] What matters to the real-life participants in the drama is less relevant: 'What matters here is what matters to the professional nomospheric technicians in their practical tasks of making (legal) sense.'[19] We recognize that, in scrutinizing conventional interpretations of property law, and seeking to open up the possibility of alternative interpretations, we are similarly 'agents of technocratic form',[20] or nomospheric technicians, but this only emphasizes the significance of the generic role as academic. It also emphasizes the ambition of the task that awaits us. This is the way Valverde describes the task:

> In order to avoid sociological reductionism and better understand the 'how' of legal mechanisms, analyses need to be simultaneously inside and outside law, simultaneously technical and theoretical, legal and socio-legal. Doctrinal 'technicalities' would be as important in such a study as sociological analyses of power effects.[21]

There we have it: an ethnographic task as a way of doing property/place/home law.

---

[16] T. Ross, 'The Rhetoric of Poverty: Their Immorality, Our Helplessness' (1991) 79 *Georgetown Law Journal* 1499, 1509; and the work of Dawn Watkins on narrative, identity and law.

[17] W. Parsons, *Public Policy: An Introduction to the Theory and Practice of Policy Analysis* (Edward Elgar, 1995) p. 87.

[18] See D. Delaney, *Nomospheric Investigations: The Spatial, The Legal and the Pragmatics of World-Making* (Routledge-Glasshouse, 2010) ch. 6; and see G. Douglas, 'Cohabitation and Conveyancing Practice: Problems and Solutions' (2008) 72(5) *Conv* 365.

[19] Delaney, n. 18, p. 163.

[20] See A. Riles, 'A New Agenda for the Cultural Study of Law: Taking on the Technicalities' (2005–6) 63(4) *Buffalo Law Review* 973.

[21] M. Valverde, 'Jurisdiction and Scale: Legal "Technicalities" as Resources for Theory' (2009) 18(2) *Social and Legal Studies* 140.

INDEX